Energiepolitik und Klimaschutz.
Energy Policy and Climate Protection

Series Editors

Lutz Mez, Berlin Centre for Caspian Region Studies, Freie Universität Berlin, Berlin, Germany

Achim Brunnengräber, Environmental Policy Research Centre, Freie Universität Berlin, Berlin, Germany

Diese Buchreihe beschäftigt sich mit den globalen Verteilungskämpfen um knappe Energieressourcen, mit dem Klimawandel und seinen Auswirkungen sowie mit den globalen, nationalen, regionalen und lokalen Herausforderungen der umkämpften Energiewende. Die Beiträge der Reihe zielen auf eine nachhaltige Energie- und Klimapolitik sowie die wirtschaftlichen Interessen, Machtverhältnisse und Pfadabhängigkeiten, die sich dabei als hohe Hindernisse erweisen. Weitere Themen sind die internationale und europäische Liberalisierung der Energiemärkte, die Klimapolitik der Vereinten Nationen (UN), Anpassungsmaßnahmen an den Klimawandel in den Entwicklungs-, Schwellen- und Industrieländern, Strategien zur Dekarbonisierung sowie der Ausstieg aus der Kernenergie und der Umgang mit den nuklearen Hinterlassenschaften.

Die Reihe bietet ein Forum für empirisch angeleitete, quantitative und international vergleichende Arbeiten, für Untersuchungen von grenzüberschreitenden Transformations-, Mehrebenen- und Governance-Prozessen oder von nationalen „best practice"-Beispielen. Ebenso ist sie offen für theoriegeleitete, qualitative Untersuchungen, die sich mit den grundlegenden Fragen des gesellschaftlichen Wandels in der Energiepolitik, bei der Energiewende und beim Klimaschutz beschäftigen.

This book series focuses on global distribution struggles over scarce energy resources, climate change and its impacts, and the global, national, regional and local challenges associated with contested energy transitions. The contributions to the series explore the opportunities to create sustainable energy and climate policies against the backdrop of the obstacles created by strong economic interests, power relations and path dependencies. The series addresses such matters as the international and European liberalization of energy sectors; sustainability and international climate change policy; climate change adaptation measures in the developing, emerging and industrialized countries; strategies toward decarbonization; the problems of nuclear energy and the nuclear legacy.

The series includes theory-led, empirically guided, quantitative and qualitative international comparative work, investigations of cross-border transformations, governance and multi-level processes, and national "best practice"-examples. The goal of the series is to better understand societal-ecological transformations for low carbon energy systems, energy transitions and climate protection.

Reihe herausgegeben von
PD Dr. Lutz Mez
Freie Universität Berlin

PD Dr. Achim Brunnengräber
Freie Universität Berlin

Maarten Arentsen · Rinie van Est
Editors

The Future of Radioactive Waste Governance

Lessons from Europe

Editors
Maarten Arentsen
Terborg, The Netherlands

Rinie van Est
Rathenau Instituut
The Hague, The Netherlands

ISSN 2626-2827   ISSN 2626-2835 (electronic)
Energiepolitik und Klimaschutz. Energy Policy and Climate Protection
ISBN 978-3-658-40495-6   ISBN 978-3-658-40496-3 (eBook)
https://doi.org/10.1007/978-3-658-40496-3

© The Editor(s) (if applicable) and The Author(s) 2023. This is an Open Access publication.
Open Access This book is licensed under the terms of the Creative Commons Attribution 4.0 International License (http://creativecommons.org/licenses/by/4.0/), which permits use, sharing, adaptation, distribution and reproduction in any medium or format, as long as you give appropriate credit to the original author(s) and the source, provide a link to the Creative Commons license and indicate if changes were made.

The images or other third party material in this book are included in the book's Creative Commons license, unless indicated otherwise in a credit line to the material. If material is not included in the book's Creative Commons license and your intended use is not permitted by statutory regulation or exceeds the permitted use, you will need to obtain permission directly from the copyright holder.

The use of general descriptive names, registered names, trademarks, service marks, etc. in this publication does not imply, even in the absence of a specific statement, that such names are exempt from the relevant protective laws and regulations and therefore free for general use.

The publisher, the authors, and the editors are safe to assume that the advice and information in this book are believed to be true and accurate at the date of publication. Neither the publisher nor the authors or the editors give a warranty, expressed or implied, with respect to the material contained herein or for any errors or omissions that may have been made. The publisher remains neutral with regard to jurisdictional claims in published maps and institutional affiliations.

This Springer VS imprint is published by the registered company Springer Fachmedien Wiesbaden GmbH, part of Springer Nature.
The registered company address is: Abraham-Lincoln-Str. 52, 65189 Wiesbaden, Germany

Preface: The Future of Radioactive Waste Governance: Lessons from Europe

This volume examines the radioactive waste management (RWM) policies of ten European countries. An important proportion of the radioactive waste must be stored safely for people and nature for hundreds of thousands of years. The decision-making process thus needs to take into account an extreme long-term perspective. This places high demands on the storage location, the way in which that location is chosen and how society is involved.

None of the countries under scrutiny in this volume has an operational deep geological disposal facility. Various countries are at various stages in the policy process. Some countries are still in the process of policymaking, while others have already made decisions about where to site the geological disposal of their radioactive waste. Finland is furthest along in the process, and its deep geological disposal facility at Onkalo is currently under construction.

Especially with respect to siting geological disposal facilities, many European countries have been confronted with great social resistance since the 1970s. In response, in recent decades countries have paid more attention to involving societal actors in decision-making on RWM. This volume offers insight into how this participative turn in the policy of various European countries took place.

The Rathenau Instituut initiated this volume. The Dutch government established this institute some 35 years ago in order to stimulate political and societal debate on the influence of science, technology, and innovation on society. Currently approximately 60 people work here.

At present, the Rathenau Instituut is working on policy advice on how the Netherlands can organise the decision-making process about the final storage of its radioactive waste. We do this at the request of the Dutch Ministry of Infrastructure and Water Management. This comparative edited volume is part of this assignment. In addition, we examine how knowledge is created, shared, and maintained in relation to RWM, and scrutinise legal aspects concerning RWM. We previously published a historical study on how Dutch decision-making on RWM took shape since 1945.

We quite often collaborate with researchers outside of our institute, as with this volume. I therefore would like to sincerely thank the authors of the respective country studies. A special thanks goes out to Maarten Arentsen (University of Twente) for playing a key role in coordinating and editing this volume.

The book concludes with 17 lessons based on the national case studies. Those lessons will likely find their way into the advice we will provide to the Dutch government in 2024. I hope the insights will also provide inspiration for other countries.

October 3, 2022
Prof. Dr. Ir. Eefje Cuppen
Director Rathenau Instituut

Contents

1 **Introduction: The Governance Challenge of Radioactive Waste Management**... 1
Rinie van Est, Maarten Arentsen und Romy Dekker

2 **Long-Term Radioactive Waste Management in the Netherlands: Seeking Guidance for Decision-Making**............ 25
Romy Dekker, Vincent Lagendijk, Roos Walstock und Rinie van Est

3 **Nuclear Waste Governance in Italy: Between Participation Rhetoric and Regionalism**................................. 51
Maria Rosaria Di Nucci und Andrea Prontera

4 **Do You Care About High-Level Radioactive Waste and Spent Nuclear Fuel? Opportunities for Co-Constructing an Appropriate Governance-Ecosystem in Belgium**................ 85
Anne Bergmans, Catherine Fallon, Ron Cörvers und Céline Parotte

5 **The Long Road Towards the Soft Nuclear Repository State: Nuclear Waste Governance in Germany**................ 113
Maria Rosaria Di Nucci und Achim Brunnengräber

6 **The Melancholic Lock: High-Level Radioactive Waste Governance in Spain**.. 141
Josep Espluga-Trenc und Ana Prades

7 **Who Decides What is Safe? Experiences from Radioactive Waste Governance in Switzerland**....................... 169
Sophie Kuppler, Anne Eckhardt und Peter Hocke

8   UK Nuclear Waste Policy: 50 Wasted Years 199
    Stephen Thomas

9   The Governance Ecosystem of Radioactive Waste Management
    in France: Governing of and with Mistrust 231
    Markku Lehtonen

10 Radioactive Waste Management in Sweden: Decision-Making
    in a Context of Scientific Controversy 259
    Johan Swahn

11 The Finnish Solution to Final Disposal of Spent Nuclear Fuel 287
    Jarmo Vehmas, Aleksis Rentto, Jyrki Luukkanen, Burkhard
    Auffermann und Jari Kaivo-oja

12 European Lessons for the Governance of Long-Term
    Radioactive Waste Management 319
    Rinie van Est und Maarten Arentsen

Editors and Contributors

About the Editors

Dr. Maarten Arentsen was Associate Professor of Innovation in Energy Supply at the University of Twente in the Netherlands until his retirement in 2020. He has a degree in political science and a PhD in engineering sciences. His many years of research focused on change and innovation in European energy markets, among others, the transition towards renewable energy. He has published numerous articles, papers and book chapters, and has co-edited several books on the topics. He is a member of REFORM, an international academic network on innovation and change in energy markets.

Rinie van Est is a research coordinator at the Rathenau Instituut, the Dutch parliamentary technology assessment (TA) and science systems assessment (SciSA) organisation in The Hague. He has a degree in applied physics and public administration, and a PhD in political science. He is a global expert in the field of TA, politics of innovation and public participation. For more than twenty-five years he has been involved in the energy and digital transitions, with special attention to the role of emerging technologies, such as robotics and AI. He is part-time Professor of Technology Assessment and Governance at Eindhoven University of Technology.

Contributors

Dr. Maarten Arentsen Emeritus University of Twente, Terborg, Netherlands

Dr. Burkhard Auffermann University of Turku, Finland Futures Research Centre, Tampere, Finland

Prof. Dr. Anne Bergmans Faculty of Social Sciences, University of Antwerp, Antwerp, Belgium

Dr. Achim Brunnengräber Freie Universität Berlin, Forschungszentrum Für Nachhaltigkeit (FFN), Berlin, Germany

Dr. Ron Cörvers Maastricht Sustainability Institute, Maastricht University, Maastricht, Netherlands

Romy Dekker MA Rathenau Instituut, The Hague, Netherlands

Dr. Maria Rosaria Di Nucci Freie Universität Berlin, Forschungszentrum Für Nachhaltigkeit (FFN), Berlin, Germany

Dr. Anne Eckhardt risicare GmbH, Zollikerberg, Switzerland

Dr. Josep Espluga-Trenc Institute of Government and Public Policies (IGOP) & Department of Sociology, Universitat Autònoma de Barcelona, Barcelona, Spain

Prof. Dr. Catherine Fallon Département de Sciences Politiques – Faculté de Droit, Université de Liège, Liège, Belgium

Dr. Peter Hocke Institute for Technology Assessment and Systems Analysis (ITAS), Karlsruhe Institute of Technology, Karlsruhe, Germany

Dr. Jari Kaivo-oja University of Turku, Finland Futures Research Centre, Tampere, Finland

Dr. Sophie Kuppler Institute for Technology Assessment and Systems Analysis (ITAS), Karlsruhe Institute of Technology, Karlsruhe, Germany

Dr. Vincent Lagendijk Rathenau Instituut, The Hague, Netherlands

Dr. Markku Lehtonen Universitat Pompeu Fabra, Barcelona, Spain

Dr. Jyrki Luukkanen University of Turku, Finland Futures Research Centre, Tampere, Finland

Prof. Dr. Céline Parotte Département de Sciences Politiques – Faculté de Droit, Université de Liège, Liège, Belgium

Dr. Ana Prades Socio-technical Research Centre (CISOT-CIEMAT), Centro de Investigaciones Energéticas, Medio Ambientales y Tecnológicas (CIEMAT), Barcelona, Spain

Dr. Andrea Prontera Department of Political Science, Communication and International Relations, University of Macerata, Macerata, Italy

Aleksis Rentto B.Sc. University of Turku, Finland Futures Research Centre, Tampere, Finland

Dr. Johan Swahn MKG, Swedish NGO Office for Nuclear Waste Review, Göteborg, Sweden

Prof. Stephen Thomas Public Services International Research Unit (PSIRU), University of Greenwich, London, UK

Prof. Dr. Ir. Rinie van Est Rathenau Instituut, The Hague, Netherlands

Dr. Jarmo Vehmas University of Turku, Finland Futures Research Centre, Tampere, Finland

Roos Walstock MA./MSc Kirkman Company, Baarn, Netherlands

Abbreviations

ABWR	Advanced boiling water reactor
AC	Alternative Current
ACRO	Association pour le contrôle de la radioactivité à l'Ouest
AE	Autorité environnementale (Environment Authority)
AFCN-FANC	Belgium Federal Agency for Nuclear Control
AGP	Deep Geological Warehouse (Almacenamiento Geológico Profundo)
AGR	Advanced Gas-cooled Reactor
AkEnd	Working Group on the Selection Procedure for Repository Sites (Arbeitskreis Auswahlverfahren Endlagerstandorte)
AMAC	Association of Municipalities Affected by Nuclear Power Plants
ANCCLI	National umbrella organisation of local information committees (Association Nationale des Comités et Commissions Locales d'Information)
Andra	The French National Agency for Radioactive Waste Management
ANPA	National Agency for Environment Protection and Technical Services
AREVA	Regulatory Authority for Energy, Networks and the Environment
ARPA	Regional environmental agencies
ASN	French Nuclear Safety Authority
ASN	Agenzia per la Sicurezza Nucleare
ATC	Centralised Temporary Waste Store (Almacén Temporal Centralizado)
ATI	Temporary Individual Warehouses
BASE	Federal Office for Safety of Nuclear Wate Management (Bundesamt für die Sicherheit der nuklearen Entsorgung)

BGE	Federal Company for Radioactive Waste Disposal (Bundesgesellschaft für Endlagerung mbH)
BNFL	British Nuclear Fuels Limited
BUND	German Federation for the Environment and Nature Conservation
BWR	Boiling Water Reactor
CEA	Commissariat of Atomic Energy
CGN	China General Nuclear
CHN	High-Level Committee author to advise name
CIEMAT	Center for Energy, Environmental and Technological Research
Cigéo	Centre industriel de stockage géologique
CIRPS	Interuniversity Research Centre for Sustainable Development
CLIS	Local information and liaison committees author to advise name
CNAI	National Charter for suitable areas
CNAPI	National Map of Potentially Suitable Areas
CNDP	National Commission on Public Debate
CNE2	National Assessment Board
CNR	Consiglio Nazionale delle Ricerche
COESDIC	Comité d'Expertise et de Suivi de la Démarche d'Information et de Consultation
CoRWM	Committee on Radioactive Waste Management
COWAM	Community Waste Management Spain initiative
CRIIRAD	Commission de recherche et d'information indépendantes sur la radioactivité
CSN	National Safety Council (Consejo de Seguridad Nuclear)
DAD	Decide-Announce-Defend
DBE	Federal Company for Radioactive Waste Disposal (Bundesgesellschaft für Endlagerung mbH)
DGD	Deep Geological Disposal
DGEC	Directorate General for Energy and Climate
DiP	Decision-in-principle
DUP	Declaration of Public Utility
EdF	Électricité de France
EIA	Environmental Impact Assessment
ELDS	Local Encounters for Sustainable Development
EndKo	Commission for the Disposal of High-Level-Waste (Endlager-Kommission)
ENEL	Ente Nazionale Energia Elettrica
ENRESA	National Radioactive Waste Company (Empresa Nacional de Residuos Radioactivos S.A)

Abbreviations

EPR	European Pressure Reactor
EPR	European Pressurised Reactors
EPWR	European Pressurised Water Reactor
FBR	Fast Breeder Reactor
FKTG	Fachkonferenz Teilgebiete (Sub-areas Conference)
FSC	OECD Nuclear Energy Agency's Forum for Stakeholder Confidence
GDF	Geological Disposal Facility
GDR	German Democratic Republic
GIP	Groupement d'intérêt public
GNS	Company for nuclear service (Gesellschaft für Nuklear Service)
HCTISN	High Commission for Transparency and Information on Nuclear Security
HLW	High-level nuclear waste
HSE	Health & Safety Executive
IAEA	International Atomic Energy Agency
IC	Inter-ministerial Commission
ILW	Intermediate level nuclear waste
INFN	Istituto Nazionale di Fisica Nucleare
IRSN	Nuclear safety authority's technical support organisation – author to advise name
ISIN	Ispettorato Nazionale per la Sicurezza Nucleare e la Radioprotezione
IVO	Voima Oy, predecessor of Fortum (shareholder of Posiva)
JEN	Spanish Nuclear Energy Board (Junta de Energía Nuclear)
JYT	Publicly funded research programme on nuclear waste [Julkisrahoitteinen ydinjätetutkimus]
KBS-3V	Technology for disposal of high-level radioactive waste developed in Sweden by Svensk Kärnbränslehantering AB [KärnBränsleSäkerhet]
KTH	Swedish Royal Institute of Technology
KYT	National Research Programme on Nuclear Waste [Kansallinen ydinjätteen tutkimusohjelma]
LILW	Low or intermediate-level waste
LLW	Low level nuclear waste
MEE	Ministry of Economic Affairs and Employment
MITERD	Ministry for the Ecological Transition and the Demographic Challenge
MKG	The Swedish NGO Office for Nuclear Waste Review
MOX	Mixed Oxide fuel
NAC	US National Academy of Sciences

NBG	The National Citizens' Oversight Committee (Nationales Begleitgremium)
NDA	Nuclear Decommissioning Authority
NEA/OECD	Nuclear Energy Agency/Organisation for Economic Co-operation and Development
NGO	Non-Governmental Organization
Nirex Ltd	Nuclear Industry Radioactive Waste Executive
NPP	Nuclear Power Plants
NRC	US National Research Council
NWM	Nuclear waste management
NWS	Nuclear Waste Services
OECD NEA	Nuclear Energy Agency/Organisation for Economic Co-operation and Development
ONR	Office of Nuclear Regulation
ONDRAF-NIRAS	Belgian radioactive waste management agency
OPECST	The Parliamentary Office of Science and Technology
PGRR	General Radioactive Waste Plan (Plan General de Residuos Radioactivos)
PIP	Public Information and Participation procedure
PP	Popular Party (Partido Popular)
PSC	Catalan socialist party (Partit dels Socialistes de Catalunya)
PSOE	Spanish socialist party (Partido Socialista Obrero Español)
PWR	Pressurised Water Reactor
R&D	Research and development
R&D+i	Research and Development plus Innovation
RD&D	Research, development and demonstration
RWM	Radioactive waste management
SEPI	Sociedad Estatal de Participaciones Industriales
SCK CEN	Belgian Nuclear Research Centre
SKB	Swedish Nuclear Fuel and Waste Management Company
SKI	Swedish Nuclear Power Inspectorate (historic)
SMR	Small Modular Reactor
SNF	Spent nuclear fuel
SNWMF	State Nuclear Waste Management Fund
SOGIN	Società Gestione Impianti Nucleari
SSM	Swedish Radiation Safety Authority
StandAG	Repository Site Selection Act

STUK	Finnish Radiation and Nuclear Safety Authority [Säteilyturvakeskus]
THORP	Thermal Oxide Reprocessing Plant
TVO	Teollisuuden Voima Oy, shareholder of Posiva
UKAEA	UK Atomic Energy Authority
URL	Underground Research Laboratory TBC
VLLW	Very Low Level Waste
VSLLW	Very short-lived waste
VTT	Technical Research Centre of Finland [Valtion Teknilinen Tutkimuskeskus]
VVER	Water-water energized reactor (Soviet-based pressurized water reactor)
WNWR	World Nuclear Waste Report
ZEPA	Specially Protected Bird Area

Introduction: The Governance Challenge of Radioactive Waste Management

Rinie van Est, Maarten Arentsen and Romy Dekker

1.1 An Extreme Long-Term Governance Challenge[1]

In 1989, the US federal government initiated research into how future generations could be warned and protected against the hazards of an isolated high-level nuclear waste disposal site. One project focused on the risks posed to the site. Scientists from various prestigious American universities designed imaginary future worlds surrounding the site and assessed the probability and impact of a list of possible future risks. A second project investigated how to mark the site in such a way that people in the future would understand the kind and hazards of the materials stored in the location. Experts, among them artists, made suggestions for the design of markers. The first study concluded that in the long-term human intrusion of the waste disposal site was unavoidable (Hora et al., 1991), while the second study looked at how markers could be used to prevent such human intrusion (Trauth et al., 1993).

---

[1] The authors would like to thank Anne Bergmans and Vincent Lagendijk for their very helpful comments on earlier versions of this chapter.

R. van Est · R. Dekker
Rathenau Instituut, The Hague, The Netherlands
e-mail: q.vanest@rathenau.nl

R. Dekker
e-mail: r.dekker@rathenau.nl

M. Arentsen (✉)
Emeritus University of Twente, Terborg, The Netherlands
e-mail: m.j.arentsen@utwente.nl

© The Author(s) 2023
M. Arentsen and R. van Est (eds.), *The Future of Radioactive Waste Governance*, Energiepolitik und Klimaschutz. Energy Policy and Climate Protection, https://doi.org/10.1007/978-3-658-40496-3_1

The fascinating thing about the studies was their timeframe: 10,000 years from now. It was concluded that governmental control of the site is highly unlikely over the entire time period of 10,000 years. The survival of information on the content and hazards of the site was considered best preserved when it becomes part of a legend or a myth. The experts stated that the conservation of incomplete information is the most dangerous: "Knowing that something is there, but not knowing what it is or what its value may be, may serve to attract investigations such as archaeological digs or salvage operations" (Hora et al., 1991, ES-8).

This US research shows that the challenges and uncertainties incorporated in the long-term disposal of radioactive waste are multifold. This book focuses specifically on how ten European countries are dealing with the long-term disposal of radioactive waste (also see Box 1.2). Long-lived radioactive waste needs to be disposed of safely for extremely long periods, mainly due to various unique characteristics of radioactive waste. It emits ionized radiation (energy) that can destroy (and disturb) the mitosis of all living organisms, and can remain dangerous for time periods up to hundreds of thousands of years, depending on the composition of a radioactive atom (UNSCEAR, 2000). Therefore, radioactive waste needs to be managed to protect humans and the environment until it is no longer harmful.

Although radioactive waste is mainly associated with the production of electricity in nuclear power plants (NPPs), it is also generated during other applications of nuclear technology, such as in health care, non-destructive research and military activities. At present, there is no standard universal categorization of radioactive waste; however, it is usually categorized as low-level waste (LLW), intermediate-level waste (ILW) and high-level waste (HLW). Which waste should be stored in a long-term repository depends not only on the degree of radioactivity, but also on how long the waste will remain radioactive. This can differ between countries since they can decide for themselves on how they categorize and deal with different types of radioactive waste. This book therefore focuses on all radioactive waste that is part of a nation's long-term management policy, regardless of how it is produced (i.e. in a research facility, NPP etc.) and how long and intensely it will be radioactive. We note, however, that in all ten countries studied, nuclear-based power generation contributes the largest share of HLW. Moreover, historically, the public debate about radioactive waste management (RWM) has become strongly intertwined with the often polarised discussions about nuclear energy. Recently, the debate on nuclear energy has become topical again in various European countries (cf. Schneider & Frogatt, 2020) due to the climate crisis (Rogner, 2010), and in 2022 the gas supply crisis due to the Russian invasion of Ukraine.

Currently, deep geological disposal (DGD) is the dominant preferred option in ongoing research on final disposal options being considered internationally (IAEA, 2003). The assumption is that disposal of radioactive waste for a time period of hundreds of thousands of years should be possible from a geophysical perspective. However, there are various uncertainties and disputes: to this day, no geological disposal site is in operation, and there are concerns about the adequacy of various—natural or geological, technical, and social—barriers that a geological repository must maintain (cf. Di Nucci & Brunnnengräber, 2019).

From a societal and political perspective, it is hard to imagine how the world will look some 10,000 years from now—e.g. in the year 12,023—let alone in 100,000 years or longer. This is however, the timeframe we are facing when it comes to political decision-making about the long-term disposal of radioactive waste. These decision-making processes are ongoing in most European countries. The history of RWM shows that when specific sites are designated for the establishment of a (deep geological) repository, most European countries face domestic resistance from significant segments of the population (cf. Thurner et al., 2017). Such resistance illustrates that RWM is not just a technical, but rather a "wicked" sociotechnical issue (Brunnengräber, 2019). Section 1.2 presents ten characteristics of the challenges of RWM.

Faced with considerable social resistance, and a consequent standstill in the implementation of the chosen RWM policy, many European countries have started looking for new approaches. This change in governance style is sometimes typified as the 'participatory turn' in RWM governance strategy (Bergmans et al., 2014). More attention is being paid to the input of local authorities, social organisations and citizens in decision-making processes, but also in the production and use of scientific and technological knowledge. But in addition to this participatory turn, the new governance style in the field of RWM also involves recalibrating institutions and jointly establishing policy principles, including in legislation and regulations. The premise of this book is that the ten countries described have been renewing their decision-making processes and the institutions that support them over the past two to three decades. Thus, the central question of this book is: What lessons do the country studies teach us about the governance of long-term RWM?

To address this question, we use a comprehensive framework, which will be introduced in Section 1.3. The assumption behind this multi-level governance ecosystem framework is that decision-making takes place within a complex field of political, social, scientific, technological, economic and legal actors and institutions from different levels of government (from international and European to national, regional and local). The function of the framework is twofold: analysing current problems in different national contexts in a comparative way, and identifying approaches and strategies for advancing the democratic decision-making process around RWM.

The authors of the ten country chapters have been asked to analyse the state-of-the-art of the governance of radioactive waste in each setting by means of the governance ecosystem framework. Such an approach identifies the strengths and weaknesses of the current institutional setting for democratic decision-making on final disposal in several European countries. Chapter 12 addresses the question: What lessons do the country studies teach us about the governance of long-term RWM? Based on the ten country descriptions and analyses it aims to distill productive ways to improve democratic decision-making on RWM.

This introductory chapter ends with a reader's guide to the contents of the book.

1.2 Ten Challenges of Radioactive Waste Management

The three previous books on nuclear waste governance published in this Springer VS series on energy policy and climate protection provide a good picture of the nature of the problem of radioactive waste: *Nuclear waste governance: An international comparison* (Brunnengräber et al., 2015), *Challenges of nuclear waste governance* (Brunnengräber et al., 2018), and *Conflicts, participation and acceptability in nuclear waste governance an international comparison* (Brunnengräber & Di Nucci, 2019). In particular, the third book in the series (Brunnengräber & Di Nucci, 2019) provides an elaborate understanding of the specificities of nuclear waste siting as a highly complex, a so-called "wicked planning problem" (Rittel & Webber, 1973) or "intractable controversy" (Hisschemöller & Hoppe, 1995) along ten dimensions. Five of those dimensions refer to the nature of the issues at stake, while another group refers to questions of how to deal with those issues.

With regard to the nature of the issues, Brunnengräber (2019, pp. 336–352) identifies the following five dimensions. First, nuclear waste siting concerns problems that are not only characterized by facts, but are socially constructed, and in which *changing narratives* (with a central role for visions, values and expectations) play an important role. Second, it is not just a technical challenge, but a *sociotechnical challenge*. And given the complex interplay between social and technical issues, a blueprint for solving the problem does not exist. Third, Brunnengräber talks of a *double jeopardy situation* because radioactive waste disposal raises both safety and security issues, and responses to safety concerns may strengthen security concerns. Fourth, in dealing with radioactive waste *systemic risks* are involved, that arise from the interaction between technology, politics, society and economics. Fifth, the radioactive waste problem is characterized by *vast time scales*.

With regard to organising the governance of long-term RWM, Brunnengräber presents five dimensions. First of all, the governance task is specific to each country, because it depends on the national context, and the political, social and cultural background. Second, it presents a *multi-level governance* challenge, which implies that radioactive waste disposal is part of a system of international, supranational, and country-specific institutions and policies. Third, a multiplicity of actors is involved in the decisions regarding the management of radioactive waste at different levels of governance. Various actors bring in different ideologies and interests, which leads to a *landscape of conflicting actors*. Fourth, dealing with the radioactive waste issue requires inter- and transdisciplinary research and thus crosses the *boundaries of different scientific fields*. Last but not least, radioactive waste governance forms a *democratic challenge,* which is ultimately about "reshaping state authority, a shift in responsibility and the integration of civilian knowledge and experience" (Brunnengräber, 2019, p. 350).

This book draws on these entry points by exploring how countries in Europe are currently organising or planning decision-making regarding long-term RWM, explicitly acknowledging that this is a deeply challenging issue. In addition to continuing the analysis and explanation of problems, we intend to suggest approaches and strategies for advancing the democratic decision-making process around RWM.

1.3 Multi-Level Governance-Ecosystem Framework

Knowing that societal resistance in combination with (scientific and technological) uncertainties on radioactive waste disposal options are central issues in national debates, our analysis focuses on trust-building policy measures and socially robust institutions that are capable of shaping a continuous process of interaction between politics, law, science and technology, and society over a long period of time, far beyond electoral periods. To thoroughly analyse and compare these decision-making processes we use a governance ecosystem approach. Below we introduce its conceptual background and the design of the multi-level governance ecosystem framework, which is based on an historical review of how the Netherlands has dealt with ethical and social issues surrounding various new technologies, like biotechnology, ICT, clinical trials and animal experiments (Kool et al., 2017).

1.3.1 Conceptual Background

The governance ecosystem framework combines two concepts. While the concept of governance has a social science background, the concept of ecosystem originates from biology and ecology.

Multi-level governance
The concept of governance implies that the government is not seen as the only guardian of public interests, but that public services can be delivered by a diverse set of actors in the public and private sectors, ranging from organisations at different levels of government (from international and European to national, regional and local) to companies, scientific institutions, non-governmental organizations (NGOs), and citizens (Kersbergen & Waarden, 2001). There will therefore often be so-called *multi-level governance*, within which we can make an analytical distinction between vertical, horizontal and diagonal interactions. Vertical interactions take place between the public authorities of different administrative layers. Horizontal and diagonal interactions are interactions between public and private actors, respectively, within a particular tier of government and across different tiers of government. Moreover, governance does not just take place through formal instruments such as legislation and regulation, but is also about creating and reproducing shared principles, social norms and institutions by means of public debate, negotiations, collaboration, joint vision development, etc. (Kersbergen & Waarden, 2004, pp. 151–2). In short, governance is about achieving public goods and services in a society by the interplay of public and private actors in the context of a configuration of social, economic, political and legal institutions.

Ecosystem approach
The *Cambridge Dictionary* gives two meanings of the word ecosystem as 1) "all the living things in an area and the way they affect each other and the environment", and 2) "any complicated system consisting of many different people, processes, activities, etc., especially relating to technology, and the way that they affect each other". From a biological perspective, ecosystems are composed of organisms living together in symbiotic relationships allowing them and the ecosystem they are part of to survive. The living organisms of the ecosystem are plants, animals and micro-organisms. The ecosystem is able to survive through

the exchange of matter and energy between the composing organisms and their environment: soil, water and air. The social sciences, including public and business administration, have adopted the ecosystem concept as a biological metaphor to analyse the structure and organisation of (parts of) the social, political, economic and technological world, with interdependence and interaction between the constituent components as major explanations for reaching outcomes. The second definition of ecosystem in the *Cambridge Dictionary* refers to this. Adner (2017) suggests the following definition of a social science-focused ecosystem: "The ecosystem is defined by the alignment structure of the multilateral set of partners that need to interact in order for a focal value proposition to materialize" (Adner 2017, p. 42). Adner's corporate business strategy-oriented paper distinguishes four dimensions of a business-oriented ecosystem. First the *alignment structure* for analysing how positions and flows in the system are organised and accepted. *Multilaterality* of dependencies as a second dimension refers to the type of dependencies in an ecosystem, which are multisided by definition. The third dimension, *set of partners*, refers to the idea that outcomes are the result of a collective of actors. The fourth and final dimension refers to what the ecosystem is heading for, in Adner's paper, a certain value proposition; the normative outcome of the ecosystem. In our framework, the goal of democratic decision-making is to achieve public values, where "public value is the combined view of the public about what they regard as valuable" (Talbot, 2011, p. 28).

1.3.2 Multi-Level Governance-Ecosystem Framework

In combination, the governance ecosystem can be conceptualised as the institutional setting in which societies deal with specific problems and challenges, which need democratic decision-making. This conceptualisation implies that in a society several governance ecosystems can be identified. A specific governance ecosystem, therefore, is demarcated by a specific public problem or challenge. In this book, the governance of long-term RWM demarcates the governance ecosystem of interest. The conceptualisation of a multi-level governance ecosystem is displayed in Fig. 1.1.

The framework consists of four mutually dependent societal domains: "politics and administration", "science and technology", "laws and regulations", and "civil society". These four domains form the alignment structure of the ecosystem, defining the positions, interactions and flows which shape decision-making and lead to outcomes. But each of the four domains is also an independent institutional setting, with its own history, structures, cultures and routines. In the

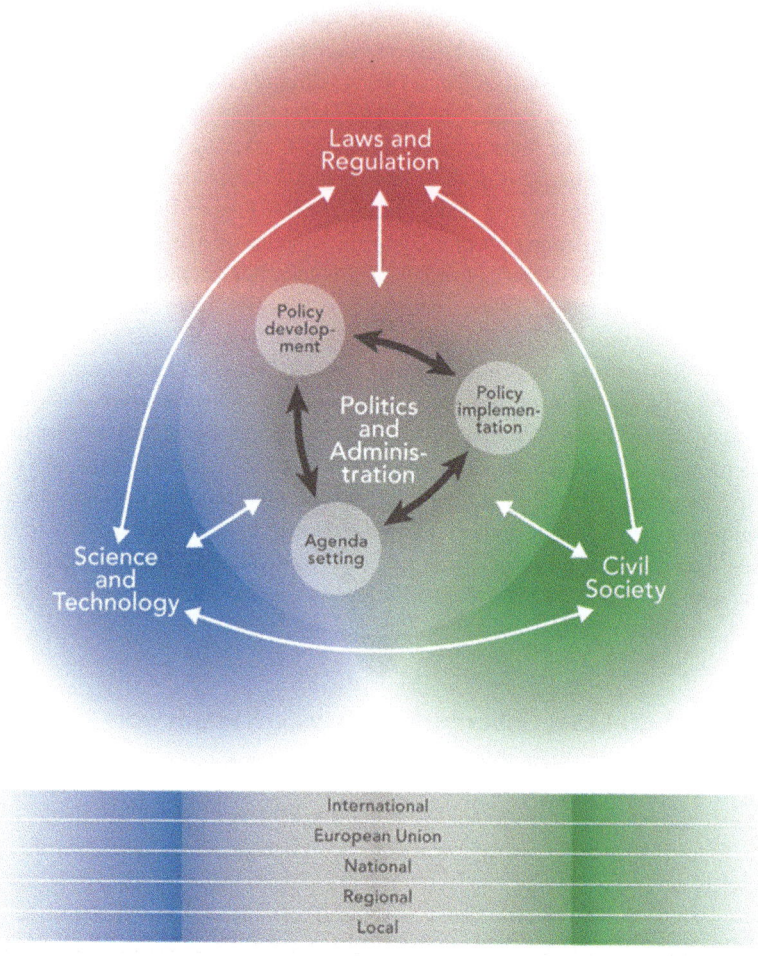

Fig. 1.1 Multi-level governance-ecosystem framework (Adapted from: Kool et al., 2017, p. 95). The figure shows both a top view and front view of the governance ecosystem, with the top view showing the four social domains and their (horizontal) interactions and the front view showing the multi-level nature of the governance ecosystem

ecosystem conceptualisation the alignment of the four domains is multilateral, meaning that all four are mutually influencing and crucial to reach outcomes. The four domains also define the set of actors carrying the interactions between the domains, and the inertia and dynamics of the decision-making processes. Below, we elaborate on the four domains and the interactions between them to provide examples that give the reader a clearer idea of the role of the various domains and the interplay between them. While the domains are distinguished analytically here, there is a strong overlap between them, as shown in Fig. 1.1, and as also appears in the ten country descriptions.

Science and technology
The safe management of risks to humans and the environment from radioactive waste is highly dependent on scientific knowledge and technological expertise, capabilities and instruments. Science and technology play at least three roles in political decision-making (cf. Beck, 1992, p. 163). First, the industrial use of science and technologies creates social benefits and risks. With regard to political decision-making, science and technology can provide practical solutions to societal problems. For example, in the case of long-term RWM, a geological storage facility is often put forward as a possible long-term option. Second, science and technology provide means to recognise and measure physical risks, but also indicate and articulate social and ethical issues related to technologies. And third, science and technology can be used to deal with risks in the best possible way. Accordingly, many technologies and scientific fields, both physical and social, may play a valuable role in the decision-making process on long-term RWM. For the physical sciences, this varies from physics, chemistry to geology, ecology and medical sciences. Here, the focus is on science and technology in the field of radioactive materials and safety. These areas of knowledge have become highly institutionalised internationally and play a central role in national legislation and regulations (see Box 1.1).

The social sciences play a less institutionalised role in the field of RWM, although more attention has been paid to this in recent decades. For example, the work of the Radioactive Waste Management Committee (RWMC), as part of the Nuclear Energy Agency (NEA) within the Organization for Economic Cooperation and Development (OECD), also covers societal aspects of nuclear waste management, in particular stakeholder involvement in decision-making on management issues. According to the NEA website: "The decision-making process for RWM, as well as for decommissioning and legacy management, is couched in a socio-political context, in which issues of public concern and stakeholder engagement must be addressed. This especially comes into play when considering final disposal and deep geological repositories" (RWMC website, 2022). In 2000, the RWMC established the Forum on Stakeholder Confidence (FSC) "to foster learning about stakeholder dialogue and ways to develop shared confidence, informed consent and acceptance of RWM solutions" (ibid.) There is thus an understanding that RWM is not just a technical issue but a socio-technical issue, which requires all kinds of social scientific knowledge, ranging from ethics and public administration to legal knowledge.

> **Box 1.1 Coordination of International and National Governance of Radiation Protection and Nuclear Safety**
>
> Science and technology in the field of radiation protection and nuclear safety have become organised along three pillars: radiology and radiological protection, nuclear installation safety, and radioactive waste disposal. The history of radiological protection is well-documented (Clarke & Valentin, 2008). Figure 1.2 shows how scientific knowledge feeds into recommendations at multiple levels of governance. The International Commission on Radiological Protection (ICRP) plays a central role. The ICRP was established in 1928 to study the implications and effects of the discoveries of X-ray and radioactivity (Clarke & Valentin, 2008, p. 77). The ICRP is an independent, international, non-governmental organization, with the mission to protect people, animals, and the environment from the harmful effects of ionizing radiation. Since the 1950s, epidemiological research of people being exposed to radioactivity due to radioactive fallout from atomic bomb tests in the atmosphere provides the scientific grounding of the safety standards. The United Nations Scientific Committee on the Effects of Atomic Radiation (UNSCEAR)—established by the General Assembly of the United Nations in 1955 to assess and report levels and effects of exposure to ionizing radiation—published its first report on human safety and protection in 1958, and the second in 1962 (https://www.unscear.org/unscear/about_us/history.html).
>
> With regard to nuclear safety, the radiological protection standards are translated into nuclear technologies, and technologies for the safe application of radioactive materials in medicine, food safety and non-destructive research. Research and safety guidelines of the International Atomic Energy Agency (IAEA)—an autonomous organization of the United Nations, which seeks to promote the safe, secure and peaceful use of nuclear technologies—provide the base for the global safety standards. In the European Union (EU), the safety standards have been codified through the European Union's Directive on Nuclear Safety. The IAEA monitors and reviews the safety of operational nuclear installations globally; the Operational Safety Review Team (OSART) reviews the installations and reports on findings and recommendations.

The Organization for Economic Cooperation and Development (OECD) is the world's leading organisation with regard to the safe disposal of radioactive material and the development of scientifically grounded guidelines. The OECD's activities are organised in the Nuclear Energy Agency (NEA). Its website states that "[t]he NEA assists member countries in the development of safe, sustainable and societally acceptable strategies for the management of all types of radioactive waste". In 1975 the NEA established the Radioactive Waste Management Committee (RWMC), for supporting

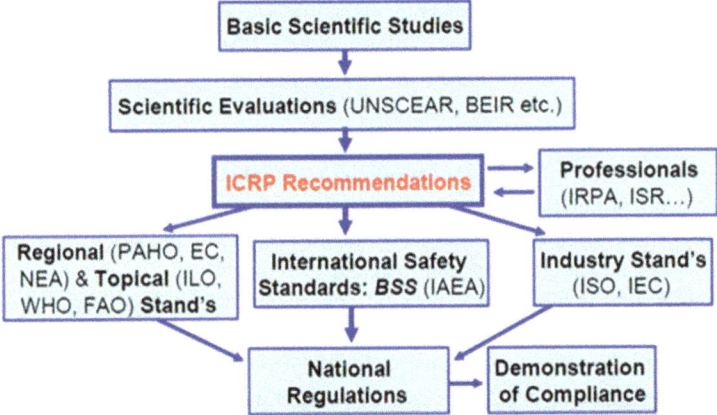

Fig. 1.2 The basis for and use of the International Commission on Radiological Protection (ICRP) recommendations on radiological protection policy. (Source: Clarke & Valentin, 2008, p. 102)

members "… in the development of safe and economically efficient management of all types of radioactive waste including spent fuel considered as radioactive waste based on the latest scientific and technological knowledge" (Nuclear Energy Agency (NEA)—Radioactive Waste Management Committee (RWMC) (oecd-nea.org)).

Civil society
Civil society includes all individuals and private organizations in a society not associated directly with the government, such as schools and universities, interest groups, professional associations, churches, cultural institutions, NGOs and

businesses. This wide array of individuals and organisations represents different groups, opinions and interests, and is thought to be essential for democracy (cf. Rosanvallon, 2008). The goal of democratic decision-making is that it leads to legitimised outcomes that are valued by many members of society. If that is the case, it may increase people's trust in the decision-making processes and provide acceptability of the outcomes.

In democratic countries, periodic national, regional, and local elections are means to influence political directions. Together with the rights to express opinions, to demonstrate and to protest, people can influence political decision-making and hence political outcomes. Civil society actors in many European countries have become heavily involved in RWM issues, especially with regard to the installation of waste disposal facilities. For example, protests have been very intense in Germany in particular, but also peaked in other European countries (Thurner et al., 2017). Civil society actors can also play a role as watchdog, and for example, with the help of technical, legal or ethical experts if required critically scrutinize the information that official knowledge institutes, companies and governments produce. Because policy is often based on scientific and technical knowledge, the presence of such public counter-expertise can strongly influence public debate and political decision-making.

As indicated above, public trust or distrust and social acceptance or non-acceptance have played a major role in decision-making on long-term RWM, which has led in many countries to a 'participatory turn' in RWM governance strategy (Bergmans et al., 2014), and thus to all kinds of top-down participatory experiments, organised by public or private organizations, to involve citizens in decision-making and in the production of knowledge. The ten country studies show various inspiring examples of this.

Laws and regulations

Laws and regulations serve many purposes. Four principal ones are establishing standards, maintaining order, resolving disputes, and protecting liberties and rights. In EU countries, the laws and regulations regarding long-term RWM are based on international law and recommendations and guidelines from three international organizations (IAEA, ICRP and NEA) and European law. In the EU, the Euratom Treaty legally grounds the peaceful applications of radioactive materials and its accompanying safety standards. The Euratom Treaty is one of the fundamental treaties of the European Union and provided the legal context for Directive 2011/70/Euratom (European Council, 2011). Under the Directive, countries are obliged to develop and design a regulatory framework for the management of the country's radioactive waste. In addition to legislative frameworks regarding nuclear technology activities, there are also relevant laws and regulations in the field of environmental protection, spatial planning, and rules on public participation and access to information and the courts.

Figure 1.2 shows how rules and regulations are fed by and embedded in international scientific research, recommendations, guidelines and rules of conduct. It shows the hierarchy in the process of developing rules and regulations and their science-based grounding. The many organisations displayed in the fourth layer of Fig. 1.2 indicate the wide range of applications of radioactive material and its accompanying safety measures, mediated by many sector organizations. Protection of the workforce and protection of the environment are the two main addressees of safety standards. The internationally agreed recommended rules and regulations are translated and implemented nationally under the ratification requirements of the agreements.

A second relevant set of international input for national regulations are the agreements made in 1998 under the Convention on Access to Information, Public Participation in Decision-making and Access to Justice in Environmental Matters, the Aarhus Convention: "In order to contribute to the protection of the right of every person of present and future generations to live in an environment adequate to his or her health and well-being, each Party shall guarantee the rights of access to information, public participation in decision-making, and access to justice in environmental matters in accordance with the provisions of this Convention (Article 1). "(UN, 1998). Article 6 under 1, obliges countries to develop and design rules in accordance with the Convention for participation in radioactive waste siting and availability of information on siting matters. Annex 1 explicitly mentions disposal of radioactive waste as one of the activities covered. The Aarhus Convention provides an international legal reference for organising and designing public participation in decision making on long-term RWM.

Politics and administration
The fourth domain is that of politics and administration. Politics can be defined as the authoritative allocation of public values (Easton, 1965). The function of politics and administration is to organise democratically legitimised decision-making and to implement effective and socially acceptable policies. With regard to long-term RWM it is about effective and democratically legitimised decision-making procedures, decisions and policies. Building an effective and trust-inspiring radioactive waste governance ecosystem is an important point of attention. Time plays an important political and policy role in the governance of long-term RWM: in essence, the governance of radioactive waste is time or temporal governance (see Box 1.2).

Within the political-administrative domain we recognize three stages: 1) Agenda-setting phase, in which public issues on new developments in science and technology are identified and articulated; 2) policy development phase, in which political decisions are prepared and made; in the latter, representatives of the people play a central role, and 3) policy implementation phase, in which the above decisions are put into practice. Figure 1.1. clearly indicates that the politics and administration domain is in strong interchange and (horizontal) interaction with the other three domains. The three other domains feed political decision-making and receive the decisions taken in the politics and administration domain. In other words, strong interference, exchange of knowledge and ideas and interaction are particular features of the relationship between the politics and administration domain and the other three domains. Policy implementation includes developing, operating and maintaining the existing infrastructure of national radioactive waste processing and storage industries. Countries applying radioactive materials have established private or publicly-owned industries responsible for the logistics, processing and storage of radioactive waste in all categories.

Box 1.2 The governance of radioactive waste as time governance
Because part of the radioactive waste can remain active for hundreds of thousands of years, this waste must be managed in such a way that it does not endanger people and the environment in the distant future, but such a long period of time presents a unique governance challenge. Scientists and policymakers see geological disposal of radioactive waste as the preferred method. Laes (2016) argues that the technological and moral legitimacy of geological disposal rests on the promise that it will enable future generations in the not-so-distant-future "to forget about radioactive waste". Because time plays such an important role in the governance of RWM, in this book we pay special attention to time or temporal governance, which refers to all time-related activities that contribute to organising or preventing collective action to reach common goals, such as the safe handling of radioactive waste.

Firstly, time can be used as a governance tool for collective action. In this case, Bornemann & Strassheim (2019) speak of "governance by time". Time can be used as a resource through, for example, time management and/or time tactics (Pollitt, 2008), such as intentional delay, making promises, fixing deadlines, seizing opportunities from a crisis (cf. Carter, 2019).

To give an example, according to current policy in the Netherlands, radioactive waste is stored above ground for a period of at least a hundred years at the Central Organization for Radioactive Waste (COVRA) in Zeeland. The government wants to make a decision about long-term RWM in the Netherlands around the year 2100. An important governance question is whether this timing of the decision-making process is sensible and, if not, what would be an appropriate time schedule, and if so, how can the period up to 2100 be used wisely?

Second, because our social and political perspective on time has an important influence on how we shape governance ecosystems, our view on time is also an important object of governance. Political terms such as sustainability, intergenerational justice, reversibility of decisions and retrievability of radioactive waste have a strong time component. And if such moral guiding principles are politically embraced, they will have a strong impact on policy shaping and, in the longer term, the entire governance ecosystem. At the same time, policy proposals often contain implicit assumptions and visions about time. For example, according to Laes (2016), implementing geological disposal is aimed at realising the 'imagination of forgetting' within a few generations. Such a time governance perspective would reduce the time horizon of the radioactive waste problem from hundreds of thousands of years to several hundred years.

Interaction between the four domains
Effective and democratically legitimised governance of RWM depends on each of the four social domains. Each domain also entails a specific condition for effective democratic decision-making. The political-administrative domain requires political legitimacy and acceptance. The remaining three domains require scientific knowledge and technological feasibility, legal admissibility and social desirability and acceptance. Due to the importance of all conditions that must be met at the same time, a constructive interaction between the domains is crucial. Here, we briefly describe the (horizontal) interactions between the four domains regarding RWM in a more theoretical way. Chapter 12 will provide a comparative empirical analysis of these dynamics based on the ten country studies.

The central role of the scientific and technological domain in dealing with radioactive waste implies that science and technology also play a central role in the three other social domains. This can, for example, lead to a scientificisation of the political decision-making process. For example, in the Spanish case, Josep

Espluga-Trenc and Ana Prades state that HLW management is used by political parties to profile themselves politically, which has led to a 'nuclearization of politics'. As part of the same dynamic, the scientific and technological domain may also become politicised.

Citizens can express their support for policy, existing regulations, or technology in many ways, but they can also critically question or actively oppose their implementation in many ways. Historian Rosanvallon (2008) argues that in addition to being a voter, citizens can fulfill three more democratic roles: as a watchdog or supervisor, as a protester or restrainer, and as users of the legal system. In these three ways, citizens (individually or collectively) can give substance to their so-called democratic mistrust, which aims "to make sure that elected officials keep their promises and to find ways of maintaining pressure on the government to serve the common good" (Rosanvallon, 2008, p. 8). In the first role, citizens watch closely and critically and make themselves heard, for example through the media, when they think things are not going well. In this role it is possible to collaborate with scientists and other experts who share this critical stance. If citizens want to block a certain development, they can also go to court—the domain of law. Finally, citizens can try to ensure through protest actions that parliamentary legitimised government policy is not or cannot be implemented.

As described above, the political and administrative domain relies on science and technology to identify RWM public problems and develop solutions. National and international legislation and policy principles guide the ways in which the government can act, and which technical options can be applied. For example, French and Dutch policy both stipulate that after disposal, the radioactive waste must be retrievable, which requires certain scientific knowledge and development of technological options. In addition, the actions of the government require not only legal legitimacy, but also social support. At the same time, politicians and policymakers have a central public responsibility for good long-term RWM. They can fulfill this role by adequately stimulating and regulating the development of science and technology. In the field of radioactive waste, science and technology are highly dependent on political support and funding. The government and representatives of the people also play a central role in developing and implementing policy, legislation and regulations, and also monitor and evaluate their application. Finally, from a democratic perspective, governments have a responsibility to properly inform citizens and to involve them in decision-making processes. This is legally required due to, for example, the Aarhus Convention (UN, 1998), which became operational in 2001, and Directive 2011/70/Euratom of the European Council (2011).

In addition to the political and administrative domain, the social domain and the science and technology domain also play a role in the development of legislation and regulations. Legal frameworks and principles provide the rules on the basis of which people act and interact in a constitutional state, and aim to protect citizens against each other and the government. That is why high-quality legislation is important. In governance in general, and the drafting and implementation of legislation and regulations in particular, the interaction between various levels of government—local, regional, national and international—plays an important role. This is referred to as multilevel governance. In the field of radioactive waste governance, international bodies such as the NEA of the OECD, the IAEA of the UN, and the EU, or Euratom all play an important role.

1.4 A Reader's Guide

The following ten chapters are devoted to the governance of long-term RWM in ten EU countries. In each of those countries long-term RWM is a societal and political challenge mainly because of the country's nuclear-based production of electricity, which is by far the largest contributor to long-lived radioactive waste (European Commission, 2019, p. 15).

The first row of Table 1.1 lists the taxonomy of three types of radioactive waste according to the IAEA: low-level waste (LLW), intermediate-level waste (ILW) and high-level waste (HLW). All countries included in the book follow this IAEA classification in one way or another. The second row lists the IAEA preferred technical option for the management, storage and disposal of each waste type. For the long-lived LLW a (near) surface storage of at least 300 years is recommended. For ILW and HLW, deep geological storage for 100,000 years and more are recommended. In all ten European countries discussed in this book, the final disposal of LLW, ILW and HLW is still work in progress. So none of the countries described (nor anywhere else in the world) has reached the operational phase of long-term final disposal as suggested by the IAEA.

Table 1.1 Taxonomy of three types of radioactive waste and suggested waste management options by the IAEA. (Source: IAEA, 2009)

Radioactive waste type	Low-level waste (LLW)	Intermediate-level waste (ILW)	High-level waste (HLW)
IAEA suggested technical option	Near surface disposal	Intermediate depth disposal	Deep geological disposal

The ten European countries included in the book are working on near surface or intermediate depth disposal options and DGD options, but the stage of development, the technological challenges and governance approach differ from country to country. The order of the chapters is mainly determined on the basis of the development phase a country is in. We start with countries that are still in a policy-making phase with regard to the final disposal of high-level radioactive waste, and end with countries that are already in the implementation phase. We therefore end with France, Sweden, and finally Finland since these three countries are clearly ahead of the other seven countries, having decided on a technology (DGD) and location, and are in the phase of developing the site for a geological disposal facility. Starting with countries that are still far from such a final solution and ending with countries closest to it, provides the reader with a rich overview of the challenges involved in the different phases of the governance of RWM.

In Chap. 2, Romy Dekker, Vincent Lagendijk, Roos Walstock and Rinie van Est describe how the Netherlands pursues a so-called 'dual strategy'—national and international—with regard to RWM. On the national level, an above-ground facility was built in the 1990s to store radioactive waste for a period of at least 100 years. By around the year 2130 a geological disposal facility is envisaged to be operational. The Netherlands also pursues an international strategy, which leaves the possibility open for collaboration with other European Union Member States to establish a shared geological disposal facility. Currently, the country's radioactive waste policy lacks a concrete step-by-step decision-making process to implement its dual strategy.

In Chap. 3, Maria Rosaria Di Nucci and Andrea Prontera explain how radioactive waste governance in Italy is characterised by complex interactions between European, national, regional and local political-territorial levels. In 2011, the European Council Directive 2011/70/Euratom (European Council, 2011) put pressure on national decision-makers to initiate an inclusive process for a suitable site for nuclear waste on the basis of socio-technical and scientific criteria. Accordingly, the nuclear waste operator SOGIN envisioned plans for the construction of a central surface repository for the temporary storage of, amongst others, HLW. Recently, after a long period of incoherent stop-and-go, local opposition to the plans and a subsequent deadlock, the mandatory search for a national site is taking shape. The national map of potentially suitable areas was released in January 2021.

In Chap. 4, Anne Bergmans, Catherine Fallon, Ron Cörvers and Céline Parotte discuss key dimensions for the future of radioactive waste governance in Belgium. They highlight elements that a diverse set of Belgian stakeholders considered of importance for a national public debate. This foresight chapter gives

1 Introduction: The Governance Challenge ...

voices to actors who compose the current HLW governance ecosystem, from concerned citizens, scientists, policymakers, civil society representatives, and public administrators to environmental associations. These actors considered five important governance principles: a flexible and stepwise approach, practicing transparency, providing clarity about the link between participation and decision-making, ensuring monitoring and control, and robust financing.

In Chap. 5, Maria Rosaria Di Nucci and Achim Brunnengräber describe that Germany has a long tradition and history in final disposal siting, but to date its governance is still work in progress. After massive societal protest, Germany decided to restart the governance process, this time from the bottom-up. Since 2013, the Repository Site Selection Act (StandAG) opened-up new opportunities, by providing a framework for the establishment of new state institutions and a participation procedure for involving civil society and stakeholder groups. The authors maintain that the StandAG leaves many unresolved issues, but permits extensive room for manoeuvre, and represents an opportunity for new and expanded forms of participation to be pursued.

In Chap. 6, Josep Espluga-Trenc and Ana Prades describe the complex interactions between central and regional governments in Spain in the search for a location for a centralised temporary aboveground repository for, amongst others, HLW. The plan to build such an intermediate aboveground disposal facility has been the subject of numerous social and political conflicts, so that it remains a difficult issue to solve. Environmental legislation, required by European directives, requires public transparency and openness to citizen participation. The authors argue that in Spain, opening the nuclear issue from the closed circles of experts and their organisations to a broad public debate has created a "nuclearization of politics", leaving limited room for counter-expertise, as nuclear-related arguments are employed opportunistically to serve broader political aims.

In Chap. 7, Sophie Kuppler, Anne Eckhardt and Peter Hocke critically discuss the basic characteristics of the Swiss governance approach to RWM. In Switzerland, the selection procedure for a nuclear waste repository site is characterized by deliberation and debate between different governmental levels, and lay persons and experts. The usual Swiss decentralised democratic model has been amended, with more centralised coordination in the decision-making process. For example, the Swiss Parliament abolished the cantonal veto rights on deep geological disposal in favor of an optional national veto right on the general license for such a repository. Moreover, it was decided in 2008 to link the decision-making process around finding a geological disposal facility to the methodology of a Sectoral Plan, which is an established spatial planning instrument of the Swiss Confederation.

In Chap. 8, Steve Thomas argues that the United Kingdom is still several decades away from building facilities that will provide a safe, permanent home for HLW. Attempts to site new facilities have repeatedly failed. In 2007, the approach changed from one driven by identifying an ideal site then implementing it, to one that placed informed consent from the hosting community at the forefront. The author estimates the new policy as risky, and has little confidence that it will identify a site for HLW that is both technically and politically acceptable.

As indicated above, France is one of the forerunners in advancing towards implementation of a repository for HLW. In Chap. 9, Markku Lehtonen describes how the state agency responsible for RWM, Andra, plans to start the construction of the Cigéo facility in 2022, with a pilot-testing phase in 2025, and operation in 2040–2050. Although supported by most parliamentarians and key stakeholders in the region, the project continues to generate controversy and recurrent clashes between opponents and the police. To deal with public distrust, the French authorities laid down the principle of reversibility by law in 2006, as a concept that allows future generations to choose between either continuing the construction and operation of disposal through successive phases, or to re-examine the earlier choices and modify the management solutions. Moreover, the government together with the nuclear industry have institutionalised counter-expertise through the establishment of permanent and ad hoc multi-stakeholder bodies, and have set up experiments at "co-creation of knowledge" by experts and citizens holding distinct types of expertise.

In Chap. 10, Johan Swahn describes how in January 2022, the Swedish government decided to allow the construction of a geological repository for SNF (the SFL). The geological waste facility is based on the KBS-3 V concept, which has three safety barriers (bedrock granite, bentonite clay, and copper canister) designed to keep the HLW isolated from the biosphere for at least 100,000 years. But the decision was controversial and may still be found to conflict with the implementation of the Swedish environmental legislation developed since the beginning of the twenty-first century. This chapter describes the long process that has led to the decision to allow the construction of a repository for SNF, and the controversies that have arisen. The most important controversy has been the copper canister corrosion issue, which has been central in the discussions of long-term safety of the repository since 2007, as well as to the repository licence review process from 2011, until the decision in January 2022.

In Chap. 11, Jarmo Vehmas, Aleksis Rentto, Jyrki Luukkanen, Burkhard Auffermann and Jari Kaivo-oja describe that Finland plans full operation of the ONKALO geological disposal facility in 2024. The ONKALO project includes an encapsulation plant and final disposal facility based on the Swedish KBS-3 V concept (see Chap. 10). The authors identify various factors that brought Finland to a forerunner position in long-term RWM, like structural corporatism and high trust in technology, nuclear expertise and politicians. Since the potential host municipality has a veto right, the critical factor was local acceptability in the municipal council of Eurajoki, which was reached after negotiations on mutual benefits with Posiva, the company established by the nuclear power companies Fortum and TVO for nuclear waste management.

We hope that the ten European country chapters contain examples of productive ways for collective decision-making, which may provide inspiration to better democratic decision-making. Thus the concluding Chap. 12 aims to address the question: What lessons do the country studies teach us about the governance of long-term RWM? Rinie van Est and Maarten Arentsen make use of the governance ecosystem framework. They show that the governance of RWM is strongly influenced by developments in the field of nuclear energy. To emphasize the multi-level nature of RWM's governance, they reflect on the interactions between international and national governmental levels, and national, regional and local levels. Next they focus on each of the four domains of the governance ecosystem framework: politics and administration, law and regulation, science and technology, and civil society. As a result the authors identify 17 lessons that may advance the democratic decision-making process around RWM.

References

Adner, R. (2017). Ecosystem as structure: An actionable construct for strategy. *Journal of Management*, 43(1), 39–58.
Beck, U. (1992). *Risk society: Towards a new modernity*. (M. Ritter, Trans.). SAGE.
Bergmans, A., Sundqvist, G., Kosc, D., & Simmons, P. (2014). The participatory turn in radioactive waste management: Deliberation and the social-technical divide. *Journal of Risk Research*, 18 (3). https://doi.org/10.1080/13669877.2014.971335.
Bornemann, B., & Strassheim, H. (2019). Governing time for sustainability: Analyzing the temporal implications of sustainability governance. *Sustainability Science*, 14: 1001–1013.
Brunnengräber, A., di Nucci, M. R., Isidoro Losada, A. M., Mez, L., & Schreurs, M. A. (Eds.) (2015). *Nuclear waste governance: An international comparison*. Springer VS.
Brunnengräber, A. & Di Nucci, M.R., (Eds.) (2019). *Conflicts, Participation and Acceptability in Nuclear Waste Governance. An International Comparison (Volume III)*. Springer VS.
Brunnengräber, A. (2019). The wicked problem of long term radioactive waste governance: Ten characteristics of a complex technical and societal challenge. In Brunnengräber A. & Di Nucci, M. R. (Eds.). *Conflicts, participation and acceptability in nuclear waste governance: An international comparison (Volume III)*. Springer VS. pp. 335–355.

Brunnengräber, A.; Di Nucci, M. R.; Isidoro Losada, A. M.; Mez, L. and Schreurs, M. (Eds.) (2018). *Challenges of nuclear waste governance: An international comparison (Volume II)*. Springer VS.

Carter, P. (2019). Time tactics: Project managing policy implementation in a network. *Time & Society*, 28(2), 721–742.

Clarke, R.H., & Valentin, J. (2008). *The history of ICRP and the evolution of its policies*. ICRP Publication 109.

Di Nucci M. R. & Brunnengräber, A. (2019). Making nuclear waste problems governable: Conflicts, participation and acceptability. In Brunnengräber, A. & Di Nucci, M. R. (Eds.). *Conflicts, participation and acceptability in nuclear waste governance: An international comparison (Volume III)*. Springer VS. pp. 3–19.

Easton, D. (1965). *A system analysis of political life*. John Wiley.

European Council. (2011). *Council Directive 2011/70/Euratom of 19 July 2011 establishing a Community framework for the responsible and safe management of spent fuel and radioactive waste*. OJ L 199/48, 2 August 2011.

European Commission. (2019). *Inventory of radioactive waste and spent fuel present in the Community's territory and the future prospects accompanying the document report from de Commission to the Council and the European Parliament on progress of implementation of Council Directive 2011/70/Euratom and an inventory of radioactive waste and spent fuel present in the Community's territory and the future prospects*. 17.12.2019 SWD (2019) 435 final.

Hisschemöller, M. & Hoppe, R. (1995) Coping with intractable controversies: The case for problem structuring in policy design and analysis. *Knowledge and Policy* 8 (4), 40–60.

Hora, S.C., von Winterfeldt, D., & K. M. Trauth. (1991). *Expert judgment on inadvertent human intrusion into the waste isolation pilot plant*. Sanda National Laboratories.

IAEA. (2003). *Scientific and technical basis for the geological disposal of radioactive wastes*. Technical Reports series No 413. International Atomic Energy Agency.

IAEA. (2009). *Safety Standards for protecting people and the environment: Classification of radioactive waste—General safety guide No GSG-1*. International Atomic Energy Agency.

Kersbergen, K. van, & van Waarden, F. (2001). *Shifts in governance: Problems of legitimacy and accountability*. NWO.

Kersbergen, K. van, & van Waarden, F. (2004). 'Governance' as a bridge between disciplines: Cross-disciplinary inspiration regarding shifts in governance and problems of governability, accountability and legitimacy. *European Journal of Political Research*, 43: 143–171.

Kool, L., Timmer, J., Royakkers, L., & van Est, R. (2017). *Urgent upgrade: Protect public values in our digitized society*. Rathenau Instituut.

Laes, E. (2016). *Een kritische analyse van het Belgische kernafvalbeleid aan de hand van Foucault*. Universiteit van Antwerpen.

Peters, B. G., & Pierre, J. (2009). Governance approaches. In A. Wiener & T. Diez (Eds.) *European integration theory* (2nd ed. pp. 91–104). Oxford University PressPollitt, C. (2008). *Time, policy, management: Governing with the past*. Oxford University Press.

Rosanvallon, P. (2008). *Counter-democracy: Politics in an age of distrust*. (A. Goldhammer, Trans.). Cambridge University Press.

Rittel, H. W. J., & Webber, M. M. (1973). Dilemmas in a general theory of planning. *Policy Sciences*, 4(2), 155–169.

Rogner, H. H. (2010). Nuclear power and sustainable development. *Journal of International Affairs*, 64 (1), 137–163.
RWMC website (2022) https://www.oecd-nea.org/jcms/pl_25191/radioactive-waste-management-committee-rwmc.
Schneider, M., & Frogatt, A. (2020). *The world nuclear industry status report 2020*. Mycle Schneider Consulting.
Talbot, C. (2011). Paradoxes and prospects of 'public value'. *Public Money & Management*, 31(1), 27–34.
Thurner, P.W., Brouard, S., Dolezal, M., Guinaudeau, I., Hutter, S., & Müller, W. C. (2017). *Conflict over nuclear energy: Public opinion, protest movements, and green parties in comparative perspective*. Oxford University Press.
Trauth, K.M., Hora, S. C., & Guzowsti, R. V. (1993). *Expert judgment on markers to deter inadvertent human intrusion into the waste isolation pilot plant*. Sanda National Laboratories.
United Nations Scientific Committee on the effects of Atomic Radiation (UNSCEAR). (2000). *Sources and effects of ionizing radiation*. UNSCEAR.
UN (1998). *Convention on Access to Information, Public Participation in Decision-Making and Access to Justice in Environmental Matters*. The United Nations Economic Commission for Europe (UNECE). https://unece.org/environment-policy/public-participation/aarhus-convention/text.

Rinie van Est is a research coordinator at the Rathenau Instituut, the Dutch parliamentary technology assessment (TA) and science systems assessment (SciSA) organisation in The Hague. He has a degree in applied physics and public administration, and a PhD in political science. He is a global expert in the field of TA, politics of innovation and public participation. For more than twenty-five years he has been involved in the energy and digital transitions, with special attention to the role of emerging technologies, such as robotics and AI. He is part-time Professor of Technology Assessment and Governance at Eindhoven University of Technology.

Maarten Arentsen was Associate Professor of Innovation in Energy Supply at the University of Twente in the Netherlands until his retirement in 2020. He has a degree in political science and a PhD in engineering sciences. His many years of research focused on change and innovation in European energy markets, among others, the transition towards renewable energy. He has published numerous articles, papers and book chapters, and has co-edited several books on the topics. He is a member of REFORM, an international academic network on innovation and change in energy markets.

Romy Dekker is a senior researcher at the Rathenau Instituut, the Dutch parliamentary technology assessment (TA) and science systems assessment (SciSA) organisation in The Hague. She has a degree in cultural anthropology and development sociology. Her research focuses on topics related to the governance of sustainability. She is a part-time PhD-candidate in the democratic governance of science and technology at Eindhoven University of Technology.

Open Access This chapter is licensed under the terms of the Creative Commons Attribution 4.0 International License (http://creativecommons.org/licenses/by/4.0/), which permits use, sharing, adaptation, distribution and reproduction in any medium or format, as long as you give appropriate credit to the original author(s) and the source, provide a link to the Creative Commons license and indicate if changes were made.

The images or other third party material in this chapter are included in the chapter's Creative Commons license, unless indicated otherwise in a credit line to the material. If material is not included in the chapter's Creative Commons license and your intended use is not permitted by statutory regulation or exceeds the permitted use, you will need to obtain permission directly from the copyright holder.

Long-Term Radioactive Waste Management in the Netherlands: Seeking Guidance for Decision-Making

2

Romy Dekker, Vincent Lagendijk, Roos Walstock and Rinie van Est

2.1 Introduction

The Netherlands currently stores its radioactive waste above ground at the Central Organization for Radioactive Waste (COVRA). With regard to the long-term management of radioactive waste and spent fuel, the Netherlands pursues a 'dual strategy'. First, there is a national route in which the government envisions a geological disposal facility (GDF) for a part of its radioactive waste and spent fuel to be operational by 2130 (Ministry of I&E, 2016). Nevertheless, the option is left open to deviate from this timeframe, as well as from the currently preferred long-term disposal method (geological disposal), if there is reason to do so. Second, the government pursues an international route with other European Union (EU) Member States for the long-term management of radioactive waste (Ministry of I&E, 2016). Although an approximate timeline has been developed, the concrete decision-making process that should lead to a solution, either nationally or internationally, has not yet been established.

R. Dekker (✉) · V. Lagendijk · R. van Est
Rathenau Instituut, The Hague, Netherlands
e-mail: r.dekker@rathenau.nl

V. Lagendijk
e-mail: v.lagendijk@rathenau.nl

R. van Est
e-mail: q.vanest@rathenau.nl

R. Walstock
Kirkman Company, Baarn, Netherlands
e-mail: r.walstock@kirkmancompany.com

© The Author(s) 2023
M. Arentsen and R. van Est (eds.), *The Future of Radioactive Waste Governance*, Energiepolitik und Klimaschutz. Energy Policy and Climate Protection,
https://doi.org/10.1007/978-3-658-40496-3_2

The Netherlands is a medium-sized country with regard to radioactive waste, characterized by a diverse nuclear technology portfolio (with four operational nuclear facilities for energy, research, uranium enrichment and the production of medical isotopes). Approximately 1,300 companies hold a license to work with radioactive materials, of which two-thirds produce radioactive waste (Ministry of I&E, 2016). In 2020, the central national facility of COVRA in Borsele contained a total of 35,411.1 m^3 radioactive waste. 110.1 m^3 of this was high-level radioactive waste (HLW), while 34,168 m^3 of the waste stored was low-level and intermediate-level radioactive waste (LILW). Some 70% of the HLW brought to COVRA annually originates from the production of nuclear energy, and 30% comes from the production of medical isotopes and from the research reactors in Delft and Petten. The LILW stems from various sources, such as nuclear reactors, research facilities, hospitals, gas- and oil-drilling, discarded smoke detectors, and the enrichment of uranium by the Netherlands branch of Urenco (COVRA, 2020a).[1] Because of the relatively small volumes of radioactive waste produced in the Netherlands, and the relative high initial costs of geological disposal, the Dutch government wants to place LILW that is still active at the time of disposal in the same location as the HLW (Ministry of I&M, 2016). This is in contrast to other countries, such as Belgium, France and the UK, where ('short-lived') LILW is to be placed in a surface or near-surface disposal facility (cf. Schröder, 2012).

At present, there is no detailed step-by-step approach to decision-making on the long-term management of radioactive waste in the Netherlands. Therefore, following the National Program Radioactive Waste (Ministry of I&E, 2016), in 2019, the State Secretary for Infrastructure and Water Management commissioned the Rathenau Instituut to provide advice in 2024 on the decision-making process regarding the long-term management of radioactive waste.[2] The Rathenau

---

[1] The classification system currently used in the Netherlands resembles the IAEA guideline of 2009 (IAEA Safety Standard, 2009), but consists of four categories instead of six: 'high-level radioactive waste' (HLW), 'low-and medium-level radioactive waste' (LILW), 'short-lived waste' (with a half-time of less than 100 days) and 'exempt waste' (COVRA, 2014). A subcategory of LILW consists of waste produced from the use of naturally occurring radioactive material (NORM). NORM waste with an activity concentration of up to ten times the exemption threshold, are disposed of as very low-level waste at special licensed dumpsites (Ministry of I&E, 2016, p. 16). In this chapter, we only focus on the long-term management of the waste stored at COVRA.

[2] The Rathenau Instituut is an independent technology assessment organization. It has been involved in research and debate about the impact of science, innovation, and technology on society for 35 years.

Instituut aims to fulfill this task by organising research and dialogue between citizens, experts and stakeholders. The authors of this chapter are involved in this advisory process, of which this book and chapter are a part.

This chapter investigates various important challenges for the decision-making process regarding the long-term management of radioactive waste in the Netherlands. To this end, we use the conceptual model of a multi-level governance ecosystem (Kool et al., 2017), as explained in the introductory chapter, which consists of four domains and their interactions: 'politics and administration', 'science and technology', 'laws and regulations', and 'civil society'. We first describe the historical development of the governance ecosystem in the Netherlands, based on a reading of parliamentary documents, publications from the national waste management organisation (COVRA), governmental organisations, NGOs, news items, previous reviews of the national nuclear sector, as well as literature on the governance of radioactive waste. Based on that overview, we reflect on the developments within the separate domains and identify current challenges for decision-making. We end by drawing several conclusions.

2.2 History of Radioactive Waste Management and Policy in the Netherlands

This section describes how the Netherlands managed radioactive waste from 1945 to 2016, and how decision-making took shape. This timeframe spans the period between the building-up of the nuclear sector to the first National Program for the management of radioactive waste. Since the management of radioactive waste is closely linked to its applications, we also take developments in the field of nuclear technologies into account. We show that over the years different waste management methods have been suggested, discussed, researched, used, regulated, banned, and/or abandoned. For each of these methods, specific decision-making processes took place, in terms of technical viability, and social and political-administrative desirability and legal admissibility.

2.2.1 Development of the Nuclear Sector and Laws and Regulations for Nuclear Safety and Radiation Protection in the Netherlands

After World War II, with the support of the United States, the Dutch government teamed up with scientists to explore the peaceful potential of nuclear technology.

To this end, the government set up a knowledge and research infrastructure, developed industrial policy, and provided information about nuclear technology to the general public (Ministerie van Economische Zaken, 1957). The Netherlands also became a shareholder in Eurochemic, an international company founded in 1957 within the framework of the Organization for European Economic Cooperation (OEEC). Its purpose was to build a factory for reprocessing spent fuel, situated in Belgium. Dutch nuclear reactors came online for research and education in Petten (1960 and 1961), Delft (1963), Wageningen (1963), and Eindhoven (1969). Nuclear power plants (NPP) became operational in Dodewaard (1968) and Borssele (1973). There was relatively little attention to radioactive waste management (RWM) during this build-up phase, which also held true for waste management in most other sectors at that time (cf. IAEA, 2002). Over the years, there was a gradual increase in attention to radioactive waste, driven by an international scientific discussion on how such waste should be handled.

In the 1950s and 1960s, new organisations were set up to promote the safe use of nuclear technology, such as the International Atomic Energy Agency (IAEA) in 1957, the European Nuclear Energy Agency (ENEA, later NEA) in 1958, and the European Atomic Energy Community (Euratom) in 1958. The Dutch government implemented legislation and regulations on nuclear safety and radiation protection due to the expected increase in the use of radioactive substances in medical, biological, industrial and agricultural fields (Radioactieve Stoffenbesluit, 1958, p. 7). On the basis of agreements within the Euratom Treaty, the Ionizing Radiation Decree (Radioactieve Stoffenbesluit, 1958) provided guidelines with regard to safety. In addition, the government used existing legislation to create the preconditions for protection against ionizing radiation for employees and the general public. In 1963 the Nuclear Energy Act was passed, that governed nuclear activities and provided regulations for nuclear safety and radiation protection (Kernenergiewet 1963). This law, which still applies, is a so-called framework law, with associated Decrees and Ordinances providing more detailed legislation.

During the first two decades of the nuclear program in the Netherlands, there was no explicit radioactive waste policy, just as there was no regular waste policy. However, a practice of managing radioactive waste did emerge (Berkers et al., 2023). In 1963, the Minister of Social Affairs and Health established a special designated service to collect LILW waste. This radioactive waste was subsequently stored above ground in Petten, near the Reactor Center Netherlands (RCN). Part of this waste was disposed in the deep sea. This latter practice was supervised by ENEA after 1965. Between 1966 and 1974, spent nuclear fuel was reprocessed at Eurochemic in Belgium, where—according to contract—the leftover HLW remained. After Eurochemic shut down in 1974, new agreements were made for the reprocessing of spent fuel with the United States, United Kingdom and France. The remaining Dutch HLW would eventually be sent back from the UK and France to the Netherlands. At the same time, social resistance to the dumping of radioactive and other high-toxic waste into the deep sea grew, both within and outside the Netherlands, and an international ban on the dumping of HLW into the sea came into effect in 1972. An international moratorium on dumping LILW was issued in 1983, followed by a complete ban in 1993.

2.2.2 Realizing an Above-Ground Interim Storage Facility for Radioactive Waste

RWM became a topic in the Dutch societal arena in the 1970s, as exemplified by the societal resistance to deep sea dumping. RWM also became a central issue in the nuclear energy debate as the anti-nuclear movement arose. Furthermore, the government at the time indicated that expanding nuclear energy was only possible after an 'acceptable solution' was found for radioactive waste (Ministerie van Economische Zaken, 1974). In line with international scientific debates, the Scientific Council for Nuclear Energy, and the Reactor Center of the Netherlands, among others, advised to examine the possibilities of disposing radioactive waste in deep underground salt domes (cf. WRK, 1972). In 1976, the government wanted to investigate the technological possibilities of disposing HLW in salt formations in the northeastern part of the Netherlands. Regional and local resistance by citizens, societal organisations, companies and politicians eventually obstructed the proposed in situ test drilling (Berkers et al., 2023).

In 1981, the government initiated a Broad Social Discussion (BMD) on energy policy in response to the political and social impasse that had arisen. Within the BMD nuclear energy and radioactive waste were important topics. In 1984, the BMD Steering Committee advised to keep existing nuclear power stations open, but concluded that expansion of nuclear energy was undesirable.[3] Despite this, the government opted for the construction of two new NPPs, leaving many nuclear-critical participants in the BMD indignant. Political support for nuclear energy disappeared after the Chernobyl accident in April 1986, and the two pro-

---

[3] This Steering Committee consisted of nine experts from political and scientific circles, and was chaired by Mauk de Brauw, a socialist politician who had been minister of academic education and research, and previously worked for various companies including Unilever.

posed NPPs were never built. During the same period, the importance of nuclear medicine grew considerably. In the Netherlands, the High Flux Reactor (HFR) at Petten began to play a central role in the (world-wide) production of medical isotopes (Vijftig jaar HFR, 2011).

These societal and political developments impacted scientific research as well as the policy process (Schröder, 2012). The Integral National Research Program Nuclear Waste (ILONA) started in 1981. ILONA consisted of various committees that examined different possibilities for the disposal of HLW: storage on land, just above or below the earth's surface, interim-storage of spent fuel elements and nuclear fission waste, disposal in salt domes in the North Sea, and disposal in geological layers beneath the deep seas (Ministerie van VROM, 1984). The research on North Sea salt domes and deep sea geological disposal was rather quickly abandoned due to higher than expected costs (Berkers et al., 2023). In 1981, the Committee Reconsidering Disposal of Radioactive Waste (Commissie Heroverweging Verwijdering Radioactief Afval, HVRA) was installed to look for alternatives for the deep sea disposal of LILW (Ministerie van VROM, 1984, p. 12). HVRA concluded in March 1983 that it had a preference for disposing LILW in salt layers, e.g. by means of deep salt cavities (Berkers et al., 2023).

The first RWM policy was presented in 1984 by the Minister of Housing, Spatial Planning and the Environment (VROM). It included two goals in the field of radiation protection. First, to comply with the ALARA (As Low As Reasonably Achievable) principle, which had been recommended by the International Commission on Radiological Protection (ICRP) in 1973 and endorsed by Euratom in 1980. This had to be done by isolating, managing and controlling the waste (in Dutch the so-called IBC-criteria). Second, the sum of the received and expected doses for humans should not exceed the established dose limits. The government also decided to set up an above-ground interim storage facility for LILW and HLW. This should be managed by COVRA, for a period of 'several decades', which was later explained during parliamentary debates and related policy documents as at least 100 years (Ministry of I&E, 2016). This temporal policy provided time to further study options for a final GDF and to explore the possibility of an international disposal facility. A designated committee under the aegis of liberal politician W.J. Geertsema was tasked with finding a suitable and acceptable location for the intended facility. This eventually led to an above-ground radioactive waste storage facility in Borsele, near the NPP. Local residents and the anti-nuclear energy movement participated in this decision-making process. By August 1989, COVRA had obtained all necessary permits and was able to start construction of the storage facility.

2.2.3 Deep Geological Disposal: Elaboration of Policy and Research

In subsequent decades, the government elaborated on its 1984 radioactive waste policy through parliamentary debates, research and public consultation. This included the formulation of an environmental policy framework, informed by a public consultation on the acceptability of geological disposal of (radioactive and highly-toxic) waste. This led to new modified principles for RWM: in line with the IBC-criteria, reversibility of the decision-making process and retrievability of the waste became requirements (Tweede Kamer, 1993). With this in mind, the national scientific Committee on Storage of Radioactive Waste (CORA) was asked by ILONA in 1996 to investigate the feasibility of retrievable disposal of radioactive waste both in salt domes and Boom Clay. In addition to technical aspects, one of its subcommittees focused on ethical and social aspects of long-term RWM in a scoping study amongst environmental organisations (CORA, 2001; Selling, 2002). This was the first time a social scientific angle was included in a national research programme on RWM in the Netherlands.

The work of international organisations influenced Dutch RWM policy and research. This concerned, for example, international agreements in the IAEA-framework, international radiation guidelines and standards by the International Commission on Radiological Protection (ICRP) (via Euratom), and the work of the Nuclear Energy Agency (NEA). The NEA developed the concept of a safety case, which 'comprises the findings of a safety assessment and a statement of confidence in these findings' (OECD, 1999, p. 22). The safety case methodology was applied in the national Research Program for the Final Storage of Radioactive Waste (OPERA), which ran from 2011 to 2016. This program was organised by COVRA, and looked in particular into the possibilities of a geological disposal facility in Boom Clay. In 2004, NEA also argued for a stepwise approach to decision-making, which was in line with the Dutch principle of reversibility. Furthermore, NEA stated that it is important that 'the public, and especially the most affected local public, are meaningfully involved in the planning process' (OECD, 2004, p. 7). With regard to the legal domain, the Aarhus Convention came into effect in 2001, and grants EU citizens the right to access to information, public participation in decision-making, and access to justice in environmental matters (UN, 1998).

Institutional arrangements also changed during this period, with several changes in the division of ministerial tasks and responsibilities in the field of nuclear energy, nuclear safety and radiation protection. For example, since 2010 the Ministry of Economic Affairs was responsible for nuclear safety and radiation protection, nuclear energy, the Nuclear Energy Act and the management of the associated organisational units. The Minister of Social Affairs and Employment (SZW) was responsible for the protection of employees, and the Minister of Health, Welfare and Sport (VWS) was responsible for protecting patients against the risks of ionizing radiation (ABDTOPConsult, 2019). Influenced by the House of Representatives and international guidelines from the IAEA, it was decided in 2015 to set up a new independent Authority for Nuclear Safety and Radiation protection under the Ministry of Infrastructure and the Environment (I&E): the ANVS. The new authority could not fall under the Ministry of Economic Affairs, which was responsible for (nuclear) energy policy (Wijzigingswet kernernergiewet, 2016). In 2019, a legal evaluation of the ANVS led to the transfer of policy responsibility for the management of radioactive waste to the Ministry of Infrastructure and Water Management (before I&E).

The EU also had an influence on the decision-making process regarding the disposal and management of radioactive waste in the Netherlands. In accordance with the 2011/70/Euratom directive, every EU Member State became obliged to draw up a National Program (European Council, 2011). In preparation for the Dutch National Program, four studies were carried out: 1) an inventory of the current and future volume of radioactive waste by COVRA; 2) an initial study into options for the long-term management of radioactive waste by engineering consultancy ARCADIS; 3) a study on public participation by the Rathenau Instituut; and 4) a study of the state of affairs concerning international research into disposal by the Nuclear Research & Consultancy Group (NRG).

Building on earlier policies, the National Program from 2016 listed the following four policy principles: 1) minimization of the generation of radioactive waste; 2) safe management of radioactive waste; 3) no unreasonable burdens on the shoulders of later generations; 4) the producers of radioactive waste are responsible for the costs of its management (Ministry of I&E, 2016). In addition, the National Program underlined the importance of public participation and the earlier mentioned dual strategy. Because the Netherlands has a relatively small volume of radioactive waste, a multinational repository was considered logical "in terms of quality, safety, knowledge sharing, care and costs" by the consultancy group of OPERA (Adviesgroep OPERA, 2017, p. 50).[4] International

---

[4] The consultancy group consisted of seven members from different backgrounds, such as regional authorities, drinking water boards and universities.

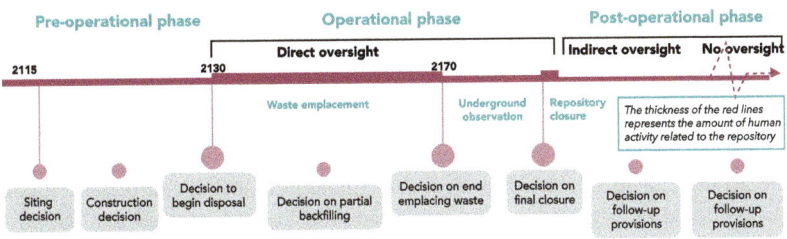

Fig. 2.1 Suggested timeline in the National Program of important decision-making moments for a GDF. (Source: OPERA, figure from OECD/NEA adapted to the Dutch situation)

collaboration is sought for this route within the European Repository Development Organization (ERDO), which has been based at COVRA since 2021. Several European Member States, including the Netherlands, work within this international association on multinational radioactive waste solutions (COVRA, 2021).

The National Program opted for interim above-ground storage for at least 100 years, followed by geological disposal. It also suggested a timeline: a political decision on a final repository will be made around 2100, and the GDF is to be operational around 2130 (see Fig. 2.1). It is however possible to deviate from this, both in terms of the timeframe and disposal method, for example due to technological developments or international cooperation. The government legitimised this policy by stating that "the relatively long period of above ground storage will provide time to learn from experiences in other countries, to carry out research and accumulate knowledge" (Ministry of I&E, 2016, pp. 4–5). This should ensure that no unreasonable burden is placed on the shoulders of future generations.

The National Program also announced the construction of a consultation group (Klankbordgroep) that would be tasked to focus on issues including:

- public participation ('identifying specific forms of participation');
- siting of radioactive waste disposal facilities ('potential suitable search areas for the disposal of radioactive waste that can be reserved, and identifying the necessary policy harmonization, given other future functions of the (deep) underground environment at those sites');
- knowledge infrastructure ('options for maintaining the necessary knowledge infrastructure in the Netherlands for the management of radioactive waste'), and;

- practical implementation of the principle of retrievability ('defining the criteria for determining the period of retrievability of radioactive waste from disposal to allow a decision on a period of retrievability supported by society'). (Ministry of I&E, 2016, p. 6)

The Ministry of I&W asked Van Soest to explore how such a consultation group process could be organisationally embedded. Van Soest concluded that the mission of such a group could be "to think through a possible participatory decision-making process aimed at a social agreement about the disposal of radioactive waste and spent fuel, and to advise relevant parties on this" (Van Soest, 2018, p. 8). As a result of this preliminary investigation, it was decided to task the Rathenau Instituut with issuing advice in 2024 on the decision-making process regarding the long-term management of radioactive waste.

2.3 Current Challenges

The long-term interim above-ground storage at COVRA provides time to work on a final solution for the long-term management of radioactive waste. While the National Program provides a tentative timeline, the step-by-step process of decision-making needs further elaboration. To better understand the challenges that need to be addressed, this section reflects on historic and current development of the four domains of the governance-ecosystem: 1) laws and regulation, 2) policy and administration, 3) science and technology, and 4) civil society. Because each domain depends on the others for their functioning, we consider their mutual interactions. Moreover, since various levels of government play a role in dealing with radioactive waste, we also consider the multi-level character of the domains.

2.3.1 Laws and Regulations

In the Netherlands, legislation and regulations regarding the management of radioactive waste are part of the legal framework for radiation protection and nuclear safety. This is covered by the Nuclear Energy Act of 1963 (Kernenergiewet 1963). This Act, and its associated decrees and ordinances, have been continuously adapted to guidelines provided by international organisations such as IAEA, Euratom, and ICRP. Various political and social developments have had an influence on international legislation and regulations. This for example has led to international bans on the dumping of radioactive waste into the deep sea, and to a European Directive for the responsible and safe management of spent fuel and radioactive waste—which pays attention to public information provisioning and public participation. Moreover, the latter is in line with more general (international) regulations such as those drawn up under the Aarhus Convention, and obligations for public participation as part of licensing (UN 1998). A study of the current legal framework for the long-term management of radioactive waste concludes that the Dutch framework complies with all international and European rules for RWM, and that most of the recommendations of the IAEA have been followed (Akerboom, 2023).[5]

2.3.2 Policy and Administration

Since the advent of nuclear technology in the Netherlands, the domain of politics and administration gradually started to pay attention to RWM. To enable the safe use of nuclear technology, the nuclear sector was institutionalized (both internationally and nationally), which led to guidelines for the management of radioactive materials, including radioactive waste. In the 1970s, RWM became part of the societal and political debate on nuclear energy. That, combined with international scientific debates on radiation protection standards, led the government to set up various research programmes and organise the Broad Societal Discussion (BMD) on energy policy. Both inputs were used to formulate the 1984 radioactive waste policy plan. This policy opted for the long-term interim above-ground storage of radioactive waste. To achieve this, COVRA had been established in 1982, and a GDF was foreseen as a long-term solution via either a national or an international route. The National Program reaffirmed this policy in 2016, and offered a timeline according to which the political decision on a final repository will be taken around 2100, and a GDF will be operational around 2130 (see Fig. 2.2). Since EU regulations require that National Programs need to be updated every ten years, a new one is scheduled for 2026.

Dutch RWM policy has been both hailed and criticized. First, the organisation of centralised long-term interim above-ground storage of radioactive waste has been deemed as 'good governance' by member states of the Joint Convention on the Safety of Spent Fuel, and on the Safety of Radioactive Waste Management, because the packaging and storage facilities are also designed with a term of 100

---

[5] This study has been conducted as part of the current assignment of the Rathenau Instituut.

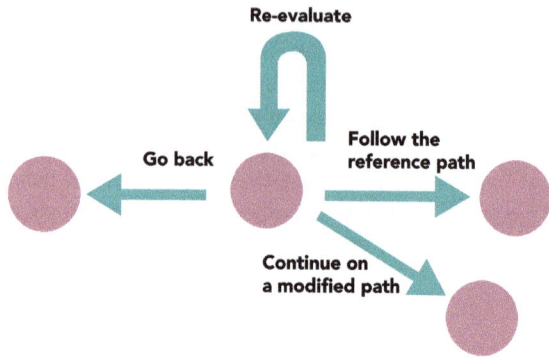

Fig. 2.2 Reversibility of decisions. (Source: National Program, adapted from OECD/NEA)

to 300 years in mind, which facilitates a high level of safety (Ministry of I&W, 2020). In line with this, the IAEA (2009) considered the incorporation of passive safety features in the design of the packaging and facilities as a 'good practice', because it makes the safety of the interim-storage less dependent on maintenance, and the packaged materials can be monitored more easily. Second, the IAEA concluded that COVRA communicates well with the public, for example through art and by organising open days, which has increased the confidence of the public regarding the activities of COVRA (IAEA, 2009).

There is also criticism, for example on the intention not to realize a GDF until 2130. According to LAKA, a Dutch documentation and research center rooted in the anti-nuclear energy movement, the long duration of this more than 100-year period can lead to a political "wait-and-see" situation in the present (LAKA, 2015). A similar point is put forward by the advisory board of OPERA.[6] They supported the century-long horizon, but remarked that this time period should be used effectively, as it could lead to a lack of urgency among contemporary politicians and policymakers. They advised to start with public participation and scientific research as soon as possible (Adviesgroep OPERA, 2017). However, the study by the Rathenau Instituut that was carried out in preparation for the

---

[6] The OPERA advisory group was asked to advice on the quality of the research and on its social relevance. In addition, they had an advisory role on the communication about the program and the results.

National Program, showed that the absence of actual decisions negatively impacts the sense of urgency amongst the public, making public participation a complex challenge (De Vries et al., 2015).

Other organisations also emphasise that the period up to 2100 should be used meaningfully. The Netherlands Commission for Environmental Assessment (NCEA) advised the designation of a number of potentially suitable search areas for possible disposal of radioactive waste, to prevent an outcome that by the year 2100 the most suitable sites for geological disposal of radioactive waste would already be occupied (Commissie m.e.r., 2015).[7] Reserving potential search areas implies an implicit choice for a disposal method and a location, for which provisional selection criteria must be determined. However, it is uncertain whether the subsurface will actually become fully occupied, in view of the current strong social resistance to and distrust of various existing and potential developments in the Dutch subsurface, which ranges from natural and shale gas extraction (Waes et al., 2014) to CO_2 storage and geothermal energy (Smink et al., 2017). Therefore, it should be made clear whether, and if so at what moment in time, search locations for a potential GDF *have* to be reserved. This challenge has been included as a point of attention in the National Program (Ministry of I&E, 2016).

Other actors have also made suggestions about how the long-term interim period should be used. In 2019, the advisory board of the ANVS suggested that the ANVS should open the discussion about bringing forward decision-making by the government regarding the type and location of a final GDF (Raad van Advies, ANVS, 2020).[8] This would allow for more time to study and evaluate the host rock, and realize the selected type of disposal in 2130. Based on experiences from other countries, this might take a long time. A study commissioned by the Ministry of I&W recently concluded that stakeholders are in need of a more detailed step-by-step plan that identifies moments for public consultation and decision-making (Berenschot, 2022). To date, there is no such plan (Ministry of I&E, 2016). The European Commission (EC) even questioned in 2017 whether the government had in fact taken reasonable and concrete steps to ensure that future generations will not have to carry the burden of radioactive waste produced in the

---

[7] The Netherlands Commission for Environmental Assessment (NCEA) advises governments on the quality of environmental information in environmental assessment reports. The NCEA does not get involved in decision-making or political considerations.

[8] The advisory board of the ANVS consists of independent experts from the Netherlands and abroad, its task is to provide the ANVS with solicited and unsolicited advice on matters related to the tasks of the ANVS.

past and present, as required by the Euratom guidelines (Tweede Kamer, 2017). In response to this question, the Minister of I&M referred to the reasons for the current policy as stated in the National Program, and to the government plan to start a consultation group. As noted, the latter gave rise to the current assignment to the Rathenau Instituut.

Although the policy intention to switch to geological disposal following a period of above-ground storage has not changed since 1984, two additional requirements have been set for the long-term management of radioactive waste. The principle of retrievability has been given a somewhat narrower interpretation in the National Program than in the 1993 Parliamentary paper, by stating that it means "that the possibility for retrieving waste (packages) must be included in the design of a facility" (Ministry of I&E, 2016, p. 26). The optimum period of retrievability is to be decided in consultation with society. In addition, as far as practically desirable, the decision-making process must be reversible. This is associated with the step-by-step approach to licensing (Ministry of I&E, 2016) and is explained as follows: "before each step is taken, consideration will have to be given to whether the step should be taken, or whether a step back should be taken in the process" (see Fig. 2.2). Although this principle offers the opportunity for flexible decision-making, according to the Committee's environmental impact assessment, the concept version of the National Program did not provide instruments or mechanisms to reassess risks and adapt to unexpected developments (Commissie m.e.r., 2015). It remains unclear to what extent decisions should be reversible—with a view to 'manageability'—and how this should be assessed.

Another important development over the last two decades is the redistribution of ministerial tasks and responsibilities. Since the 1950s, responsibility for both nuclear energy and nuclear safety in the Netherlands has rested most of the time with the Ministry of Economic Affairs. In 1994, the IAEA Convention on Nuclear Safety stipulated that each Member State had to ensure a separation between organisations in the fields of nuclear safety and nuclear energy. Currently there is a clear division between the responsibilities for energy policy that lie with the Ministry of Economic Affairs, and on the responsibilities for nuclear safety and radiation protection that lie with the Ministry of I&W. The ANVS, established in 2015, was given both policymaking and supervision responsibilities. In 2020, the responsibility for policymaking was transferred from the ANVS to the Ministry of I&W. This creates a better distinction between the duties of the Ministry of I&W, and ANVS as a supervisor and licensing authority (ABDTopconsult, 2019).

In recent years, the nuclear energy discussion has resurfaced, partially because of the climate crisis. In the wake of this discussion, radioactive waste also returned to the political and social agenda. In its coalition agreement, the current government intends to keep the nuclear power plant in Borssele open longer, to build two new NPPs, and to provide for the safe disposal of nuclear waste (Kabinetsformatie, 2021). What this will mean for the decision-making process regarding the long-term management of radioactive waste remains to be seen.

2.3.3 Science and Technology

The domain of science and technology continues to play an important role in the development of standards for radiation protection and nuclear safety. The same holds for the investigation of the viability and safety of technical options for (long-term) RWM. It thereby influences the development of legislation, regulations, and policy. Below, we describe how despite increased awareness of the importance of interdisciplinary and transdisciplinary knowledge, an integral, participatory and sociotechnical knowledge agenda is still missing in the Netherlands, and it is unclear where the institutional responsibility for such an agenda lies. Moreover, we highlight that the vitality of the science and technology domain would benefit from a long-term vision on knowledge development.

Until the 1990s, Dutch RWM research primarily focused on technical aspects, such as the technical feasibility of geological disposal in salt domes. From CORA (which ran from 1996 to 2001) onwards, ethical and social aspects of the long-term management of radioactive waste, and the role of public participation in decision-making, have received attention. Within ILONA (the research program which ran between 1981 and 1993), it was argued that social scientific research should be limited to an inventory of the processes that play a role in decision-making (Tweede Kamer, 2002). OPERA, the subsequent national research program (which ran from 2011 to 2018), set up the previously mentioned OPERA advisory group. The group dealt with the "wider societal issues of disposal, including stakeholder engagement and conditions for an inclusive process for long-term decision-making on disposal" (Verhoef et al., 2017, p. 8). The advisory group stated that this requires a participatory process and the recognition of emotions and values, which can be used to shape and direct technological development; so-called "value sensitive design" (cf. Correljé et al., 2015). In 2015, the Rathenau Instituut concluded that RWM transcends various academic disciplines (technical, geological, ethical, social, psychological, economic), and that it is therefore important "to retain sight of the issue's multidisciplinary character and the consequent need for interdisciplinary cooperation" (De Vries et al., 2015, p. 19). Despite intentions to set up a broader research program, the current long-term program at COVRA focuses primarily on technical aspects. A more integrated sociotechnical research agenda is thus still lacking.

Moreover, it is unclear where the institutional responsibility for setting up such an integral research agenda lies. According to the IAEA, the government should be responsible for ensuring that the necessary knowledge and expertise is maintained (IAEA, 2000). As seen above, since the beginning of the 1980s, the government and the nuclear sector have developed various research programmes in collaboration with a specially designated scientific committee. However, currently the government's involvement in research on the final disposal of radioactive waste is somewhat limited. After the CORA research program ended in 2001, COVRA started to play a key role in coordinating research (Berkers et al., 2023).[9] And for the first time, the current research program is not financially (co-)supported by the government, but solely financed by COVRA (COVRA, 2020b). Part of the money that COVRA receives from the producers of radioactive waste is used for this purpose.[10]

According to the consultancy firm Berenschot (2022), this and previous research programmes have been appreciated by companies and NGOs, however, they also experience a lack of insight into the current steps of knowledge development regarding disposal: "[even though] the report of the research programs are public […] it is not clear what will happen with these insights and what the next steps are. Linked to this, an overview of the lessons until now, and what we still want/need to know before a safe geological disposal facility can be realized is lacking"[11] (Berenschot, 2022, p. 19). This raises the question to what extent it is up to COVRA to provide insights into these aspects, or whether this should be a responsibility of the government, or a combination of both. In addition, stakeholders have also indicated that the lack of insight into what still needs to be investigated to realize a GDF is related to the absence of a more detailed step-by-step decision-making process (Berenschot, 2022). As mentioned before, the lack of this step-by-step plan is another challenge for the government, and part of the present assignment of the Rathenau Instituut.

---

[9] Although COVRA is fully owned by the Dutch state, it is an independent administrative body (in Dutch: Onafhankelijk Bestuursorgaan) that performs government tasks, but does not fall directly under the authority of a ministry.

[10] This is in line with the polluter pays principle. This principle assures that organisations which deliver their radioactive waste to COVRA pay for all costs related its management, including research (COVRA, 2020b).

[11] Translation from Dutch by authors.

2 Long-Term Radioactive Waste Management … 41

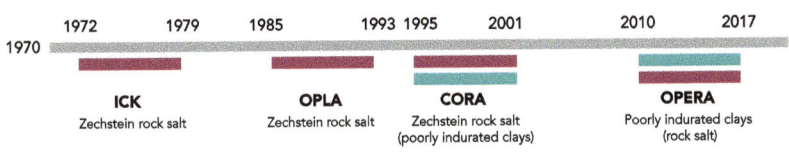

Fig. 2.3 Overview of Dutch research programs (COVRA, 2020b)

The NEA recommended that the public should be involved in the development and implementation of a safety case (OECD, 2000). The Rathenau Instituut proposed that a participatory knowledge agenda is an essential feature of knowledge assurance for decision-making on the long-term management of radioactive waste. Such an agenda should be based on "information sources originating from […] citizens, scientists in various disciplines, stakeholders and (lower tiers of) government" (De Vries et al., 2015, p. 46).[12] A transdisciplinary mode of knowledge production is seen as important in science in general (cf. Gibbons & Nowotny 2001; Nowotny, 2003) and in RWM in particular (Brunnengräber, 2019), because it may contribute to more socially robust knowledge. There has been some level of involvement in Dutch research programmes, by means of informing the public and parliament of plans and findings, and by collaborations between science, industry and policy. However, the general public has so far been absent in the design and execution of research programmes. Involving civil society actors, such as citizens and civil society organisations, remains a challenge in the Netherlands, since those actors may lack the will or resources to participate (De Vries et al., 2015). These issues should be addressed in order to develop a participatory knowledge agenda.

The permanence and vitality of the science and technology domain remains a point of attention. Successive research programmes often had gaps between them ranging up to ten years (see Fig. 2.3). In some cases, this implied that "earlier collected knowledge had to be recovered and that the research infrastructure on the geological disposal of radioactive waste had been diminished and weakened over time" (COVRA, 2020b, p. 12). To prevent this from happening in the future, COVRA's most recent research programme has a long-term scope.

From the point of view of institutional independence, checks and balances, and spreading knowledge, as well as COVRA, the Ministry of I&W, ANVS and

---

[12] While preparing the national programme, ANVS asked the Rathenau Instituut to formulate a vision on public participation in decision-making about long-term radioactive waste management, to serve as a supporting study for the national programme.

other relevant stakeholders must also continue to have access to sufficient and (independent) knowledge and expertise to continue to perform their institutional duties (cf. Raad van Advies ANVS, 2020). The Ministry of I&W is currently exploring how the knowledge landscape of nuclear technology and radiation can be strengthened, including in the long term (cf. Van de Zande et al., 2020).

2.3.4 Civil Society

Over the last few decades, the societal domain has been involved in decision-making on the long-term management of radioactive waste in several ways. In some cases, involvement was initiated by the government, and in others by civil society actors themselves. We show here that this had various outcomes, and took multiple forms: from protest and resistance to informing and consulting. Over the years, awareness of the importance of public involvement in radioactive waste decision-making has increased. It even became legally required by international and national guidelines, treaties and laws. Part of the assignment to the Rathenau Instituut is to develop an advice on a (possibly participatory) decision-making process for the final disposal of radioactive waste on behalf of the Ministry of I&W. This has been lacking until now, partly due to the absence of concrete decision-making steps, which influences willingness to participate.

Civil society has influenced both policy and research. In the 1950s, companies worked closely with scientific institutions to erect a nuclear industry in the Netherlands. In the early 1970s, governmental policy to expand the nuclear sector was criticized by an emerging anti-nuclear energy movement. Dealing with radioactive waste became a central issue in the nuclear energy debate after the government indicated that expanding nuclear energy was only possible if an 'acceptable solution' had been found for radioactive waste. At the same time, the existing practice of disposing radioactive waste in the deep sea was also met with increasing public protest, resulting in a ban for first HLW (1975), and subsequently LILW (temporary moratorium in 1983, legal ban in 1993). The announcement of in situ test drillings in salt layers in the northeastern part of the Netherlands to find potentially suitable places for a GDF, led to regional political-administrative and social resistance among both proponents and opponents of nuclear energy. To this day, conducting research in the subsurface for the geological disposal of radioactive waste remains a sensitive issue (De Vries et al., 2015).

The government has also consulted the public on policy development at various times—often under pressure from parliament, local and regional authorities, and society. This was the case during the BMD in the early 1980s, and the broad consultation regarding the desirability of geological disposal of radioactive and highly toxicological waste in the early 1990s. Local residents were also consulted by COVRA in the search for a suitable location for the interim aboveground storage of radioactive waste.

Scientific studies show that public participation can lead to higher levels of trust, but that this is not a causal relationship (cf. Wang & Wan Wart, 2007; OECD, 2017; Liu et al. 2019). The broad societal discussion on energy policy (BMD) in the Netherlands, for example, has not led to more confidence in the government among opponents of nuclear energy. The government saw the BMD as a public consultation and had clearly indicated in advance that it would not automatically follow the outcome of the BMD. At the start of the BMD, many opponents of nuclear energy had low faith in the government and saw the BMD as fake participation. After the BMD in 1984, they felt reinforced in that opinion when the government ignored the outcome of the BMD, that there should be no further expansion of nuclear energy. This experience still seems to play a role in current debates on RWM (Berkers et al, 2023). In a 2015 study (De Vries et al. 2015), the Rathenau Instituut concluded that there is "limited trust in the government with regard to this specific policy issue" (p. 7), and that there is a lack of urgency to participate because of the absence of actual decisions. The Rathenau Instituut proposed that the best way of bolstering trust and willingness to participate, is "to develop a public participation model whose subject matter and procedural design enjoys widespread support" (De Vries et al., 2015, p. 15), and concluded that decision-making on long-term RWM requires a more extensive, long-term and systematic process of public participation. To this end, it proposed the following: 1) the development of a shared plan for public participation, 2) the tailoring of issue-based participation clusters, and 3) periodic reflection to deviate from the plan if necessary.

Public participation has in fact become obligatory following the 1998 Aarhus Convention (UN 1998) and through the 2011/70/Euratom directive (European Council, 2011) and Dutch legislation (Akerboom, 2023). Rather than serving as blueprints for the participatory process, these guidelines and regulations should therefore be seen as 'minimum standards'.

2.4 Conclusions

Since the materialization of NPPs in the 1960s and 1970s, political and societal debates on radioactive waste and nuclear technology, in particular nuclear energy, have become entangled. This has made long-term RWM a sensitive issue. While the government opted for the further development of nuclear power since the opening of the nuclear power plant in Borsele in 1972, the 1986 Chernobyl accident put a stop to such plans. Recently, the political discussion on nuclear energy has resurfaced. This might influence the long-term management of radioactive waste. The entanglement is also visible from an institutional point of view. For example, the Nuclear Energy Act regulates the licensing of nuclear installations and the safe management of radioactive materials, including radioactive waste. And the division of ministerial responsibilities has shifted because of a perceived conflict of interest between the fields of nuclear energy, and nuclear safety and radiation protection, including RWM.

Over the years, societal resistance against various waste management options, such as disposal into the deep sea and exploratory drillings for geological disposal in salt layers, has influenced the political decision-making process regarding long-term RWM. Since 1984, the radioactive waste policy has resulted in the establishment of an above-ground storage facility, after which geological disposal is foreseen either nationally or internationally. The National Program in 2016 stated that a decision on a final GDF should be taken around 2100. The possibility is left open to deviate from this scenario—both in terms of the timeframe and disposal method. In this way, future generations should not be left with an unreasonable burden. In addition, various policy principles and requirements have been formulated over the years, and a legal framework has been developed that provides guidelines for the decision-making process that lies ahead. Moreover, over the past two decades the ministerial tasks and responsibilities regarding nuclear energy, nuclear safety and radiation protection are split between the Ministries of Economic Affairs and I&W, which may contribute to the checks and balances in the field of RWM.

Although there is a National Program and a suggested timeline for RWM, the road to a final solution is only partly worked out. The Dutch policy of long-term above-ground storage, followed by a GDF, is not only hailed but also criticized. It is seen as good governance and as a good practice in terms of safety and communication with the public. On the other hand, parties such as the European Commission, societal organisations and the Rathenau Instituut are concerned that the century-long period for decision-making leads to a decrease in political urgency and willingness to participate and act on the subject. Various parties, such as the NCEA and the Council of the ANVS, therefore recommend using the interim period meaningfully and to concretize and possibly bring forward the decision-making process. The National Program named several issues that should be clarified as part of the decision-making process.

1) Define the optimal period of retrievability,
2) Set up criteria to reserve potential search locations for a GDF,
3) Clarify options for maintaining the necessary knowledge landscape, and
4) Concretize the role of public participation within research and various national and decentralised political decision-making processes.

The reflections in this chapter on the separate domains bring to light four additional cross-domain issues to be addressed in the decision-making process:

5) Further elaborate the requirement of reversibility of the decision-making process to clarify to what extent decisions should be reversible and how this will be assessed.
6) Develop a long-term, integral and participatory knowledge agenda to support the decision-making process and to keep the science and technology domain vital, now and in the future.
7) Spread knowledge over various (public) institutions, so that there can be an institutionally sound knowledge landscape with sufficient checks and balances. And lastly,
8) Develop a participatory decision-making process for the final disposal of radioactive waste that enjoys broad public and political support in terms of content and procedure to bolster trust and willingness to participate. Laws and regulations in the field of participation can serve as minimum standards.

Acknowledgements The authors would like to thank Dhoya Snijders for his contribution to earlier versions of this chapter and the participants of the societal review from the societal, scientific and public administration domains for their highly appreciated feedback.

References

ABDTOPConsult. (2019). *Wettelijke evaluatie van het zbo ANVS. Algemene Bestuursdienst*. Den Haag: Ministerie van Binnenlandse Zaken en Koninkrijksrelaties.

Adviesgroep OPERA. (2017). *Van Afval naar Berging. Tijd voor Verantwoordelijkheid*. Nieuwdorp: COVRA.

Akerboom, S. (forthcoming 2023). *Rapport rechtendomein lange termijn beheer radioactief afval. Een studie naar het juridisch en governance-kader omtrent opslag en berging van radioactief afval in Nederland*. Den Haag: Rathenau Instituut.

Berenschot. (2022). *Evaluatie Radioactief afval. Een evaluatie van de Nota Radioactief afval en het Nationaal Programma Radioactief afval*. Utrecht: Berenschot.

Berkers, E., Lagendijk, V., Dekker, R., Snijders, D., en R. van Est (2023). *Een kwestie van tijd: Besluitvorming over radioactief afval in Nederland van 1945 tot 2016*. Den Haag: Rathenau Instituut.

Brunnengräber, A. (2019). The wicked problem of long term radioactive waste governance. In A. Brunnengräber, & M.R. Di Nucci (Eds.), *Conflicts, Participation and Acceptability in Nuclear Waste Governance* (pp. 335–355). Wiesbaden: Springer VS.

Correljé, A., Cuppen, E., Dignum, M., Pesch, U., & Taebi, B. (2015). Responsible Innovation in Energy Projects: Values in the Design of Technologies, Institutions and Stakeholder Interactions. In B.-J. Koops, I. Oosterlaken, H. Romijn, T. Swierstra, & J. van den Hoven (Eds.), *Responsible Innovation 2* (pp. 183–200). Springer International Publishing, Cham.

Commissie m.e.r. (2015). Nationaal uitvoeringsprogramma voor het langetermijnbeheer van radioactief afval en verbruikte splijtstoffen. Utrecht: Commissie voor de milieueffectenrapportage.

CORA. (2001). *Terugneembare berging, een begaanbaar pad? Onderzoek naar de mogelijkheden van terugneembare berging van radioactief afval in Nederland*. Den Haag: Economische Zaken.

COVRA (2014). Inventaris Radioactief Afval in Nederland. https://www.covra.nl/app/uploads/2019/08/Inventaris-radioactief-afval-in-Nederland.pdf.

COVRA. (2020a). *Jaarrapport 2020*. Nieuwdorp: COVRA.

COVRA. (2020b). *Long-Term Research Programme for Geological Disposal of Radioactive Waste. Overall research program and work program for 2020–2025*. Nieuwdorp: COVRA and Technopolis.

COVRA. (2021). *Vereniging voor Multinationale Samenwerking Radioactief Afval opgericht in Nieuwdorp: ERDO*. https://www.covra.nl/nl/organisatie/nieuws/vereniging-voor-multinationale-samenwerking-radioactief-afval-opgericht-in-nieuwdorp-erdo/.

De Vries, A., van Waes, A., van Est, R., van der Meulen, B., & Brom, F. (2015). *Enabling participation: A vision on public participation in decision-making about long term radioactive waste management*. Den Haag: Rathenau Instituut.

European Council. (2011). *Council Directive 2011/70/Euratom of 19 July 2011 establishing a Community framework for the responsible and safe management of spent fuel and radioactive waste*. OJ L 199/48, 2 August 2011.

Gibbons, M., & Nowotny, H. (2001). The potential of transdisciplinarity. *Transdisciplinarity: joint problem solving among science, technology, and society*, 67–80.

IAEA Safety Standards. (2009). *Regulations for the Safe Transport of Radioactive Material*. Vienna: International Atomic Energy Agency.

IAEA (2000) Legal and governmental infrastructure for nuclear, radiation, radioactive waste and transport safety. Vienna: International Atomic Energy Agency Specific Safety Requirements, GS-R-1.

IAEA. (2002). *Radioactive Waste Management Profiles*. Vienna: International Atomic Energy Agency.

IAEA. (2009). *Peer Review of the Radioactive Waste Management Activities of COVRA, Netherlands*. International Atomic Energy Agency: Vienna, IAEA Safety Standards Applications Series, 8.

Kabinetsformatie. (2021). *Omzien naar elkaar, vooruitkijken naar de toekomst*. Den Haag: Bureau Woordvoering Kabinetsformatie.

Kernenergiewet. (1963) *Staatsblad van het Koninkrijk der Nederlanden*, 82.

Kool, L., Timmer, J., Royakkers, R., & van Est, R. (2017). *Urgent upgrade: Protect public values in our digitized society.* Den Haag: Rathenau Instituut.

LAKA. (2015, September 8). *Pleitnotitie—Uitbreiding.* COVRA. *LAKA.* https://www.laka.org/info/uitbreiding-covra/2015-09-08_pleidooi_uitbreiding_covra_anoniem.pdf.

Liu, L., Bouman, T., Perlaviciute, G., & Steg, L. (2019). Effects of trust and public participation on acceptability of renewable energy projects in the Netherlands and China. *Energy Research & Social Science, 53,* 137–144.

Ministerie van Economische Zaken. (1957). *Nota inzake de Kernenergie.* Den Haag: Ministerie van Economische Zaken.

Ministerie van Economische Zaken. (1974). *Energienota.* Den Haag: SDU.

Ministry of I&E. (2016). *The national programme for the management of radioactive waste and spent fuel.* Den Haag: Ministry of Infrastructure and the Environment (I&E).

Ministry of I&W. (2020). *Joint convention on the safety of spent fuel management and on the safety of radioactive waste management.* Den Haag: Ministry of Infrastructure and Water Management (I&W).

Ministerie van VROM. (1984) *Radioactief afval.* Den Haag: Ministerie van Volkshuisvesting, Ruimtelijke Ordening en Milieubeheer.

Nowotny, H. (2003). Democratising expertise and socially robust knowledge. *Science and Public Policy, 30*(3), 151–156.

OECD. (1999). *Confidence in the Long-term Safety of Deep Geological Repositories. Its Development and Communication.* Paris: Nuclear Energy Agency / Organisation for Economic Co-operation and Development.

OECD. (2000). *Geological disposal of radioactive waste: Review of developments in the last decade.* Paris: Nuclear Energy Agency / Organisation for Economic Co-operation and Development.

OECD. (2004). *Stepwise approach to decision making for long-term radioactive waste management: Experience, issues and guiding principles.* Paris: Organisation for Economic Co-operation and Development, Nuclear Energy Agency.

OECD. (2017). *Trust and Public Policy: How Better Governance Can Help Rebuild Public Trust. OECD Public Governance Reviews.* Paris: Organisation for Economic Co-operation and Development.

Raad van Advies ANVS. (2020). *Advies van Raad van Advies over de rol van ANVS in relatie tot eindberging van radioactief afval.* Den Haag: Autoriteit Nucleaire Veiligheid en Stralingsbescherming.

Radioactieve stoffenbesluit. (1958). *Staatsblad van Het Koninkrijk der Nederlanden 317,* 7.

Schröder, J. (2012). *Identifying remaining socio-technical challenges at the national level: the Netherlands.* SOTEC working paper. Antwerp: University of Antwerp.

Selling, H.A. (2002). *Policy of radioactive waste disposal in the Netherlands.* https://inis.iaea.org/collection/NCLCollectionStore/_Public/33/037/33037868.pdf.

Smink, M., van den Broek, J., Metze, T., Cuppen, E., & van Est, R. (2017). In E. van de Grift, & A. van Waes (eds.), *Samen kennis aanboren: Verkenning van kennis en opvattingen over ultradiepe geothermie.* Den Haag: Rathenau Instituut.

Tweede Kamer. (1993). *Opbergen van afval in de diepe ondergrond.* Den Haag: SDU, 1992–1993, 23163–1.

Tweede Kamer. (2002). *Radioactief afvalbeleid.* Den Haag: SDU, 2002–2003, 28674–1.

Tweede Kamer. (2017). *Opwerking van radioactief materiaal.* Den Haag: SDU, 2016–2017, 25422–204.

UN. (1998). *Convention on Access to Information, Public Participation in Decision-Making and Access to Justice in Environmental Matters.* Geneva: The United Nations Economic Commission for Europe (UNECE).

Van der Zande, A., Wolterbeek, B., & C. Leijen. (2020). *Naar een Agenda en Platform Nucleaire Technologie en Straling.* Den Haag: Autoriteit Nucleaire Veiligheid en Stralingsbescherming.

Van Soest, J.P. (2018). *Diepgravende Dialogen,Bouwen aan Vertrouwen.Eindrapportage Kwartiermaker Eindberging radioactief afvalen verbruikte splijtstoffen.* Deventer: De Gemeynt.

Van Waes A., de Vries, A., van Est, R., & F. Brom. (2014). *Broadening the debate on shale gas: Guidelines for decision making based on the Dutch experience.* Rathenau Instituut.

Verhoef, E., Bartol, J., Neeft, E., Chapman, N., & McCombie, C. (2017). *Summary OPERA Safety Case.* Nieuwdorp: COVRA.

Vijftig jaar HFR. (2011). Elst: Kernvisie 6(6), 1–5.

Wang, X., & Wan Wart, M. (2007). When public participation in administration leads to trust: An empirical assessment of managers' perceptions. *Public administration review*, 67(2), 265–278.

Wijzigingswet Kernenergiewet. (2016) *Staatsblad van Het Koninkrijk der Nederlanden.*

WRK. (1972). *Vestigingsplaatsen van energiereactoren en de opslag van radio-actief afval.* Den Haag: Wetenschappelijke Raad voor de Kernenergie.

Romy Dekker is a senior researcher at the Rathenau Instituut, the Dutch parliamentary technology assessment (TA) and science systems assessment (SciSA) organisation in The Hague. She has a degree in cultural anthropology and development sociology. Her research focuses on topics related to the governance of sustainability. She is a part-time PhD-candidate in the democratic governance of science and technology at Eindhoven University of Technology.

Vincent Lagendijk is a senior researcher at the Rathenau Instituut, the Dutch parliamentary technology assessment (TA) and science systems assessment (SciSA) organisation in The Hague. He was trained as a historian and in Science and Technology Studies, and has a keen interest in infrastructures. He also is a part-time Assistant Professor at Maastricht University's Faculty of Arts and Social Sciences.

Roos Walstock works at Kirkman Company, a consultancy that helps organisations identify opportunities for truly tackling societal issues ('wicked problems') in an innovative way. In 2021, she first worked as a research intern, and from September to December as a junior researcher at the Rathenau Instituut, the Dutch Parliamentary organisation for Technology Assessment. Roos studied strategic innovation management, and philosophy and society at the University of Groningen. As part of her Masters in philosophy she researched different ways of decision-making under deep uncertainty and their connection with values.

Rinie van Est is a research coordinator at the Rathenau Instituut, the Dutch parliamentary technology assessment (TA) and science systems assessment (SciSA) organisation in The Hague. He has a degree in applied physics and public administration, and a PhD in political science. He is a global expert in the field of TA, politics of innovation and public participation. For more than twenty-five years he has been involved in the energy and digital transitions, with special attention to the role of emerging technologies, such as robotics and AI. He is part-time Professor of Technology Assessment and Governance at Eindhoven University of Technology.

Open Access This chapter is licensed under the terms of the Creative Commons Attribution 4.0 International License (http://creativecommons.org/licenses/by/4.0/), which permits use, sharing, adaptation, distribution and reproduction in any medium or format, as long as you give appropriate credit to the original author(s) and the source, provide a link to the Creative Commons license and indicate if changes were made.

The images or other third party material in this chapter are included in the chapter's Creative Commons license, unless indicated otherwise in a credit line to the material. If material is not included in the chapter's Creative Commons license and your intended use is not permitted by statutory regulation or exceeds the permitted use, you will need to obtain permission directly from the copyright holder.

Nuclear Waste Governance in Italy: Between Participation Rhetoric and Regionalism

3

Maria Rosaria Di Nucci and Andrea Prontera

3.1 Introduction[1]

Over the last 65 years nuclear power in Italy has been characterised by cyclical stop and go activities. Starting with the pioneer phase in the 1950s, and engaging at the beginning of the 1960s in various technological developments, Italy has witnessed a discontinuous nuclear research strategy, as well as incoherent technology and industrial policies to promote this "modern" source of energy. Following the Chernobyl accident in 1986, the debate on nuclear power led to a 1987

---

[1] Parts of this article draw heavily on the previous work of one of the authors. See, Di Nucci (2015). M.R. Di Nucci drafted the text at the Research Center for Sustainability (Forschungszentrum für Nachhaltigkeit, FFN) Freie Universität Berlin, as part of the TRANSENS-project "Transdisciplinary research on the management of high-level radioactive waste in Germany" (transens.de). TRANSENS is a collaborative project funded by the Federal Ministry for the Environment, Nature Conservation, Nuclear Safety and Consumer Protection and the *"Niedersächsisches Vorab"* of the Volkswagen Foundation by the Ministry of Science and Culture of Lower Saxony (FK 02E11849C).

M. R. Di Nucci (✉)
Freie Universität Berlin, Forschungszentrum Für Nachhaltigkeit (FFN), Berlin, Germany
e-mail: dinucci@zedat.fu-berlin.de

A. Prontera
Department of Political Science, Communication and International Relations, University of Macerata, Macerata, Italy
e-mail: andrea.prontera@unimc.it

© The Author(s) 2023
M. Arentsen and R. van Est (eds.), *The Future of Radioactive Waste Governance*, Energiepolitik und Klimaschutz. Energy Policy and Climate Protection, https://doi.org/10.1007/978-3-658-40496-3_3

referendum and the definitive shut-down in 1990 of all four country's nuclear power plants (NPPs). After attempts to revive the nuclear option, a second referendum three months after the Fukushima disaster in March 2011 led to the withdrawal of all Italian nuclear ambitions. However, nuclear waste stemming from the four permanently shut down NPPs, various research reactors, and reprocessing and fuel fabrication facilities represents a pressing problem.

Nuclear waste governance in Italy is characterised by complex, intertwined relationships and interaction between political-territorial levels from the national, through the regional to the local. The jurisdiction and responsibilities for nuclear waste are centralised; the governance of radioactive waste is shaped by a large number of national institutional actors and a limited number of regional and non-institutional actors, and has been characterised until recently by non-transparent top-down decisions.

The mandatory implementation at the national level of the *Council Directive 2011/70/Euratom* (European Council, 2011) put pressure on decision-makers. One of the major challenges was to initiate an inclusive process for a suitable site for nuclear waste on the basis of socio-technical and scientific criteria. Plans for the construction of a repository stayed strictly locked in the drawers of the nuclear waste operator SOGIN (Società Gestione Impianti Nucleari) for over five years. These plans envisaged the construction of a central surface repository and a technology park for the storage of both very low level (VLLW) and low-level waste (LLW) as well temporarily for intermediate-level waste (ILW) and high-level waste (HLW). However, the siting selection has been in a stalemate situation for a decade.

Recently, after a long period of incoherent stop and go, local opposition to the plans and a subsequent deadlock, the mandatory search for a national site is taking shape. The national map of potentially suitable areas was released in January 2021. The site search process should lead to the location of a site, which should house 78,000 cubic metres of VLLW and LLW, as well as temporarily 17,000 cubic metres of HLW. The latter should be stored for a maximum of 50 to 100 years and then placed in a repository for deep geological disposal (DGD), about which nothing has yet been revealed.

In this chapter, we identify the issues that dominate the governance debate on the storage and management of the Italian nuclear waste. Our analysis focuses on four domains: politics and administration; laws and regulations; science and technology, civil society, and on the interrelations between the domains. Special emphasis is laid on public participation and the involvement of local authorities, local communities and civil society in the site search procedures and planning. We look at the dynamics of the institutional actors, in particular the involved

Ministries, the regulatory authority (Ispettorato Nazionale per la Sicurezza Nucleare e la Radioprotezione, ISIN) and operator SOGIN and their interaction with civil society. They are all challenged to adopt a procedure on the basis of sociotechnical criteria, which incorporates inclusive and decentralised forms of decision-making and interaction among players and stakeholders at all levels of (risk) governance. The process is therefore expected to be cumbersome and will require a new and more democratic approach to nuclear waste management. Such an approach will not be easy to implement in a country like Italy, which is characterised by scarce trust in public institutions and a long legacy of top-down decision-making.

This chapter is structured as follows. In Sect. 3.2, we describe the evolution of the Italian waste management strategy. We provide a brief historical background and key facts on the Italian nuclear programme and illustrate recent developments that have led to the current concept for the national repository. In Sect. 3.3, we consider the political, institutional and legislative domains of Italian nuclear waste governance. In Sect. 3.4, we investigate the scientific and technological domain. Then, in Sect. 3.5, we focus on the societal domain and its interactions with the previous ones. In particular, we look at these interactions with regard to the ongoing, more participatory siting policy, for which we provide a first assessment. Finally, in the Conclusion (Sect. 3.6), we ask what we can learn from the interaction between the different domains (how are science and politics integrated, how is civil society engaged in governance, etc.) and try to delineate what is unique about the Italian case. We suggest that nuclear waste governance in the country is affected by a vicious circle of (low) trust that is difficult to break despite the changing participation approach.

3.2 Evolution of the Waste Management Strategy

3.2.1 Brief Historical Background[2]

Italy had a pioneering role in the early development of nuclear power in the 1950s. Nuclear energy was seen as the answer to the lack of domestic fossil resources. In the 1960s, following the nationalisation of the electricity sector and the establishment of the national electricity monopolist ENEL (Ente Nazionale

---

[2] The facts referred to in this section are based on Di Nucci (2009, 2015).

Energia Elettrica), and due to cheap oil prices and powerful petroleum lobbies, the nuclear option was no longer pursued (Di Nucci, 2009)· As a reaction to the oil crises of 1973 and 1979 there was a renaissance of nuclear power, and two massive nuclear development programmes were planned (Di Nucci, 2009). Nevertheless, the share of nuclear power remained marginal. Following the Chernobyl disaster in 1986, there was first a moratorium on nuclear plans, followed by a referendum in 1987, and finally a phase-out of all NPPs in 1990.

In the mid-1990s, ENEL abandoned fuel reprocessing in its own pilot facilities and opted for reprocessing abroad, and for an interim dry storage of the remaining spent fuel from its nuclear plants. Spent fuel from the British technology Magnox reactor in Latina was shipped to Sellafield in the UK for reprocessing, whilst used fuel from the other three Italian NPPs was sent for reprocessing in La Hague (France). Following reprocessing, vitrified waste will be returned to Italy.

In spite of the unambiguous results of the referendum in 1987, the debate on the nuclear option was revived in 2008 by the pro-nuclear centre-right Berlusconi government, which introduced a package of nuclear rulings and by-laws including measures to simplify the licensing of siting and construction. New legislation (Law 99/2009) was passed in July 2009, and envisaged six months to select sites for new NPPs.[3] However, this triggered a civic and institutional opposition. The regions with potentially suitable sites for new NPPs (Basilicata, Emilia-Romagna, Latium, Liguria, Molise, Marche, Calabria, Tuscany and Umbria) appealed against Law 99/2009, which they considered unconstitutional. In June 2010, the Italian Constitutional Court rejected the joint appeal by the regional governments, but the national government had to approve a new legislation on nuclear sites, in order to adjust to the decision of the Constitutional Court. Further, organised protest arose as members of the new Nuclear Regulatory Agency were named directly by the government in November 2010, without Parliament's approval. In December 2010, a joint meeting of the Parliamentary Commissions for Environment and for Industry rejected one of the nominations, halting the Berlusconi government's plans. In the aftermath of the Fukushima disaster in 2011, the initiative "Vote Yes to stop nuclear power", started by over 60 associations, promoted a referendum to repeal a number of the new laws introduced to pave the way for

---

[3] In the same year ENEL and Electricité de France (EdF) launched the joint venture Sviluppo Nucleare Italia to build at least four 1,650 MWe reactors deploying the EPWR (European Pressurised Water Reactor) technology of Areva.

new NPPs.[4] This referendum, held on 12–13 June 2011, reached a 55% voter turnout.[5] About 94% of respondents voted against restarting nuclear energy programmes. This confirmed the results of the Chernobyl referendum, showing that the majority of Italian citizens are against nuclear power.

3.2.2 The Current Dimension of the Waste Problem

Almost all the waste generated by the operation of nuclear installations is stored at the sites of origin. In addition, radioactive waste produced by R&D activities and medical and industrial uses is preliminarily stored in specific facilities. Most of this waste has been stored in untreated form, and dismantling activities, treatment and/or conditioning are on-going at NPPs and fuel cycle facilities. Concerning management of spent fuel, Italy decided to reprocess abroad. Following the stop of all nuclear power activities, the shipments of spent fuel for reprocessing terminated; the last shipment to the UK took place in 2005.

The Technical Guide 26, issued in 1987 by the former national environmental and safety agency ANPA (ANPA, 1987), subdivides waste into: Category I: very low-level waste (VLLW); Category II: low or intermediate-level waste (LILW) and Category III: long-lived and/or high-level waste (LLW/HLW). Radioactive waste of differing levels is being temporarily stored in at least 20 sites scattered throughout Italy (NEA/OECD, 2013; World Nuclear News, 2021).

Most of the radioactive waste derives from the operation of the NPPs and nuclear installations. Further radioactive waste stems from decommissioning activities, and the return of ILW and HLW from reprocessing of spent nuclear fuel abroad. The national inventory of radioactive waste, updated until 31 December 2020 by the regulator ISIN, indicates that there are approximately 31,751 cubic meters of radioactive waste, of which 14,000 cubic meters are VLLW, 12,500 cubic meters is LLW and 3000 cubic meters is ILW (ISIN, 2020, 2021a; SOGIN 2021c). To these volumes one needs to add the HLW returning after reprocessing abroad, and the medium-level radioactive waste expected from the dismantling of decommissioned nuclear plants (ENEA, n. d.). According to ISIN estimates, the waste returning in the next few years from reprocessing in UK and

---

[4] The questions posed in the referendum concerned the abrogation of about 70 regulatory and legislative measures established since 2008 in order to enable the construction of new NPPs.
[5] In Italy, legislative referenda require a turnout of over 50% of all eligible voters.

France will amount to approximately 35 cubic meters of HLW and approximately 48 cubic meters of ILW (See Table 3.1).

It has been estimated that the national repository will host 78,000 cubic meters of VLLW and LLW. Of this volume, approximately 33,000 cubic meters have already been produced, whilst the rest is expected to be produced in the future from the operation and decommissioning of NPPs, and from nuclear research facilities, nuclear medicine and industry. In addition, the national repository will also include a high activity storage complex for the temporary storage of approximately 17,000 cubic metres of IHLW. A part of this (approximately 400 cubic meters), consists of residues from fuel reprocessing carried out abroad and non-reprocessable fuel. SOGIN manages approximately 15,000 cubic meters stemming from the four NPPs and five nuclear facilities (Bosco Marengo, Casaccia, Ispra I, Saluggia and Rotondella). Additionally, NUCLECO,[6] stores temporarily 8138 cubic metres of radioactive waste in the Casaccia facilities (Deposito Nazionale, 2020). The major nuclear facilities and their locations are illustrated in Fig. 3.1.

3.2.3 Early Attempts to Develop a Waste Disposal Concept

In recent decades several attempts were made to develop and implement a radioactive waste disposal concept. In 1996, the national energy agency (ENEA) established a "Task Force for a National Site for a Radioactive Waste Repository" tasked with undertaking the conceptual and system projects and site prospection, selecting suitable sites and preparing the preliminary safety report. In 1999, the government launched a strategy for the complete decommissioning of nuclear facilities by 2020. The underlying precondition for this was the construction of a LILW repository to be used also for the temporary storage of HLW (see Di Nucci, 2015).

The Minister of Industry's timeline disclosed in December 1999 envisaged treatment and conditioning of waste from NPPs in on-site storage within ten years, with the perspective of a successive transport to a national waste repository; site selection and construction of a national repository for LILW within ten years, and decommissioning of NPPs and other nuclear facilities within 20 years.

---

[6]NUCLECO is a company belonging to the SOGIN group and acts as the operator for the collection, treatment, conditioning and temporary storage of radioactive waste and sources from nuclear medicine and scientific and technological research activities.

Table 3.1 Volume of radioactive waste according to category in 2020 and expected volume of returned waste (in m^3)

Waste category	International classification	Source	Volume in 2020 (m^3) (ISIN inventory)	(m^3) Estimated Volume*	Art of waste disposal
Category I	Very short-lived waste (VSLLW)	Industry, medical and research establishments	1,241.91		Controlled discharge
	Very low level waste (VLLW)	Industry, medical and research establishments	14,618.28	78,000	Long term surface storage in the national repository
Category II	Low level waste (LLW)	Fuel cycle facilities; NPPs, research reactors; decommissioning	12,700.07		
Category III	Intermediate Level waste (ILW)	NPPs, nuclear facilities, research reactors	3,141.83	17,000	Temporary storage in the national repository waiting for emplacement in a DGD
	ILW	Reprocessing of spent fuel, vitrified ILW returning from Areva	47.6	of which 400 m^3 reprocessed fuel	
	High Level waste (HLW)	Vitrified HLW returning from BNFL	19	and non reprocessable fuel	
	HLW	Vitrified HLW returning from Areva	15.4		

*SOGIN estimates reported in Deposito Nazionale (2020) (https://www.depositonazionale.it/consultazione-pubblica/progetto-preliminare/pagine/stima-dei-rifiuti.aspx)
(Source: Compiled and adapted from Di Nucci (2015), ISIN (2021) and SOGIN (2021c). Estimates until 2020)

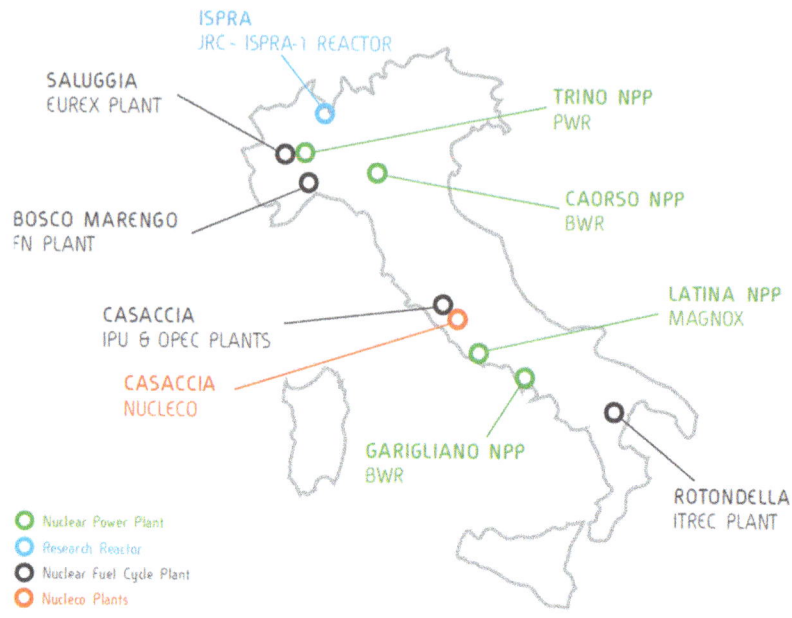

Fig. 3.1 Location of nuclear facilities where waste is temporarily stored. (Source: SOGIN (2020))

In 1999, an agreement between the government, regions and autonomous provinces was signed to define and initiate measures to promote the safe management of radioactive waste. In the framework of this agreement a working group was set up with the aim of preparing a document encompassing technical options and participatory procedures for the local population. The document was approved in January 2002 by the Conferenza Stato-Regioni—the body for horizontal coordination between the national government and regions (SOGIN, 2003, p. 24).

In 2001, the "Task Force Site" submitted to the environmental agency ANPA (later renamed ISPRA), which was acting as interim regulatory authority, a first draft of the conceptual and system projects designed for a repository for LLW, with the aim of starting a preliminary evaluation and testing the acceptability of directives and methodologies for the safety analysis. In 2002, the "Task Force

Site" also considered the near surface option. Following the selection criteria, around 33 areas for a surface facility were identified. (Di Nucci, 2015). However, in the end, the siting process failed in the wake of increasing local opposition (see Section 3.5).

3.2.4 Recent Developments and Design of the National Repository

The current disposal concept—as stated in the *Legislative Decree* 31/2010—focuses on a waste storage solution. It specifies the construction of a central repository as a surface structure (with reversibility and retrievability options) to store approximately 78,000 m^3 of VLL and LLW, as well as approximately 17,000 m^3 of HLW (Deposito Nazionale 2020). For the latter, a deep geological disposal (DGD) is considered necessary, and therefore high activity waste will be stored only temporarily (50–100 years) in a special area of the repository, and will then be permanently transferred to a DGD (Deposito nazionale n.d).

The decision for a centralised surface repository was based on the assumption that transferring the waste into a central structure could guarantee maximum safety for people and the environment, and could allow for the complete restoration of environmental systems, optimising time and costs and eliminating the need for temporary storage sites (Di Nucci, 2015).

The concept for a national repository also includes a technology park with a centre for R&D and innovation in the field of decommissioning and radioactive waste management on-site. The dedicated official portal on the repository explains the design of the facility. The repository will extend over 150 hectares, of which 40 hectares are foreseen for the technology park. The conditioned encased solid waste (or solidifying liquid waste, in cement or glass) is to be sealed inside steel drums filled with cementite. The drums will be sealed in reinforced concrete boxes, and all the boxes will be placed in a large cement aboveground tank which will be covered with a layer of soil and turf. These tanks will be sealed for 300 years. The total investment for the construction of the national repository and technology park is estimated to reach 900 M € (but could rise to 1.5 Bn € with related works), and will be financed through the electricity bill (the so-called A2RIM tariff component), which already covers the costs of dismantling nuclear plants (www.depositonazionale.it).

3.3 Nuclear Waste Politics, Administration and Legislation

3.3.1 Institutional Framework and Main Actors

Italy has a rather complex organisation and institutional setting. At the national level, a number of ministries share responsibilities in the nuclear waste area. We focus on the major institution with competence for regulations and for issuing the operating licence for nuclear and radioactive facilities. The Ministry of Ecological Transition, established in 2021, is responsible (under the technical advice of ISPRA) for assessing and inspecting nuclear facilities and activities involving the use of radiation sources, for technical recommendations and legally binding requirements. Moreover, its Department of Ecological Transition and Green Investments—DG for Waste, performs functions to ensure protection of the soil, air and water. Two further key institutional actors are: the Regulator ISIN and the Operator SOGIN. The former is the independent nuclear safety authority in charge of the regulation and control of nuclear installations safety and radiation protection.

The operator is responsible for decommissioning NPPs and fuel cycle plants and the disposal of LLW/ILW as well as the temporary storage of HLW. Other actors are the regional administrations where the sites are located, the Parliament, the national Regulatory Authority for Energy, Networks and the Environment (ARERA), and ISPRA. Additionally, there are consulting bodies such as the Conferenza Stato-Regioni in charge of discussing issues where competence is shared between central and regional governments. Under the Italian constitution, the opinion of this body is non-binding, but it represents a clear political message for the central government.

3.3.2 The Long Road to the Establishment of an Independent Regulator

Art. 5.2 of the Nuclear Safety Directive (Council Directive 2009/71/Euratom of 25 June 2009) requires European Union Member States to establish and maintain a competent regulatory authority functionally separated from any organisation associated with "[..] the promotion or exploitation of nuclear energy or radioactive material; the production of electricity using isotopes; the management of spent fuel and radioactive waste". The fact that such activities in Italy were for long time under the jurisdiction of the Ministry of Economic Development (an actor traditionally closely connected with the nuclear industry) has been considered as a very critical issue (Di Nucci, 2015).

Indeed, the execution of regulatory and safety functions in Italy has a troubled history characterised by a continuing change of agencies. It started in 1964 with the creation of Comitato Nazionale per l'Energia Nucleare (CNEN) as regulatory agency using safety criteria from the UK and USA, and later was taken over by the Nuclear Safety and Health Protection Directorate, a department of the National Energy Agency ENEA (ENEA-DISP) (WNA 2021).[7] In line with Law 99/2009, a new Agency for Nuclear Safety (ASN, Agenzia per la Sicurezza Nucleare) was to be established with staff from ISPRA and ENEA-DISP. Following the cancellation of the ASN through Legislative Decree 201/2011, its functions were temporarily assigned to ISPRA, which de facto acted as the national nuclear safety authority.

ISPRA, established in 2008 as a governmental institute with administrative and financial autonomy under the supervision of the then Ministry of Environment, was in charge of the control and supervision of nuclear facilities and radiation protection. ISPRA's authorisation was required for detailed designs of any structure, system and component relevant to safety in any nuclear plant. Within ISPRA, the duties of the regulatory body were carried out by the Nuclear, Technological and Industrial Risk Department.

Legislative Decree No. 45 of 2014 finally provided for the establishment of a national independent nuclear regulatory authority responsible for nuclear safety and radiation protection, in accordance with the Directives 2009/71/Euratom and 2011/70/ Euratom (European Council, 2011). However, the Italian regulatory authority (ISIN) only began to operate in August 2018. ISIN is a technical body governed by public law and enjoys operational and administrative autonomy. It is responsible for the regulation and supervision (by inspection) of nuclear installations in matters of nuclear safety and radiation protection.

The bodies of ISIN are the Director, the Council (composed of three experts, one of whom has organisational coordination functions within ISIN) and the Board of Auditors. Both the Director and the Council are appointed by decree of the President of the Republic, after deliberation of the Council of Ministers. The Inspectorate took up all the functions concerning nuclear safety and

---

[7] In 1994, the responsibility for safety and licensing was transferred to ANPA, National Agency for Environment Protection and Technical Services (renamed APAT in 2002, and later in 2009, ISPRA).

radiation protection that over the course of decades had been attributed by the national legislation to several different agencies. The structure of ISIN is made up of about 65 units with proven expertise in the specific areas covered by the regulator, and stem mostly from staff of ISPRA's Nuclear, Technological and Industrial Risk Department, and other public administrations and research bodies.

ISIN is responsible for the authorisation processes and the technical assessments, control and supervision of the nuclear installations, including research reactors, plants and activities related to the management of radioactive waste and spent nuclear fuel, protection of nuclear materials and installations, use of ionizing radiation sources (www.isinucleare.it). Moreover, the remit of ISIN includes the issue of technical guides in matters of transport and certifications of radioactive materials.

3.3.3 Operator/Implementer

There is a long history of industrial interdependencies leading to the birth of the state-owned nuclear waste management and disposal company SOGIN. SOGIN started operating in 2001, but became a group in 2004 after the acquisition of a 60% stake in NUCLECO SpA, the operator responsible for collecting and conditioning as well as for the temporary storage of radioactive waste from nuclear medicine and R&D activities. Apart from management and decommissioning of NPPs, spent fuel and nuclear materials, SOGIN is also in charge of designing, constructing and operating the national repository for LILW and the interim storage for HLW. SOGIN operates according to the strategic guidelines of the Italian government. Authorisations are granted by the Ministry of Ecological Transition, on the basis of the technical advice of ISIN.

The company is financially solid and has approximately 1,150 employees.[8] At the end of the 2020 financial year, there has been an increase in the volume of decommissioning activities that grew from 48.3 M € in 2019 to 72.5 M € in 2020 (SOGIN, 2021a).

---

[8] In the past, due to its non-transparent management, its personnel recruiting practices, consulting services abroad and high expenses, SOGIN has been the object of various parliamentary interrogations, and has also been criticised by the Court of Auditors (Corte dei Conti) as well as by the Energy Regulatory Authority. See Rovai (2009) and Di Nucci (2015).

3.3.4 The Legal Framework

There is a high number of laws and rulings (mostly decrees) regulating nuclear activities and radioactive waste.[9] A milestone is *Law 282/2005*, promulgated for the Italian ratification of IAEA's "Joint Convention on the Safety of Spent Fuel Management and on the Safety of Radioactive Waste Management". Further major references are the *Legislative Decree 230/95* (implementation of various Euratom directives) later integrated and modified by the *Legislative Decree 241/2000*, as well as the *Legislative Decree 314/2003*, modified and converted in *Law 368/2003*, as well as *Law 239/2004*. Other important legal and normative references are Law *99/2009*, and the *Legislative Decree 31/2010*, with their subsequent amendments.

Legislative Decree 31/2010 ("Discipline of the storage systems for radioactive fuel and waste as well as economic benefits [...]") belongs to the primary nuclear legislation. In the case of nuclear waste, this decree regulates steps and scheduling of the siting procedures of the national repository, including also public consultations. Art. 22 provides built-in provisions related to the funding of the decommissioning activities and compensation measures for the municipalities hosting nuclear facilities. Art. 4 states that construction and management of nuclear facilities are activities of state interest, are subject to a single authorisation upon request of the operator and are granted (in terms of *Legislative Decree 66/2010*)— and subsequent to a consultation with the Ministry of Defence and the respective region of the site in accordance with the "Unified Conference" (Conferenza Unificata)[10]— by decree of the Ministry of Economic Development in agreement with the Ministries of Environment, Infrastructures and Transportation. The response of the region is mandatory, but not binding, and is to be delivered within 90 days after the request for authorisation. Should there be no reaction after this time, the Conferenza Unificata will examine the matter. This Legislative Decree assigned to SOGIN the task of implementing the storage

---

[9] It would be an enticing task to list with references all relevant legislation. We therefore refer to the website of the Italian Parliament (http://www.parlamento.it), 'Laws' section,where it is possible to consult the laws, decree-laws and legislative decrees approved since the 13th Legislature (9 May 1996).

[10] The "Unified Conference" is a governance body consisting of a state-region conference, state-municipalities and autonomous bodies' conference, i.e. regions, provinces, municipalities, etc. Its aims are to enhance cooperation between the state activities and other bodies' and examine issues of common interest.

concept and made it also responsible for construction and operation of the national repository. Finally, it provides—along with Law 241/1990 and the Directive of the Presidency of the Council of Ministries 2/2017—the framework for the participation process that is organised around a 'National Seminar'. This process is open to all parties identified on the basis of the provisions of Art. 27, and to all those who participate in the public consultation by submitting comments and technical proposals, which should be made available on a dedicated website.

As anticipated, *Legislative Decree* 45/2014 that implemented the Euratom directive 2011/70 (European Council, 2011), provided for the establishment of the regulator ISIN. A joint Ministerial Decree (by the Ministry of Economic Development and the Ministry of Environment) of 7 August 2015, then implemented other Euratom directives providing for a renewed classification of nuclear waste. The legislative framework was subsequently upgraded with Legislative Decree 137/2017 and Legislative Decree 101/2020, which also improved the role of the new regulator.

3.4 The Science & Technology Domain

Italy has a long tradition in nuclear research, which dates back to the pioneering work of Enrico Fermi in the 1930s. This legacy is still reflected in the Italian research community and institutions. The dynamics between science, technology and society have been evolving over recent decades. On the one hand, policymakers manifested an increased need for scientific advice (science-policy interface). On the other hand, science continuously interacts with society. In his analysis of the risk society, Beck (1986) pointed out the importance of the inclusion of different expertise and forms of knowledge for gaining new insights.

Due to the many unanswered questions about nuclear waste disposal, multidisciplinary expert knowledge is required as a productive source for making the best possible decisions in balancing risk technologies with societal interests and concerns. Since the 1970s, opposition to the Italian nuclear programme has also been animated by an important part of the scientific community that developed contacts with environmental movements and NGOs (Baracca, 2008).

After the abandonment of the nuclear programme, the Italian nuclear research community has maintained a niche role. This role has occasionally expanded in conjunction with the re-launch of the nuclear option in the political agenda, especially under the centre-right government of Berlusconi in the late 2000s. However, the simple fact that Italy no longer has a nuclear power programme in place has favoured the separation between civil society and the niche of the nuclear research community. Moreover, the public debate on nuclear waste is no longer influenced by the debate on the role of nuclear power in the country's energy mix. On the one hand, this situation has simplified the debate on nuclear waste management. On the other hand, however, the lack of a nuclear power programme has reduced the visibility and salience of the nuclear waste issue for Italian public opinion at large, with the exception of the local communities directly affected by the site location process.

The research community involved with nuclear waste includes various universities and research institutes as well as dedicated agencies. Theoretical nuclear research is performed by laboratories belonging to Consiglio Nazionale delle Ricerche (CNR) and Istituto Nazionale di Fisica Nucleare (INFN). All of the INFN's research activities are undertaken within a framework of international cooperation, in close collaboration with Italian universities. The leading agency for applied nuclear research is ENEA, which performs dedicated nuclear research, and manages research centres at Casaccia (Latium), Bologna, and Brasimone (Emilia Romagna).[11]

Research and emerging technologies in the field of decommissioning and waste management are carried out by SOGIN alone, as well as in cooperation with universities and research centres. They all participate in cooperative projects on nuclear safety, waste management and decommissioning within the framework of the Euratom Research and Training Programme. SOGIN participates in a number of European projects. Additionally, there is a number of international cooperation projects running within programmes and schemes of the OECD/NEA and the IAEA.

The scientific community is involved in nuclear waste management in different ways. First, experts from governmental agencies lay down the technical normative framework on the matter. The *Technical Guide 26* (ANPA, 1987), provides waste classification as well as the technical requirements. The *Technical Guide no. 29*, issued in 2014 by ISPRA defines the criteria for the location of a surface disposal facility for LLW and ILW. It identifies 15 exclusion criteria including: volcanic and seismic activities, geomorphological and hydraulic risk, altitude above 700 m, distance from the coast line within 5 km, unsuitable distance from residential areas, distance from motorways, suburban roads and railway lines, proximity to industrial activities, airports and military facilities, hydrology and

---

[11] For an account of the Italian nuclear R&D organisations and cooperation activities, see IAEA (2021).

hydro-resources; importance of biodiversity. Among the investigation criteria are the presence of secondary volcanic and tectonic activities, presence of erosion phenomena, weather and climatic conditions, soil and groundwater conditions, hydrogeological parameters, natural habitat, availability of transport infrastructures, presence of strategically important infrastructures, etc. (ISPRA, 2014).

A proposal for the *Technical Guide no. 32*, 'Safety and Radiation Protection Criteria for Engineered Surface Disposal Facilities of Radioactive Waste', has been published on the ISIN website and was subject to consultation with the public and interested companies, bodies and organisations for a period of 60 days. The criteria stipulate that the site qualification, design, construction, operation, closure and post-closure of disposal facilities must be planned and conducted in accordance with criteria that guarantee the safety and radiation protection of members of the public and workers, as well as the protection of the environment in the vicinity of the installation (ISIN, 2021c).

In addition, experts from the research community are involved in the decision-making and the participatory process for site location. This involvement exposes the interactions between science and society.

3.5 The Societal Domain and Its Interactions with the Political-Administrative and Scientific Domains

3.5.1 Italian Society and Nuclear Energy: An Evolving Relation

Italian citizens have twice manifested their opposition to nuclear energy through referendums. The relation between Italian society and nuclear energy, however, is more complex than these results suggest. The outcomes of the 1987 and 2011 referendums have been strongly influenced by international negative events, namely the Chernobyl and Fukushima nuclear disasters. Surveys from the late 2000s showed that about 46% of Italians were in favour of building nuclear power plants in the country, whereas 44% were against (European Commission, 2010).[12] The number of opponents increased to 50% when people were asked if they were willing to have a NPP in their province. Younger people and centre-left voters were more against the nuclear option, which was mainly supported by

---

[12] See the data available at http://www.demos.it/a00231.php (accessed 25 October 2021).

elderly people and voters from centre-right political parties. The Fukushima disaster represented the turning point. After that event, opponents of nuclear energy increased. Surveys show that the number of citizens against nuclear energy has been constantly over 60% since 2012.[13] In 2021, this figure reached 67%. Interestingly, among those against nuclear energy, 60% motivated their opinion by worries about possible mismanagement in the treatment of nuclear waste. This figure is even larger than the number of opponents that were worried about possible accidents in NPPs (49%). This apparent paradox has its roots in the low level of trust citizens have in public institutions in charge of environmental safety and protection. The trust in national institutions has progressively reduced over the last decade, and is lower than the average in OECD countries; a trend that correlates with the emergence and reinforcement of populist parties. In 2020, only 37% of the respondents trusted the government, and merely 28% of citizens trusted the Italian parliament.[14] Moreover, this paradox is also linked to the legacy of the past top-down nuclear waste siting policy, which was a failure.

3.5.2 The Failure of the Past Top-Down Siting Policy

In Italy, the direct involvement of civil society in (large) infrastructural projects is still in an infant stage. Until a few years ago, siting processes have been inspired by Decide-Announce-Defend (DAD) strategies, even at time when the designation of a national site for waste disposal represented a political priority.

As anticipated, the "Task Force Site" created by ENEA in 2002, identified 33 areas with favourable physical and territorial characteristics for a national repository (Ventura, 2003). The list of potentially suitable national sites did not find a consensus. After a technical evaluation, a site in the region Basilicata (Scanzano) was selected by the government, and was included in the *Legislative Decree 314/2003* ("Urgent Dispositions for the collection, disposal and storage of radioactive waste"). This Decree also established an extraordinary Commissioner in charge of the validation of the site, the approval of the economic and financial plan, as well as the procurement and tenders for planning and constructing the national repository (Cianciullo, 2003a, b). The Government then mandated the

---

[13] See the data available at https://nucleareeragione.org/2021/07/05/sondaggio-swg-oltre-un-italiano-su-due-possibilista-sui-nuovi-reattori-nucleari/ (accessed 29 October 2021).
[14] See https://www.statista.com/statistics/1264813/citizens-who-express-trust-in-public-institutions-in-italy/ (accessed 31 May 2022).

Chairman of SOGIN, a former army General acting as "Extraordinary Commissioner", to select a location for radioactive waste of category I and II. Experts identified underground salt caverns in Scanzano Jonico as a potentially suitable repository for HLW at 700 m depth (La Repubblica, 2003; Di Nucci, 2015). This location had been selected in spite of criticism about the high population density and the proximity to the sea. Local residents had not been consulted (Cianciullo, 2003b). Zinn (2007) talks about "militarisation" of the project. The site was defined as a military defence installation of national property. Some of the press, praised *Decree 314* and considered it a courageous move which represented a break with the modus operandi of postponing difficult choices, described as typically Italian.

Indeed, the top-down, militaristic procedure triggered harsh reaction. For nearly two weeks, residents blocked motorways and shut down shops and businesses. Approximately 150,000 people marched in what was described as the largest demonstration held in the southern region of Basilicata (Rossano, 2003). The regional, provincial and municipal administrations of Basilicata opposed *Decree 314*. The regional council declared the area a denuclearised zone and initiated a lawsuit against the government decree. As a result of the protest, the Berlusconi government was forced to withdraw from the decision to make Scanzano Jonico the site of the main nuclear waste repository in Italy. It amended the decree (deleting the name of the designated location), and commissioned SOGIN to undertake the search for a new site.

3.5.3 Site Identification and Participatory Siting Procedures

The popular revolt in Scanzano has gained an iconic status for civic protest. The resistance was articulated at two parallel and complementary levels, institutional and popular, and was characterised by a deep and continuous discourse exchange (Zinn, 2007). The lessons learned are that siting procedures require an open, democratic process, where all stakeholders' interests can be discussed and where both residents' opinions and scientific arguments are considered, rather than *de lege* enforcement (Di Nucci, 2015).

Currently, the newly started siting procedures try to focus on transparency and openness, but the legacy of the past represents a serious hurdle to create the trust necessary for such a process. Politicians and authorities have often given misinformation in the past, and these mistakes represent a critical burden. After a long stalemate, and with over five years delay, on 5 January 2021 a new map was published with potential sites considered suitable to host the surface repository to store all radioactive waste. Elaborated by SOGIN, the National Map of Potentially Suitable Areas (CNAPI) proposal has been validated by the regulator ISIN, and subsequently by the responsible ministries. The release of the documents represents the first step on a new participatory path that should lead to the identification of the single site at national level where to realise the national repository and technology park.

The CNAPI proposal identifies the areas whose characteristics meet the location criteria defined by the regulator ISIN in *Technical Guide no. 29* (ISPRA, 2014). The CNAPI proposes a grouping of the 67 potentially suitable areas subdivided into four sets, with decreasing order of suitability with "equal safety conditions" (A1, A2, B and C). This classification has been reached by considering socio-environmental, logistic and seismic aspects. For each of the potentially suitable areas identified, a report on the geological, naturalistic and anthropic characteristics at a regional scale has been prepared and made available online.

The map identifies 67 locations in seven regions (Piedmont, Tuscany, Latium, Apulia, Basilicata, Sardinia and Sicily) (Table 3.2). A1 sites are located only in two regions: Piedmont (7) and Latium (5), which also host 3 A2 sites. Several A2 sites are located between Apulia and Basilicata. Sardinia and Sicily, mainly due to their insular positions, only host B and C sites. A table attached to the map indicates the 69 municipalities involved. The most likely are expected to be in two areas in the province of Turin (Caluso and Carmagnola), five in the province of Alessandria (including Bosco Marengo and Novi Ligure), and in the province of Viterbo.

Table 3.2 Number/category of potential sites for the national repository in each Region. (Source: Authors' elaboration on the data available at www.depositonazionale.it/documentale/documenti_proposta_cnapi/ordine_di_idoneita/dngs00226_procedura_risultati_classificazione_aree.pdf)

Region	A1	A2	B	C	Tot.
Piedmont	7	1			8
Latium	5	2		15	22
Apulia/Basilicata		6		11	17
Tuscany		2			2
Sardinia			14		14
Sicily			1	3	4
Tot.	12	11	15	29	67

Phase	Date	Year	Event
Phase 1: Public consultation	5 January	2021	Publication of the National Map of Potentially Suitable Areas (CNAPI), starting of public consolation (180 days) (website: depositonazionale.it)
	5 July	2021	End of the public consultation
Phase 2: National seminar	3 August	2021	Promotion of the National Seminar
	7 September	2021	Opening of the National Seminar (website: seminariodepositonazionale.it)
	14 September	2021	First national session of the Seminar
	28 September	2021	Territorial session of the Seminar (Sardinia)
	26 October	2021	Territorial session of the Seminar (Basilicata and Apulia)
	3 November	2021	Territorial session of the Seminar (Tuscany)
	9 November	2021	Territorial session of the Seminar (Latium)
	15 November	2021	Territorial session of the Seminar (Piedmont)
	15 December	2021	Closing of the National Seminar and publication of its results (stakeholders can submit additional observations within 30 days)
Phase 3: Localisation of the national deposit	15 March	2022	National Charter for suitable areas (CNAI) submitted by Sogin within 60 days from the closing of the public consultation. Pending approval by Ministry of Ecological transition
	Summer	2022	
	??		Expression of interest to host the national repository and science park
	2025 ???		Localisation of the national deposit and the science park

Fig. 3.2 Timeline of the consultation process. (Source: Authors' elaboration on the data available at www.depositonazionale)

The publication of the potential sites marked the start of a two-month phase of public consultation of the documents, which were made available on a dedicated website (i.e. depositonazionale.it) (Fig. 3.2). This was followed after four months by a national debate (the National Seminar) involving local authorities, trade associations, trades unions, environmental NGOs, universities and research bodies, as well as citizens. During this phase, all aspects of the proposed facility were analysed, including the possible economic benefits and related territorial development. Subsequently, regions, provinces and municipalities have been allowed to submit observations regarding the map. On 7 September 2021, the national seminar began, with the aim of reaching a shared decision on the location of the site for the national repository. The seminar was organised on a dedicated website (https://www.seminariodepositonazionale.it/) and was articulated into seven work sessions, one national and six territorial, which covered the potentially suitable areas in the regions involved (Table 3.2). ISIN guaranteed the correct application of national and international criteria (ISIN, 2021b).

At the end of this process, SOGIN updated the CNAPI. On 15 December 2021, the results of the seminar were presented (Deposito Nazionale 2021). Subsequently SOGIN needed to skim further through the candidate territories, arriving at a new map: the National Charter for suitable areas (CNAI). This provides the final shortlist of sites from which to choose the future location of the national repository. At the end of the National Seminar, a second stage of the public consultation started and lasted thirty days, during which any further observations and technical proposals could be sent. The procedure was finalised by 14 January 2022.

On 15 March 2022, the CNAI has been submitted by Sogin to the Ministry of Ecological Transition within the within 60 days from the closing of the public consultation, as envisaged by Legislative Decree 31/2010. In the next step, the Ministry of Ecological Transition following ISIN's technical opinion will approve the map by its own decree. The map will then be published (Deposito Nazionale, 2022c).

The final draft of the CNAI will need the approval of the ministries involved in nuclear decommissioning, and from the regulator ISIN which will review comments and documents received by SOGIN to arrive at a shortlist of suitable sites. Following the publication of the CNAI, municipalities will be able to submit expressions of interest for hosting the storage facility. The interesting point is that Legislative Decree 31/2010 recognises that these expressions of interest are non-binding until the final identification of the site, which is a procedure resembling the "decision in principle" from Finland (Di Nucci 2019). The final decision rests in the hands of the Ministry for Ecological Transition (in accordance with the Ministry of Transport and Infrastructures) who will identify the area with a decree, after a Strategic Environmental Assessment is performed. The goal is to build the repository by 2025.

3.5.4 Participation in the Consultation Process and Position of the Main Actors

The first phase of the consultation process following the publication of CNAPI lasted 180 days. Several institutional and civil society actors took part in this process, submitting documents, technical reports and expressing their positions and concerns. Overall, 318 participants were involved in this phase. The largest group were regional and local governments (62%), followed by associations and

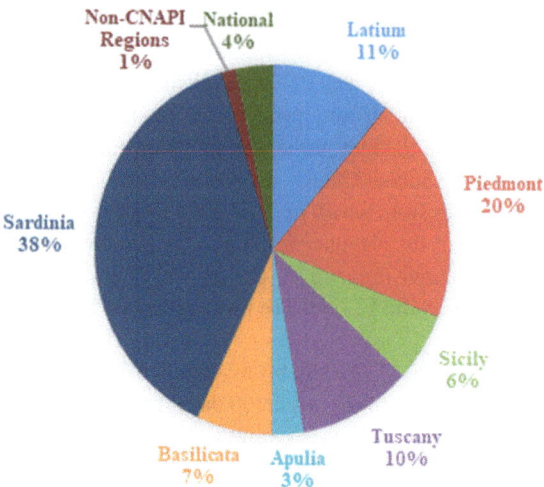

Fig. 3.3 Territorial distribution of the participants in the consultation stage. (Source: Authors' elaboration on the data available at www.depositonazionale)

civic committees (20%), citizens (13%) and companies (4%) (Deposito Nazionale 2022a, b). The territorial distribution of the participants reflects, in part, the distribution of the geographical areas possibly affected by the siting of the national repository (Fig. 3.3).

Participation has been particularly high in Sardinia and Piedmont. This fact is not surprising, as seven out of twelve of the A1 sites are located in Piedmont. In Sardinia however, there are no A1 and A2 sites, although there are 14 C sites. In the Southern regions (Sicily, Basilicata, Apulia), participation has been lower. This is likely because they host fewer potential areas for siting the national repository, and because these regions are generally characterised by lower levels of public participation than those located in Northern and Central Italy.

Overall, the position of the main actors has manifested dissent with regard to the CNAPI proposals. Regions involved have expressed their firm opposition, both within the framework of the consultation process and in institutional bodies, such as the Conferenza Stato-Regioni. This opposition came from both regions governed by centre-right (Piedmont, Sardinia, Sicily, Basilicata) and centre-left (Apulia, Latium, Tuscany) political parties. Several regions have contested the CNAPI proposal, pointing to technical gaps in the selection process of the sites, which they claim have underestimated several important risks. For example, Sicily pointed to the very high risk posed by the sea transportation of nuclear waste. Besides, many regions have highlighted the 'incompatibility' between the national repository and local development strategies based on tourism, agriculture and the valorisation of local traditions and landscape. For example, Apulia and Basilicata protested that their areas are unsuitable to build a national repository, as they are of particular natural value. Similar arguments were put forward by other regions with a strong tourism sector, such as Tuscany and Sardinia. For these assessments, regions have involved their technical bodies, experts and regional environmental agencies (the ARPA). Some regions have established 'Scientific and Technical Committees' with experts from universities and the research community.

The mayors of several municipalities throughout Italy also stressed the unsuitability of their respective territories to host nuclear waste. Concerns about the potentially negative impact of the national repository on agriculture, tourism and places of high natural value have represented the most common observations submitted during the consultation phase, both by local governments and civil society organisations.

In addition, some regions, along with civil society organisations, pointed to their limited involvement in the process that led to the CNAPI formulation (Deposito Nazionale, 2022a, b). The governor of the Piedmont Region, for example, complained that the CNAPI map was drafted without actively involving the region and the mayors of the areas affected. Piedmont is the region that already hosts the majority of nuclear waste.[15]

Worries about potentially underestimated risks were further expressed by environmental NGOs and civil society organisations. For example, WWF-Italy provided 73 pages of observations, in which they indicated fundamental limits and gaps in the CNAPI. Legambiente, the largest environmental NGO in Italy, underlined that the single national repository should be chosen wisely, objectively and transparently, in full compliance with the exclusion and investigation criteria. They reiterated that the identification of a single site for the safe storage of LILW radioactive waste is the only way to ensure the proper treatment and disposal of radioactive waste.

Finally, among the research community, criticisms have been expressed by two important organisations including experts from universities and research

---

[15] It is estimated that 75% of radioactive activity from nuclear waste is concentrated in the area where there are three nuclear sites of Saluggia, Trino Vercellese and Bosco Marengo.

institutions, i.e. the Scientific Commission on Decommissioning (established in 2014) and the Interuniversity Research Centre for Sustainable Development (CIRPS). Both these organisations criticised the choice to apply the criteria of *Technical Guidelines no. 29* (ISPRA, 2014)—which was drafted for LLW and ILW—to HLW, as well as the limited independence of ISIN and SOGIN from the government.

3.5.5 Plans vs. Reality: A Preliminary Assessment of the Participation Process

According to SOGIN (2020), the siting process is based on three fundamental principles: transparency, information and participation. But how transparent and genuinely participatory is the search process?

The National Seminar can be considered as the first public consultation in Italy regarding an infrastructure of national importance. Invited parties had to register by 30 September 2021, according to the procedures indicated in the letter sent on 10 August 2021. Information and transparency can be considered as partly achieved. The National Seminar, which took place online, was subdivided into nine working sessions (three national sessions and six regional sessions). Each meeting was broadcast live via streaming, and was made accessible from the page dedicated to each event. Each session was moderated by an expert in participatory processes, and envisaged an hour in which the operator SOGIN commented on the observations and technical proposals received during the first phase of the process (which were available on the dedicated website). Other members of the scientific community were also invited to illustrate specific elements of the project, such as experts from ISIN, NUCLECO or researchers from universities, particularly from the Polytechnic University of Milan. The rest of the time was left for discussion. Spokespeople from the local communities had ten minutes and five slides at their disposal, other comments or questions could be sent by email. Moreover, citizens could use this channel for questions or comments or to get involved in a dedicated chat on the event platform. Experts commented and replied to these inputs at the end of the session (a total of 66 questions were asked during all the events) (SOGIN, 2021b). In addition, after each session, all the material has been made available on the dedicated website of the National Seminar together with a summary of the session. SOGIN considers this format as an assurance in terms of transparency and information sharing. But are the formats chosen also participatory? Can the future operator both lead the participation process and be perceived as neutral?

3 Nuclear Waste Governance in Italy: Between ... 75

Table 3.3 Number and groups of actors involved in the territorial sessions of the National Seminar.

Regional session	Regional governm	Local governm	NGOs	Civic Committees*	Citizens	Ass.**	RI^	Others	Tot
Piedmont	1	16	4	4	5	5	–	2	37
Latium	–	7	4	2	4	7	–	4	28
Apulia/ Basilicata	1	6	1	1	–	4	2	3	18
Sardinia	1	6	1	7	1	–	–	1	17
Tuscany	1	2	1	–	–	1	–	1	6
Sicily	1	0	1	–	1	–	–	–	3
Tot.	5	37	12	14	11	17	2	11	109

(Sources: Authors' elaboration on the data available at https://www.seminariodepositonazionale.it/. Notes: (*) Including committees against nuclear waste (e.g. Comitati No Scorie). (**) Ass. = associations (e.g. trade unions, business associations, business tourism associations); (^) RI = Research institutions (e.g. Universities, national research agencies). The sessions of Latium and Piedmont lasted two days)

Overall, more than 100 stakeholders took part in the regional sessions (see Table 3.3). Participation has been higher in those regions where the majority of A1 potential sites are located, i.e. Piedmont and Latium (see Table 3.2).

In Apulia/Basilicata and Sardinia participation has also been significant. These regions host respectively 17 and 14 potential sites, although no A1 site is present in their territories. Finally, Tuscany and Sicily show the lower level of stakeholders' involvement, but they are also the regions with fewer potential sites.

Local governments (municipalities and provinces) have been the most active parties in the regional sessions (34%), followed by associations representing several organised interests (e.g. business associations, business tourism associations) (16%), civic committees (e.g. committees created to oppose the siting of the national repository) (13%), and environmental NGOs (11%) (Fig. 3.4). Among the latter, Legambiente has been the most active and joined each regional session. A few citizens and other actors (e.g. companies, park authorities) also took part in the regional sessions, along with research institutions which participated only in the Apulia/Basilicata session. Regional governments have been involved in almost all the territorial sessions.

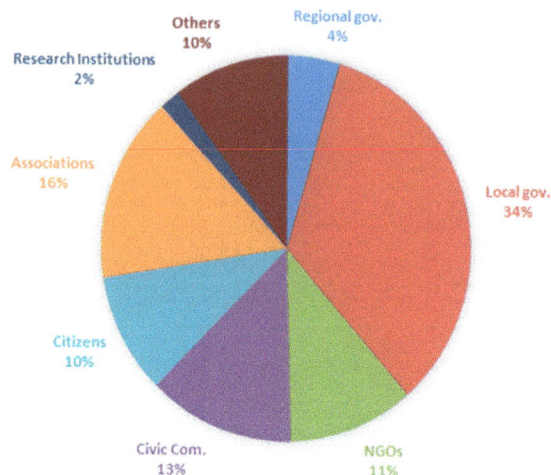

Fig. 3.4 Actors' participation in the regional sessions. (Source: Authors' elaboration on the data available at https://www.seminariodepositonazionale.it/)

As in the previous stage of the participatory process, local governments and associations have generally contested the selection of the sites and criticised the scarce consideration for the socio-economic impact of the national repository, often by highlighting the limited compatibility of the national repository with local development strategies based on agriculture or tourism. Some actors also disputed site decisions, pointing to technical shortcomings in addressing specific risks, such as ground water, seismic criteria or environmental issues. Environmental NGOs also pointed to technical shortcomings in the selection of the sites. Concerning the Piedmont region, it has been noted that especially the areas around the Saluggia and Trino sites already host notable radioactive volumes and that a further site would involve a concentration of health and environmental risks for local population, thus rendering this area a hot-spot from the nuclear risk point of view (see also Borgogno-Mondino et al., 2021).

Only Confindustria, the general Italian industry confederation, has shown support for the national repository and the technological park. Trades unions have been mostly critical, although in some cases they have been sensitive to the potential positive impact of the repository on jobs. Local governments have often coordinated their actions with regional governments, civic committees and local associations in order to build a common front to oppose the siting procedure. Nonetheless, the large majority of stakeholders showed a positive attitude towards the new participatory process and SOGIN's role. SOGIN in turn appreciated the process and claimed that the new information and data provided by the participants would be duly taken into consideration when drafting the CNAI.

3.5.6 Voluntarism as an Option to Break the Stalemate?

With the approval of the CNAI a phase of voluntary expression of interest will be initiated. According to this voluntarist perspective, which is the first option in the current nuclear waste management framework, SOGIN will check whether any municipality is interested in hosting the national repository. But what are the prerequisites to make the procedures understandable and to gain political and societal acceptance for a repository at regional and local level? Is voluntarism, as in the Scandinavian countries, a path that can also be followed in Italy? Are the planned compensation measures attractive enough to persuade the affected population to host a repository?

Compensation mechanisms are provided for the communities involved. In particular, economic compensation for the territory is subdivided according to criteria set in Art. 23 of the Legislative Decree 31/2010, and is to be paid by SOGIN according to criteria to be set by the Ministry of Economic Development in agreement with the Ministries of Environment and of Finance, depending on the level of radioactivity. There are additional expected benefits for the hosting area of the national repository.[16] These include an employment impact for over 4000 people (of which 2000 are direct) per year during the four years of construction. In addition, in the operating phase lasting 40 years, direct employment is estimated on average at around 700 employees, whilst downstream activities could help increasing employment for around a thousand people.

Yet, the first reaction from regions and local communities to the CNAPI proposal has been a firm 'No'. No regional or local government has explicitly considered claiming the compensation mechanisms provided by the legislation or appears attracted by the direct and indirect benefits connected with the repository and technology park. This strong reaction is common within the majority parties supporting regional and local governments as well as within the opposition. The leeway for changing this position during the next phase of the participatory process appears rather limited.

---

[16] See the data available at https://www.depositonazionale.it/deposito-nazionale/pagine/quali-sono-i-benefici-del-deposito.aspx#territorio (accessed 26 October 2021).

3.6 Conclusion

Fierce opposition over three decades and a contradictory nuclear policy have provoked a stalemate, and still render the mandatory search for a national repository site for nuclear waste in Italy a political and societal challenge. In the last few years progress has been made, at least on the institutional side. The legal framework and main governance bodies for nuclear waste management are in place and are becoming robust. It was certainly a success that after so many years ISIN could be established in 2018 as the competent licensing authority and as a body independent of economic interests, and that there is a clear demarcation between the regulatory authority and the developer/operator.

However, the reinforcement of a competent and independent authority that can be considered trustworthy by the largest majority of stakeholders and by the entire society, as well as the initiation of an unambiguous participation process that deserves public confidence remain the Gordian knot in Italy as elsewhere in the European Union (Di Nucci et al. 2021). The "independence" and distribution of roles and responsibilities are partly disputable, especially because of the direct dependence of the regulator ISIN on the Executive. Moreover, the double involvement of the operator SOGIN as implementer and future operator of the repository, and as the main actor responsible for the whole public participation process does not help to make it trustworthy to the sceptical or opposing local authorities and population.

In the consultation and participation process, SOGIN represented the official technical and scientific standpoint. Its technical competence is acknowledged by a wide spectrum of stakeholder groups, but the search for a nuclear repository is only partly a technical and scientific matter. Especially in siting issues, the affected population has built up knowledge over decades. For these reasons, siting strategies can no longer rely merely on "official" scientific knowledge. SOGIN technical expertise has been increasingly confronted with lay expertise, e.g. citizen science and alternative expert opinions. There have been criticisms about the suitability of many territories selected by SOGIN in the national map. For example, in a recent analysis of siting criteria adopted by SOGIN, Borgogno-Mondino et al. (2021, p. 20) point out that a site in Piedmont is located in a critical area as the depth of the ground water table can interfere in a substantial way with the vault of the repository.

Social conflicts and opposition are deeply rooted and are exacerbated by the fact that in the past technical approaches have neglected socially relevant questions and have not been made transparent. It appears that in this most recent attempt, Italy is also risking the opportunity to address real and potential conflicts in a rigorous and open way by failing to integrate the potentially affected local authorities and local residents in the decision-making process. Finding a nuclear waste disposal option requires iterative learning, addressing societal conflicts, and the possibility of readjusting strategies. Following the disclosure of the generally suitable sites, it should have been necessary to gather the consensus of the communities concerned and local institutions, through a more full-fledged public consultation, eventually extended over a longer period of time. However, the participation remained limited to a few hundred people and was concentrated over approximately three months.

The site search procedure could have represented an opportunity for structuring a process in which science and society together cultivate a new art of discourse and are prepared to learn from each other. SOGIN as the responsible actor for the consultation could have gone beyond just informing the public comprehensively, and could have tried to involve the potentially affected territories in the selection process as "co-designers". Such an innovation could have helped to overcome the difficult legacy of the past that has triggered what can be described as a vicious circle of (low) trust. Indeed, the previous top-down approach and the limited involvement of local communities has undermined citizens' trust in public institutions in charge of nuclear waste policy. In general, the relationship between the state and civil society is fundamental to generate and maintain public trust in governmental institutions, and often implies the willingness to delegate negotiation of agreements to them, as this is perceived to be in the public interest (Di Nucci et al., 2021). Exactly this lack of perceived communities' interests makes the new participatory approach problematic, as the standard reaction of the social and institutional local actors involved is a firm 'No', followed by the persistent "protection" of competing local interests. Hence, there is a risk that also decision-makers may lose confidence in the process. No matter how this process is designed and implemented, it can be expected that the actors involved will not change their initial negative stance. They are confronted with other stakeholders and political decision-makers who see little room for manoeuvre in their own logic and standpoints, and this generates mutual distrust. Distrust is also triggered and reinforced by technical, social and political uncertainties and complexities.

Although the whole procedure somehow depended on SOGIN's goodwill, in a preliminary assessment the consultation and role of SOGIN can be considered as fair. The stakeholders expressed their satisfaction, especially with respect to transparency and openness of communication and of the procedures, and were prepared to have confidence in SOGIN's declaration that criticism is going to be taken into consideration.

A timely solution for the waste problem is urged by the Euratom directive (European Council, 2011). However, against this background, 2025 as the point in time envisaged for the localisation is totally illusory. Moreover, it appears that in spite of the good intentions, the initial steps taken towards transparency and openness are not sufficient to instigate trust in the process and in the institutional actors in charge of it. There are no signals of the intention to open up a phase of co-decision for the local communities in the designated sites on the short list. This would be an important step to build confidence in the procedures and to break the enduring stalemate situation. In spite of the potential compensation mechanisms for the affected communities it is unlikely that there will be successful cases of voluntary candidates for the repository, not even by municipalities close to existing nuclear sites. If no candidature is put forward, SOGIN will have to promote bilateral negotiations to find a shared solution. The final decision rests in the hands of the Ministry for Ecological Transition. The worst-case scenario would be for the government to revert to its old reflex and, justified by the pressure to implement the Euratom directive, move back to the old Decide-Announce-Defend strategy. But history has shown that this will not solve the problems and could end up increasing mistrust between society and the government and further hindering the implementation of Italian nuclear waste governance. A more radical way to involve local communities, interest and visions is needed to avoid this rollback and to make steps forward.

References

ANPA (1987). *Guida tecnica n. 26. Gestione dei rifiuti radioattivi.* https://www.depositonazionale.it/raccoltadocumenti/linee-guida/guida_tecnica_N26_gestione_rifiuti_radioattivi.pdf.
Baracca, A. (2008). *L'Italia torna al nucleare. I costi, i rischi, le bugie.* Jaca Book.
Beck, U. (1986). *Risikogesellschaft. Auf dem Weg in eine andere Moderne.* Surkamp.
Borgogno-Mondino, E., Borgia, A. & Cigolin, C. (2021). Locating the Italian Radioactive Waste Repository: Issues and Perplexities Arisen from Open Data-Based Analyses about the TO-10 Site (NW Italy). *Land,* 10, 932. https://doi.org/10.3390/land10090932.
Cianciullo, A. (2003a, June 25). Cimiteri nucleari: slitta la decisione. *La Repubblica.*
Cianciullo, A. (2003b, October 15). Tutti i rischi del cimitero nucleare, *La Repubblica.*
Deposito Nazionale (n. d.). https://www.depositonazionale.it/ Accessed 24 February 2022.
Deposito Nazionale (2020). Stima dei rifiuti radioattivi da conferire al Deposito Nazionale. Rapporto Tecnico: https://www.depositonazionale.it/documentale/progetto_preliminare/sicurezza_del_deposito_nazionale/dnsm00007_stima_rifiuti_radioattivi_da_conferire_al_deposito_nazionale.pdf Accessed 29 October 2021.
Deposito Nazionale (2021). Deposito nazionale rifiuti radioattivi: gli atti del seminario Sogin. https://www.recoverweb.it/deposito-nazionale-rifiuti-radioattivi-gli-atti-del-seminario-sogin/ Accessed 22 February 2022.

3 Nuclear Waste Governance in Italy: Between ...

Deposito Nazionale (2022a). Procedura di localizzazione del "Deposito Nazionale eParco Tecnologico" ex D.lgs. n.31/2010 e ss.mm.ii. Atti conclusivi del seminario nazionale. https://www.depositonazionale.it/seminario_nazionale_documenti/atti-conclusivi-seminario-nazionale.pdf Accessed 24 February 2022.

Deposito Nazionale (2022b). Proposta di Carta Nazionale delle Aree Potenzialmente Idonee. https://www.depositonazionale.it/consultazione-pubblica/proposta-di-cnapi/pagine/default.aspx Accessed 30 May 2022.

Deposito Nazionale (2022c). Deposito Nazionale scorie radioattive: al MiTE la mappa delle aree idonee https://www.recoverweb.it/deposito-nazionale-scorie-radioattive-al-mite-la-mappa-delle-aree-idonee/ Accessed 30 May 2022.

Di Nucci, M. R. (2009). Between Myth and Reality: Development, Problems and Perspectives of Nuclear Power in Italy. In L. Mez, M. Schneider, & S. Thomas (Eds.), *International Perspectives on Energy Policy and the Role of Nuclear Power* (pp. 279–300). Multi-Science Publishing.

Di Nucci, M. R. (2015). Breaking the stalemate. The Challenge of Nuclear Waste Governance Italy. In: A. Brunnengräber, M. R. Di Nucci, A. M. Isidoro Losada, L. Mez, & M. Schreurs (Eds.), *Nuclear Waste Governance. An International Comparison* (pp. 299–322) Springer VS.

Di Nucci, M. R. (2019). Voluntarism in Siting Nuclear Waste Disposal Facilities: Just a Matter of Trust? In: Brunnengräber A. & Di Nucci M.R. (2019). *Conflicts, Participation and Acceptability in Nuclear Waste Governance*. Springer VS, 145–174.

Di Nucci, M. R., Isidoro Losada, A. M., & Themann, D. (2021). Confidence gap or timid trust building? The role of trust in the evolution of the nuclear waste governance in Germany. *Journal of Risk Research*, (1–19).

ENEA. (n.d.) *Situazione in Italia*, https://www.enea.it/it/seguici/le-parole-dellenergia/fissione-nucleare/i-rifiuti-radioattivi-1/situazione-in-italia. Accessed 15.10.2021.

European Commission. (2010). *Europeans and Nuclear Safety Report*. Eurobarometer 324.

European Council. (2011). Council Directive 2011/Euratom of 19 July 2011 establishing a Community framework for the responsible and safe management of spent fuel and radioactive waste. 1/199/48 *Official Journal of the European Union*, Brussels.

ISIN. (2020). *Inventario nazionale dei rifiuti radioattivi. Aggiornamento al 31 Dicembre 2019*. https://www.isinucleare.it/sites/default/files/contenuto_redazione_isin/inventario_isin_aggiornato_al_dicembre_2019.pdf. Accessed 7 January 2022.

ISIN (2021a). Inventario nazionale dei rifiuti radiottivi, aggiornato al 31 Dicembre 2020. : https://www.isinucleare.it/sites/default/files/contenuto_redazione_isin/inventario_nazionale_rifiuti_radioattivi_al_dicembre_2020_0.pdf. Accessed 12 December 2021.

ISIN (2021b). *National seminar, one of the most important experiences of public debate at national level*. ISIN guarantor of the correct application of national and international criteria. https://www.isinucleare.it/en/news/national-seminar-one-of-the-most-important-experiences-of-public-debate-at-national-level-isin. Accessed 8 September 2021.

ISIN (2021c). Guida Tecnica n. 32. Criteri di sicurezza e di radioprotezione per impianti ingegneristici di smaltimento in superficie di rifiuti radioattivi. October https://www.isinucleare.it/sites/default/files/contenuto_redazione_isin/all_2_gt32_ottobre_consultazione_pubblica.pdf. Accessed 8 December 2021.

IAEA (2021). *Italy*. https://cnpp.iaea.org/countryprofiles/Italy/Italy.htm. Accessed 15 October 2021.

ISPRA (2014). *Guida Tecnica n. 29, Criteri per la localizzazione di un impianto di smaltimento superficiale di rifiuti radioattivi a bassa e media attività*. http://www.isprambiente.gov.it/files/nucleare/GuidaTecnica29.pdf. Accessed 4 September 2021.

La Repubblica (2003, November 19). Scorie a Scanzano Jonico entra in vigore il decreto.

Nuclear Energy Agency – NEA/OECD. (2013). *Radioactive waste management and decommissioning in Italy (Report)*. https://www.oecd-nea.org/jcms/pl_33730/radioactive-waste-management-and-decommissioning-in-italy?details=true. Accessed 11 October 2021.

Rossano, A. (2003, December 1). Scanzano, la vittoria della piazza e la forza della comunicazione, *La Gazzetta del Mezzogiorno*.

Rovai, D. (2009). L' eredita nucleare SOGIN, un'esperienza allarmante. http://www.nonukes.it/nonukes/sogin.htm. Accessed 2 September 2021.

SOGIN. (2003). *Studio per la localizzazione di un sito per il deposito nazionale centralizzato dei rifiuti radioattivi*. PDN RT 002. http://www.archivionucleare.com/files/studio-sogin-deposito-nazionale-2003.pdf. Accessed 12 October 2021.

SOGIN. (2020). *Company Profile, April*. https://www.sogin.it/uploads/governanceetrasparenza/SoginCompanyProfile_apr2020_EN.pdf. Last accessed 12 October 2021.

SOGIN. (2021a). *Relazione_sulla_Gestione_e_Bilancio_Esercizio_2020 (Consolidated Financial Statement 2020)*. https://www.sogin.it/en/group/economicdata/Pagine/default.aspx https://www.sogin.it/SiteAssets/uploads/2021/societa-trasparente/Bilanci/Sogin_Relazione_sulla_Gestione_e_Bilancio_Esercizio_2020.pdf.

SOGIN. (2021b). *Atti conclusive del seminario nazionale*. https://www.depositonazionale.it/seminario_nazionale_documenti/atti-conclusivi-seminario-nazionale.pdf. Last accessed 18 December 2021.

SOGIN. (2021c). *Rapporto Tecnico. Stima dei manufatti di rifiuti radioattivi da conferire al Deposito Nazionale. Rev. 4 Rapporto Tecnico ELABORATO DN SM 00007. Status 30.12.2020*. www.depositonazionale.it/documentale/progetto_preliminare/sicurezza_del_deposito_nazionale/dnsm00007_stima_rifiuti_radioattivi_da_conferire_al_deposito_nazionale.pdf. Accessed 7 January 2022.

Ventura, G. (2003). *Sistema Informativo Geografico per il sito del Deposito Nazionale dei Materiali Radioattivi*. ENEA GSP3 SITO. http://www.archivionucleare.com/files/studio-gsp3-sito-deposito-nazionale-2003.pdf. Accessed 11 October 2021.

World Nuclear Association. (2021). Nuclear Power in Italy. https://world-nuclear.org/information-library/country-profiles/countries-g-n/italy.aspx. Accessed 18 September 2021.

World Nuclear News. (2021, January 29). *Italy begins search for national radwaste storage site*. https://www.world-nuclear-news.org/Articles/Italy-begins-search-for-national-radwaste-storage. Accessed 15 October 2021.

Zinn, D. L. (2007). Il caso di Scanzano: la ragione di stato e le ragioni di una ribellione. *Quaderni di Sociologia*, 44, 151–174.

Maria Rosaria Di Nucci is an energy economist and a Senior Researcher at the Department of Political and Social Sciences, Freie Universität Berlin. Currently she is the principal investigator of the Horizon 2020 research project COME RES on community energy. Previously she coordinated a Horizon 2020 project on acceptance of wind energy and cooperated in the project TRANSENS: "Transdisciplinary research on the management of high-level radioactive waste in Germany", and other projects on nuclear waste governance (ENTRIA and SOTEC-radio). She is co-editor of a number of volumes on nuclear waste issues and authored several articles on nuclear waste governance. Rosaria's research interests comprise: Multi-level governance, regulation of energy markets, comparative nuclear and energy policy and politics, support instruments for renewable energy, acceptance of contested technologies.

Andrea Prontera is a political scientist and an Associate Professor at the Department of Political Science, Communication and International Relations of the University of Macerata (Italy). He has a degree in economics and social sciences, and a PhD in political science. His main research interests lie in the areas of energy policy and politics, international political economy, comparative public policy and European politics.

Open Access This chapter is licensed under the terms of the Creative Commons Attribution 4.0 International License (http://creativecommons.org/licenses/by/4.0/), which permits use, sharing, adaptation, distribution and reproduction in any medium or format, as long as you give appropriate credit to the original author(s) and the source, provide a link to the Creative Commons license and indicate if changes were made.

The images or other third party material in this chapter are included in the chapter's Creative Commons license, unless indicated otherwise in a credit line to the material. If material is not included in the chapter's Creative Commons license and your intended use is not permitted by statutory regulation or exceeds the permitted use, you will need to obtain permission directly from the copyright holder.

4

Do You Care About High-Level Radioactive Waste and Spent Nuclear Fuel? Opportunities for Co-Constructing an Appropriate Governance-Ecosystem in Belgium

Anne Bergmans, Catherine Fallon, Ron Körvers and Céline Parotte

4.1 Introduction

On April 2, 2022 the Belgian radioactive waste management agency, ONDRAF-NIRAS, and the federal minister of Energy announced a "major national dialogue" to be a launched in the near future on what should happen to the high-level and long-lived radioactive waste from the country's nuclear power plants (NPPs) (Winckelmans, 2020). This would be the second consultation around this matter. In 2009–2010, ONDRAF-NIRAS conducted a Strategic Environmental Assessment (SEA), flanked by a societal consultation involving expert and stakeholder dialogues and a citizen forum, before issuing its Waste Plan in 2011 (ONDRAF-NIRAS, 2011) calling for a decision in principle on geological disposal (ONDRAF-NIRAS, 2012). A subsequent political decision did not materialise until a decade later (see Section I), opening the floor for a public debate on how to organise a "step-by-step plan to further the R&D activities for deep disposal" (Council of Ministers, 2022a).

This chapter discusses key dimensions for the future of high-level radioactive waste governance (HLW) in Belgium. It highlights elements that a diverse set of stakeholders considered to be of importance for a national public debate, and puts them in the context of the theoretical notion of 'caring', as developed by Maria Puig De La Bellacassa. Drawing on the work of feminist thinkers exploring the concept of care in various scientific disciplines, Puig de la Bellacasa focuses on care as a relational concept between humans and non-humans: "Care is a force distributed across a multiplicity of agencies and materials and supports our worlds as a thick mesh of relational obligation." (Puig de la Bellacasa, 2017, p. 20). Facts can be established, but they can also be unclear or disputed. Concerns and interests that feed knowledge production can differ and possibly clash. Even though caring can be enacted in a variety of ways, introducing a care perspective holds a stronger promise of common ground, of a basis to start from. Based on empirical data from the Belgian case, this chapter explores the added value of a caring approach for the long-term governance of materials such as radioactive waste.

What follows is not an attempt to update previous works describing Belgian radioactive waste management from the 1920s (see e.g., Schröder & Bergmans, 2012; Lits, 2015; Parotte & Delvenne, 2015; Schröder et al., 2015), or to identify nuclear events that sustain the (dis)continuities in the HLW programme (Parotte, 2019). This contribution is a foresight chapter that gives voices to actors who compose the current governance ecosystem of HLW (and spent nuclear fuel—SNF)—from concerned citizens, scientists, policymakers, civil society representatives, and public administrators to environmental associations. These 'voices' were collected during a research project between June 2018 and December 2019, the largest part of which was dedicated to a two round enquiry into the problem definitions of those concerned actors, including their expectations regarding a future multi-stakeholder governance process.

This chapter is structured in three sections. Section 4.1 introduces the past and current situation of Belgian radioactive waste. Section 4.2 presents the key (future) dimensions identified by Belgian stakeholders for the HLW long-term governance process. It offers insights regarding planning, policy development and implementation these stakeholders desire. However, the aim is not to highlight what perspective every type of actor develops, often resulting an emphasis on points of disagreement and conflict. Rather, the perspectives are considered as an interrelated collective in which each has its own merits and reasons for existence. It can be argued that these perspectives keep each other in balance. From that position, Sect. 4.3 develops recommendations to consider a future HLW governance process by introducing the notion of 'matter of care' as a conceptual framework. This offers the context for focusing on the commonality of the problem rather than divisiveness over the solution, as well as on the interrelations beyond those between human actors. Concrete elements are suggested to recognize potential joined pathways when considering possible futures of HLW long-term governance, and to organize collective action by allowing for multiple ways of 'caring'. In the conclusion, we link back to the governance ecosystem framework presented in the introductory chapter of this volume.

4.2 Radioactive Waste and Nuclear Activity

Radioactive waste in Belgium comes from various sources, but the bulk is related to nuclear energy production, resulting from seven pressurized water reactors (PWR) on two different sites, four in Doel (municipality of Beveren, Flanders region) and three in Tihange (municipality of Huy, Walloon region). In 2021, together both NPPs provided 21.3% of net energy generation and 49.7% of electricity production in Belgium (FEBEG, 2022).

4.2.1 From Past to Present

Belgium's nuclear history has its roots in the 1920s, with the exploitation of uranium mines in Katanga, at that time a province in the colony of Congo. In return for supplying the US and UK with uranium for the Manhattan project, an agreement was signed in 1944 enabling Belgium to start its own nuclear research programme. Experimentations with nuclear reactors for civil energy production began in the 1950s with the support of a national nuclear research centre, now the Belgian Nuclear Research Centre (SCK CEN), situated in the Flanders region. In the following decades, the area around the nuclear research centre attracted nuclear companies, such as an experimental reprocessing plant (the Eurochemic plant was operational from 1966 to 1974), MOX-fuel production plants, and a waste treatment facility.

Since January 2003, Belgium has a "gradual nuclear phase out" policy (Phase Out Law, 2003). The maximum life span of a number of reactors has meanwhile been extended. Current regulations (various amendments to the Phase Out Law) still stipulate 2025 as the year all nuclear power production in Belgium will end (AFCN-FANC, 2022). However in 2022, Belgium still has no clear plan to secure energy supply after the nuclear phase out, and lacks a long-term vision regarding a national energy policy. In response to the current energy crisis, the federal government decided on March 18, 2022 to "take the necessary steps" to extend the lifetime of two reactors (Doel 4 and Tihange 3) by ten years (Prime Minister of Belgium, 2022). Whether this will prove to be more than a decision in principle will depend on ongoing negotiations with the owner of the NPPs, Engie Electrabel.

4.2.2 Radioactive Waste Management Today

Belgium deals with a relatively large amount of radioactive waste, given the size of the country, as it has depended on nuclear energy for a long time. ONDRAF-NIRAS, the national agency for radioactive waste management, founded by law in 1980–1981 as a government agency and implemented by Royal Decree, distinguishes three categories of radioactive waste, classified according to the half-life and level of activity (ONDRAF-NIRAS, 2021; National Programme Committee, 2015):

- category A for low- and medium-level, short-lived conditioned waste (equivalent LLW—IAEA 2009);
- category B for low- and medium-level, long-lived conditioned waste (equivalent ILW—IAEA 2009);
- category C for high-level, short- and long-lived conditioned waste (equivalent HLW—IAEA 2009).

In addition, the waste manager also identified five types of waste labelled as "other" given their specific properties, which are managed differently.

Both category B and C waste, (further referred to as HLW), demand a different long-term management strategy than LLW or category A (National Programme Committee, 2015, p. 28). For category A waste, a long-term management strategy, namely surface disposal in the municipality of Dessel, has been developed through a participatory governance process launched in 1998. In 2006, this strategy was confirmed by the Federal government, after which the project's blueprints were refined. Meanwhile, various technical and societal subprojects have materialized, such as a long-term health study (2011), a quay for transporting building materials over water (2013), a local fund (2016), a visitor center and exhibition space (2021), and an encapsulation and caissons plant (2022). However, the licence application for the disposal facility itself has been under review since 2013 by the regulator, the Federal Agency for Nuclear Control (AFCN-FANC).

While the program for category A waste is quite advanced, the management of HLW remains the key challenge in Belgium. As indicated before, the radioactive waste management agency, ONDRAF-NIRAS, issued a Waste Plan for HLW in 2011 (ONDRAF-NIRAS 2011), preceded by a SEA and a social consultation. Based on this plan, ONDRAF-NIRAS suggested the Federal government take a decision in principle regarding geological disposal in poorly indurated clay as the long-term management option for HLW, including non-reprocessed SNF. ONDRAF-NIRAS considered the SEA to have determined geological disposal as the way forward. Reference was made to international consensus on this long-term management solution. Also a citizen forum, organised by the independent Roi Baudouin Foundation, had judged the ONDRAF-NIRAS' solution to be acceptable under a number of conditions, such as the establishment of an appropriate decision-making process guaranteeing 'more transparency, and more interaction with society', or the technical reversibility of the facility for at least 100 years (KBS, 2010, pp. 7–8). The emphasis on poorly indurated clay stemmed from the fact that research for the last 50 years had focussed on this particular type of host rock and that review processes (e.g., by the OECD's Nuclear Energy Agency, NEA) of this research programme had so far been positive. However, in its advice to the Federal government, AFCN-FANC acknowledged geological disposal as the reference solution to manage the HLW waste safely, but considers it premature to take a decision regarding the geological host formation (FANC, 2011).

The European Waste Directive (2014) was transposed into Belgian legislation (Transposition Law, 2014), stipulating (in Art. 4) that any national policy regarding a long-term radioactive waste management strategy should be based on disposal by means of a concept of passive safety. It holds ONDRAF-NIRAS responsible for proposing a location for such a facility, and suggests the possibility for installing an "independent, multi-disciplinary body" to follow-up the national policy. A National Programme, was subsequently adopted in 2015 describing the situation with regard to the legal and regulatory framework, concerned actors and their respective responsibilities, the state of the waste inventory, existing management practices, plans for the long-term, and financial provisions (National Programme Committee, 2015).

In 2018, the Federal Minister of Energy asked ONDRAF-NIRAS to update its SEA from 2009. A public enquiry on this updated SEA was organized from April–June 2020 during the first COVID-19 lockdown. This led to a new request to the Federal Government to take a decision in principle on geological disposal, leaving the issue of the geological host formation open. In April 2022, the Federal Government agreed on a draft Royal Decree and Draft Law regarding the national policy for the long-term management of HLW, requiring ONDRAF-NIRAS to "draw up a step-by-step plan for the R&D activities for deep disposal in Belgium of high-level and/or long-lived waste", to "sound out neighbouring and other interested countries about the possibility of developing shared disposal facilities", and "to organise a participatory process and public debate" (Council of Ministers 2022a, April 1). Another Draft Law regarding the provisions for the decommissioning of the NPPs and the management of SNF was also agreed. This law aims to tighten the existing rules regarding the management of the nuclear provisions, including the establishment of an independent oversight body (Council of Ministers 2022b, April 1).

Much will depend on further implementation, but both Federal Government decisions have the potential to be a next step in closing the gap between research, policy and practice (Schröder et al., 2015). Under pressure from the regulator, the issue of the geological host formation is most likely to feature prominently in ONDRAF-NIRAS's future R&D plans. What the topics of the "major national dialogue" will be, and how this process, announced as "deliberative" by an ONDRAF-NIRAS spokesperson (Winckelmans, 2020) will influence the course of events remains to be seen.

4.3 Imagining the Future for a Long-Term Governance Process in a Participatory Way

Our study consisted of three tiers: (a) extensive desktop research, consisting of 22 in-depth interviews with key Belgian and Dutch stakeholders, and two focus group discussions with local actors directly concerned with nuclear sites (Meyermans & Bergmans, 2019); (b) two rounds of a bilingual online Delphi survey consisting of 109 items, in which 242 Belgian stakeholders participated (Parotte & Fallon, 2020); (c) three scenario workshops with ONDRAF-NIRAS senior staff and management (Rijkens-Klomp & Cörvers, 2020).

The starting point was the deadlock situation in which the process of developing the Waste Plan of 2011 had ended, without a political decision being taken. Therefore, the questions regarding respondents' expectations for a governance process were focused on general principles and "What next?"; rather than how to govern the implementation of a specific long-term management option, in particular geological disposal. By continuously approving (either explicitly or implicitly) the direction of ONDRAF-NIRAS' R&D program over the last 50 years, implicit steps towards disposal (with geological disposal clearly in the minds of the decision-makers) have been taken long before the 2022 decision by the Council of Ministers. This has framed future national policy, as well as the mindset of several of the respondents.

4.3.1 Framing the (Start of) the Debate(s) ... Again: What Are the Problems?

Initially more than 580 persons were targeted. All had either been involved in extra public consultations organized by ONDRAF-NIRAS (2009–2010), participated in a legal public consultation (2010), made public statements in the media on the nuclear waste plan between 2009 and 2011, or shown an interest in HLW issues through participation in seminars, workshops, etc. over the previous decade. The 242 respondents presented themselves mainly as 'citizens' and 'scientific experts', though some were also members of environmental associations or trades unions, healthcare professionals, or federal/regional/local civil servants (Parotte & Fallon, 2020, p. 8).

What do Belgian stakeholders have in common regarding their views on the future of the country's HLW? Those who responded to our interactive survey generally recognised that the radioactive waste is already out there; that the way it is stored today may be considered safe for now, but cannot go on for ever; and that the European Waste Directive requires Member States to put an appropriate long-term policy in place.

So far, the 2010 Citizen Forum's request for 'more transparency, and more interaction with society' has not been met. Neither the Transposition Law (2014), nor the National Programme (2015) attracted much public or media attention. Both passed as low key, inner-circle events, to settle formal EU obligations, and no public connection was made to the Waste Plan debate initiated by ONDRAF-NIRAS in 2011 (Parotte & Delvenne, 2015; Schröder et al., 2015). Although the SEA public enquiry in Spring 2020 appears to have attracted record numbers of responses (ONDRAF-NIRAS, personal communication, September 29, 2021), one could question the appropriateness of such outreach in the unprecedented time of the full lockdown during the first wave of the COVID-19 pandemic (Parotte, 2020b).

Our results show that in Belgium, awareness of the problem of radioactive waste in general and HLW in particular appears to be limited amongst actors who do not see themselves as directly linked to or particularly interested in the nuclear sector (regardless of whether they position themselves as supportive, critical or neutral). Such findings are in line with those of the most recent SCK-CEN Barometer, which demonstrates that people in general have little knowledge of how high-level (or other) radioactive waste is currently managed. About half of the respondents to that public survey reported believing that it is already stored underground (Turcanu et al., 2018).

Of the respondents to our more targeted survey, more than half regarded geological disposal as the 'most realistic' solution, and more than half were of the opinion that 'doing nothing' (i.e. delaying any steps towards implementation) was not a solution. Nevertheless, a large majority of the respondents insisted that the future of HLW management should not be discussed without addressing the entire nuclear production chain, the role of new nuclear technologies, and the status of SNF, in addition to exploring the possibility of multi-state joint management solutions. There were some similarities between the more informed respondents participating in our study and the sample of the public invited to respond to the SCK-CEN Barometer. In the Barometer, almost as many respondents (66%) reported believing that geological disposal should be implemented as soon as possible, and 57% did not think that geological disposal would solve the HLW problem (Turcanu et al., 2018, pp. 47–49). This indicates potential for discussing geological disposal without pretending that going down that path instantly solves the HLW problem.

Our respondents also considered that uncertainty remains regarding the radioactive waste inventory (related to the ambiguous status of SNF, and lack of clarity about the nuclear phase-out). While most insisted that a full overview of this inventory would be needed before deciding on a strategy for all waste types, many also acknowledged that shifts may occur in the future and that developments in technology and/or policy may call for changes.

In combination with the reasons that a number of stakeholders provided for refusing to take part in our research project, the results point to a general feeling that the focus of geological disposal is excessively restricted as the definitive solution to the problem of HLW in Belgium. Respondents regarded the problem as multi-dimensional and argued that the governance process should aim to incorporate these dimensions as much as possible, rather than screening out some from the start. Therefore, re-framing the issue of radioactive waste would seem recommended: starting from the problem, rather than from an envisioned solution, inviting societal actors and stakeholders to participate in a debate on the question of

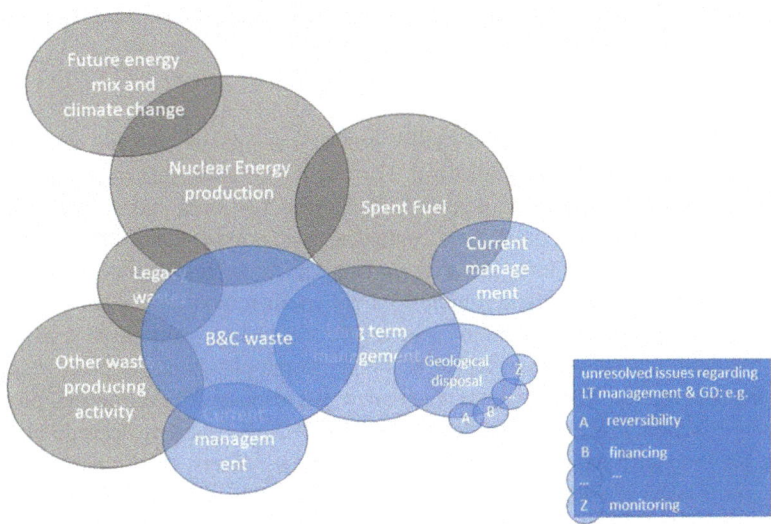

Fig. 4.1 The multiple dimensions of the HLW problem. (Source: Bergmans et al., 2020, p. 11)

high-level and long-lived radioactive materials present in society—some declared as waste, others not (yet). This debate should not be restricted to technical management features or the financial cost of the disposal project, but should also consider related environmental, ethical, socio-political, financial and legal issues regarding the entire production chain.

Figure 4.1 provides an overview of the themes associated by the respondents to the issue of HLW (or category B&C waste). The themes in blue directly relate to ONDRAF-NIRAS' realm of competence, for the themes in grey, other actors have a leading role.

4.3.2 How to Organize the (Future) HLW Governance Process?

We also asked respondents what core principles and main organisational features they considered important for HLW governance. Their answers could be clustered around the following five governance principles: (1) a "flexible and stepwise" approach, (2) "practising transparency", (3) providing "clarity about the link between participation and decision-making", (4) ensuring "monitoring and control" and (5) "robust financing".

Flexible and Stepwise

Given the long-term nature of the HLW problem, a reflexive, flexible and stepwise governance process is called for. For our respondents, this meant that an overall framework should be prepared, identifying key steps and general principles to ensure participation on a continuous basis. Many indicated a preference for this to be laid down in law to provide some guarantee. However, a clear demand for continuous participation does not mean respondents expect this to take the same form throughout the process. On the contrary, they insist it should be regularly reassessed and adapted according to the phases of the process and audiences targeted. These insights are not new, but resonate with the general principles and specific actions identified by the NEA in 2004 regarding decision-making for long-term radioactive waste, inspired, among others, by the partnership approach taken in Belgium for the long-term management of category A waste (NEA, 2004; Pescatore & Vari, 2006). Our respondents considered the federal level to be the most appropriate for organising such a debate on criteria regarding location, technical options, (economic) incentives, public and stakeholder involvement, etc., with an important role for the regulator, AFCN-FANC.

Practising Transparency

More clarity and transparency is expected from ONDRAF-NIRAS and other responsible actors on the management of HLW. Regarding our respondents' request for transparency, three clear expectations could be summarized from the interviews and the survey: (1) active sharing of information on the issues, (2) traceability of the (decision-making) process, and (3) a varied information system. Our respondents explicitly pointed out that making information accessible is one thing; actively sharing it, is something else. During the interviews in particular, more effort was requested regarding outreach and making people aware and knowledgeable. Outreach activity by ONDRAF-NIRAS was seen as too fragmented, both in time and vis-à-vis stakeholder groups. From the Delphi survey the suggestion came to set up a high-quality and varied information system, bringing together contributions from multiple sources, including what respondents referred to as "contradictory expertise". Making explicit who the concerned actors are and what they stand for with regard to the question of HLW waste was also seen as important.

Regarding the traceability of the process, respondents' expectations not only concerned the process ahead. How the current situation was reached is important to know for people who consider becoming engaged in HLW governance.

However, the related legislative history appears to be characterised by a relatively high level of obscurity. Starting with the creation of ONDRAF-NIRAS in 1980, the framework for a national waste management policy and its institutional organisation were 'buried' in one dedicated article (Art. 179) of a law on budget proposals (Budget Law, 1980).

Finally, the survey respondents connected the need for a varied information system with their demand to organize the traceability of decisions. They suggested putting into place a "Pluralist Documentation Centre" (Parotte & Fallon, 2020, pp. 50–55), to collect and preserve relevant information from a variety of sources (public agencies, NGOs and the research community), and to distribute this to diverse audiences: politicians and civil society, but also the scientific community and professionals in the field. Independence from the nuclear sector was considered important almost unanimously, but opinion was divided on how to realise this in practice. Some argued for joint management by a broad range of stakeholders. Others considered this a role for a public body.

Being Clear about the Link Between Participation and Decision-making
Our respondents asked for more clarity on the role of participation in the decision-making process. In general, they expect politicians at the appropriate levels of government to decide about the management of radioactive waste. But they also insist that a broad range of actors should be (more) actively involved in preparing those decisions. A feeling that "backroom politics" dominated the decision-making process on radioactive waste was often recorded, which can be linked to the perceived lack of transparency.

The participatory approach to local partnerships for category A waste was referred to by several interviewees as an example of how things can be done differently (without saying a future process for HLW should be designed identically) and is seen as an exemption to the rule. This can also be deduced from the section on "transparency and participation" in the National Programme for the Management of Spent Fuel and Radioactive Waste (National Programme Committee, 2015, pp. 16–17). So far, the Belgian legislator has not invested in providing a legislative framework for public participation, other than the general obligations regarding public access to government, and access to information and public participation in decision-making on environmental matters (often imposed through transposition into Belgian law of international laws and conventions).

However, the lack of legal obligation does not mean one cannot set up a participatory process with stakeholders. In Belgium, both the partnership approach (Bergmans, 2008) and ONDRAF-NIRAS activities in 2009 and 2010 for elaborating the 2011 Waste Plan (Parotte & Delvenne, 2015) highlight how it is possible to envision supplementary participatory initiatives aimed at specific stakeholder groups, experts, and citizens, beyond what the law prescribes. However, policy practice thus far provides an inconsistent pattern when it comes to public and stakeholder participation. A closer look at the information provided in the National Programme as 'transparency and participatory practices' (National Programme Committee, 2015, pp. 20–21, 25, 41–44, 46–49) makes this clear. The partnership approach for category A waste, and the societal consultation for the 2011 Waste Plan notwithstanding, the current practices listed are passive ways of making information available, and the related communication is almost solely directed at official bodies. Our respondents clearly expect more. They insisted that public and stakeholder participation as a key feature of long-term governance of HLW is only valid if a genuine connection is ensured with the institutional decision-making process. Therefore, at the start of the decision-making process, it should be clear what the purpose of participation is, when participation is possible, what is open for discussion, and how the input by stakeholders will be taken up in the decision-making process.

Ensuring Monitoring and Control

The survey respondents expressed a number of expectations that can be categorised under the heading of 'monitoring and control'. It is important to stress that they see a combined need for monitoring and follow-up of both the long-term management strategy and the related governance process, which they consider as intrinsically linked.

A majority of respondents insisted on monitoring of the governance process, which stems from their requirement for such a process to be flexible and adaptive. They expect both technical and societal aspects to be jointly addressed in the governance process, and therefore also by any control mechanisms. In line with expectations regarding the role of the regulator, respondents suggest making this more active in terms of providing information, adopting regulations, and organising debates on safety aspects. In support, many respondents consider it useful to establish an independent mixed pluralist body at the federal level. The possibility for setting up such an entity is foreseen in the Transposition Law (1980). Our respondents did not express clear views or expectations regarding the composition of such a body, but expect it to work closely with the public authorities to assess the HLW management process at strategic level. To a lesser extent, respondents thought it could also be responsible for evaluating the operational process and public consultations. The possibility for enrolling counter-expertise, particularly for affected communities (present or future) at the local level, was also put forward as an important feature of a system of monitoring and control.

Robust Financing

The respondents insisted on ensuring the principles of reliable financial management for HLW. For them, in the case of insolvency, the State is ultimate responsibility and should be clearly organised, by considering the evolving nature of the costs, presenting a risk analysis about producers' insolvency scenarios, and ensuring strict control of the sufficiency of funds at the national and European level. At the national level, respondents suggested organising financial control attached to the parliament (in the spirt of the Court of Auditors).

Regarding these suggestions, how to envision the long-term governance process of radioactive waste in Belgium? Combining the views collected from the stakeholders with the authors' past research in a European and international setting, and putting this in a perspective of considering radioactive waste as 'matter of care', Sect. 4.3 identifies three overall principles for building a long-term governance process HLW (and SNF) in Belgium.

4.4 Building a Long-Term Governance Process Based on the Notion of 'Caring'

From the field of science and technology studies we have learned that no technology is value-free and that science and technology development does not deal solely with facts, but also with interpretations, with cognitive, practical and financial boundaries, etc. These values and interpretations impact relations between human actors, but also interactions with non-human actors, in this case most particularly the waste, and any technology developed to manage it. How to manage these materials is not only a matter of established techno-scientific facts, but also a matter of interests, a "matter of concern(s)", as Bruno Latour would put it. Facts and concerns are intimately interrelated, as concerns "add reality" to facts (Latour 2004, p. 232). Therefore, concerns tie and hold together matters of fact. They contribute to "enrich and affirm their reality by adding further articulations" (Puig de la Bellacasa, 2011, p. 89). ONDRAF-NIRAS, like all other actors involved in the radioactive waste management program, produces matters of concern or appreciations, strongly entangled with, and sometimes also presented as, facts. The exclusive research focus on poorly indurated clay, for example, mainly stems from the availability of that host rock in SCK-CEN's backyard. That in itself is not necessarily problematic, as long as it is recognised as such.

As Puig de la Bellacasa (2011, 2017) points out, often we are dealing with more than interrelated matters of facts and concerns; a situation she refers to as "matters of care". Caring in this sense takes being concerned (or having an interest) in a particular issue or fact to another level. Our practices, discourses and engagement regarding a particular issue or situation differ, depending on whether we ask ourselves: "Is it a fact?", "Am I concerned?", "Do I care?". Applied to radioactive waste, an answer to each of these questions could be "The waste is already here and it must be managed", "I'm concerned about what will happen with these radioactive materials", and "I care about the way they are handled".

Caring is about projection onto another (even where that other is the self or a non-human entity); it is an outbound activity, whereas concerns and interests are directed inward. One will undoubtedly find acts and considerations of care in the current radioactive waste management approach by the responsible agency or other actors concerned when analysing discourses and practices. But the emphasis has so far remained on providing facts (based on the persisting idea that facts are neutral) and on weighing, and at best balancing, interests.

This is not unique to radioactive waste management. It is symptomatic of the way we deal with various complex societal questions, in particular in the field of urban planning, and regarding environmental and technological risk. Many participatory practices remain instrumental, and limited to what is legally required. But many of the more voluntaristic initiatives continue to be guided by Fischhoff's (1995) famous plea for inclusive risk management, which he represented as consecutive stages of development (see Fig. 4.2).

Although 'treating people nice' (Fischoff's sixth developmental stage) is a way of caring, it is not a matter of care, as put forward above. Analysing 20 years of evolution in risk management, Fischhoff argued that this practice should, ideally, be guided by the facts. However, what is recognised as facts is often limited to the "sizes of the risks and benefits involved", while "changes in political and social status that arise from the risk-management process" should also be taken

- All we have to do is get the numbers right
- All we have to do is tell them the numbers
- All we have to do is explain what we mean by the numbers
- All we have to do is show them that they've accepted similar risks in the past
- All we have to do is show them that it's a good deal for them
- All we have to do is treat them nice
- All we have to do is make them partners
- All of the above

Fig. 4.2 Developmental Stages in Risk Management (Fischhoff, 1995, p. 138)

into account as facts. In that way, Fischhoff saw the social contract between those who create and those who have to bear risks (at least partly) fulfilled. Not through eliminating conflict, but as a way of "having fewer, but better conflicts" (Fischhoff, 1995, p. 144). Twenty-five years on, it may be time to reflect on whether adding concerns as another layer onto facts (still too often interpreted as either technical facts, or social and political concerns) and creating spaces in which these could be discussed, is enough to tackle complex questions of environmental and technological risk.

Before returning more explicitly to what it could mean in practice to approach radioactive waste as matter of care, we consider three features of a related long-term governance process that have been given attention by social sciences, and that were put forward by our respondents. For each we will indicate how we see it linked to a perspective of care.

4.4.1 Long-Term Radioactive Waste Management is and will Remain a Socio-Technical Challenge

Many of the Belgian stakeholders we questioned stressed the interconnectedness of social and technical aspects and the need to integrate the socio-technical challenge into one approach. This is also the 'Leitmotiv' of ONDRAF-NIRAS' official communication. However, when it comes to public and stakeholder participation, this is often mainly directed at what is considered the social aspects (Bergmans et al., 2015; Hietela & Geysmans, 2020). Therefore, it is worthwhile to consider four observations on the interconnections between those dimensions that directly relate to our respondents' expectations (Kallenbach-Herbert et al., 2014, pp. 27–31).

First, the process of radioactive waste management is composed of a broad variety of interactions between humans and non-humans (the environment and other living entities, but also created artefacts), in various constellations, spread over space as well as over time. However robust or stable such a process may seem at a certain point in space or time, reconfigurations of these interactions and players will inevitably occur due to changes in the socio-political or economic context, the accumulated knowledge base, technical development, etc.

Second, wider societal involvement means more than offering citizens a way to express democratic values or getting approval for an already elaborated technical fix. It means that new inputs could feed the technical project and vice versa.

Third, if taken seriously, opening up to wider societal involvement has the potential to bring in alternative perspectives that could contribute to the creation of new knowledge and the identification of new solutions which could influence technical choices.

Fourth, concerned societal actors could and should be invited to participate more explicitly in the technical debate, and be encouraged to contribute to this debate beyond discussing the local impact of implementing a specific technology at a specific location.

The technical and social, but also ecological, ethical, financial, dimensions of radioactive waste management are not mutually exclusive. They are seldom the exclusive competence of one particular stakeholder, and every stakeholder should have the possibility to take part in the debate on each dimension. However, in practice people who genuinely care and have a legitimate interest (e.g. those living close to existing waste infrastructure or NPPs), often refrain from entering such a debate (particularly when this is framed as about 'technical choices'). This is largely because it tends to be centred around facts, and many do not feel competent enough or are reluctant to start an engagement process by studying large files with graphs and technical information. With respect to interests or concerns, when aiming for early and "upstream" engagement (Stirling, 2008), people may not yet fully comprehend the extent to which they are concerned. But they may care nevertheless. A perspective of care means one does not start from a proposed technical solution, but from the perceived problem, and how that matters to various stakeholders. In that way, it could lower the threshold for participation and serve as leverage to emphasise the social in the technical, and the entanglement of all relevant dimensions.

4.4.2 The Long-Term Management Solution is and will Remain Experimental by Nature

The term "experimental" was not one the respondents offered. Still, several interviewees pointed out that long-term radioactive waste management is a first of its kind endeavour, which cannot yet rely on past experience. This calls for a particular type of governance to deal with uncertainty over a long period of time. However, interviewees also indicated that even with regard to a specific technical solution such as geological disposal, different interpretations exist of what this implies as a practice (e.g. regarding notions of reversibility and retrievability, the need for monitoring). They expect these differences in interpretation to continue, which could be seen as positive, because it creates room for dialogue.

Various authors have labelled this as "experimental" or as "an on-going process of technological innovation" (see e.g., Barthe & Lindhart, 2009; Felt et al.,

2007; Kallenbach-Herbert et al., 2014; Landström and Bergmans, 2015; Parotte, 2018, 2020a). Considering the associated time-scales clearly acknowledged by most respondents, it is unlikely that at present we are able to envisage all changes or potential problems that could arise over time.

This calls for a governance approach to deal with uncertainties and give room for (social) learning. The respondents' comments are thus in line with observations from previous research, proposing to understand the implementation of a long-term management programme as "a (scientifically) controlled, open-ended exploration towards a possible solution" (Kallenbach-Herbert et al., 2014, p. 29).

This implies maintaining the capacity for technical innovation and scientific knowledge, and the continuation of the research programmes as part of the implementation process, as explicitly indicated by the respondents. It also means letting go of a classical project-based approach with a clear beginning and endpoint (Fallon et al., 2013, Kallenbach-Herbert et al., 2014; Parotte, 2018). Lastly, it implies identifying regular or milestone 'meeting points' rather than a rigid roadmap (Barthe et al., 2010; Kallenbach-Herbert et al., 2014; Parotte, 2018). Those milestones could also be understood as a momentum to assess the ongoing process and to steer a process of progressive participation, as called for by our respondents.

Approaching radioactive waste as matter of care and striving for 'communities of care' rather than 'host communities' could be meaningful. It allows the debate to unfold over the thing all care for, namely the waste and its safe future, not a particular waste management solution. A care perspective offers more opportunity for those who may not agree with, or have reservations about, the path taken to participate in the governance process. Furthermore, it holds a promise of allowing such governance processes to be truly adaptable or reversible, as new care perspectives will inevitably develop over time and generations.

4.4.3 A Transparent and Democratic Way of Addressing This Challenge

Our research results show there is a tendency to see the (Belgian) HLW governance process as participatory technology assessment to be applied in various phases of decision-making, and at various levels of government. According to the respondents, such a process could be piloted by an interdisciplinary committee of scientists and representatives from different stakeholder groups, including directly concerned local communities. Around particular aspects (or dimensions, as presented in Fig. 4.1), specific consultations could be held at specific points, targeted at a diverse range of stakeholders or existing advisory bodies.

The Transposition Law (1980, Art. 4) provides for an "independent multidisciplinary body" to follow-up the National Policy on radioactive waste and SNF. Our findings indicate that engaging such a committee in co-constructing the National Policy would be in line with stakeholder expectations. Building on suggestions from the respondents to the Delphi survey, one option could be to install a long-standing committee with rotating membership linked to parliament with an advisory role (at the Federal level and potentially also the Regional Government), reporting back on its activity at distinctive moments throughout the process.

Such a multi-level approach could be embedded in a broader ambition to strive for multiple debates in multiple interconnected arenas. This is not a task for ONDRAF-NIRAS alone. It would be extremely challenging, if not impossible, to address the multiple dimensions of HLW in one process or arena. Therefore, rather than incorporating all dimensions into a single debate on a governance process for the long-term management of HLW, one could envisage a different framework, within which different actors are mandated to organise a broad stakeholder debate on one (or more) aspect(s). These would not need to keep the same pace, nor engage the same actors at the same levels of government. But it could put the question of the long-term governance of HLW in a broader perspective and help to meet the range of related expectations from various actors.

In an ideal scenario, such a governance process is either preceded or accompanied by a public debate on national energy policy, as in Germany where the (re)launch of the radioactive waste debate came a few years after "a collective project for the future" for the country's energy transition was discussed and presented by a transdisciplinary Ethics Commission for a safe energy supply (BMU, 2011). Our respondents acknowledge it is not ONDRAF-NIRAS's role to organise such a public debate, and that the radioactive waste debate cannot be postponed indefinitely. Nuclear energy and radioactive waste are undeniably interconnected, as claimed by the respondents and other observers (e.g., Laes, 2015). In this respect, the decision of the Belgian Constitutional Court in March 2020 (Cour Constitutionnelle, 2020) to quash the decision to extend the lifetime of reactors Doel 1 and 2 could be seen as an opportunity for public consultations which couple nuclear energy and radioactive waste policy.

A recognition of the interconnectedness between nuclear energy and radioactive waste should be made more explicit by paying (more) attention in the HLW debate to the impact of various future scenarios for nuclear energy production, other nuclear technologies, and the management of SNF on the HLW inventory and related strategies. This would meet a primary concern expressed by our respondents of the need to raise awareness among a variety of stakeholders and engage them in (joint) problem definition and the analyses of potential solutions.

Our respondents had a clear focus on well-defined processes for participation with a clear purpose. However, despite inclusive principles that may lie behind a formal participatory process, some stakeholders may remain (purposely or not) outside such a structure. Therefore, a flexible and adaptive governance process should not only look inside (invited participation), but should be aware of what goes on outside (uninvited participation). It should continuously monitor its environment in order to be responsive to opinions raised, new issues arising, or new stakeholders emerging, or when new stages in the process are reached (see e.g., Chilvers, Pallet & Hargreaves, 2018; Cuppen, 2018).

An opportunity could lie in making the waste the object of care. Caring is not about providing one pre-fixed initial programme, but ensuring the waste is being taken care of by means of a collective and open decision-making and governance process. Since caring is an outward activity, it enables engagement with all who care, and in particular those directly affected, such as local (site) communities and citizens. This process of caring will inevitably span decades and generations of stakeholders. Intergenerational engagement should be aimed for, but this can only be reached by starting with the present generation.

4.4.4 Considering Belgian HLW and SNF as Matters of Care

Considering HLW and SNF as matters of care changes the way concerned actors are engaged in the programme and the way they frame it. According to Puig de la Bellacassa (2011, 2017), 'caring' has three concrete consequences. First, and related to concern, care has strong affective ethical connotations. Concern denotes worry and thoughtfulness about an issue, while care adds a strong sense of attachment. Second, the more you care, the more you are actually engaged in the process: arguably, the individual or organisational commitment to the object thus becomes stronger, also potentially criticism. And third, one could assume that those who 'care' develop a stronger sense of responsibility and a particular vision of the current state and future of things, enabling going beyond "past responsibilities" to create continuity in such a responsibility.

Each of these consequences cuts across the three features of a long-term HLW governance process described above, and makes caring substantially different from managing. A perspective of caring does not require a legal mandate, related position, nor expertise. Caring can be highlighted by actions (what people do), promoted by ethics (how people justify actions) or the labour of maintenance (invisible daily practices) (Puig de la Bellacasa, 2017). There are multiple ways of caring as well as different 'carers', people who care. The notion of 'caring' requires regular re-assessment: "Who cares and what are their concerns?", "What are the critical standpoints?", but also "Who will do the work of care, as well as how to do it and for whom?" (Puig de la Bellacasa, 2011). From the perspective of a waste management agency, 'caring' about what happens to the waste does not mean 'controlling' an entire process. It means being in charge, and 'taking care' in spite of all the unexpected things that might change.

The waste management agency does not care alone. As became clear from the survey responses, multiple committed people and organisations are willing to challenge or support the programme. They are as engaged in 'caring', as ONDRAF-NIRAS, even if 'how to care' and 'what dimensions to focus on' varies. Engaging other stakeholders in waste governance from a perspective of care allows entry to other forms of caring. A commitment to 'caring' means to "remain speculative" and not let "a situation or a position […] define in advance what is or could be" (Puig de la Bellacasa, 2011, p. 96). This is in contrast to an instrumental approach to engagement with a strong focus on finding acceptance for a pre-defined solution. Introducing care "requires critical standpoints that are careful", and that "… manifest visions that have become possible by learning to care for some issues more than others" (Puig de la Bellacasa, 2011, p. 96). It should not be decided up-front whether or not positions or standpoints are relevant to a programme. One must 'care' for the different standpoints, keeping in mind that it could have been otherwise. In the context of long-term radioactive waste governance, the objective is not only to expose or reveal care practices and matters of concern; it is also to generate them. This means there is no fixed future for these wastes, but there are multiple ways of caring about the future(s) of the programme. Our study clearly highlighted who are the stakeholders who care and what dimensions matter to them, including those who did not participate, who criticize the process from the outside and contribute to it in other ways.

Lastly, there is no monopoly of caring narratives. Beyond recognition of forms of care, the challenge is to allow forms of care to co-exist. Therefore, it would be recommended for a future HLW governance process not to be the reflection of one dominant narrative. We suggest the key question for ONDRAF-NIRAS should be: how to allow multiple care narratives to co-exist in one long-term governance programme for HLW (and SNF).

4.5 Conclusion: Time for a Paradigm Shift?

Expectations regarding the long-term governance of HLW depend on the concerned actors' framing of the radioactive waste problem, which may or may not include a pre-conceived idea about a solution. Our research made clear that some respondents seem to be willing to support ONDRAF-NIRAS to take further steps with regard to geological disposal of HLW as (part of) a long-term solution. However, others do not support this solution (and may never will), and those who do, do not necessarily share the same problem definition on which they base their conclusion. Therefore, it will be very difficult, if not impossible, to define a one-sided governance approach that covers virtually all dimensions and expectations from all stakeholders in a satisfactory way. Multiple efforts and a mix of initiatives and responsive actions towards new developments will be needed to ensure engagement and maximum transparency in the long-term governance process of Belgian HLW.

As described in the introductory chapter to this volume, planning a governance process for the long-term management of radioactive waste, and particularly HLW, is a long-haul process. The importance of a reflexive, flexible and stepwise collective governance approach cannot be emphasised enough. This means the governance ecosystem will be in constant flux. Its composition and institutional setting will evolve over time, potentially leading to a shift in structure, changes in culture and the adoption of new routines.

In this chapter we reflected on what constitutes a long-term governance approach. We have drawn on the opinion of actors as a sample of the Belgian HLW governance ecosystem and on the theoretical concept of 'care'. There appears little contestation (in academic literature, nor in the opinion of concerned actors) that long-term HLW management is and will remain a socio-technical challenge, that any solution will remain to some extent experimental in nature, and that it is our moral duty to ensure a transparent and democratic way of addressing this challenge. On how to ensure that, opinions and expectations tend to differ, and interests come into play.

We have argued for a perspective of care in order to lower the threshold for participation and to serve as leverage to emphasise the social in the technical. Such a governance approach requires an empathic attitude towards the needs and expectations of all current and future stakeholders in the nuclear energy and radioactive waste debate. In the framing and enacting of the announced public debate, ONDRAF-NIRAS and other stakeholders have the opportunity to show how they care. Caring means assuming that sociotechnical uncertainties will remain, regardless of the preferred long-term option for radioactive waste. Caring is also about allowing real spaces for others who care to express what they care about and how they desire to do so. Caring is not about providing one pre-fixed initial programme, but is about ensuring the waste is being taken care of by means of a collective and open decision-making and governance process.

Putting forward a perspective of care does not mean disregarding facts and interests or concerns. However, the COVID-19 pandemic has shown that conflicts over facts are often not the 'better' type of conflicts Fischhoff wanted, and that balancing interests is in some cases an impossible mission. We clearly need more than "all of the above" (see Fig. 4.2 here).

Figure 4.2 Rather than adding 'caring' as an additional stage in Fischhoff's list, we strongly recommend taking a care perspective first, before addressing facts and concerns. A practice of care as a more profoundly different approach to addressing environmental and technological risk could be a way forward. It is not our intention to claim that a perspective of care will prove to be the magic formula for dealing with 'reluctant stakeholders', or 'inconsiderate project developers' under all circumstances. However, we do consider this a worthwhile path to follow.

Addressing radioactive waste as matter of care means a paradigm shift at three levels. First, it means acknowledging there are multiple ways of caring that can co-exist. Rather than aiming to establish agreement on facts, and which facts matter first, establishing common ground from a perspective of care is better served by starting from identifying and acknowledging that uncertainties of various types will remain. Second, it appears recommended to talk about waste before talking about waste management solutions. This allows establishment of a community across the whole governance ecosystem of those who care about the waste, not only those who care about a particular endpoint for it. Third, since caring is an outward activity, it enables engagement with all who care, and in particular those directly affected, such as local (site) communities and citizens. This process of caring will inevitably span several decades and generations of stakeholders, and intergenerational engagement should be aimed for, but this can only be reached by starting with the present generation in a collective and open decision-making and governance process.

In support of such a paradigm shift in governance practice, further research into the consequences of addressing radioactive waste as matter of care would be helpful. The need for a closer understanding of the affective, ethical, and practical engagements of caring remains, both in terms of human interactions (the classical focus of governance studies) and of interactions between humans and non-human actors.

Another thing that remains is the waste and the need for it to be taken care of.

References

AFCN-FANC. (2022, February 24). Kerncentrales in België. Retrieved May 4, 2022, from https://fanc.fgov.be/nl/dossiers/kerncentrales-belgie.

Barthe, Y., Callon, M., & Lascoumes, P. (2010). De la décision politique réversible: histoire d'une contribution inattendue de l'industrie nucléaire (française) à l'instauration de la démocratie dialogique. Brazilian Journal of Urban Management. 2(1): 57–70.

Barthe, Y., & Lindhart, D. (2009). L'expérimentation: un autre agir politique. CSI working papers series, 13: Article halshs-00352411. https://halshs.archives-ouvertes.fr/halshs-00352411/document.

Bergmans, A. (2008). Meaningful communication between experts and affected citizens on risk: challenge or impossibility?. Journal of risk research, 11(1/2): 175–193.

Bergmans, A., Sundqvist, G., Kos, D., & Simmons, P. (2015). The participatory turn in radioactive waste management: deliberation and the social-technical divide. Journal of Risk Research, 18(3): 347–363.

Bergmans, A., Parotte, C., Fallon, C., Rijkens-Klomp, N., & Cörvers, R. (2020). Building Blocks for the Long-term Governance of B&C Waste in Belgium. UAntwerpen: Research report commissioned by ONDRAF-NIRAS. Retrieved October 13, 2021, from https://repository.uantwerpen.be/docstore/d:irua:5877.

BMU. (2011, May 30) Deutschlands Energiewende—Ein Gemeinschaftswerk für die Zukunft. Abschlussbericht der Ethikkommission „Sichere Energieversorgung". Retrieved May 2, 2022, from https://www.bmuv.de/download/deutschlands-energiewende-ein-gemeinschaftswerk-fuer-die-zukunft.

Budget Law. (1980). Law of August 8, 1980 regarding budget proposals 1979–1980 (1). Moniteur Belge 15/08/1980: 1980080802.

Chilvers, J., Pallet, H. & Hargreaves, T. (2018). Ecologies of participation in socio-technical change: The case of energy system transitions. Energy Research & Social Science, 42: 199–210.

Council of Ministers. (2022a, April 1). Nationale beleidsmaatregel inzake langetermijnbeheer van hoogradioactief en/of langlevend afval. news.belgium. Retrieved May 2, 2022 from https://news.belgium.be/nl/nationale-beleidsmaatregel-inzake-langetermijnbeheer-van-hoogradioactief-enof-langlevend-afval.

Council of Ministers. (2022b, April 1). Verzekeren van de voorzieningen voor de ontmanteling van kerncentrales en het beheer van de verbruikte splijtstof—Tweede lezing. news.belgium. Retreived May 2, 2022 from https://news.belgium.be/nl/verzekeren-van-de-voorzieningen-voor-de-ontmanteling-van-kerncentrales-en-het-beheer-van-de-0.

Court Constitutionelle. (2020). Arrêt n°34/2020 du 5 mars 2020. Numéro du rôle: 6328. Retrieved October 13, 2021, from https://www.const-court.be/public/f/2020/2020-034f.pdf.

CSS-HGR. (2021, October 26). Report 9576—Nuclear risk, sustainable development and energy transition. Retrieved (available in French or Dutch) October 28, 2021, from https://www.health.belgium.be/en/report-9576-nuclear-risk-sustainable-development-and-energy-transition.

Cuppen, E. (2018). The value of social conflicts. Critiquing invited participation in energy projects. Research & Social Science, 38: 28–32.

FANC. (2011). Advies van het FANC betreffende NIRAS documenten: ontwerp van Afvalplan en bijhorende SEA. Nota nr.010-149N. Retrieved October 13, 2021, from, https://fanc.fgov.be/nl/system/files/advies-fanc-afvalplan-2011.pdf.

Fallon, C., Parotte, C., Zwetkoff, C., Bergmans, A., & Van Berendoncks, K. (2013). Socio-Political Processes and Plan Management in Controversial Settings applied to the Plan for the Long-Term Management of Type B&C Waste—Summary Report. University of Liège & University of Antwerp. Retrieved October 13, 2021, from https://repository.uantwerpen.be/link/irua/117042.

FEBEG. (2022). Jaarverslag 2021. Retrieved May 4, 2022, from, https://www.febeg.be/jaarverslag-2021.

Felt, U., Wynne, B., Callon, M., Gonçalves, M. E., Jasanoff, S., Jepsen, M., Joly, P.-B., Konopasek, Z., May, S., Neubauer, C., Rip, A., Siune, K., Stirling, A., & Tallacchini, M. (2007). Taking European Knowledge Society Seriously. Luxembourg: Office for Official Publications of the European Communities. Retrieved October 13, 2021, from https://ec.europa.eu/research/science-society/document_library/pdf_06/european-knowledge-society_en.pdf.

Fischhof, B. (1995). Risk Perception and Communication Unplugged: Twenty Years of Process. Risk Analysis, 15(2): 137–145.

Hietela M., & Geysmans, R. (2020). Social sciences and radioactive waste management: acceptance, acceptability, and a persisting socio-technical divide. Journal of Risk Research, 25(4): 423–438.

Kallenbach-Herbert, B., Brohmann, B., Simmons, P., Bergmans, A., Barthe, Y. & Martell, M. (2014). Addressing the Long-Term Management of High-level and Long-lived Nuclear Wastes as a Socio-Technical Problem: Insights from InSOTEC. EC: InSOTEC Deliverable 4.1. Retrieved October 13, 2021, from https://www.researchgate.net/publication/312198353_Addressing_the_Long-Term_Management_of_High-level_and_Long-lived_Nuclear_Wastes_as_a_Socio-Technical_Problem_Insights_from_InSOTEC.

KBS (2010). Publieksforum 'Hoe beslissen over het langetermijnbeheer van hoogradioactief en langlevend afval?'—Eindrapport. https://www.kbs-frb.be/nl/Virtual-Library/2010/295082.

Laes, E. J. W. (2015). Een ethisch-hermeneutische benadering van het Belgische kernafvalbeleid. Ethische Perspectieven, 25(4):288–300.

Landström, C., & Bergmans, A. (2015). Long-term repository governance: a socio-technical challenge. Journal of Risk Research, 18(3): 378–391.

Latour, B. (2004). Why Has Critique Run out of Steam? From Matters of Fact to Matters of Concern. Critical Inquiry—Special issue on the Future of Critique, 30 (Winter 2004): 225–248.

Lits, G. (2015). La gestion des déchets hautement radioactifs belges à l'épreuve de la démocratie : contribution à une sociologie des activités décisionnelles. Thèse de doctorat en sciences politiques et sociales, Université catholique de Louvain.

Meyermans, A., & Bergmans, A. (2019). Stakeholder mapping en verkennende actorenbevraging (september 2018 – maart 2019). UAntwerpen: Onderzoeksrapport i.o.v. NIRAS. Retrieved October 13, 2021, from https://repository.uantwerpen.be/docstore/d:irua:5864.

National Programme Committee. (2015). Kingdom of Belgium, National Programme for the Management of Spent Fuel and Radioactive Waste. PS Economy, S.M.E.s, Self-employed and Energy—Directorate General for Energy, Nuclear Energy Division: First edition, October2015—Courtesy translation. Retrieved October 13, 2021, from https://economie.fgov.be/sites/default/files/Files/Energy/National-programme-courtesy-translation.pdf.

NEA. (2004). Stepwise Approach to Decision Making for Long-term Radioactive Waste Management. Experience, Issues and Guiding Principles. OECD: NEA No. 4429. Retrieved October 13, 2021, from https://www.oecd-nea.org/rwm/reports/2004/nea4429-stepwise.pdf.

ONDRAF-NIRAS. (2011). Executive Summary van het Afvalplan voor het langetermijnbeheer van geconditioneerd hoogradioactief en/of langlevend afval en overzicht van verwante vragen. Moniteur Belge 30/09/2011 (Ed 2): 2011018333.

ONDRAF-NIRAS. (2012). Onze opdracht: u beschermen. Jaarverslag 2012.

ONDRAF-NIRAS. (2021). Soorten Radioactief afval. Retrieved October 13, 2021, from https://www.niras.be/soorten-radioactief-afval.

Parotte, C. (2018). L'Art de gouverner les déchets hautement radioactifs. Liège : Presses Universitaires de Liège—Ed. Science Technologie et Société.

Parotte, C. (2019). La trajectoire du programme nucléaire et de ses déchets entre moments de rupture et continuités: quelles perceptions des acteurs belges engagés? Dynamiques. Histoire sociale en revue, 11. https://www.carhop.be/revuescarhop/index.php/category/revue-0/revue11/.

Parotte, C. (2020a). The Power and Limits of Classification: Radioactive Waste Categories as Reshaped by Disposal Options. Nuclear Technology, 0: 1–14.

Parotte, C. (2020b). A nuclear real-world experiment: Exploring the experimental mindsets of radioactive waste management organisations in France, Belgium and Canada. Energy Research and Social Science, 69: Article e101761.

Parotte, C., & Delvenne, P. (2015). Taming uncertainty: towards a new governance approach for nuclear waste management in Belgium. Technology Analysis & Strategic Management, 28(8), 986–998.

Parotte, C., & Fallon, C. (2020). Les futurs de la gestion à long terme des déchets hautement radioactifs et des combustibles usés en Belgique. Résultats de l'enquête Delphi (Avril–Novembre 2019). ULg : Centre de Recherches Spiral. Retrieved October 13, 2021, from https://orbi.uliege.be/handle/2268/246178.

Pescatore, C., & Vári, A. (2006). Stepwise Approach to the Long-Term Management of Radioactive Waste. Journal of Risk Research, 9(1), 13–40.

Phase Out Law (2003) Law of January 31, 2003 regarding the gradual discontinuation of industrial nuclear power generation, Moniteur Belge 28/02/2003 (Ed 3): 2003011096. http://www.ejustice.just.fgov.be/eli/wet/2003/01/31/2003011096/staatsblad.

Prime Minister of Belgium. (2022, March 18). Lifetime extension of Doel 4 and Tihange 3 nuclear power plants. Retrieved May 2, 2022, from https://www.premier.be/en/lifetime-extension-doel-4-and-tihange-3-nuclear-power-plants.

Puig De La Bellacasa, M. (2011). Matters of care in technoscience: Assembling neglected things. Social Studies of Science. 41 (1): 85–106.

Puig De La Bellacasa, M. (2017). Matters of care: Speculative Ethics in More Than Human Worlds. University of Minnesota Press.

Rijkens-Klomp, N., & Cörvers, R. (2020). Nuclear Waste B&C Scenarios and Governance Challenges. Unpublished Report WP2.

Schröder, J., & Bergmans, A. (2012). Identifying remaining socio-technical challenges at the national level: Belgium. EC: InSOTEC Working paper WP1-MS3. Retrieved October 13, 2021, from https://drive.google.com/viewerng/viewer?a=v&pid=sites&srcid=a W5zb3RlYy5ldXxpbnNvdGVVjfGd4OjYzNmZhZjNiYjVmM2RhZA.

Schröder, J., Bergmans, A., & Laes, E. (2015). Advanced research, lagging policy: nuclear waste governance in Belgium. In A. Brunnengräber, M.R. Di Nucci, A.M. Isidoro Losada, L. Mez, & M.A. Schreurs, (Eds.), Nuclear Waste Governance (pp. 141–155). Springer VS.

Stirling, A. (2008). 'Opening up' and 'closing down': Power, participation and pluralism in the societal appraisal of technology. Science, Technology and Human Values, 33(2): 262–294.

Transposition Law. (2014). Law of June 3, 2014 amending article 179 of the law of August 8, 1980 regarding the budget proposals 1979–1980 in view of the transposition into national law of Directive 2011/70/Euratom of July 19, 2011 establishing a Community framework for the responsible and safe management of spent fuel and radioactive waste. Moniteur Belge 27/06/2014: 2014011342. http://www.ejustice.just.fgov.be/eli/wet/2014/06/03/2014011342/staatsblad.

Turcanu, C., Perko, T., Schröder, J., & Abelshausen, B. (2018). The SCK-CEN Barometer 2018. Nuclear technologies and society: a survey among the Belgian population. SCK-CEN. Retrieved October 13, 2021, from https://publications.sckcen.be/portal/en/publications/the-sckcen-barometer-2018(79527b1c-1ffc-4cf1-8cb2-5614dc6cb69).html.

Verwimp, L., & Verledens A. (Eds.). (2002). The Belgian Nuclear Research Centre 1952–2002. SCK CEN.

Waste Directive (2014). Council Directive 2011/70/Euratom of 19 July 2011 establishing a Community framework for the responsible and safe management of spent fuel and radioactive waste. OJ L 199, 02/08/2011, p. 48–56. https://eur-lex.europa.eu/legal-content/GA/TXT/?uri=CELEX:32011L0070.

Winckelmans, W. (2020, April 2). Discussie nucleair afval komt weer boven water. De Standaard. https://www.standaard.be/cnt/dmf20220401_97761318.

Anne Bergmans holds a PhD in sociology and is Associate Professor and Guest Professor in Sociology of Risk and Safety, and Societal Resilience at the University of Antwerp (Belgium). Her main field of study is the interface between society and technology and the governance of risk. She has particular experience in research on informed and inclusive decision-making on environmental and technological risk, such as regarding the siting of contested facilities, (participatory) technology assessment and (responsible) innovation; both in terms of public and company policy. Most of Anne's research is policy oriented action-research, mainly qualitative in design and based in Science and Technology Studies (STS), with a strong focus on system and network analysis, including both humans and non-humans as actors in the risk and safety discourse.

Catherine Fallon was first trained in natural science and obtained a MSc in Biochemical Engineering (MIT, USA). After several years in the industry and in the European Commission, she earned her PhD in political sciences and invested the field of "Science and Society" by doing research in the social and political aspects of technological development and risk governance. She works on the governance of civil security-related organisations. She is Professor in Public Administration and Policy Evaluation at the Université de Liège (Belgium). Areas of expertise include: instruments of public policy; public policy evaluation; expertise; science policy; emergency planning & crisis management.

Ron Cörvers is Associate Professor of Governance for Sustainable Development at Maastricht University. He is programme leader of the Fair and Smart Data spearhead—the Currency for Global Sustainability (www.maastrichtuniversity.nl/fsd), and project owner of the Education in the Sustainable UM2030 programme. He has a degree in environmental geography and holds a PhD in public administration. He has an interest in multi-stakeholder governance, participatory processes, and the role of science and knowledge in dealing with sustainability issues. He was scientific director of the Maastricht Sustainability Institute from 2013–2021.

Céline Parotte is an Associate Professor at the Spiral Research Center, RU Cité in the Department of Political Science at the University of Liège, Belgium. She holds a PhD in political and social science, an MSc in public administration and a Certificate on Public Policies Evaluation. Her current research areas involve high-risk infrastructures management and control (e.g., nuclear facilities, radioactive waste, windmills), participatory and qualitative methods, and controversial public policy analysis and evaluation.

Open Access This chapter is licensed under the terms of the Creative Commons Attribution 4.0 International License (http://creativecommons.org/licenses/by/4.0/), which permits use, sharing, adaptation, distribution and reproduction in any medium or format, as long as you give appropriate credit to the original author(s) and the source, provide a link to the Creative Commons license and indicate if changes were made.

The images or other third party material in this chapter are included in the chapter's Creative Commons license, unless indicated otherwise in a credit line to the material. If material is not included in the chapter's Creative Commons license and your intended use is not permitted by statutory regulation or exceeds the permitted use, you will need to obtain permission directly from the copyright holder.

5

The Long Road Towards the Soft Nuclear Repository State: Nuclear Waste Governance in Germany

Maria Rosaria Di Nucci and Achim Brunnengräber

5.1 Introduction

The decision-making processes in the field of high-level radioactive waste (HLW) in the Federal Republic of Germany (and the former German Democratic Republic (GDR) until 1989) have been dominated by the decide-announce-defend (DAD) strategy. This approach, which endured until the beginning of the last decade, led to conflicts with civil society, mistrust of authorities and blockages, and can be epitomised by the expression "nuclear state", a term coined by Robert Jungk (1986). Nuclear policy decisions were also enforced with police coercion. Consequently, massive resistance from the anti-nuclear-movement developed against the state and the planned final geological repository waste

---

This text was written at the Research Center for Sustainability (Forschungszentrum für Nachhaltigkeit, FFN) Freie Universität Berlin, as part of the TRANSENS-project "Transdisciplinary research on the management of high-level radioactive waste in Germany" (transens.de). TRANSENS is a collaborative project funded by the Federal Ministry for the Environment, Nature Conservation, Nuclear Safety and Consumer Protection and in the "*Niedersächsisches Vorab*" of the Volkswagen Foundation by the Ministry of Science and Culture of Lower Saxony (FK 02E11849C).

M. R. Di Nucci (✉) · A. Brunnengräber
Freie Universität Berlin, Forschungszentrum Für Nachhaltigkeit (FFN), Berlin, Germany
e-mail: dinucci@zedat.fu-berlin.de

A. Brunnengräber
e-mail: Achim.Brunnengraeber@FU-Berlin.de

© The Author(s) 2023
M. Arentsen and R. van Est (Eds.), *The Future of Radioactive Waste Governance*, Energiepolitik und Klimaschutz. Energy Policy and Climate Protection, https://doi.org/10.1007/978-3-658-40496-3_5

site at Gorleben. A stop and go policy came after each decision, characterised by court orders allowing construction followed by occupation of the site by the anti-nuclear movement (Roth and Rucht 2008; Rucht 1980).

Commencing in 2010, after more than 60 years of nuclear energy deployment, the political balance of power in the energy sector in Germany has fundamentally changed. The movements against nuclear power and the transport as well as storage of radioactive waste have grown stronger over the decades and are now key political actors in the current siting process for deep geological disposal (DGD). Part of the anti-nuclear movement has integrated into the institutions, e.g. political parties and the German Bundestag, and contributed significantly to the decision in 2011 to completely phase out nuclear power.

Subsequent to the decision in 2011 to phase out nuclear power plants (NPPs) in Germany by 2022, and with insight into the failures of the past, an ambitious *Repository Site Selection Act* (StandAG) was passed in 2013, and amended in 2017. This Act provides the framework for the establishment of new state institutions and a far-reaching participation procedure involving civil society and stakeholder groups.

The search for a DGD site that offers the greatest possible safety and security potential was started with a blank map, potentially considering the whole of Germany. In September 2020, following the release of a preliminary report evaluating regions with potentially suitable host rock formations for a DGD, the Federal Company for Radioactive Waste Disposal (Bundesgesellschaft für Endlagerung mbH (BGE)), acting as the operator, designated around 90 potential areas across Germany (BGE 2020). The overall geological situation in Gorleben was assessed as "unfavourable" and the site was eliminated in this first round, putting an end to a decades-old conflict. Yet the process is still confronted with significant resistance and hence challenges. It was planned to find a suitable, socially acceptable location by 2031 and to dispose of all HLW by 2080. In November 2022, the operator BGE announced that the search for the site would take much longer and indicated a timeframe between 2046 and 2068. It is expected that Germany will now have to elaborate a concept for a long-term interim storage facility as is already the case in several European countries.

This chapter analyses the multi-level governance of HLW in Germany by focusing on the following domains: (1) legislation, politics & administration, (2) science & technology, (3) civil society and (4) the interactions between them. The chapter is structured as follows: In Section 5.2, we provide a short historical account of German nuclear waste management and discuss the wickedness (Brunnengräber 2019b) of the waste problem. In Sect. 5.3, we address governance aspects and analyse the legal, political and institutional domains. We focus on legal aspects of the StandAG, especially those providing the framework for the other domains. Section 5.4 is dedicated to the scientific and technological domain, and we analyse in particular the role and function of experts. In Sect. 5.5, we turn to the societal domain and its interactions with the other domains and focus on the current participatory process for a DGD siting. In the conclusion we emphasise that procedural fairness and inclusiveness of the process remain important and necessary prerequisites for building public confidence and for the social acceptability of the political siting decisions. We maintain that the legal framework and the StandAG leave many unresolved issues, but this permits extensive room for manoeuvre and represents an opportunity for new and expanded forms of participation to be pursued.

5.2 From the Hard Nuclear State to More Participatory Approaches

5.2.1 Historical Context[1]

The Federal Republic of Germany had an early start in the use of nuclear power. Between 1961 and the end of the 1980s, 36 NPPs entered into commercial operation. In 2005/2006 Germany's 17 NPPs supplied almost one-third of the country's electricity, but this share has fallen steadily. In 1998, the newly elected Social Democratic/Green government radically changed the previous nuclear policy, and in 2000 announced the nuclear consensus (Atomkonsens) that enabled the phase-out of NPPs within two decades. In 2009, the subsequent conservative Christian Democratic/liberal government announced a 12-year extension of the scheduled phase-out, which provoked harsh protests, especially from the Green Party and the anti-nuclear-movement. In the aftermath of the Fukushima disaster in 2011, the same government reversed its previous plans and decreed the definitive phase-out by 2022. (World Nuclear Association 2022). Following the Russian invasion of the Ukraine and the subsequent turmoil on the energy markets, the shutdown of the last three NPPs still in operation has been postponed until April 2023.

---

[1] For reasons of space we can only supply a brief historical account of the nuclear waste policies in Germany, thus for the early years of nuclear development and waste treatment, we refer to a number of important publications (see among others Blowers (2017, 2019), Hocke and Renn (2009); Kamlage et al. (2019); Radkau and Hahn (2013). This Section builds heavily upon Di Nucci et al. (2021b).

The advance and decline of nuclear power in Germany has been characterised by conflicts and intractable disputes. Public opinion widely opposed building NPPs, and public debate, the extra-parliamentary opposition and the anti-nuclear movement enjoyed broad societal and partially political support (Rucht 2008). The anti-nuclear movement emerged from the peace movement, but the dangers and risks of nuclear energy triggered the wider mobilisation of civil society.[2] The search for a DGD site for HLW has equally been accompanied by strong public opposition.

The roots of the problem date back to the 1970s, when plans for an integrated reprocessing and waste disposal site in Gorleben, a village in a rural area in the northern German state of Lower-Saxony with salt rock geological conditions, were announced. While plans for the reprocessing plant were discarded, Gorleben remained the designated site for a waste repository (Blowers, 2017; Tiggemann 2019). Di Nucci et al. (2021b) argue that the German government strategy until 2013 rested heavily on a politically driven top-down approach. The fact that all nuclear waste sites for HLW and LLW (Gorleben, Asse, Konrad and Morsleben) were designated top-down by government decisions triggered conflicts and polarisation and led to a growing mistrust of state institutions (Di Nucci et al. 2021b).

The loss of trust in state and federal state authorities by the anti-nuclear movement and the population directly affected by nuclear facilities can be attributed, among other reasons, to a process described as "messy muddling through" (Hocke and Renn 2011). Government institutions and responsible political actors had no coherent action plan and reacted to protests with harsh and repressive measures (Roth and Rucht 2008). The failure of the "nuclear state" in governing and regulating nuclear waste can be partly ascribed to earlier political-administrative control concepts, economic interests, and repressive attitudes towards local and civil protests (Kamlage et al. 2019). Di Nucci et al. (2021a) point out that the long-standing dualistic role of state institutions as both advocates and watchdogs in the nuclear field rendered a neutral moderating position problematic, if not impossible, for example with regard to civil society demands for participation and transparency in decision making.

However, an adaptation of political institutions, the expansion of renewable energies and the introduction of new participatory elements in policymaking has taken place. Following the change from the conservative Christian Democratic-

---

[2] It is interesting to note that the very large public demonstrations, especially in 1979, were induced by both national and international events; the international expert hearing about Gorleben in Hanover, Germany, and the Three Mile Island accident in Harrisburg in the USA. See Rucht (1980).

Liberal coalition in 1998 and the establishment of a red-green cabinet, revision of the nuclear policy culminated in a moratorium in 2000. The agreement of 14 June 2000 between the federal government and the energy companies for the phasing out of nuclear energy, also agreed a moratorium on the planned repository at Gorleben. This put exploratory activities for a DGD at Gorleben on hold for a period of three to ten years. The moratorium's goal was to settle questions, especially about the feasibility of the salt dome (Tiggemann 2019, p. 79).

Under the red-green government, the potential for the moratorium to induce trust remained rather limited, and the initial government-industry consensus led to a rather limited engagement of opposition groups in discussing a possible disposal strategy (Di Nucci et al., 2019). In the political process, the positions of the various interest groups hardened and the lines of conflict became more rigid, so that no progress could be made. It was only in 2011 that the conflictual relationship between the state and civil society, and between the opposing parties, was somehow smoothed by the Fukushima nuclear reactor disaster and the subsequent nuclear phase-out. One could claim that the divide between nuclear power advocates and opponents became less dramatic following the phase-out decision. Nevertheless, despite the significance of this decision and its potential to build trust between political actors and create confidence in a fresh start for nuclear waste policies, conflicts did not vanish entirely. One of the reasons for this could be that the phase-out decision was triggered by an exogenous event, and was not reached through a critical consideration of past development paths, or because of an intrinsic and endogenous awareness of the problem (Di Nucci et al. 2021b). Yet, with the adoption of the StandAG in 2013, the German Bundestag made a first move to revise the technical path dependency of a research and nuclear waste policy exclusively oriented towards DGD in salt rock formations. In the ongoing process, clay and crystalline rock formations are also taken into consideration.

5.2.2 The Nuclear Waste Problem Today

To date, there has not been a complete survey of the volume of radioactive waste produced in Germany or of the amount that can be expected in the future. The inventory of radioactive waste is difficult, because different sources use different designations for the volume of waste, and different units (tonnes, cubic meters, etc.) for its measurement. The classification of waste is thus rather complex and is also dependent on the method of disposal (e.g. surface or DGD). Because the plans envisage the disposal of all radioactive waste types in DGD, following the dose rate, it is the (related) heat generation during radioactive decay that is key for the classification and hence the inventory in Germany. Germany has used its own classification system since the mid-1980s, and distinguishes between heat-generating waste and waste with negligible heat generation. Differing slightly from the International Atomic Energy Agency (IAEA) classification, nuclear waste is thus categorised into high-level radioactive waste (HLW), intermediate-level active waste (ILW) and low-level active waste (LLW). Heat-generating waste includes HLW and part of ILW. Waste with negligible heat generation corresponds to the categories of LLW and to the major part of ILW, i.e. the IAEA classification of very low-level waste (VLLW) and low-level waste (LLW), and intermediate-level waste (ILW) (BASE 2016).

According to the BGE, Germany has accumulated approximately 27,000 cubic meters of HLW (BGE n. d.). Currently, nuclear waste with different radioactive levels is scattered across different federal states. The majority of it is hosted in facilities at the nuclear reactor sites, at interim storage facilities or at the facilities for packaging and repackaging. Non-reprocessed spent fuel is stored in twelve interim storage facilities; vitrified reprocessed waste and spent fuel is stored at the three centralised storage facilities at Gorleben, Ahaus and Lubmin (see Fig. 5.1). Waste produced through the reprocessing of fuel in the UK and France has partially been returned to Germany or is expected to be returned in the near future. In addition, about 300,000 cubic meters of LLW and ILW are expected from NPPs, research centres, industry and medical facilities (BASE 2020). Furthermore, 100,000 cubic meters stem from the uranium enrichment facility at Gronau, and 220,000 cubic meters from Asse rock salt mine (Asse II, see below). The size of the future DGD facility cannot be decided until the host rock and the according container concept have been determined.

The former iron ore mine, Konrad, in Lower Saxony, is licensed as a final repository for LLW and ILW. Starting in 2007, it was converted into a repository and is expected to be put into operation by 2027. Between 1976 and 1978, Asse II, in Lower Saxony, was used to dispose, at a depth of 650 m, 125,787 drums and casks with LLW and ILW, and a further 1300 drums with ILW from NPPs and the Karlsruhe nuclear research facility (BMUV 2021). Every day, 12,000 L of water trickle into the mine and have to be pumped out. Therefore, the casks stored there are to be retrieved by 2033. The final closure of the Asse II mine is expected by 2050 at the earliest, but a roadmap is not available yet (Niedersächsische Staatskanzlei 2021).

Following the reunification of Germany in 1990, responsibility for the former repository for LLW/ILW of the German Democratic Republic (GDR) in Morsleben (ERAM) was transferred to the Federal Republic of Germany. The emplacement of radioactive waste took place until 1998, and has been completed. Approximately 37,000 cubic meters of LLW and ILLW are stored here at a

5 The Long Road Towards the Soft Nuclear Repository State … 119

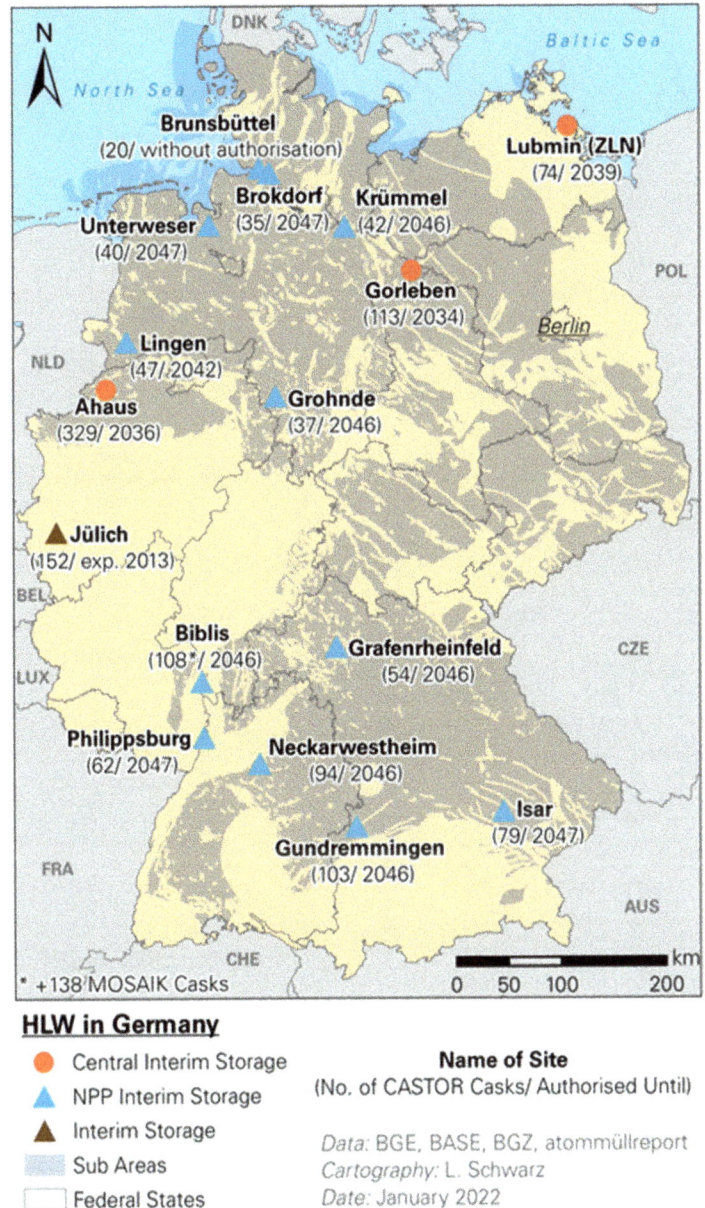

Fig. 5.1 Location of nuclear facilities where HLW is temporarily stored

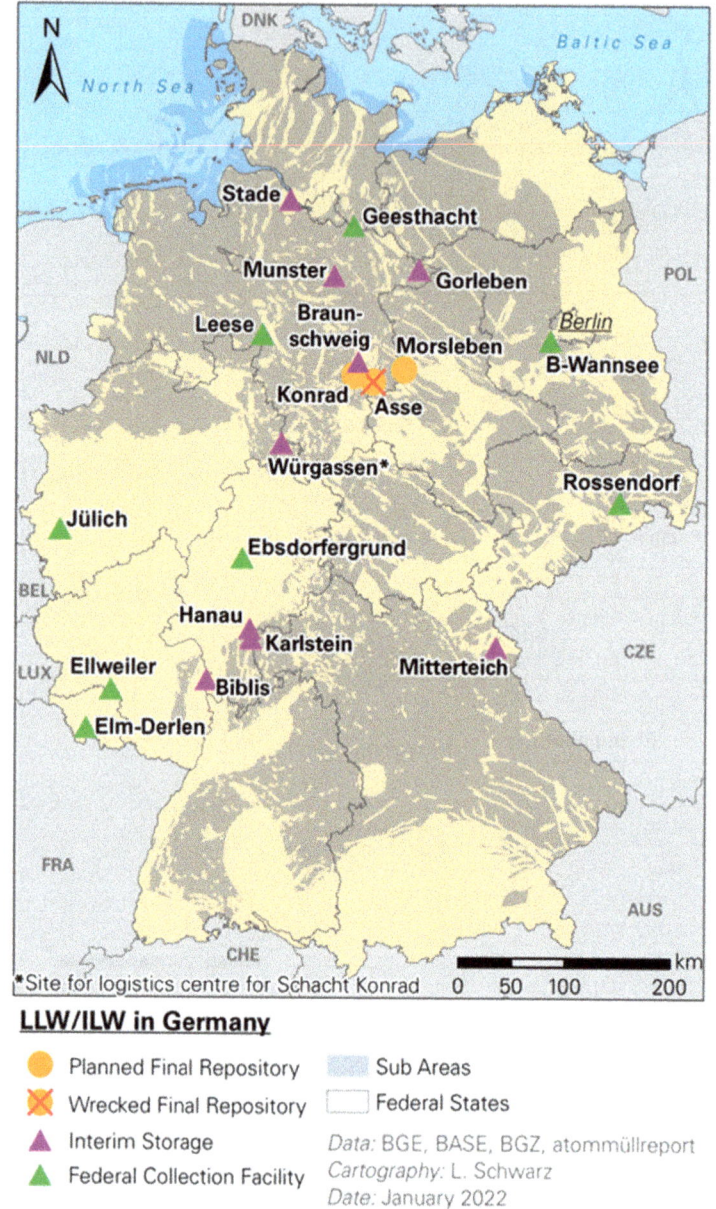

Fig. 5.2 Location of nuclear facilities where LLW/ILW is temporarily stored

depth of around 480 m. Stabilisation measures have been carried out since 2003. Morsleben is the first German repository that is to be decommissioned under the German Atomic Energy Act, with the waste being retained.

5.3 Nuclear Waste Governance: Legislation, Politics, Administration

5.3.1 The Legal Framework

The major instrument of the legal framework for HLW is represented by the *Repository Site Selection Act* (StandAG 2017). In spite of widespread critique, the law represented a novelty in the German legislative system, which had not previously regulated the siting process (Hocke and Kallenbach-Herbert 2015). This Act sets out exclusion criteria, minimum requirements and consideration criteria as well as requirements for the organisation, the procedure of the selection process, the examination of alternatives and public participation. Moreover, it establishes a transparency norm. It was the outcome of a long procedure made possible through a compromise between political parties and other involved stakeholders about a stepwise approach for siting a DGD (Smeddinck 2019).

Starting from a blank map, the site for the final disposal of HLW should be found through a science-based and transparent procedure, and is to be carried out in a participatory, science-based, transparent, self-questioning and learning process (StandAG 2017, §1(1)). In principle, all three host rocks (salt, clay and crystalline) can be considered. The best possible site should be selected in a comparative procedure and should be able to guarantee the safe containment of the waste for a period of one million years. However, the repository should be sealed with the possibility of retrieval for the duration of the operating phase for 500 years after closure.

5.3.2 The Political Dimension, Institutional Framework and Main Actors

German nuclear waste governance is shaped by several socio-technical interdependencies at various levels (Brohmann et al. 2021). We find ministries of the German Federal Government (Bund) and the federal state governments (Bundesländer), local authorities (mayors, city councils), and civil society (environmental organisations, anti-nuclear movement, citizens' initiatives). The political feedback between these levels of action and decision-making (from federal to local and vice-versa) are not always transparent. These interdependencies will continue to play a role in the future, as recent developments already show as the relationship continues to be characterised by conflicts and different approaches of how to handle the *wicked problem* of nuclear waste (Hocke and Brunnengräber 2019). Such a problem is difficult or impossible to solve due to incomplete, contradictory and changing requirements that are often difficult to identify.

The enactment of the StandAG in 2013 was the result of a compromise between the political parties at the national level which was agreed in the Bundestag. However, the consensus became fragile. At the federal state level, there has been no explicit backing for a restart of site selection, as only Baden-Wuerttemberg, Lower Saxony and Schleswig–Holstein supported the siting for a DGD in the following years. By contrast, other federal states declared that they would not qualify for siting. This shows that the search for the best location will not only be science-based, but also politically influenced.

A multiplicity of actors is involved in the decisions regarding multi-level governance of nuclear waste. Häfner (2016) identified 300 institutional actors from a wide range of spheres, subdivided into state, market, science and civil society actors. The state includes state decision-making bodies, ministries, supervisory and authorising authorities. The market consists mainly of the nuclear industry and the electric utilities that operate NPPs and their respective lobbies and think-tanks, as well as several energy companies. However, responsibility for final disposal was handed over to the state. In addition, civil society includes various environmental, peace and anti-nuclear organisations, as well as many regional and site-specific citizen initiatives (Häfner 2016).

Federal states, especially Lower Saxony, where Gorleben is located, took a central role. At the central federal governmental level, in the past, HLW fell within the remit of various federal ministries and the subdivision of responsibilities changed over time. As of June 2022, major responsibilities lie within the Ministry of Environment, Nature Protection, Nuclear Safety and Consumer Protection (BMUV). The Ministry for Economy Affairs and Climate Action (BMWK) and the Ministry of Education and Research (BMBF) also share responsibilities. The BMUV is the supervisory authority and thus the highest federal authority in the siting process. This means that all decisions by the regulator in its area of responsibility must be taken in accordance with the requirements of the Ministry, be continuously reviewed, and may be amended by the BMUV at any time.

5.3.3 The Institutional Actors

Germany established its new governance structure fairly recently in response to EU Directive 2011/70/EURATOM (European Council 2011). The StandAG mandated the reorganisation of the existing institutional structures and procedures, and ensured the required functional separation of the supervisory and licensing authority from all other government agencies or organisations involved in waste management. The StandAG stipulates a clear separation between the regulatory authority and the developer /implementer. However, the new waste governance is based on reformed rather than new institutions. As a result of this restructure, two powerful actors emerged: the Federal Office for the Safety of Nuclear Waste Management (BASE, Bundesamt für die Sicherheit der nuklearen Entsorgung[3]) as supervisory and licensing authority, and the Federal Company for Radioactive Waste Disposal (BGE, Bundesgesellschaft für Endlagerung mbH) as the operator responsible for the implementation.

The Regulator BASE
BASE is a higher federal authority under the supervision of the Federal Ministry BMUV, and independent of economic interests. It was established in 2014 on the basis of a provision of the StandAG (2013, § 7), and finally took up its duties in July 2016.[4] The authority is tasked with:

- regulation, licensing and supervision in the field of long-term nuclear waste storage, interim storage and the handling and transport of radioactive waste,
- process management and enforcement monitoring in the site selection procedure for the long-term nuclear waste storage facility,
- the organisation of public participation in the search for a site.

BASE's responsibilities are the overall site selection procedure and the overall organisation of public participation. Within the competence of BASE we also find review of the quality of the information provided by the BGE and the release of its proposals (as BGE itself is not allowed to do this). Consequently, BASE has the legal obligation to prepare and distribute "comprehensive and systematic" information for the public, which is required by law.

The fact that ultimate responsibility for the site selection procedure and for public participation lies within the same authority is controversial. BASE itself

---

[3] Formerly the Federal Office for Safety of Nuclear Disposal (BfE, Bundesamt für kerntechnische Entsorgungssicherheit).
[4] Act on the Establishment of a Federal Office for Nuclear Waste Management of 23 July 2013 (Gesetz über die Errichtung eines Bundesamtes für kerntechnische Entsorgung vom 23. Juli 2013—BGBl. I S. 2553, 2563).

has addressed this problem, and declared that it finds itself caught between the legally required control of the procedure and the necessary cooperation with the other actors. The fact that in other countries, such as Belgium or Canada, this responsibility has been defined differently, and other bodies are responsible for public participation, shows that this is not, nor has to be, a core task of the regulatory authority (Di Nucci et al. 2021a).

The Operator BGE

BGE was established in December 2016 by merging three other institutions: the Federal Company for Radioactive Waste Disposal (DBE) was founded in 1979 as a company in charge of the planning, exploration, construction and operation of facilities for securing and disposing of radioactive waste. DBE, together with Asse-GmbH and parts of the BfS, were transferred to the BGE in 2017. It is important to note that since 2008, two-thirds of the DBE belonged to GNS (Gesellschaft für Nuklear-Service), which in turn belongs to the German NPP-operators. The DBE had been responsible for the operation and maintenance of the exploration mine in Gorleben, the construction of the storage facility for low and intermediate level radioactive waste in the mine Konrad, and decommissioning of the former DDR deep storage facility in Morsleben.

The BGE is under the supervision of BASE and is 100% owned by the BMUV.[5] Gaßner et al. (2018) explain in this context that the technical supervision of the BGE under organisational law is the responsibility of the federal government and not BASE. Thus, the regulatory authority can neither influence nor control the fulfilment of the BGE's tasks. The BGE acts in accordance with StandAG (2017, § 3), and is responsible for operational activities (establishment and operation of DGD facilities), and implementation of the repository site selection procedure and informing the public about the initiated steps and measures of the process. In the first phase of the procedure (see Sect. 5.2) the BGE designated sub-areas in which host rock formations can potentially be found (Fig. 5.3). In the second phase, potential regions are to be explored by the BGE. During the final phase, it is responsible for site-related exploration programmes and assessment criteria.

---

[5] Section 9a (§ 3) of the Atomic Energy Act (AtG) stipulates that the Federal Government "shall entrust the performance [of the securing and disposal of radioactive waste] to a third party, which shall be organised in a private legal form and of which the Federal Government is the sole shareholder".

5 The Long Road Towards the Soft Nuclear Repository State … 125

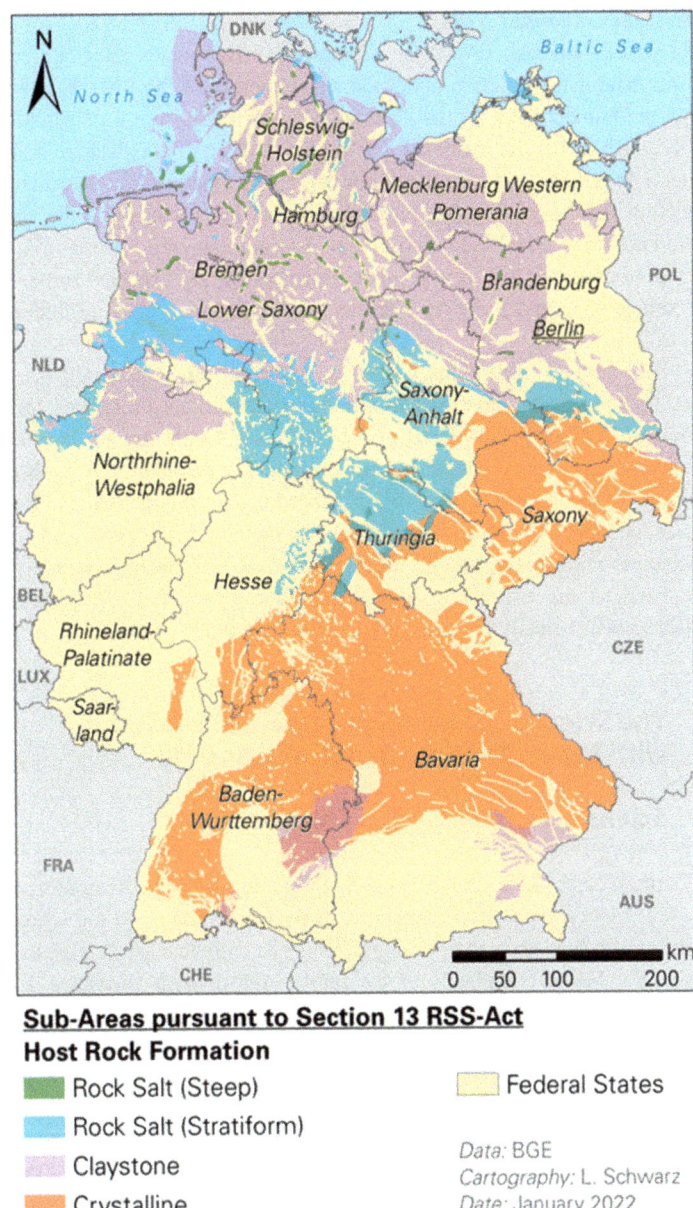

Fig. 5.3 Potential sub-areas according to host rock formation

The Oversight Committee NBG

The National Citizens' Oversight Committee (Nationales Begleitgremium, NBG) was established in 2016 under the responsibility of the BMUV. It was set upe upon recommendation by the "Commission for the Disposal of High-Level-Waste" (EndKo 2016). Its members may neither belong to a legislative body nor to a federal or provincial government, nor can have any economic interests in the site selection (Di Nucci et al., 2021b). In addition, lay persons and the younger generation are represented. Some observers maintain that participation of lay citizens on this board can help restore trust, as laypeople are expected to be driven less by self-interest and more by concern for the common good (Schreurs and Suckow 2019).

The NBG advises institutions in the site selection procedure until the siting decision. Its tasks encompass mediating the process and accompanying the public participation process. The focus of the NBG is not only monitoring the process; it also sees its task as building and continuously maintaining trust between the actors involved. However, the NBG is subordinate to the BMUV and thus not entirely independent. Until now, the NBG has had little influence, and its recommendations representing public input so far have only been marginally considered. Parts of the anti-nuclear-movement have considered the work of the committee rather critically from the very beginning (Ehmke 2020).

5.4 The Science & Technology Domain. Dealing with Expert/lay Knowledge and Society

5.4.1 Science, Technology and Civil Society

In the German case, "safety first" remains the main principle. Attributing priority to safety aspects over other criteria in all decisions related to the search and construction of a final repository is imperative. The technical safety aspects point to the socio-technical complexity of the challenging disposal measures. Factors to be considered range from political issues related to conditions for retrievability (in the first 500 years), to different types of host rock or the so far very limited standardisation of containers.

The scientific community and expert panels have tended to regard such complexity primarily as a technical challenge that can be dealt with through established forms of scientific and engineering research and development (R&D). The rationale is that any risks arising can be reduced to an acceptable degree by taking adequate measures. In the selection process, social science and techno-scientific criteria are alleged to have an important role. Yet, the so-called exclusion criteria such as earthquakes, fault zones, volcanic activity or influences from current or past mining activity, and minimum requirements such as thickness of the inclusion-effective rock mass area or the preservation of the barrier effect, are purely determined by technical and scientific criteria. The social-science based criteria are only applied at a later stage during the evaluation of the sub-areas.

Complex and *wicked problems* associated with the long term management of radioactive waste (Brunnengräber 2019b) require an integrative analysis and contextualised planning. Debates within society and science are nowadays expressions of uncertainties, both at the scientific and normative levels. This makes it difficult to define a clear long-term strategy. It is not possible to understand all the dynamics of such complex systems, in which *known unknowns* and *unknown unknowns* are frequently found (Eckhardt and Rippe 2016). To offer solutions or to possess extensive knowledge is no longer considered an exclusive capability of scientists. Due to the many unanswered questions about DGD (which repository concept, which host rock, which container? etc.), interdisciplinary expert knowledge and transdisciplinary research is called for as a productive source for making the best possible decision in balancing risk technologies with societal interests and concerns.

BASE conducts research to fulfil its duties in the field of the tasks assigned to it by the StandAG. Research is carried out at two levels: firstly, BASE is involved in the implementation of the BMUV's research (BASE 2019), which forms the scientific advisory basis for political decisions; secondly, BASE has a specific research budget for nuclear safety. Furthermore, additional research projects can be supported through third-party funding, e.g. from the European Union. The research priorities and central goals are defined in the research strategy and agenda under the BASE research budget (BASE 2019). For this, BASE appoints external experts and/or participates in third-party funded projects and research networks. This procedure has been criticised, but BASE's own R&D is justified by the need to maintain its own supervisory expertise and by the need for competent and independent examination of the operator's proposals and arguments. The OECD/NEA also points out that scientific and technical expertise is strengthened when relevant R&D is carried out directly by the regulator (OECD-NEA 2010).

5.4.2 The Role of Experts and Committees

In the field of radioactive waste governance there is a tradition of interdisciplinary expert committees that have advised various governments. Isidoro Losada et al.

(2019) examined the work and background of five advisory bodies and tried to shed some new light by juxtaposing the way these commissions provided expert advice and enlarged the level of understanding of the socio-technical challenges connected to nuclear waste. They stated that the design and performance of advisory bodies has started to change, and to show a slow development towards more openness and plurality to increase robustness in decision-making (Isidoro Losada et al. 2019).

Amongst the most prominent committees in Germany we find the ad-hoc working group on the "Selection Procedure for Repository Sites", known as AkEnd, which was established in 1999 as an interdisciplinary expert advisory body and was in charge of analysing scientifically proven criteria for searching for a repository site. In its final report in December 2002, AkEnd recommended a number of criteria for site selection and new forms of participatory governance. AkEnd was the first expert board to point out the importance of socio-political criteria and of participation for the siting process, and of public involvement in the decision-making process, traceability and transparency of the information, as well as the acceptance of the affected population (AkEnd 2002).

In 2014, a new site selection commission for a repository, EndKo, was set up. It consisted in total of 34 representatives from the political and scientific communities as well as civil society, and its tasks were defined by the StandAG. This commission represented a milestone, marking a new beginning in the relation between state and society. Its main task was to work out the basic principles for decision-making concerning site selection for a DGD. These included the definition of procedural steps within the selection process, the development of criteria used for the site selection as well as the design of the process of public participation (EndKo 2016; BASE 2021). In its constituent meeting in 2014, the Commission stressed its intention to build upon the work of AkEnd, especially with respect to the aim of a systematic and transparent development of criteria for the search of a repository as well as public participation.

There appear to be strong similarities between the recommendations of EndKo and those put forward ten years earlier by AkEnd, especially with regard to the selection criteria (Isidoro Losada et al. 2019). For both commissions, concepts of safety and risk played an important role, and both considered natural science and technical criteria to be key to the identification of a potential repository site. This is not surprising, as there was also a strong continuity between the two commissions, ensured among other things by a number of experts that served on both commissions and who, however, brought along a number of old areas of conflicts. Nonetheless, both AkEnd and EndKo recommended a site selection procedure with a participatory process that goes beyond basic participation, which was later agreed upon in the StandAG.

The selection and participation of the experts in the new commission and the limited opportunities to influence the outcome have been widely rebuked by the anti-nuclear movement, and by a large number of environmental organisations and initiatives (Brunnengräber 2019a, 110 ff). Thus, the enactment of the StandAG and the work of EndKo showed once again that conflicts have historical roots, and the legacy of the past affects the work and discussion towards the search for solutions.

5.5 The Civil Societal Domain and Its Interactions with the Institutional and Scientific Domains

5.5.1 German Civil Society and the Nuclear Issue

Both the construction of NPPs and the DGD option have been controversial in Germany. The anti-nuclear movement was formed in the early 1970s, but fundamental demonstrations against nuclear power started as early as 1968, in Würgassen. Further milestones of the movement were the occupation of the Whyl construction site in 1975, mass demonstrations in Grohnde, Brokdorf and Kalkar in 1976 and 1977, and the resistance against the planned reprocessing plant in Wackersdorf between 1981 and 1989 (Radkau 2011; Rucht 2008). The names of these sites are still iconic for the movement regarding the strong polarisation of West German society in dealing with nuclear power. The mass protests against the Castor transports[6] to Gorleben between 1977 and 2000 denounced the risks of nuclear energy and of the inadequate disposal programme of the various federal state governments. Through the establishment of the Green Party in 1980, anti-nuclear protests became institutionalised in the political party system of West Germany (Kolb 2007).

Indeed, Gorleben remained a synonym for German nuclear conflicts, and has been a permanent subject of the discourse on nuclear issues (Blowers 2019; Blowers and Lowry 1997). More recently, nuclear opponents considered the initial non-exclusion of the Gorleben site from the current siting process as a signal for the path continuity of the nuclear policy of conservative parties and governments. Even after the enactment of the StandAG in 2013, due to the distrust

---

[6] "Castors" are special containers for storing and transporting highly radioactive materials, for example spent fuel elements from NPPs or vitrified waste from reprocessing.

accumulated under the previous disposal policy there was a strong concern that the "politically driven" selection of Gorleben could be legitimised through the new participation procedure (Di Nucci 2019). The citizens' initiatives of the Gorleben region persistently pointed out that—because of the intensive exploration in the past—the Gorleben salt dome should have been excluded from the new search (Kamlage et al. 2019; Tiggemann 2019).

Large infrastructure projects call for robust decision-making procedures; this is especially true in the case of the final disposal of radioactive waste, in particular because of the extremely long-time horizon involved. Over the years there have been growing social expectations and a quest for participatory elements. This is especially linked to the legacy of the past top-down nuclear waste siting policy, which provoked enormous damage to public confidence vis-a-vis the state institutions.

The StandAG stipulates that [t]he public participation procedure shall be further developed accordingly. For this purpose, the parties involved may make use of further forms of participation beyond the minimum requirements stipulated by law. The suitability of the forms of participation shall be reviewed at "appropriate intervals." This provides an incentive for a critical reflection on the participatory process. If the public is not involved, it will be unlikely to "find a solution that is supported by a broad social consensus and can thus also be tolerated by those affected" (StandAG, 2017, Sect. 5.5 (1)).

5.5.2 Participation and Consultation in the Site Selection Process

An important feature of the StandAG is the opening up of the path for the institutionalisation of public participation in nuclear waste governance (Hocke and Smeddinck 2017), even though the process leading to the entering into force of the law was itself not sufficiently participatory. The StandAG provides for transparent and dialogue-oriented public participation in the search for the best possible site.

In the public participation concept "Information, Dialogue, Public Participation in the Initial Phase of the Repository Search", the regulatory authority points out that "transparent, open and confidence-building participation" is only possible if in particular the three stakeholders BASE, NBG and BGE (…) and in the further course of the procedure the regional conferences cooperate on a permanent basis (BfE 2019, p. 4), (BASE 2021). Actors from civil society and NGOs, such as the German Federation for the Environment and Nature Conservation

5 The Long Road Towards the Soft Nuclear Repository State ...

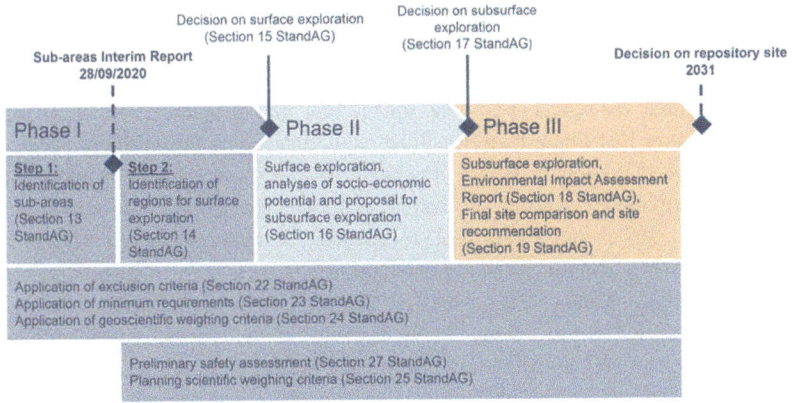

Fig. 5.4 Overview of the three phases of the site selection procedure. (Source: BGE 2020, p. 33)

(BUND), mistrusted the new approach and feared a low degree of openness with regard to their concerns (Schwarz et al. 2021a, b).

Against the background of previous experiences, it was declared that participation should not be limited to information and consultation modes (StandAG 2017). Instead, concerned citizens and stakeholders should be empowered to participate in a way that goes beyond previous participation patterns. (Themann et al. 2021a) remarked that such an approach requires an institutionalisation of and new forms of participation, but above all co-determination rights, as well as the provision of support measures for concerned citizens.

In the original intentions, the site for a DGD for HLW was to be found by 2031. As shown in Fig. 5.4, the site selection procedure in these plans could be subdivided into three phases. Against the newest postponement of the siting for the repository, the figure below is no longer realistic, but still provides a good overview of the phases and steps of the siting process. The operator BGE has refrained from further concretisation of the steps and timeline beyond 2031. Any further time estimate would be highly speculative and would only reflect a range of several possible scenarios.

- Phase I: Sub-regions and proposal for siting regions
- Phase II: Surface exploration
- Phase III: Underground exploration
- Final Phase: Site proposal and site decision.

In the first step of Phase I, the operator BGE carried out assessments on the basis of the exclusion criteria, minimum requirements and geo-scientific weighting criteria, and subsequently identified the so-called sub-areas, i.e. those areas with favourable geological conditions for the safe final disposal of HLW. At the end of this step 1 of Phase I, BGE published the interim report on the sub-areas. Subsequently, the regulator BASE organised the first standardised procedure for public participation, the so-called Sub-areas Expert Conference. This consisted of three conferences and was in part co-organised by major stakeholders, potentially affected municipalities and regional authorities, scientists, representatives of social organisations and citizens. This first step of Phase I was concluded in 2021.

Due to COVID-19 restrictions, BASE organised the kick-off event of the Sub-Areas Conference (Fachkonferenz Teilgebiete, FKTG) as an online event on 17 and 18 October, 2020. The FKTG was the regulator´s first formal participatory event of Phase 1 (see Fig. 5.4) in the site selection procedure, and was intended to open up space for the participation of a broad public. It started with the first of three consultation meetings foreseen by the StandAG in February 2021. Expectations were correspondingly high. The aim of the kick-off event was to present the "Sub-areas Interim Report" published shortly before by the operator (BGE 2020) and to give all interested citizens, municipal representatives and civil society organisations the opportunity to ask questions about the report and the procedure. There was discussion about how the exclusion and consideration criteria as well as the minimum requirements were being applied, and about how the site search was going to move into the future. However, during the presentation of the results of the interim report on sub-areas, there were hardly any opportunities for critical questions or specific discussions of the questions formulated by the participants. Instead the moderator passed on selected and often bundled questions from the panel to the representatives of the BGE (Themann et al. 2021b).

The second consultation of the FKTG took place in June 2021, and the third in August 2021. These events concluded the first step in Phase 1. The use of learning elements, transparency, self-questioning and science-based criteria envisaged by the StandAG marked significant differences vis-a-vis the hard nuclear state approaches that previously shaped nuclear policy in Germany. Themann et al. (2021a, b, c) analysed the various events belonging to step 1 by conducting participatory, qualitative and quantitative observations based on the concept of *power over*, *power to* and *power with* (Partzsch 2017). The authors asked how power manifests itself while using the concept of the soft nuclear repository state as a normative orientation. They highlighted in particular heterogeneous public stakeholders, power asymmetries between state actors and civil society in the process, and the withdrawal of civil society actors who were not satisfied with the process.

Because the FKTG was not considered sufficient for the first phase of the site search, at the end of 2021 the Forum Endlagersuche was launched (Schwarz et al. 2021b). This, however, was not envisaged in the StandAG. The Forum is supposed to critically reflect on the work's progress and to discuss the way the state institutions develop siting regions for the coming phase of the procedure. It represents a forum for meeting, information, exchange, opinion-forming and co-shaping, with the goal to increase willingness to participate while providing an introduction to the topic of siting. As a preparatory step, members for the advisory and planning group of the Forum Endlagersuche were elected by the participants at a public event on 13 November, 2021. This group was kept in place until the first meeting/consultation of the Forum. BASE offered organisational support for the work of the forum and the advisory and planning group, and provide the resources necessary for the work.

In step 2 of Phase I, following publication of the interim report on the sub-regions, representative preliminary safety studies will be prepared for the sub-regions in question. According to § 27 of the StandAG, in the preliminary safety investigations the repository system is considered as a whole, and its safety is assessed in accordance with the state-of-the-art in science and technology. Preliminary safety investigations are key for the decision whether an area will be considered further in the selection procedure.

At the end of this complex assessment, the operator will propose to the regulator BASE siting regions to be explored above ground. The Bundestag and the Federal Council will then decide which siting regions are to be explored above ground. As soon as the siting regions have been designated by the BGE, BASE will initiate the establishment of so-called regional conferences. The regional conferences have extensive information and control rights in the further site selection procedure.

In Phase II, the BGE is expected to explore the siting regions whilst BASE reviews and approves these exploration programmes. On the basis of the exploration results, the BGE carries out further preliminary safety investigations according to the requirements and criteria defined in the StandAG. The BGE will then prepare socio-economic potential analyses in the siting regions, which will be discussed by the regional conferences. Subsequently, BASE will assess the proposals and determine exploration programmes and assessment criteria. At this point, the Bundestag and the Bundesrat will decide which sites are to be explored underground, and how. Thereupon, a judicial review is also possible before the Federal Administrative Court.

In Phase III, the underground exploration starts. The BGE explores the sites selected and prepares comprehensive preliminary safety assessments on the basis of the exploration results and the requirements and criteria defined in the StandAG. On the basis of the results, which also include a comparative assessment of the sites, BASE performs an environmental impact assessment.

In the final phase, BASE assesses the BGE proposal, considering all concerns and the results of the participation procedure, to determine the site with the best possible safety. BASE will then submit the site proposal to the Federal Ministry for the Environment and Nuclear Safety. The final decision on the site is taken by the Bundestag and the Bundesrat.[7]

5.6 Conclusions

The socio-technical complexity of the nuclear waste governance and multilevel structures indicate that the political regulation of siting a DGD cannot be based on a singular understanding of the problem. Within the various stakeholder groups, up to now the definition of the problem, the social perception and attitudes to problem-solving are highly divergent and have been shaped by the legacy of the past, formal as well as informal rules, and political constraints. In the past, as well as during the ongoing siting procedure for a DGD, political regulation and the interests of the state actors, in particular BASE and BGE, were brought to the fore. However, their preferences and logics of action did not always match the preferences and expectations of civil society and NGOs, who have been active in the anti-nuclear movement in Germany for decades.

A lot has been done; governance mechanisms to improve participation have been set-up and reinforced, whilst state actors endeavour to engage the interested public more intensively. The siting procedure is required to be self-questioning, science-based, reversible, transparent, mutually learning and fostering participation on an equal footing between state and civil society. However, as long as a number of stakeholders (in particular the environmental NGOs and civil society groups) continue to perceive the participation procedures as little more than unidirectional communication, the state institutions run the risk that once again civil society will distrust the entire process. In fact, the level of participation remained below expectation due to the withdrawal of NGOs such as the German Federation for the Environment and Nature Conservation (BUND) in the middle of the process in 2021, and low public interest in the first Beteiligungskonferenz in May

---

[7] For further details of all phases and steps, see the website of the operator BGE, https://www.bge.de/de/endlagersuche/standortauswahlverfahren/.

2022. Amongst the 300 participants from various stakeholder groups, only a little more than a dozen citizens took part in the event (BGE 2022).

Alongside the existing economic and technical problems, the root of the current difficult siting process is the way the various governments managed the siting process in the past. Consequently, politics and policies continue to be constrained by past development paths and events and stakeholders that have shaped this past. This continuity and persistence, combined with uncertainty and a long timeline are part of the difficult socio-technical challenges facing the siting process. In addition, the present development is characterised by the fact that as of December 2022, half of the area of Germany could still be suitable for siting, and therefore there is not yet a directly "affected" population. Yet, in the course of recent years, there have been changes within the state institutions and among civil society actors. Institutions are learning how important it is to take the concerns and fears of the potentially affected population and interest groups earnestly and give them a voice. This increases the chances for a debate that is taken seriously by all parties and can thus potentially lead to "acceptable" results. Moreover, the participation of younger generations as new actors in the process might open-up a new window of opportunity.

The site search process is proceeding along the trajectories of the StandAG, which defines the tasks for the involved actors and specifies all key criteria and requirements. Although the ongoing process is experiencing a stall, potentially there is some room for manoeuvre. Whilst the intention of the legislator was ground-breaking and forward-looking, the StandAG (2017) leaves extensive space for interpretation, and therefore implementation. The fact that the law leaves many issues open should not be considered as a flaw, but on the contrary as an opportunity to reflect on the success or failure of the current participation procedures and to influence the process towards an acceptable solution. It remains to be seen to what extent and with which formats the participation of interested people will be enabled.

Hocke and Brunnengräber (2019) have pointed out that more attention should be paid to the different national, regional and local levels of action. Novel forms of multi-level governance must be developed and implemented to ensure that the knowledge and concerns of civil society are actually listened to, taken up and integrated into state-driven and -steered processes. Initiatives at regional and local level are now forming and they demand a role and a voice in the process. For the next steps in the site selection procedure envisaged by the legislator, i.e. the Regional Conferences and the Council of the Regions (see Fig. 5.4), more far-reaching participation formats could be developed and coordinated. Further elements of a bottom-up approach could be integrated into the procedure.

In spite of the progress made, the DGD issue will remain a thorny matter for at least a century. We have learnt that a generally acceptable procedure depends on trust and willingness within civil society to cooperate with the state. Fairness and inclusiveness of the process remain important and necessary prerequisites for confidence-building, and for the acceptability of the siting decisions. Ultimately, even if the state actors (BASE and BGE) are perceived as independent, competent and credible, new forms of participation, and dialogue on an equal footing, remain key. The participation processes initiated in the first of the three phases of the site selection represent an initial step towards a potential historical course-setting, through which the "hard nuclear state" and the social polarisation of past decades can be overcome.

Despite all the criticism of the first phase of the site selection and the need for improvement, the fulfilment of this possibility is linked to the clarification of many downstream issues concerning state intervention in the process. At the same time, it is necessary to master a balancing act in the design of participation corridors. Whilst participation should be thematically focussed on the final disposal in order to do justice to complex challenges, it is paramount to open up new arenas for a transparent discourse. This challenging task needs to be mastered before phases II and III of the selection process begin.

References

AkEnd. (2002). Auswahlverfahren für Endlagerstandorte. Köln.
BASE. (2016). Waste types. BASE. https://www.base.bund.de/EN/nwm/waste/types/types_node.html;jsessionid=C10DFAEDF0A90497E3E69F67A5DD896C.1_cid391. Accessed 1 August 2022.
BASE. (2019). Unsere Forschungsstrategie. https://www.base.bund.de/SharedDocs/Downloads/BASE/DE/broschueren/bfe/forschungsstrategie_final.pdf?__blob=publicationFile&v=8. Accessed 23 November 2021.
BASE. (2020). Zwischenlager für hochradioaktive Abfälle: Sicherheit bis zur Endlagerung. Berlin.
BASE. (2021). Änderungsanträge zur Geschäftsordnung (FKT_Bt2_004). https://www.endlagersuche-infoplattform.de/SharedDocs/Downloads/Endlagersuche/DE/Fachkonferenz/Dok_FKT_2.Beratungstermin/FKT_Bt2_004_Aenderungsantraege_GO.pdf?__blob=publicationFile&v=4.
BfE. (2019). Information, Dialog, Mitgestaltung: Öffentlichkeitsbeteiligung in der Startphase der Endlagersuche. Berlin.
BGE. (n. d.). Types of waste and how they are generated. BGE. https://www.bge.de/en/radioactive-waste/types-of-waste-and-how-they-are-generated/.
BGE. (2020). Sub-areas Interim Report pursuant to Section 13 RSS-Act (StandAG). https://www.bge.de/en/sitesearch/sub-areas-interim-report/. Accessed 5 August 2021.

BGE. (2022). Meldung—Standortsuche: BGE-Geschäftsführer Steffen Kanitz betont den Wert der Beteiligung an der Methodenentwicklung. https://www.bge.de/de/aktuelles/meldungen-und-pressemitteilungen/meldung/news/2022/5/726-endlagersuche/. Accessed 1 August 2022.

Blowers, A. (2017). The Legacy of Nuclear Power. Oxon, New York: Routledge.

Blowers, A. (2019). The Legacy of Nuclear Power and What Should Be Done About It: Peripheral Communities and the Management of the Nuclear Legacy. In A. Brunnengräber & M. R. Di Nucci (Eds.), Conflicts, Participation and Acceptability in Nuclear Waste Governance: An International Comparison Volume III (pp. 55–68). Wiesbaden: Springer Fachmedien Wiesbaden.

Blowers, A., & Lowry, D. (1997). Nuclear conflict in Germany: The wider context. Environmental Politics, 6, 148–155. https://doi.org/10.1080/09644019708414345.

BMUV. (2021). Herkunft der in der Schachtanlage Asse II eingelagerten radioaktiven Abfälle und Finanzierung der Kosten: Hintergründe und Fakten. BMUV. https://www.bmuv.de/fileadmin/Daten_BMU/Download_PDF/Endlagerprojekte/hintergrundbericht_finanzierung_schachtanlage_asse_bf.pdf.

Brohmann, B., Brunnengräber, A., Hocke-Bergler, P., & Isidoro Losada, A. M. (Eds.). (2021). Robuste Langzeit-Governance bei der Endlagersuche—Soziotechnische Herausforderungen im Umgang mit hochradioaktiven Abfällen. Bielefeld: transcript.

Brunnengräber, A. (2019a). Ewigkeitslasten: Die "Endlagerung" radioaktiver Abfälle als soziales, politisches und wissenschaftliches Projekt (2nd ed.). Baden-Baden: Bundeszentrale für politische Bildung (BpB), Band 10361.

Brunnengräber, A. (2019b). The Wicked Problem of Long Term Radioactive Waste Governance: Ten Characteristics of a Complex Technical and Societal Challenge. In A. Brunnengräber & M. R. Di Nucci (Eds.), Conflicts, Participation and Acceptability in Nuclear Waste Governance: An International Comparison Volume III (335-355). Wiesbaden: Springer Fachmedien Wiesbaden.

Di Nucci, M. R. (2019). Voluntarism in Siting Nuclear Waste Disposal Facilities. In A. Brunnengräber & M. R. Di Nucci (Eds.), Conflicts, Participation and Acceptability in Nuclear Waste Governance (pp. 147–174, Energiepolitik und Klimaschutz. Energy Policy and Climate Protection). Wiesbaden: Springer Fachmedien Wiesbaden.

Di Nucci, M. R., Isidoro Losada, A. M., & Laes, E. (2021a). Institutionelle Herausforderungen bei der Endlagerung hochradioaktiver Abfälle. In B. Brohmann, A. Brunnengräber, P. Hocke-Bergler, & A. M. Isidoro Losada (Eds.), Robuste Langzeit-Governance bei der Endlagersuche—Soziotechnische Herausforderungen im Umgang mit hochradioaktiven Abfällen (pp. 265–297). Bielefeld: transcript.

Di Nucci, M. R., Isidoro Losada, A. M., & Themann, D. (2021b). Confidence gap or timid trust building? The role of trust in the evolution of the nuclear waste governance in Germany. Journal of Risk Research, 1–19.

Eckhardt, A., & Rippe, K. P. (2016). Risiko und Ungewissheit bei der Entsorgung hochradioaktiver Abfälle (1st ed.). Zürich: vdf Hochschulverlag.

Ehmke, W. (2020). Das Nationale Begleitgremium (NBG) ist komplett. https://www.bi-luechow-dannenberg.de/2020/03/23/das-nationale-begleitgremium-nbg-ist-komplett/. Accessed 1 August 2022.

EndKo. (2016). Verantwortung für die Zukunft- Ein faires und transparentes Verfahren für die Auswahl eines nationalen Endlagerstandortes: Abschlussbericht der Kommission Lagerung hoch radioaktiver Abfallstoffe .

European Council. (2011). Council Directive 2011/70/Euratom of 19 July 2011 establishing a Community framework for the responsible and safe management of spent fuel and radioactive waste. OJ L 199/48, 2 August 2011.

Gaßner, H., Groth, K.-M., & Siederer, W. u. C. (2018). Zum Verhältnis zwischen BGE und BfE im Standortauswahlverfahren: Rechtsgutachten im Auftrag der Bundesgesellschaft für Endlagerung mbH (BGE).

Häfner, D. (2016). Screening der Akteure im Bereich der Endlagerstandortsuche für hoch radioaktive Reststoffe in der Bundesrepublik Deutschland: Das "Who is who" eines sich verändernden Konfliktfeldes. ENTRIA-Arbeitsbericht-04 (Transversalprojekt Technikfolgenabschätzung und Governance). Berlin.

Hocke, P., & Brunnengräber, A. (2019). Multi-Level Governance of Nuclear Waste Disposal: Conflicts and Contradictions in the German Decision Making System. In A. Brunnengräber & M. R. Di Nucci (Eds.), Conflicts, Participation and Acceptability in Nuclear Waste Governance: An International Comparison Volume III (pp. 383–401). Wiesbaden: Springer Fachmedien Wiesbaden.

Hocke, P., & Kallenbach-Herbert, B. (2015). Always the Same Old Story?: Nuclear waste Governance in Germany. In A. Brunnengräber, M. R. Di Nucci, A. M. Isidoro Losada, L. Mez, & M. A. Schreurs (Eds.), Nuclear Waste Governance: An International Comparison (pp. 177–202, Energiepolitik und Klimaschutz. Energy Policy and Climate Protection). Wiesbaden: Springer VS.

Hocke, P., & Renn, O. (2009). Concerned public and the paralysis of decision-making: nuclear waste management policy in Germany. Journal of Risk Research, 12, 921–940.

Hocke, P., & Renn, O. (2011). Concerned Public and the Paralysis of Decision-Making: Nuclear Waste Management Policy in Germany. In U. Strandberg & M. Andrén (Eds.), Nuclear Waste Management in a Globalised World (pp. 43–62). Abingdon: Routledge.

Hocke, P., & Smeddinck, U. (2017). Robust-parlamentarisch oder informell-partizipativ? Die Tücken der Entscheidungsfindung in komplexen Verfahren. GAIA—Ecological Perspectives for Science and Society, 26, 125–128.

Isidoro Losada, A. M., Themann, D., & Di Nucci, M. R. (2019). Experts and Politics in the German Nuclear Waste Governance: Advisory Bodies between Ambition and Reality. In A. Brunnengräber & M. R. Di Nucci (Eds.), Conflicts, Participation and Acceptability in Nuclear Waste Governance: An International Comparison Volume III (pp. 231–259). Wiesbaden: Springer Fachmedien Wiesbaden.

Jungk, R. (1986). Der Atom-Staat: Vom Fortschritt in die Unmenschlichkeit (Rororo, 7288: rororo-Sachbuch). Reinbek bei Hamburg: Rowohlt.

Kamlage, J.-H., Warode, J., & Mengede, A. (2019). Chances, Challenges and Choices of Participation in Siting a Nuclear Waste Repository: The German Case. In A. Brunnengräber & M. R. Di Nucci (Eds.), Conflicts, Participation and Acceptability in Nuclear Waste Governance: An International Comparison Volume III (pp. 91–110). Wiesbaden: Springer Fachmedien Wiesbaden.

Kolb, F. (2007). Protest and Opportunities. The Political Outcomes of Social Movements. Frankfurt am Main: Campus Verlag.

Niedersächsische Staatskanzlei. (2021). Abo-Service Landeskabinett benennt Gesamtkoordinator für Rückholung der Asse-Fässer. Niedersächsische Staatskanzlei. https://www.stk.niedersachsen.de/startseite/presseinformationen/landeskabinett-benennt-gesamt-koordinator-fur-ruckholung-der-asse-fasser-196082.html. Accessed 1 August 2022.

OECD-NEA. (2010). Partnering for Long-Term Management of Radioactive Waste: Evolution and Current Practice in Thirteen Countries. Paris.

Partzsch, L. (2017). 'Power with' and 'power to' in environmental politics and the transition to sustainability. Environmental Politics, 26, 193–211.

Radkau, J. (2011). Eine kurze Geschichte der deutschen Antiatomkraftbewegung. Aus Politik und Zeitgeschichte (APuZ), 61(46–47), 7–15.

Radkau, J., & Hahn, L. (2013). Aufstieg und Fall der deutschen Atomwirtschaft. München: oekom.

Roth, R., & Rucht, D. (Eds.). (2008). Die sozialen Bewegungen in Deutschland seit 1945: ein Handbuch. Frankfurt am Main: Campus Verlag.

Rucht, D. (1980). Von Wyhl nach Gorleben. Bürger gegen Atomprogramm und nukleare Entsorgung. München: Beck.

Rucht, D. (2008). Anti-Atomkraftbewegung. In R. Roth & D. Rucht (Eds.), Die sozialen Bewegungen in Deutschland seit 1945: ein Handbuch (pp. 246–266). Frankfurt am Main: Campus Verlag.

Schreurs, M. A., & Suckow, J. (2019). Bringing Transparency and Voice into the Search for a Deep Geological Repository: Nuclear Waste Governance in Germany and the Role of the National Civil Society Board—Nationales Begleitgremium (NBG). In A. Brunnengräber & M. R. Di Nucci (Eds.), Conflicts, Participation and Acceptability in Nuclear Waste Governance: An International Comparison Volume III (pp. 293–310). Wiesbaden: Springer Fachmedien Wiesbaden.

Schwarz, L., Themann, D., & Brunnengräber, A. (2021a). Räume erobern, öffnen und verteidigen: Über die Wirkung von Macht beim dritten Beratungstermin der Fachkonferenz Teilgebiete. Forschungsjournal Soziale Bewegung Plus, 34(4).

Schwarz, L., Themann, D., & Brunnengräber, A. (2021b). Von Machtasymmetrien zu flachen Hierarchien im Standortsuchprozess für ein Endlager?: Über die Wirkung von Macht beim zweiten Beratungstermin der Fachkonferenz Teilgebiete. Forschungsjournal Soziale Bewegungen Plus, 34(3), 1–26.

Smeddinck, U. (2019). Sanfte Regulierung: Ressourcen der Konfliktlösung im Standortauswahlverfahren für ein Endlager. Deutsches Verwaltungsblatt(12), 744–751.

StandAG. (2017). Gesetz zur Fortentwicklung des Gesetztes zur Suche und Auswahl eines Standortes für ein Endlager für Wärme entwickelnde radioaktive Abfälle und anderer Gesetzte: StandAG.

Themann, D., Brunnengräber, A., Di Nucci, M.R., & Schwarz, L. (2021a). From a 'hard nuclear state' towards a 'soft nuclear repository state': Participation, Co-design, Learning, and Adaptation by the German 'Repository Site Selection Act'? ECPR.

Themann, D., Di Nucci, M. R., & Brunnengräber, A. (2021b). Alles falsch gemacht? Machtasymmetrien in der Öffentlichkeitsbeteiligung bei der Standortsuche für ein Endlager. Forschungsjournal Soziale Bewegung Plus, 34(1), 1–10.

Themann, D., Schwarz, L., Di Nucci, M. R., & Brunnengräber, A. (2021c). Power over, power with und power to bei der Standortsuche für ein Endlager: Über die Ausübung von Macht beim ersten Beratungstermin der Fachkonferenz Teilgebiete (FKTG). Forschungsjournal Soziale Bewegungen Plus, 34(3), 1–23.

Tiggemann, A. (2019). The Elephant in the Room: The Role of Gorleben and its Site Selection in the German Nuclear Waste Debate. In A. Brunnengräber & M. R. Di Nucci (Eds.), Conflicts, Participation and Acceptability in Nuclear Waste Governance: An International Comparison Volume III (pp. 69–87). Wiesbaden: Springer Fachmedien Wiesbaden.

World Nuclear Association. (2022). Nuclear Power in Germany. World Nuclear Association. https://www.world-nuclear.org/information-library/country-profiles/countries-g-n/germany.aspx. Accessed 1 August 2022.

Maria Rosaria Di Nucci is an energy economist and a senior researcher at the Department of Political and Social Sciences, Freie Universität Berlin. Currently she is the principal investigator of the Horizon 2020 research project COME RES on community energy. Previously she coordinated a Horizon 2020 project on acceptance of wind energy and cooperated in the project TRANSENS: "Transdisciplinary research on the management of high-level radioactive waste in Germany", and other projects on nuclear waste governance (ENTRIA and SOTEC-radio). She is co-editor of a number of volumes on nuclear waste issues and authored several articles on nuclear waste governance. Rosaria´s research interests comprise: Multi-level governance, regulation of energy markets, comparative nuclear and energy policy and politics, support instruments for renewable energy, acceptance of contested technologies.

Achim Brunnengräber is a political scientist and an Associate Professor at the Department of Political and Social Sciences, Freie Universität Berlin. At the Research Center for Sustainability (Forschungszentrum für Nachhaltigkeit, FFN) he presently coordinates the research project TRANSENS: "Transdisciplinary research on the management of high-level radioactive waste in Germany" (transens.de). Additionally, he was engaged in other projects on nuclear waste governance (ENTRIA and SOTEC- radio). He is co-editor of a number of volumes on nuclear waste issues and has authored numerous articles on nuclear waste governance. His research and teaching interests comprise: Global governance, multi-level governance and socio-ecological transformation. His special focus is on nuclear policy, national, European and global energy, environmental, renewable and climate policy and politics.

Open Access This chapter is licensed under the terms of the Creative Commons Attribution 4.0 International License (http://creativecommons.org/licenses/by/4.0/), which permits use, sharing, adaptation, distribution and reproduction in any medium or format, as long as you give appropriate credit to the original author(s) and the source, provide a link to the Creative Commons license and indicate if changes were made.

The images or other third party material in this chapter are included in the chapter's Creative Commons license, unless indicated otherwise in a credit line to the material. If material is not included in the chapter's Creative Commons license and your intended use is not permitted by statutory regulation or exceeds the permitted use, you will need to obtain permission directly from the copyright holder.

6 The Melancholic Lock: High-Level Radioactive Waste Governance in Spain

Josep Espluga-Trenc and Ana Prades

6.1 Introduction

Nuclear waste management shows the Spanish evolution from top-down, unidirectional strategies applied in the earlier decades since the 1960s, to more comprehensive, bidirectional and participative approaches for interacting with society since the end of the 1990s. The internalisation of European Directives has increasingly required more public transparency and openness to citizen participation. This has been reflected in the approach to managing the location of the repository for high-level nuclear waste (HLW), so far without success due to the peculiar structure of the nuclear conflict in Spain, which relegates the role of science and technology to marginal positions in the debate. This process, initiated in 2004 by national politics but as yet unfinished, illustrates the challenges that inclusive nuclear waste governance entails in a country with a multi-level governance system, characterised by a complex and intertwined political decision-making process, where the nuclear issue is used instrumentally by political parties (for electoral purposes), and in a social context with highly sceptical public opinion towards nuclear energy.

J. Espluga-Trenc (✉)
Institute of Government and Public Policies (IGOP) & Department of Sociology, Universitat Autònoma de Barcelona, Barcelona, Spain
e-mail: joseplluis.espluga@uab.cat

A. Prades
Socio-technical Research Centre (CISOT-CIEMAT), Centro de Investigaciones Energéticas, Medio Ambientales y Tecnológicas (CIEMAT), Barcelona, Spain
e-mail: ana.prades@ciemat.es

© The Author(s) 2023
M. Arentsen and R. van Est (eds.), *The Future of Radioactive Waste Governance*, Energiepolitik und Klimaschutz. Energy Policy and Climate Protection, https://doi.org/10.1007/978-3-658-40496-3_6

The Spanish institutional context leaves little room for fact-based argumentation based on experience. In this way, instead of opening up the nuclear issue to a broad public debate, counter-expertise has tended to be excluded from formal debates, finding its leading role in social conflicts outside institutional frameworks. Factors leading to public acceptance of radioactive waste repositories go beyond the competence and capabilities of Spanish institutions, since none of them is in a position to prevail in the political game and prevent the partisan use of the nuclear waste issue, which means that, no matter how much technical data they can offer, this will never be enough to win the public's trust. As we will see in this chapter, without substantial structural changes in the Spanish political and institutional system, the conflicts surrounding nuclear waste management will continue for a long time.

6.2 The Spanish Nuclear Program in Context

Despite being a relatively poor country under a dictatorship regime, Spain belonged in the mid-1950s to the group of pioneering nuclear countries, connecting its first nuclear reactor to the grid by 1968. This happened due to the full support of the government, the commitment of the private utilities which controlled the oligopolistic electricity market, and the transfer of technology and funds, mostly from the United States but also from France and Germany (Rubio-Varas et al., 2018). The geopolitical position of the Spanish dictatorship (Francoism) during the first part of the Cold-War period (1947–1962) favoured its integration into the Western-capitalistic bloc, allowing international recognition of the regime and access to US commercial funds and technology in exchange for American military sites in Spain, among other diplomatic commitments.

An ambitious nuclear programme, set up in the 1960s and 1970s, foresaw the construction of almost 40 nuclear reactors. By the mid-1970s, the government pre-authorised the installation of over 15,000 MWe. Yet, a combination of economic, political and social factors led to the contraction of the Spanish nuclear program to only 10 reactors connected to the grid by 1988, with just over 7,500 Mwe; at that time around 35% of national electricity consumption. The 7 reactors still in operation in 2022 provide about 20% of Spanish electricity.

The early nuclear projects faced barely any opposition. Yet competing uses of territory and resources (tourism along the coast, and agricultural water needs inland) brought critical voices and administrative complaints through the late 1960s and 1970s (Lemkow, 1984; Rubio-Varas et al., 2018). The dictatorship regime forbade civil activism, but informal and unstructured social antinuclear groups arose from the mid-1970s, led by a handful of people, mainly to defend local livelihoods such as tourism and agriculture (Costa Morata, 2001).

The oil crises in the 1970s contracted the economy and the expected electricity demand, increasing the financial burden of nuclear projects and making them unsustainable for the private utilities. So, beyond the social critical voices at the local and regional level, the national and international economic and political cycle played a crucial role in slowing and eventually paralysing the expansion of the Spanish nuclear program. The economic crisis was paired with the uncertainties of the transition to democracy (1977–1982), and the nuclear program was drastically reduced in 1979 by the first elected parliament in 40 years.

In this context, democratic Spain emerged as one of the societies most opposed to nuclear power in Europe, with a latent public opposition acknowledged by all actors (Espluga et al., 2017; Rubio-Varas et al., 2018). Nuclear development was targeted for a long time as a dictatorship project, so the popular struggle against nuclear energy (expanding throughout the Western world since the Three Mile Island incident in the US in 1979) was equated with the struggle against Francoism. All the left-wing opposition political parties relied on the antinuclear flag (despite the fact that some of them had been earlier supporters of nuclear energy). This sociopolitical dynamic influenced the public image of nuclear energy in Spain for decades, and is still shaping some of the contemporary responses to radioactive waste management.

In 1984, the Spanish government, then ruled by the socialist party (PSOE), approved a moratorium for the nuclear programme, for which the private utilities obtained large compensation. After the abandonment of the programme, the nuclear industry opted to keep a low public profile, focusing its efforts on taking advantage of the accumulated technical expertise and human capital, becoming a strong international player in engineering services and components. The moratorium generated some local and national debate during the 1980s, yet waste management and the reactor lifetime extensions remained the only truly contentious issues in recent times.

Much of these debates have been related to the search for a location for a centralised repository (Almacén Temporal Centralizado; ATC), an unfinished process that has been greatly influenced by deep-rooted institutional mistrust, in a country with a complex multi-level governance system that favours permanent tensions between central and regional governments, whose political parties tend to leverage comparative grievances in the distribution of risks and benefits between regions or territories, often for instrumental purposes.

Although it has been possible to establish a permanent site for low- and medium-level nuclear waste (LILW), it has not been possible so far to do the

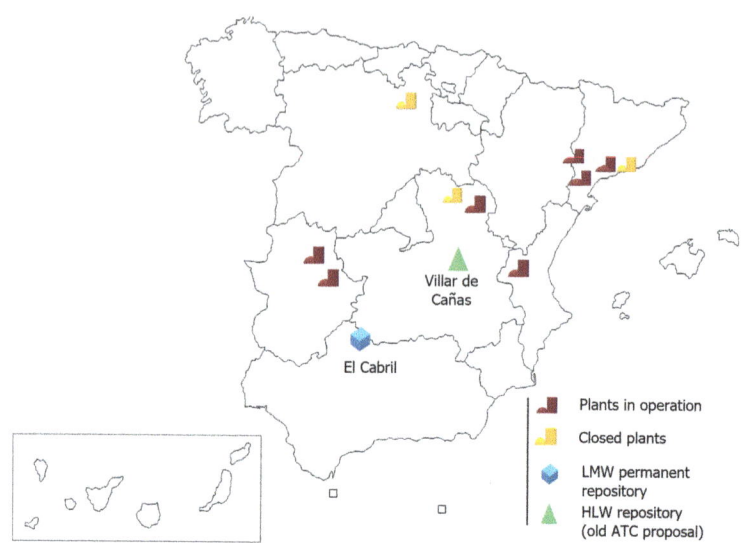

Fig. 6.1 Spanish nuclear power plants and waste repositories sites. (Source: authors)

same for HLW. An ambitious plan to build a centralised temporary warehouse, which could house all this type of waste, started almost two decades ago, and has been the subject of numerous vicissitudes and social and political conflicts, so that it remains a pending and difficult issue to solve (Fig. 6.1).

6.3 Evolution of Radioactive Waste Management in Spain

The generation of radioactive waste in Spain began in the 1950s as a result of early research into the use of radioactive isotopes in medicine, industry and agriculture, as well as in particular research centres. Since 1968, nuclear power plants (NPPs) have become the main source of radioactive waste production, due both to normal operation and the dismantling of some NPPs. Spain currently has 7 reactors in operation, in 5 locations. In addition, there are 3 shut down reactors, which are in different administrative situations (figure 6.1). The Vandellós I NPP, which ceased operation in October 1989 after a serious incident, is currently in a dormant phase after partial decommissioning, pending total decommissioning. The José Cabrera NPP (a.k.a. Zorita) ended operation in April 2006, and is currently in the total decommissioning phase. The Santa María de Garoña NPP, which has been shut down since December 2012, ceased operation in August 2017, pending decommissioning.

Other radioactive waste-generating facilities in Spain include a fuel assembly factory, research centres, universities, hospitals, industries, etc. The uranium oxide fuel assembly factory for light-water reactors (LWRs)—like pressurised water reactors (PWRs), their Russian counterpart Vodo-Vodjanoi Energetitsjeski Reactor (VVERs), and boiling water reactors (BWRs)—located in Juzbado, Salamanca province, started operation in 1985, with an annual production capacity of about 500 tons of enriched uranium (by 5%) (MITERD, 2020, p. 19). In addition, the public National Radioactive Waste Company, (Empresa Nacional de Residuos Radioactivos; ENRESA), has signed collection contracts with 934 Spanish companies and facilities, and also manages waste from conventional companies, mainly from the steel industry and metal recovery (MITERD, 2020, p. 19).

It is also necessary to manage spent nuclear fuel (SNF) produced by all Spanish NPPs, both those in operation and those in shutdown, with the exception of the SNF produced at the Vandellós I NPP, which was sent to La Hague (France) to be reprocessed and should have been returned to Spain years ago.

In Spain, LILW has had a consolidated and efficient management system for years. But that is not the case with regard to HLW, the management of which is still a pending issue, and likely to be troublesome in the future, as is also the case in most countries with nuclear installations (Di Nucci et al. 2018).

6.3.1 Low- and Intermediate-Level Radioactive Waste: Learning on the Job

The management of LILW in Spain is based on an integral and consolidated system with a centralised permanent repository in El Cabril, a former uranium mine located in the municipality of Hornachuelos, in the Province of Córdoba. El Cabril dates back to 1935 when uranium ore was discovered, intensively exploited from the 1940s until its closure in 1959, and had informally operated as a repository since the 1960s. From 1961, the Nuclear Energy Board (JEN) started to use the former uranium mine for storing low-level radioactive waste (LLW). Storage was first regulated by the Nuclear Energy Law of 1964. In October 1975, El Cabril was formally licensed as a deposit for radioactive waste, with more than 3000 drums already stored (Rubio-Varas et al., 2018), and it was at this time, when the existence of the deposit became public, that the first social protests took place.

In the 1990s, the waste stored at El Cabril was moved from the mine into new buildings, becoming a near-surface disposal facility with engineering barriers, taking the French Centre de L'Aube as reference. Designed by INITEC Nuclear (Westinghouse Electric Spain), preparatory work started in 1986, construction in January 1990, and authorisation for start-up was granted in October 1992. ENRESA, the public company in charge of radioactive waste management, has operated El Cabril since then, when it began to receive LILW. El Cabril is considered by the United States Nuclear Regulatory Commission (NRC) as a good model for other countries (ENRESA, 2017).

As of 2018, it is calculated that more than three quarters of the low-, very low- and medium-level waste generated in Spain are permanently deposited in El Cabril (69% of the 22,457 m^3 of radioactive waste of very low activity, and 83% of the 40,300 m^3 of LILW) (MITERD, 2020, pp. 20–21).

Six decades of operation of the El Cabril repository has entailed different phases and types of management, from initial secrecy, through timid attempts at transparency in the 1990s, to the recent implementation of deliberative actions with local society. In this sense, the management of LILW has been an interesting learning field for all the involved institutions (also for civil society and social movements). The sparse available evidence on public perception indicates that, at first, in a context of lack of information and, consequently, distrust towards ENRESA, the facility was perceived as being imposed on local residents. The media echoed this distrust, emphasising the fear of the unknown. The Anti Cabril movement, supported by environmentalists, politicians and trades unions, argued that the facility has hindered the development of the region. This opposition included anti-ENRESA demonstrations outside the main entrance of El Cabril (years 1987–1989).

During the licensing process of El Cabril in the late 1980s and early 1990s, the legislation in force requested an environmental impact assessment to evaluate the suitability of the site. That assessment was carried out in the context of the construction authorisation of an existing facility which was expanded. A number of local institutions were involved in this communication process, although the Town Council played the main role. One of the first actions was the opening of an information bureau to explain the details of the disposal facility, and its socioeconomic impacts (such as job-related opportunities, and requirements for workers and contractors). In this way, ENRESA, in collaboration with the local authorities, provided training to the local population and gave priority to local companies in any service contract (Molina, 1996).

From 1989, ENRESA commissioned several studies to track public perceptions of the facility and its economic and social impacts in the area (in 2009, 2010 and 2014). In addition, the Chair on Sustainability created at Cordoba University in 1996, has been active in promoting deliberative workshops in the area of influence of El Cabril (Local Encounters for Sustainable Development; ELDS). Thus, stakeholders who believed they could contribute to the sustainable development of their villages were invited to present opinions and proposals and discuss them with local institutions, including ENRESA.

In terms of economic compensation, measures to provide financial allocations to the municipalities have been in force since 1988. Such financial allocations were taken from the Fund to perform the activities of the General Radioactive Waste Plan (Plan General de Residuos Radioactivos; PGRR), managed by ENRESA. Besides Hornachuelos (the municipality hosting El Cabril), the Spanish legislation provides financial allocations to villages located up to 8 km from the facility. Studies on the economic impact of El Cabril indicate a positive effect. This indicator is manifested in the index of job creation and the impact on the remuneration of the work of residents in the local municipalities, as well as the direct allocations linked to the operating company ENRESA (Rubio-Varas et al., 2018).

Key findings from the local participatory workshops show that the original local rejection was mainly based on the perceived negative socio-economic impact in nearby villages, which felt they were not sufficiently compensated. Notably, dissatisfaction was not limited to El Cabril, with other local matters also perceived to be restricting the sustainable development of the area (public policies on natural environment or rural development). The environmental mediation led by the local university allowed the integration of ENRESA's representatives in local debates for the first time. This change in the institutional image of ENRESA fostered the creation of the 'Group for active social dialogue towards local sustainable development'. Tensions were reduced, and smooth interactions were promoted between ENRESA and local residents. Finally, following suggestions by the ELDS-mediators, any change in El Cabril activities that may provoke social destabilisation or damage the fruitful relationship between ENRESA and the local communities would require special communication and engagement actions at the local level. In fact, although with a low profile, new and limited social opposition appeared when the economic funds transferred to the municipalities in the area were reduced from 2014 onwards.

Recent debates on lengthening the operating time for Spanish NPPs has put local social movements on the defensive, as they fear the repository will receive more waste than planned. This fear is coupled with concern that the Spanish government is unable to find a place to store HLW, and that HLW will also be deposited in El Cabril in the long term. This, together with the reduction of economic funds for nearby municipalities, has reactivated local opposition to El Cabril in recent times (since 2014), although the social climate is still calm and the facility can operate normally (Table 6.1).

Table 6.1 Decision-making process around low- and intermediate-level radioactive waste management in Spain

Time	Event
1951	Establishment of the Spanish Nuclear Energy Board (Junta de Energía Nuclear, JEN)
1961	The Nuclear Energy Board (JEN) started to use the former uranium mine in El Cabril (Córdoba) for storing low-level radioactive waste. No regulation at that time
1964	Nuclear Energy Law, first attempt to regulate nuclear waste storage
1975	El Cabril was formally licensed as a deposit for radioactive waste (ending the period of illegality). Start of early social protest
1978	New democratic system in Spain led to the adoption of international standards on nuclear management. Increasing social protests against El Cabril
1980	Establishment of National Safety Council (CSN), independent regulatory body
1984	(scientific body) and the Sociedad Estatal de Participaciones Industriales (SEPI) (a conglomerate of public companies that depend on the government)
1986	Establishment of the Center for Energy, Environment and Technical Research (CIEMAT), the scientific body ENRESA takes over the El Cabril facilities
1988	Start of economic compensation for the surrounding municipalities
1992	Start of operation of the new near surface disposal site (inspired by the French Centre of l'Aube) Start of a new phase of social protest mobilisations (lasting several years)
1996	Setting of El Cabril Information Center
2004–2012	Deliberative workshops with local society (led by the ENRESA Chair of the University of Córdoba)
2008	Facilities expanded with complementary modules
2016	Facilities expanded again with more complementary modules

6.3.2 High-Level Radioactive Waste: The Great Unfinished Business

The situation for HLW is quite different. After decades without planning or taking any action, the 6th Spanish Plan for the Management of Radioactive Waste (released in 2006) considered the centralised temporary waste store (ATC) as a suitable transitional strategy for the management of HLW and SNF (MITC, 2006). It was argued that the ATC option was economically, strategically and technically better than the Individualised Temporary Stores at the NPPs, as it provides more time to adopt 'final solutions' and reduces the number of nuclear installations.

The decision to build the ATC seems to be initially related to the Spanish Government's obligation to prepare the return of radioactive waste reprocessed in France (with a contract expired in 2011) (Costa Morata & Baños, 2010), originated by the dismantling of the Vandellós I NPP (13 m^3 of vitrified HLW). Thus, the Spanish Parliament approved in December 2004 a resolution urging the government to solve this pressing problem by installing an ATC. It was assumed that the ATC would provide the system with a framework of sufficient reliability and flexibility during the time necessary for the development of the definitive management program (MITERD, 2020, pp. 23–24). To this end, the government created an Inter-ministerial Commission (IC) and a Dialogue Table to determine the most suitable location; a complex process illustrative of the sociopolitical conditioning factors of nuclear management in Spain, which is analysed (Sect. 6.3) from a governance-ecosystem perspective (Kool et al., 2017).

Meanwhile, SNF has been temporarily deposited in the storage pools of NPPs and in individual dry warehouses (Temporary Individual Warehouses; ATI) located in the NPPs. Despite the absence of a more definitive location, the government always warned that these ATIs were only complementary to ATC, not substitutes. However, in November 2022, the Spanish Ministry of Ecological Transition published a amended version of the 7th General Plan for Radioactive Waste draft. In this new versión, the centralized temporary warehouse (ATC) project seems to be definitively rejected, and replaced by seven decentralized temporary repositories (ATD), one for each nuclear plants site. These decentralized temporary warehouses will include, in an expanded form, the current individual temporary warehouses (ATI) of the respective nuclear plants. The 7th General Plan for Radioactive Waste is (Februrary 2023) still pending approval by the Spanish Parliament, so it is not definitive yet, although it seems reasonable to think that it will remain as it is now.

On December 31, 2018, the total volume of nuclear fuel elements in the NPP pools or the ATIs was approximately 7300 m^3. Forecasts indicate that the 7 reactors in operation will produce an additional 3100 m^3 of HLW. Altogether, it is expected that those with high activity will account for 4% of the total volume of radioactive waste in Spain (MITERD, 2020, p. 29).

6.4 The Actors

Following the scheme proposed by Kool et al. (2017, p. 95), in this section we describe the main actors corresponding to the four social domains of the governance-ecosystem: politics & administration, laws and regulations, science & technology, and civil society. Later, we address the complex interactions between these actors and domains around the ATC development, which have led to the current situation of political stalemate.

6.4.1 Politics and Administration

The political and administrative actors involved in the management of radioactive waste in Spain have evolved over time. In a first phase, during the Francoist dictatorship, everything related to nuclear energy was managed by a single institution of a military nature, the Spanish Nuclear Energy Board (Junta de Energía Nuclear, JEN), formally created in 1951. With the transition to a democratic regime, with the Spanish Constitution of 1978 and after the dissolution of the JEN, several key institutions were created to adapt the sector to international standards, which are those in force today.

In 1980, the Nuclear Safety Council (Consejo de Seguridad Nuclear; CSN) was set up as the regulator of the Spanish nuclear sector. It is a public body, independent from the General State Administration, with legal personality and its own assets, and is not accountable to the government, but to the Spanish Parliament. The mission of the CSN is to protect workers, the population and the environment from the harmful effects of ionising radiation, ensuring that nuclear and radioactive facilities are operated safely by licensees, and establishing prevention and correction measures against radiological emergencies. It has the power to propose regulations on nuclear safety and radiological protection to the government, and to adapt the national legislation to international requirements. The CSN can also dictate mandatory regulations, which may determine the immediate cessation of the activity of nuclear facilities. The Plenary board of the CSN is made up of a president and four councillors, normally well-known experts, who are elected for six years after consultation with the Industry Commission of the Spanish Parliament. This institutional design favours substantial changes in its composition, depending on the ruling parties at each legislative stage.

At present, the Ministry for the Ecological Transition and the Demographic Challenge (MITERD, formerly the Ministry of Industry) is in charge of the radioactive waste management policy of the Spanish Government, with particular prominence by the Secretary of State for Energy, and the Secretary of State for the Environment.

The other two basic institutions in the field of radioactive waste management are ENRESA, established in 1984, and the Center for Energy, Environmental and Technological Research (CIEMAT), created in 1986 as a public body dedicated to R&D on energy and its environmental impacts. These institutions, due to their design, function in a coordinated manner, the first being a management body and the second a research body.

ENRESA was established to provide services and special facilities for storage, transportation, disposal and handling of radioactive waste. It was set up as a state-owned limited liability company, independent of waste producers, and is supervised by the government. It also deals with decommissioning disused nuclear and radioactive facilities and the environmental restoration of uranium mines. ENRESA's shareholders are CIEMAT and the Sociedad Estatal de Participaciones Industriales (SEPI) (a conglomerate of public companies that depend on the government). ENRESA is obliged to periodically inform the Spanish Parliament on its activities and projects, to express its legislative needs, and to report on technological innovations that arise in its field of action. ENRESA is funded by the contribution of companies that generate radioactive waste and, ultimately, by citizens through the electricity bill.

6.4.2 Science and Technology

The main scientific institution in Spain producing knowledge about radioactive waste management is CIEMAT, although ENRESA has a wide scientific competence and devotes important resources to R&D activities too. It is important to keep in mind that the activities of these two entities are strongly interrelated.

Both CIEMAT and ENRESA, in collaboration with various research groups (mainly from the Polytechnic Universities of Madrid, Barcelona, Valencia, among others), have developed an important scientific-technical program around nuclear energy, including waste. For example, since 1987 numerous studies have been carried out on the geology of Spanish territory and its different types of lithologies (in particular granite, clay and salt), to propose designs for deep geological storages, and evaluate the behaviour of the land in the very long-term (MITERD, 2020), which has allowed the establishment of potential territorial areas to host a future deep geological repository.

These scientific groups have also participated in the dismantling of uranium ore treatment facilities (such as the old uranium factory in Andújar/Jaén, or La Haba/Badajoz and Saelices el Chico/Salamanca), as well as the restoration of mining operations, the deferred partial dismantling of the Vandellós I nuclear NPP, the closure of two research reactors (Argos, in Barcelona, and Arbi, in Bilbao), or the dismantling of research facilities of CIEMAT itself (PIMIC plan). Since 2010, they have been involved in the dismantling of the José Cabrera NPP.

Two research areas in CIEMAT explicitly address the issue of nuclear waste. The Scientific Area of Ionising Radiations carries out Research and Development plus Innovation (R&D+i) programmes and technical services related to radiological protection of the public and the environment. Their expertise is on methodologies for the recovery and rehabilitation of contaminated land, and on processes that affect the migration/retention of radionuclides in the natural environment or in radioactive waste storage barriers. The CIEMAT Nuclear Fission Area provides scientific and technical support to the management of radioactive waste, through activities such as its radiological and physicochemical characterisation, or the analysis and evaluation of the stability and separation of high-activity waste from nuclear irradiated materials.

As far as radiological characterisation is concerned, non-destructive methods for determining the activity in medium-to-low activity waste containers are being developed and applied at CIEMAT itself (as support to other divisions and decommissioning), at ENRESA-El Cabril Storage Centre, and at Spanish NPPs. Destructive characterisation methods have also been developed, and sample and chemical separation procedures are being applied to over 20 low and/or medium-energy alpha, pure beta and gamma radionuclide emitters, in addition to spectrometric procedures for high-energy.

In the field of HLW, CIEMAT carries out research on the stability of high-activity waste (irradiated nuclear fuels) under storage conditions (temporary or final), and studies radionuclide separation. Thus, CIEMAT provides scientific and technological support to the main Spanish nuclear entities, mainly NPPs and ENRESA.

ENRESA also dedicates part of its activities to scientific-technical research. ENRESA's 8th Research and Development Plan (2019–2023) is divided into four technical work areas and a fifth horizontal one: i) activities related to the physical and chemical properties of the components of radioactive waste, as well as their temporal evolution and the influence of their irradiation history; ii) actions related to the conditioning of radioactive waste before its deposit, to reduce its volume and radiotoxicity, or those other actions applicable to the dismantling of nuclear or radioactive facilities; iii) materials and containment systems, with the aim of acquiring and expanding knowledge and technologies related to the materials used in storage facilities as barriers between the waste and the biosphere, such as cement, clays, metals, etc., considered both individually and collectively; and iv) radiation protection and safety studies, such as improvement of the numerical models used in evaluations of the safety of storage facilities in the short-, medium- and long-term. Additionally, ENRESA has developed activities of support, coordination and knowledge management, in order to integrate existing research results and transfer them to potential recipients (scientific-technological dissemination).

ENRESA currently has the Mestral Technological Center, dealing with the dismantling and decommissioning project for the Vandellós I NPP in Tarragona, whose lines of research are related to the exchange of experiences in the dismantling of nuclear facilities. In the future, ENRESA plans to start up another Technology Center associated with the hypothetical ATC, with the aim of developing the R&D projects necessary for the correct management of SNF. This is one of the main assets argued to convince potential host municipalities that the ATC will mean the creation of quality jobs in the area.

Given the "long periods of management, development, operation and surveillance" (MITERD, 2020, p. 85) inherent to the management of radioactive waste, ENRESA expresses serious concern about the management of the knowledge generated through the different R&D programs. A design of institutional mechanisms to ensure knowledge transfer to new generations of technicians (from ENRESA itself) has already been suggested.

In addition, both ENRESA and CIEMAT participate in initiatives and projects of international organisations such as NEA/OECD and IAEA, and other national and European R&D forums related to the generation of knowledge on radioactive waste management. In addition, both institutions actively participate in the Spanish R&D platforms CEIDEN (Fission Nuclear Energy Technology Platform), PEPRI (National R&D Platform in Radiological Protection), and in the European IGD-TP (European Platform for geological storage), SNE-TP (European Platform for Sustainable Fission Energy), as well as other European R&D platforms in radiation protection.

6.4.3 Laws and Regulations

The legislative domain plays an important role in the long-term governance of nuclear waste management. Directives of the Council of the European Union (Council Directive 2011/70/Euratom of 19 July 2011 establishing a Community framework for the responsible and safe management of spent fuel and radioactive waste; and Council Directive 2009/71/Euratom of 25 June 2009 establishing a Community framework for the nuclear safety of nuclear installations) impose a series of obligations for the establishment of a national nuclear safety framework applied to nuclear installations.

In Spain, the Law 25/1964, of April 29, on nuclear energy (LEN), contains the requirements and basic principles for the management of radioactive waste, providing that the management of radioactive waste and SNF, and the dismantling and closure of nuclear facilities, constitute an essential public service that is reserved to the ownership of the State, as stated in the Spanish Constitution of 1978 (Article 128.2). ENRESA is entrusted with the management of such public service, its activities and financing system, as set out in Royal Decree 102/2014, of February 21, for the responsible and safe management of spent fuel and radioactive waste. The financing system of this public service consists of a system of four rates, due to the producers of radioactive waste. Law 24/2005 of November 18, of reforms to boost productivity, regulates the fees for the provision of its services, the collection of which will be used to provide the Fund for the financing of the activities of the General Radioactive Waste Plan (PGRR).

The government is responsible for approving the regulatory developments of the laws approved by Parliament, and MITERD is currently the ministerial department in charge of processing regulatory proposals in the field of nuclear energy. When the proposals refer to matters that may affect nuclear safety or radiological protection, the initiative corresponds to the CSN, which transmits the proposals to MITERD for processing.

The PGRR collects the strategies and activities to be carried out in Spain in relation to radioactive waste, the dismantling of facilities and its economic-financial study. It is approved by the government and is periodically reviewed and updated. Since ENRESA was created in 1984, there have been six PGRRs, which have set the lines of action and objectives for a comprehensive waste management system that the company has been developing and implementing. The 6th PGRR, currently in force and approved in 2006, was the first to undergo a public information and consultation process with the Autonomous Communities (regional governments). This illustrates the changes in the radioactive waste management practices in Spain over time. This PGRR established the need for an ATC for the management of SNF and HLW generated in Spain.

In more detail, the 6th PGRR (MITC, 2006) contemplates the following strategies:

- Maintaining LILW management, in particular to the definitive storage in El Cabril.
- Maintaining the unified temporary management strategy for spent fuel, HLW and special waste in a single facility, the most important milestone being the start-up of the ATC.
- Providing additional radioactive waste storage capacity in those NPPs requiring it (either in operation or decommissioning), while the ATC is not built.
- Developing technological and social acceptance capabilities to guide and implement the future definitive storage solution for high-activity radioactive waste and SNF in a Deep Geological Warehouse (AGP, by Almacenamiento Geológico Profundo, in Spanish).
- Maintenance of the dismantling and closure strategy of nuclear facilities until the release of their sites in the shortest possible time, in accordance with the criteria of minimising doses and protecting human health and the environment.

The recent draft of the 7th Radioactive Waste Management Plan (still preliminary and pending approval) establishes that most of these strategic approaches will continue to be valid in the future and, consequently, will remain as the foundation of the new PGRR, varying its timeframe (MITERD, 2020). However, in November 2022, the MITERD aproved a new updated versión of the 7th PGRR draft, with the great novelty that the centralized temporary storage (ATC) is left aside, and instead it is proposed to create seven decentralized temporary repositories, one at each nuclear site. It is a temporary strategy with the purpose of finding a deep geological storage for the year 2073.

6.4.4 Civil Society

Spanish public opinion tends to be largely anti-nuclear. The scant longitudinal evidence at the country level (based on data from Eurobarometer and the Spanish Sociological Research Center, ranging from the early 1990s to the present) shows that the majority of Spaniards (around 2/3) tend to be against nuclear energy (Espluga et al., 2017). Data from the last Eurobarometer on public attitudes towards nuclear (Eurobarometer, 2010) shows 73% of Spaniards consider that NPPs represent a risk rather than a benefit. Spain shows the highest percentage, together with Greece and France, which all score above the 52% average for Europe.

After the turbulent decades of the 1970s and 1980s, with numerous antinuclear mobilisations during the transition to democracy, from the 1990s the social pressure decreased considerably. In recent years, the most intense popular mobilisations in this field have been directed against the ATC site. The announcement of the participatory procedure for the location of the ATC in 2006 (see below) triggered numerous local social movements, either for or against, depending on the interests they claimed to defend. At the same time, the main environmental organisations, such as Greenpeace, Ecologistas en Acción, or Amigos de la Tierra (local branch of Friends of the Earth), actively re-engaged in the social conflicts related to nuclear energy, which originally gave them prominence in the 1980s and allowed their expansion and consolidation as large and influential environmental social movements. These processes will be further developed in the following sections.

Another key actor representing civil society is the Association of Municipalities Affected by Nuclear Power Plants (AMAC). Formed in 1990, it brings together a series of municipalities geographically close to the Spanish NPPs, to demand greater safety measures and guarantees of future economic diversification. Although AMAC has become a key actor in the Spanish nuclear sector, some authors consider it is not a classic environmental social movement, as it tends to instrumentalise a process based on "(1) arguing fear and unsafety, (2) asking for money and investments and, after obtaining it, (3) prolong this spiral strategy, exploiting the circumstances to the maximum and always bartering, ultimately, material compensation in exchange for their conformity with regard to nuclear safety. In short, it thus becomes an invaluable aid to the nuclear sector; companies, Government and, singularly, ENRESA" (Costa Morata & Baños, 2010, pp. 153–154). However, AMAC claims that a large part of its activity focuses on generating alternative economic paths, and that it has established fruitful and sustainable economic development programmes in all nuclear areas. AMAC provides consultancy and coordination services to facilitate access opportunities that may arise, for example, in the current context of the energy transition. AMAC has been a pioneer of exchanges between nuclear municipalities in different European countries, and as such was a leading promoter of a network of European nuclear municipalities known as GMF (Group of European Municipalities with Nuclear Facilities). In any case, AMAC has become a powerful actor without whom it is very difficult to legitimise decisions on nuclear issues, especially in relation to the management of radioactive waste.

6.5 High-Level Nuclear Waste Management: The Vicissitudes of the ATC

The 2006 6th PGRR, drawn up by ENRESA, gave priority to the ATC. Notably, a major requirement was that the decision-making process should comply with the principles of voluntarism, transparency and openness; something really new in the nuclear management approach in Spain. This is a substantial milestone, when issues like transparency, trust, and reliable information and communication—including new forms of engagement and participation—became essential elements for the new institutions in their communication strategies and missions for interacting with society. Lessons learnt at El Cabril repository could probably contribute to inspire this new approach.

In this context, a relevant antecedent was the creation of the Dialogue Board for the evolution of nuclear energy in Spain ("Mesa sobre energía nuclear") in 2005. The Dialogue Board was chaired by the General Secretary of Energy and included representatives from all political parties in Congress and Senate, public bodies in charge of nuclear, environmental and industrial matters, trade unions, municipalities, consumers and environmental groups. The Dialogue Board concluded that the ATC was a need for the country, with only the environmental groups disagreeing. It should be noted that as long as there are NPPs in operation in the country, the Spanish environmental groups refuse to participate in any negotiation on waste management policy. Their precondition is first to have agreed to the closure of the Spanish nuclear program (Costa Morata & Baños, 2010).

Another milestone was the launch of the Community Waste Management (COWAM) Spain initiative (2004–2006) with the involvement of AMAC, the CSN and ENRESA. Based on the COWAM experiences at the EU (and its methodology to search suitable candidate sites), AMAC announced its commitment to support the government in the ATC siting process, and organised a number of information meetings, seminars and debates in the nuclear areas (Vila d'Abadal, 2006).

Taking into account these institutional, political and social contexts, we now look at the evolution of the process, where the interactions between the four social domains of the governance-ecosystem (Kool et al., 2017) become highly visible.

6.5.1 Phase 1: The Preparation

The need for an ATC was fully debated in, and supported by parliament on at least three occasions between 2004 and 2006. Thus, in April 2006, an Inter-ministerial Commission (IC) for the ATC was set up by the government to look at the transparency and openness of the decision-making process around the siting of the ATC (RD 775/2006). With the support of a Technical Advisory Committee, the IC defined the basic criteria for the ATC and facilitated all the necessary information to municipalities and entities potentially interested in hosting the ATC. This preparation phase took place with a ruling socialist government (PSOE).

In December 2009, a public call was launched which gave any interested municipality a month to apply as candidate to host the ATC. The call defined the basis and the procedure of the decision process, specifying that the Spanish Government would designate the ATC site once the process ended. The IC deployed a series of informative and support actions to help potentially interested municipalities. All documents produced by the IC during the selection process were uploaded to the web (www.emplazamientoatc.es). In February 2010, the IC reported on the selection process and presented the final list of selected candidate sites. It should be noted that most candidate municipalities were rural, isolated, underdeveloped areas, and/or already nuclear areas.

A month later, a Public Information and Participation (PIP) procedure was opened so that any interested party could present arguments and request clarifications on the decision-making process. In addition, individual notifications on the PIP procedure were sent to municipalities, councils, Autonomous Communities (regional governments), the Spanish Federation of Municipalities and Provinces, associations and organisations.

Finally, and taking into account the considerations (if any) by the Autonomous Communities, in September 2010, the IC published a report with the proposed candidate sites. A total of 8 municipalities from 5 Autonomous Communities were finally accepted. The accepted sites were then evaluated against the pre-defined quantitative and qualitative criteria that had been favourably valued by the CSN. The IC concluded that although all sites were technically viable, Zarra, Ascó, Yebra and Villar de Cañas (in this order) were the most suitable, with little technical differences among them.

6.5.2 Phase 2: The Decision

Although the most feasible candidates seemed to be Yebra and Ascó (Ansede, 2010) due to their geographical position, communications, proximity to existing nuclear facilities, and a population accustomed to living with them, both cases ran into political opposition that made their candidacy difficult. The Catalan village of Ascó, which was probably the main candidate because it had 2 reactors in operation and a railway line, collided with the refusal of the autonomous Catalan government, then in the hands of the socialist party (PSC, the Catalan branch of PSOE), with a President (José Montilla) who a few years before had been the Minister of Industry who launched the ATC project (which gives an idea of the interference of the political system in the matter).

On December 30th 2011, the Spanish Government (ruled by PP, the right-wing Popular Party since December 20th) designated Villar de Cañas, a very small rural municipality in the province of Cuenca, far from nuclear facilities and without rail communication, as the site to host the ATC. It should be noted that the regional government (of Castilla-La Mancha Autonomous Community) was also in the hands of the Popular Party (PP), since May 2011.

ENRESA started the licensing process by sending the corresponding formal request to the Ministry of Industry, Energy and Tourism (currently MITERD). The process took over 4 years. In July 2015, the CSN issued the favourable siting license report and established the limits and conditions to be met in terms of nuclear safety and radiological protection. By law, all the information related to the nuclear-related ATC licensing process was made available at the CSN website (www.csn.es/almacen-temporal-centralizado).

The Plenary Session of Villar de Cañas City Council unanimously agreed to present its candidacy to host the ATC. The first and main argument was the need to stop the increasing depopulation in the area. But as in other candidate sites, platforms and movements emerged at the local level to both support and reject the ATC candidacy. On the one hand we find the 'Platform Yes we want the ATC in Villar de Cañas' and the Association of Companies of Villar de Cañas; on the other, the 'Platform against the nuclear repository in Cuenca'.

The pro-ATC collective claims that the facility is the best solution for the huge depopulation problem in Villar de Cañas. They argue that ATC will transform the area in an internationally recognised research, development and innovation reference in the search for solutions to radioactive waste management. The Yes Platform became very active throughout the decision-making process, collecting signatures and presenting their arguments.

The 'Platform against the nuclear repository in Cuenca' rejects the ATC, not only for Villar de Cañas but for any other municipality in the region (Castilla—La Mancha), and commits to mobilising citizens to avoid it. It was formed by 49 organisations, including public and private bodies. A key argument in their manifesto relates to the decision-making process. They argue that in a complex, long-term, and global issue (such as radioactive waste management), the final responsibility cannot be assigned to local entities. They support a new energy model based on renewables, sustainable tourism, and high-quality foodstuffs; a model that enhances local values and resources (historical, archaeological, natural, etc.). They claim to represent the opinion of a majority of Cuenca's society. The anti-platform was also very active throughout the process, organising protests, demonstrations, and deliberative workshops at the local and regional level.

At the wider level, Spanish environmental groups are opposed to any type of radioactive waste policy, as long as NPPs are in operation. Two of the main environmental NGOs (Greenpeace Spain and Ecologistas en Acción) were also actively engaged in the ATC decision-making process. For instance, Ecologistas en Acción presented a request for a negative Environmental Impact Assessment for the ATC at the Government Delegation in Cuenca. Their request was mainly grounded on the need to preserve the Natura 2000 network, and on the lack of appropriate geological or accident risk assessments. In 2015, Greenpeace asked the government to recognise that the ATC is not a viable option, and to definitively cancel the project. They argued for a dialogue process to find a solution for radioactive waste, involving the whole society, which should start with an agenda to close the NPPs. Greenpeace also published a document highlighting the ATC transport risks: radioactive waste will pass through 216 municipalities in the way from the NPPs to the ATC. Lastly, and in line with the Anti Platform at Villar de Cañas, a relevant argument in the environmentalist narrative is that radioactive waste management is a global, transboundary, issue which cannot be just "confined to a limited piece of land" (Costa Morata and Baños, 2010, p. 151). In their view, as for other techno-environmental problems, social legitimacy does not necessarily come together with the municipal-administrative one.

6.5.3 Phase 3: The Stalemate

A crucial element in the licensing process was a combination of the complex Spanish political system and the changing position of the affected Regional Government (Castilla-La Mancha). In February 2010, the Regional Parliament, ruled by the socialist party (PSOE), declared that no ATC (or any other nuclear facility) should be installed in any of the provinces or municipalities under their control, as they supported a sustainable development model based on renewables. In 2012, with the conservative Popular Party (PP) now ruling the region, the ATC was fully supported. Yet, in July 2015 the PSOE took over power in the region again, ousting the conservative Popular Party, which rules at the national level, and the ATC was (once again) fully rejected at the regional level. The collision of interests between the national and the regional government was set. The regional government strategy focussed on expanding a Specially Protected Bird Area (ZEPA in Spanish) known as Laguna del Hito (from 1000 Ha to 25,000 Ha) to include ATC land.

ENRESA insisted on the arguments of job creation, economic investment, and a pioneering technological infrastructure. The Spanish Government, in turn, argued that stopping the work would cause economic losses, €51 million per year (and an increase in the electricity bill of 25–30%), and insisted that the decision had been made with an important social, territorial and institutional consensus.

However, the regional government (of Castilla-La Mancha) argued irregularities in the planning, warned about contradictory external reports on safety guarantees, highlighting the need to expand the ZEPA zone. The Official College of Geologists and experts from the CSN (Earth Sciences Area) also expressed their doubts about the viability of the site, warning of possible additional economic costs.

The pro-ATC platform reacted against the extension of the ZEPA area proposed by the Autonomous Community. Signatures were collected through the change.org platform, and citizens travelled to the province capital (Cuenca) to demonstrate against the uncertainty created by such a 'stand-by' situation, and its implications for the local economy. More than 1500 individual allegations were presented at Villar de Cañas municipality.

Nearby town councils expressed their concern about the expansion of the ZEPA, as it could cause losses to farmers and to the development of the ATC. The mayor of Alconchel de la Estrella (neighbouring municipality) affirmed that ENRESA offered them 12,000 euros per year until the ATC began to function. Meanwhile, Greenpeace and Ecologistas en Acción continued to argue their position against the ATC.

This decision by the regional government of Castilla La Mancha was challenged by the (central) State's Attorney, and the final statement by the Courts is still pending, but ENRESA finally revoked to continue with the process. After long negotiations between the national and regional governments, following multiple swings in political power constellations, the project was on hold for a long time, and ENRESA was looking into alternatives. Even in 2022, the project has been officially suspended, and a new PGRR is currently being drawn up that will try to find new solutions (Table 6.2).

Table 6.2 Decision-making process around high-level radioactive waste management in Spain

Time	Event
2004	The Spanish Parliament urged the Government to solve the pressing problem of HLW by installing a Centralised Temporary Waste Repository (ATC)
2005	Creation of the Dialogue Board for the evolution of nuclear energy in Spain, which included representatives from all political parties in Congress and Senate, public bodies in charge of nuclear, environmental and industrial matters, trades unions, municipalities, consumers and environmental groups
2004–2006	Community Waste Management Initiative (COWAN, which was formed in 1990; part of European GMF: Group of European Municipalities with Nuclear Facilities), including Association of municipalities affected by NPPs (AMAC), CSN (Nuclear Safety Council), ENRESA
2006	6th Spanish Plan for the Management of Radioactive Waste (PGRR published by ENRESA). Announced the wish to develop a Centralised Temporary Waste Storage for HLW (ATC). The first plan to undergo a public information & consultation process
2009	A public call was launched to search for interested municipality candidates to host the ATC. Institutional participative process
2010	Inter-ministerial Commission and Dialogue Table publish the final list of selected candidate sites. 8 municipalities meet the criteria, from which 4 were the most suitable
2011	Choice for Villar de Cañas (province of Cuenca) City Council agreed. 'Platform Yes we want the ATC in Villar de Cañas' (solution for huge depopulation trend) versus 'Platform against the nuclear repository in Cuenca' (procedural argument: such a discussion should not be based on local decision; content: there is a need for a new energy and economic model)
2012	Regional government: Conservatives fully supported ATC
2015	Regional government: Socialist ruled and fully rejected the ATC. Expansion of a Specially Protected Bird Area (ZEPA) to make it impossible
2020	Draft of the 7th PGRR (still pending approval). Commitment to the ATC is maintained, suggesting restarting all the procedures to search for a suitable location
2022	HLW remain stored at the respective NPPs in the so-called 'individualised temporary storage' (Decentralised storage of HLW), waiting for the approval of the 7th PGRR (which will supposedly dismiss the ATC and promote decentralized storage).

6.6 Conclusion: Interactive Dynamics within the Country's Governance Ecosystem

Radioactive waste management shows the Spanish evolution from top-down, unidirectional, strategies applied in the earlier decades since the 1960s to more comprehensive, bidirectional and participative approaches for interacting with society since the end of the 1990s. In that sense, the management of the near surface disposal site of LILW at El Cabril from the early 1990s exemplified how continuous and direct contacts with local populations, incorporating some participatory methods, contributed to generate local trust-building processes, although resistance from local environmental groups remains active.

In turn, the decision-making process for siting the ATC for HLW, initiated in 2004 by national politics but yet unfinished (and probably discarded in the future management plan), illustrates the challenges that inclusive nuclear waste governance entails in a country with a multi-level governance system, characterised by a complex and intertwined political decision-making process, where the nuclear issue is used instrumentally by political parties (for electoral purposes), and in a social context with sceptical public opinion towards nuclear energy, inheritance of the social movements of transition from dictatorship to democracy during the 1970s.

Despite the willingness to define and implement an inclusive decision-making process (based on public information and participation procedures, and open and transparent principles), the final result of the process—the selection of Villar de Cañas—did not obtain the expected support, and the ATC remained politically blocked for long time. In the Spanish case, HLW management seems to be weaponised in national and regional political struggles, and the Spanish political party system seems willing to take advantage, for its own electoral benefit. This has made it difficult to decide on the location of the ATC: The central national government launched the process to decide on the location, and several municipalities presented their candidacy. One of these municipalities (Ascó) was located in the territory of the Autonomous Community of Catalonia, whose regional government (ruled by a political party other than the central one) decided to oppose it, arguing unfair imbalances between what the central government offers and takes, and blaming it for imposing its decisions over regional self-government. Meanwhile, general elections were celebrated and a new political party took over the central government, which decided to locate the ATC in a municipality in the Autonomous Community of Castilla-La Mancha, ruled then by the same party. When the procedure was already underway, regional elections occurred and the regional government fell in the hands of the political party which previously launched the ATC process at national level, which was now totally opposed to the ATC being installed there, arguing unfair distribution of territorial risks and benefits. The paradox about the case is that all these political parties are, in principle, in favour of nuclear energy, but in practice they alternatively support or oppose it for reasons of electoral tactics.

In Spain, a deep mistrust of state institutions and instrumentalisation of nuclear issues for political purposes can be found (Espluga et al., 2018), which limits the space for fact-based argumentation based on expertise, which would correspond to what Ylönen et al. (2017) call "depoliticization" of nuclear issues. Depoliticization can be defined as the scientisation, technicisation, economisation and/or legalisation of issues, which are thus transferred from the public sphere to the "closed circles of experts and their organisations". Through depoliticization, political actors express and seek to build trust in technical and matter-of-fact arguments. Politicisation, by contrast, would be a strategy designed to open up the issue at stake to a broad public debate, facilitating democratic deliberation on the various technical and non-technical issues (Ylönen et al., 2017). As stated by Lehtonen et al. (2021), in the Spanish case, mistrust of institutions has been spurred by the view that the state has granted undue privileges to the private utilities, and by the instrumental use of nuclear issues in battles between the central and regional governments, with politicians shifting their positions on nuclear according to political constellations. According to the available data on the Spanish case, instead of a "politicization of nuclear issues", which would have led to opening the nuclear issue to a broad public debate, in Spain a "nuclearization of politics" has taken place, leaving limited room for counter-expertise, as nuclear-related arguments are employed opportunistically to serve broader political aims (Lehtonen et al., 2021, p. 15).

Another issue to take into account in the Spanish case is the tension between territories with different development models. It is no coincidence that ATC sites are always located in economically depressed areas, with little industrialisation and distant from large conurbations. As seen in the case of the LLW (El Cabril), local pressure decreased significantly when the surrounding municipalities obtained economic compensation allowing them new economic activity options. Often, the arguments to oppose any nuclear facilities, not only the disposal of waste, have to do with the attempt to maintain certain types of economic activities and ways of life (agricultural, tourism, etc.), which are perceived as threatened by the new nuclear infrastructures. This brings us back to the delicate public sensibility regarding the fair distribution of risks and benefits, and the hard and complex game between political parties and their different territorial levels.

One of the main lessons of the Spanish case is that the principles of transparency and participation are not easy to put into practice, at least regarding finding a place for HLW temporary centralised storage, and that much more long-term work is required to generate trust between actors. In the case of LILW, public acceptance has been more favourable, and a timid participative approach has allowed better management, although its location has also suffered conflictive episodes in the past, especially with local environmental groups, which are still monitoring any changes in the management of radioactive waste.

Nuclear waste management in Spain has been influenced by environmental legislation that increasingly requires more public transparency and openness to citizen participation, mainly due to the internalisation of European Directives. This has been reflected in the way of managing the location of the repository for HLW, without success so far due to the peculiar structure of the nuclear conflict in Spain, which relegates the role of science and technology to marginal positions in the debate.

It seems clear that currently, the Spanish context does not allow a discussion based on data (and expertise), since actors respond to logic based on the mobilisation of emotions and feelings of grievance in the public sphere. The generally negative public perception of nuclear energy that prevails in Spanish society may be conditioning the erratic behaviour of political parties, which despite being mostly in favour of nuclear energy, do not dare to maintain this option in public in the long-term, especially in territories that they consider sensitive for their electoral interests. Generating trust between actors becomes quite difficult in a political-institutional context in which nuclear issues have already been used too many times in a tactical and instrumental way by political parties, in accordance with their conjunctural electoral interests at each historical moment.

The stalemate has become melancholic because the process entailed a loss of enthusiasm by the most active professionals in institutions in charge of radioactive waste management, as they had high expectations of the (limited) new participatory and transparent procedures. It became clear that the factors that can lead to public acceptance of a radioactive waste repository go beyond the competence and capabilities of the involved institutions, since none of the institutions in charge of managing nuclear waste in Spain, much less ENRESA, is in a position to prevail in the political game and prevent the partisan use of nuclear waste, which means that, no matter how much technical data they can offer, this will never be enough to win the public's trust.

Looking to the future, the management of radioactive waste in Spain could only be carried out through a serious investment of resources dedicated to building trust between the different actors, on at least two levels: On the one hand, trying to minimise territorial tensions (the perception of comparative grievances between territories) through a redesign of the political and institutional system that currently promotes and favours them. On the other hand, it would be necessary to build trust between public administrations and social movements around nuclear issues, which would require a long-term process of mutual recognition and potential convergence of objectives. However, it is foreseeable that all this would require long-term planning and temporal rhythms that neither the political system nor the nuclear management may have.

Finally, a novelty in this scenario is that from 2019 the Spanish government will close all NPPs as their operational life is considered fulfilled. This was one of the essential conditions for environmental groups to agree to discuss the management of radioactive waste, which may lead to a new scenario more favourable to the management of HLW. However, the future scenario also foresees a decarbonisation of the European economies (in 2022 pushed by the war in Ukraine and the associated energy requirements) that, indirectly, may favour an extension of the NPPs' operational life, which in turn could shift that window of opportunity over time.

Acknowledgements This chapter has partially benefited from the H2020 research project History of Nuclear Energy and Society (GA 662268).

References

Ansede, M. (2010, June 6). Ascó y Yebra, favoritos para el ATC, *Público*. https://www.publico.es/ciencias/asco-y-yebra-favoritos-atc.html.
Costa Morata, P. (2001). *Nuclearizar España*. Troya.
Costa Morata, P., & Baños, P. (2010). Sociología e ideología de los residuos radiactivos: la sociedad contra la técnica. *Argumentos de Razón Técnica*, 13, 137–158.
Di Nucci, M.R., Isidoro Losada, A.M., Schreurs, M., Brunngräber, A., & Mez, L. (2018). The Technical, Political and Socio-Economic Challenges of Governing Nuclear Waste a Comparative Perspective. In A. Brunngräber, M. Di Nucci, A. Isidoro Losada, L. Mez, & M. Schreurs (Eds.), *Challenges of Nuclear Waste Governance*. Springer. https://doi.org/10.1007/978-3-658-21441-8_1.
ENRESA. (2017). Un modelo de gestión con 25 años de historia: El Cabril, *Dinamo*, 14 (special issue), 6–15.
Espluga, J., Medina, B., Presas, A., Rubio-Varas, M., & De la Torre, J. (2017). Las dimensiones sociales de la percepción de la energía nuclear. Un análisis del caso español (1960–2015). *Revista Internacional de Sociología*, 75 (4), Article e075.
Espluga, J., Medina, B. & Konrad, W. (coords.) (2018). Case Studies Reports; In-Depth Understanding of the Mechanisms for Effective Interaction with Civil Society: Selected

Case Studies, in *History of Nuclear Energy and Society (HoNESt) Consortium Deliverable n. 4.3*, Retrieved July 7, 2022, from https://perma.cc/5SDY-LKCK.

Eurobarometer. (2010) *Europeans and Nuclear Safety*. Special Eurobarometer 324. Retrieved July 7, 2022, from https://europa.eu/eurobarometer/surveys/detail/769.

Kool, L., Timmer, J., Royakkers L., & van Est, R. (2017). *Urgent upgrade: Protect public values in our digitized society*. Rathenau Instituut.

Lehtonen, M., Prades, A., Espluga Trenc, J., & Konrad, W. (2021). The emergence of mistrustful civic vigilance in Finnish, French, German and Spanish nuclear policies: ideological trust and (de)politicization. *Journal of Risk Research*, 25(5).

Lemkow, L. (1984). *La protesta antinuclear*. Mezquita.

MITC (Ministerio de Industria, Turismo y Comercio). (2006). *6º Plan General de Residuos Radioactivos*. Retrieved July 7, 2022, from https://www.enresa.es/esp/inicio/conozca-enresa/plan-general-de-residuos-radiactivos.

MITERD (Ministerio de Transición Ecológica y Reto Demogràfico). (2020). *Borrador del 7º Plan General de Residuos Radioactivos*. Retrieved July 7, 2022, from https://energia.gob.es/es-es/Novedades/Paginas/primer-borrador-del-7-plan-general-de-residuos-radiactivos.aspx.

Molina, M. (1996). *The role of local authorities in the process of siting the Spanish repository for low and intermediate-level radioactive waste*. Nuclear Energy Agency of the OECD (NEA), OECD Publications.

Rubio-Varas, M., De la Torre, J., Espluga, J., & Presas, A. (2018). *Spain: Short Country Report. HoNESt project deliverable D3.6*. Retrieved July 7, 2022, from https://academica-e.unavarra.es/xmlui/handle/2454/38269.

Ylönen, M., Litmanen, T., Kojo, M., & Lindell, P. (2017). The (de)Politicisation of Nuclear Power: The Finnish Discussion after Fukushima. *Public Understanding of Science* 26 (3), 215–260.

Vila d'Abadal, M. (Ed.). (2006). *La gestión democrática de los residuos radiactivos*. Programa COWAN España, AMAC.

Josep Espluga-Trenc, PhD in sociology, he is Associate Professor at the Department of Sociology of the Universitat Autònoma de Barcelona (UAB), and a senior researcher at the Institute of Government and Public Policies (IGOP) of the same university. His research interests are focused on the relationships between health, work, environment and territory, with particular attention to the social perception of technological risks, socioenvironmental conflicts and participatory methods.

Ana Prades holds a PhD in sociology and is Head of the Sociotechnical Research Centre of the CIEMAT (Centro de Investigaciones Energéticas, Medio Ambientales y Tecnológicas) in Barcelona. Her research has focused on the field of public risk perception and communication, as well as on instruments for citizen engagement in the context of energy technologies. The implications of these processes in the development and implementation of environmental policies is another of her research areas. She has been the European Coordinator of Social Studies in Fusion, within the framework of the WPSES (Socioeconomic Studies on Fusion) of EUROfusion.

Open Access This chapter is licensed under the terms of the Creative Commons Attribution 4.0 International License (http://creativecommons.org/licenses/by/4.0/), which permits use, sharing, adaptation, distribution and reproduction in any medium or format, as long as you give appropriate credit to the original author(s) and the source, provide a link to the Creative Commons license and indicate if changes were made.

The images or other third party material in this chapter are included in the chapter's Creative Commons license, unless indicated otherwise in a credit line to the material. If material is not included in the chapter's Creative Commons license and your intended use is not permitted by statutory regulation or exceeds the permitted use, you will need to obtain permission directly from the copyright holder.

7 Who Decides What is Safe? Experiences from Radioactive Waste Governance in Switzerland

Sophie Kuppler, Anne Eckhardt and Peter Hocke

7.1 Introduction

Switzerland is one of the countries that experienced failures in its original approach to identifying one or several sites for nuclear waste repositories. In consequence, the country initiated a new site selection procedure in 2008, based on a blank map. Since then, despite some delays, good progress has been made towards the goal of granting a general license for one or two deep geological repositories in 2031. So far, the different actors involved in the selection process have cooperated effectively and without major disruptions. Emerging conflicts can be solved in a way that does not threaten the implementation of the site selection procedure according to plan. Nevertheless, it is worth taking a critical look at some aspects of the process—especially with regard to future governance aspects.

In this contribution, we will show how the Swiss democratic model was modified for nuclear waste governance, how this affected the actors involved, and what role different actors play within the site selection process. This also includes a debate on how the participatory elements are integrated into decision-making,

S. Kuppler (✉) · P. Hocke
Institute for Technology Assessment and Systems Analysis (ITAS),
Karlsruhe Institute of Technology, Karlsruhe, Germany
e-mail: sophie.kuppler@kit.edu

P. Hocke
e-mail: hocke@kit.edu

A. Eckhardt
risicare GmbH, Zollikerberg, Switzerland
e-mail: anne.eckhardt@risicare.ch

for example who is involved in what kinds of tasks and decisions, and how the borders are drawn between experts and the public, particularly with regard to the debate on safety. We will discuss how the actors communicate and interact along and across those borders. We draw conclusions about how successful the Swiss approach to decision making is in dealing with conflicts and moving towards safe disposal of nuclear waste. The results presented in this contribution are based on our research in several inter- and transdisciplinary research projects on nuclear waste governance. The focus lies on interactions and cooperation between the responsible collective actors.

7.2 Radioactive Waste Management in Switzerland

7.2.1 Origins of Waste and Interim Storage

Four nuclear power plants are currently in operation in Switzerland, Beznau I and II, Gösgen and Leibstadt. A fifth power reactor, Mühleberg, finally terminated its commercial operations in 2019 and is now being decommissioned. Today, the nuclear power plants produce around one third of the electricity generated in Switzerland (Swissnuclear, 2021). All nuclear power plants are predominantly owned by the public sector. This presumably promotes the perception of waste disposal as a collective task to be solved by Switzerland as a whole. After the severe Fukushima reactor accident in 2011, the Swiss government, the Federal Council (Bundesrat) and the Parliament decided that Switzerland should phase out the use of nuclear energy. However, the existing nuclear power plants may continue to be operated as long as they are safe.[1] New nuclear power plants can no longer be licensed, but this does not signify an absolute ban on nuclear technology.

The use of nuclear energy in Switzerland is controversial. In 2013, 57% of Swiss citizens were opposed to energy production by nuclear power plants (TNS opinion, 2013). However, about two thirds of the Swiss consider the nuclear power plants (NPPs) in their own country to be 'safe' or 'rather safe' (Swissnuclear, 2021). Various referendums calling for a phase-out or a faster phase-out of nuclear power have failed over the last twenty years, most recently the

---

[1] A nuclear power plant is considered safe if the legal safety requirements are met. Demands on the implementation of the legal safety requirements are substantiated by the Swiss Federal Nuclear Safety Inspectorate (ENSI) in guidelines and, if necessary, in additional subordinate specifications.

"Atomausstiegsinitiative" (nuclear phase-out initiative). This wanted to ban the construction of new NPPs in Switzerland at the constitutional level and limit the operating lives of the five existing Swiss NPPs. In 2016, it was rejected by Swiss voters with 54.2% of the vote against it (DETEC, 2016).

The radioactive waste in Switzerland, especially the ca. 1500 m^3 of high-level radioactive waste, originates mainly from the nuclear power plants. Medicine, industry and research account for about 30% of the total volume of low- and intermediate-level radioactive waste which amounts to 56,000 m^3, including disposal containers (Nagra, 2022). Facilities for the conditioning and interim storage of the radioactive waste that is produced during operation are located at the nuclear power plants. A central interim storage facility, ZWILAG, accommodates all types of radioactive waste. Aside from storage buildings it encompasses a conditioning plant as well as an incineration and smelting plant. Waste originating from the medical, industrial and research sectors is stored temporarily in a federal interim storage facility. This facility is located at the site of the Paul Scherrer Institute (PSI), the largest research institute for natural and engineering sciences within Switzerland. PSI has also facilities for the treatment of its own radioactive waste and of radioactive waste from the medical, industrial and research sectors. The ZWILAG- and the PSI-sites are located in the immediate vicinity of each other in the canton of Aargau (ENSI, 2021b).

7.2.2 The Recent Evolution of Radioactive Waste Disposal

The Swiss governance ecosystem for the long-term management of radioactive waste has changed considerably over the past 20 years. The transformation started in 2000 with the societal and political agreement on the concept of deep geological repositories, as described in the final report of the Expert Commission on Disposal Concepts (Expertengruppe Entsorgungskonzepte für radioaktive Abfälle, EKRA) (EKRA, 2000).[2] This concept was novel at the time and contains specific features, like the so-called pilot repository, which are unique to Switzerland. Further, the original plan of the implementer, the National Cooperative for the

---

[2] Members of the EKRA discussed this concept with NGOs, industry and safety authorities and addressed their concerns before publication of the report. The report was widely acknowledged and the concept it described laid the basis for further planning activities in Switzerland.

Disposal of Radioactive Waste (Nagra), to start underground investigations for a repository for low- and intermediate-level waste at the Mount Wellenberg site had to be abandoned due to two cantonal vetoes against this endeavour. The agreement on geological repositories for high-level and low- and intermediate-level radioactive waste, together with the events at the Wellenberg site and other developments, paved the way for new nuclear energy legislation which went into force in 2005.

This legislation envisaged regulating the site selection procedure with a Sectoral Plan. A Sectoral Plan is an established spatial planning instrument of the Swiss Confederation (Kreusch et al., 2019; Jud, 2014), which is used for any activities affecting or altering space within federal responsibility. Other Sectoral Plans exist, for example, for transport infrastructure and transmission lines for electricity (ARE, 2021). Usually, they provide a framework and guidelines for the planning activities of the cantons and—in contrast to the Sectoral Plan for Deep Geological Repositories—do not entail additional participatory elements. At the same time, the lead management of the site selection procedure was transferred from the implementer, Nagra, to the Swiss Federal Office of Energy (SFOE) and thus to the public administration—a step that fostered confidence in the procedure among the Swiss population.

The conceptual part of the "Sectoral Plan for Deep Geological Repositories" (SFOE, 2008) entered into force in 2008. There, a step-wise site selection process is fixed, which aims at identifying one or several repository sites for radioactive waste produced in Switzerland in a transparent and comprehensible manner while ensuring safety and security (Hocke & Kuppler, 2015). Stage 1, the selection of suitable geological areas, was concluded on December, 1st 2011 when the Federal Council gave its consent to the result report issued by the SFOE. In stage 2, the public was invited to participate in the siting of the surface facilities. Further, the responsible actors had to select at least two sites that would be subject to extended exploration in order to identify suitable sites at the end of stage 3. Stage 2 was concluded in 2018. In September 2022, Nagra announced that a combined site in the siting area of Nördlich Lägern would be the safest option according to their current assessments (Nagra, 2022a). Stage 3 is expected to be concluded in 2031 with the approval of the Federal Council's decision on the general licenses by Parliament and a possibly subsequent referendum (SFOE, 2008, see Fig. 3). After this, construction, operation and closure of the repository have to be decided upon and carried out.

7.3 A Federalist Governance Ecosystem

Switzerland has developed over centuries from a network of various alliances into a federal state whose national borders were internationally recognised in 1815. The political system dates back to the Federal Constitution of 1848. The federal state consists of 26 cantons. Each canton has its own cantonal constitution and its own legislative, executive and judicial authorities.

The federal structure of Switzerland is deeply rooted in the self-concept, the political culture and the legislation of the country (cf. for example Maissen, 2015). The cantons are responsible wherever the Federal Constitution does not explicitly delegate responsibilities to the Confederation. Therefore, the Confederation has a primarily coordinating effect in many policy areas. In the case of nuclear energy, the responsibility lies with the Confederation according to the Federal Constitution. Nevertheless, the cantons and regions are strong actors that clearly shape the process. Their influence on agenda setting, policy development and policy implementation is significant; in practice, the federal government cannot act without the cantons. In addition, direct democratic elements are implemented in Swiss political decision-making, which comprise for example the right to call for public votes on certain legislations.[3] The Swiss governance ecosystem can only be understood if this specificity is taken into account. This characteristic is also referred to as multilevel governance, which implies that in governance in general the interaction between various levels of government—local, regional, national and international—may play an important role. For the analysis in this chapter, Switzerland's governance ecosystem therefore requires a subdivision of the political sphere into the level of the Confederation and the other two levels of government: the cantons and the municipalities (see Fig. 7.1). They are grouped together here for the sake of clarity (see also Fig. 7.2).

Over the course of time, the governance ecosystem established due to the enforcement of the Sectoral Plan has shown some dynamics that have helped to mitigate conflicts, but have also led to new conflicts emerging. In the following, we first give a short overview of the actors involved in the different societal domains, which form the governance ecosystem, to then analyse their interaction and dynamics.

---

[3] For detailed information on the Swiss democratic system see for example Linder and Mueller (2021).

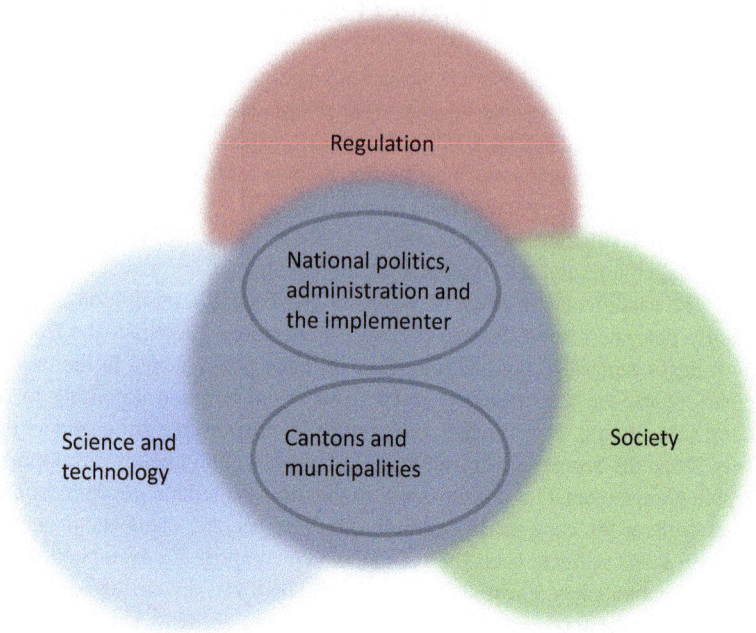

Fig. 7.1 The governance ecosystem framework for Switzerland. (Adapted from Kool et al., 2017)

7.3.1 Laws and Regulations

The main legal documents guiding nuclear waste governance in Switzerland are the Nuclear Energy Act (SNEA, 2021) and the Nuclear Energy Ordinance (SNEO, 2019), which entered into force in 2005. In the previously applicable Federal Act on the Peaceful Use of Atomic Energy (or Atomic Energy Act), radioactive waste, referred to there as residues, was mentioned only in passing (1959). In the present nuclear energy law three leading principles are stipulated (SNEA, 2021, Art. 30):

1. Radioactive substances shall be handled in such a manner as to ensure that as little radioactive waste as possible is produced.
2. All radioactive waste produced in Switzerland shall, as a general rule, be managed in Switzerland.
3. Radioactive waste shall be managed in such a manner as to ensure the permanent protection of humans and the environment.

7 Who Decides What is Safe? Experiences from Radioactive Waste …

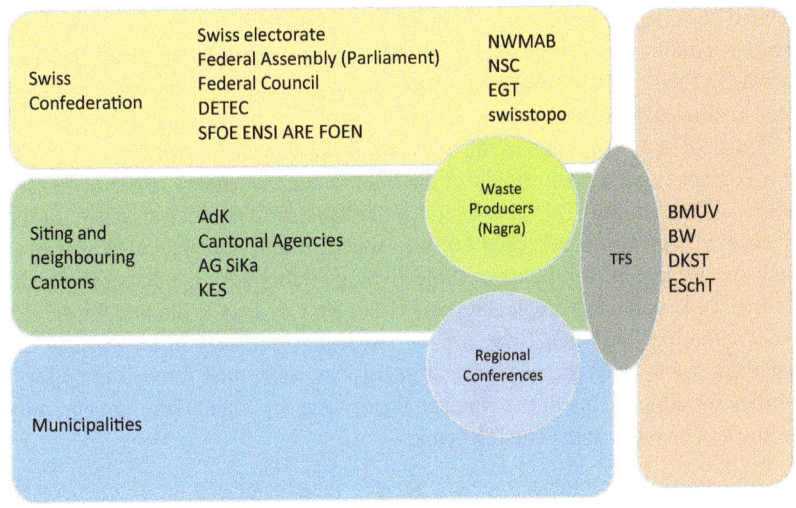

Fig. 7.2 Main institutions involved in the site selection procedure. (Adapted from SFOE, 2019)
AdK: Siting Cantons Coordination Committee
AGSiKa: Cantonal Safety Working Group
ARE: Federal Office for Spatial Development
BMUV: Federal Environment and Consumer Protection Ministry
BW: Federal State Baden-Wuerttemberg and its districts
DETEC: Federal Department of the Environment, Transport, Energy and Communications
DKST: German Coordination Office for Swiss Deep Geological Repositories
EGT: Expert Group on Deep Geological Disposal
ESchT: Expert Group Swiss Deep Geological Repositories
FOEN: Federal Office for the Environment
KES: Cantonal Expert Group on Safety
NSC: Nuclear Safety Commission
NWMAB: Nuclear Waste Management Advisory Board
SFOE: Swiss Federal Office of Energy
Swisstopo: Federal Office of Topography TFS: Technical Safety Forum

These principles do not differ substantially from the way the waste was handled before 2005. What is new is that they became legally binding. The implementation of the first principle can essentially be left to the waste producers, as it is in their own interest to keep the amount of radioactive waste that has to be disposed of at high cost as low as possible. The second principle is sporadically challenged politically with ideas of disposing of radioactive waste abroad, but these ideas have so far never found significant resonance. The third principle is to be implemented sustainably with deep geological disposal. Further important principles are the 'polluter pays' principle, the prohibition of reprocessing spent fuel elements, and the explicit obligation to dispose of all types of radioactive waste in deep geological repositories.

The Federal Constitution of the Swiss Confederation states that the Confederation is responsible for legislation in the field of nuclear energy (Federal Constitution, 2021, Art. 90). This also includes the legislation on nuclear waste. In the Nuclear Energy Ordinance (SNEO), it is specified that the "federal government shall specify in a Sectoral Plan the objectives and criteria for the disposal of radioactive waste in deep geological repositories which are legally binding for the relevant authorities" (SNEO, 2019, Art. 5). The legal framework in Switzerland has remained stable since the new nuclear energy law came into force. The political hurdles for adjustments to the Nuclear Energy Act are high. There are currently no signs of changes in the coming years.

7.3.2 Population and Civil Society

In Europe, the Swiss case is often considered a special case from which it is not straightforward to draw lessons learned for other countries. The main reason for this is the Swiss model of democracy, which Linder (2004) classifies as "semi-direct", and which is unique in Europe. Due to the direct-democratic elements in the political system, citizens entitled to vote play a particularly important role in political issues such as the disposal of radioactive waste. In common Swiss parlance, the community of those entitled to vote, is therefore also referred to as the sovereign («Souverän»).

When taking a closer look at the way decision-making processes take place in cooperation between the political and the public domains, it becomes clear that for example the Swiss electorate's veto rights can fulfil a similar function as for example extra-parliamentary protests in representative democracies, such as Germany (Kuppler, 2016). At the same time, in view of the "participatory turn", the Swiss political domain has the clear advantage of being familiar with consultations with a wide variety of actors in policy processes (cf. Linder, 2004; Saurugger, 2010; Linder & Mueller, 2017, 2021.

Representative surveys, for example based on the Eurobarometer studies, show that about half of the general population of Switzerland has a rather critical and rejecting attitude towards the disposal of radioactive waste as it is planned today. The other half is more in favour of the disposal in deep geological repositories as it is planned currently. About 50% of Swiss citizens agree that deep geological disposal is the most appropriate solution for long-term management of high-level radioactive waste. At the same time, over 80% think that there is no safe way of getting rid of this waste (TNS opinion, 2013). The proportion of those who would take a negative view of a deep geological repository in the vicinity of their own place of residence declined from 2012 to 2018. In 2018, it was around 65% (SFOE, 2018b, p. 15).

There are several citizens' initiatives in Switzerland actively lobbying against the construction of a nuclear waste repository at specific sites or, more generally, advocating for modifications in the site selection process.[4] The larger environmental NGOs, such as the Schweizerische Energie-Stiftung or Greenpeace, seem to not consider nuclear waste as one of their main fields of activity as no larger campaigns on this topic could be observed in Switzerland. One reason for this is that Switzerland is now phasing out nuclear energy. As the use of nuclear energy—due to the danger of a strong uncontrolled nuclear reaction—is associated with a far higher disaster potential than the disposal of radioactive waste, these NGOs have already reached their most important goal. Another reason might be that the path currently being followed for disposal can build on a broad consensus among the population and politicians (see below). Therefore, the opportunities to mobilise opponents are limited.

In the past, the citizens' initiatives have regularly organized protest activities. Several of their members also participate in the regional conferences ("Regionalkonferenzen"), which are the official participatory bodies in the potential siting regions. The motivations of the various NGOs have not been well studied. It is assumed that both the concern not to have a repository in one's own neighbourhood (NIMBY arguments, e.g. Kraft & Clary, 1991) and values that differ from those of other actors play a role.

---

[4]Those include for example KLAR! Schweiz ("for a life without atomic risks", https://www.klar-schweiz.com/), LIKE Weinland ("no repository in the Weinland", http://www.likeweinland.ch/go/), KAIB ("no nuclear waste in Bözberg"), NOE ("Niederamt without repository", http://www.kaib.ch/), LOTI ("Nördlich Lägern without repository", https://loti2010.ch/). All slogans in brackets were translated by the authors (see also Alpiger 2019: 191).

7.3.3 Politics and Administration I—Cantons, Municipalities and Regions

Socio-economic issues associated with a deep geological repository affect not only the siting municipality, but a specific region. This also applies to other issues, such as the transport of radioactive substances or the long-term safety of the repository.

Therefore, regional participation is a pivotal element of the Sectoral Plan. The core of regional participation is the regional conferences, founded in 2011. They consist of around 90 to 100 members from diverse backgrounds, such as local stakeholder representatives, civil society representatives and representatives from the German communities bordering the potential repository sites. In stage 2 of the Sectoral Plan, they expressed (among others) their views on where the facilities above ground of a deep geological repository should be built. In stage 3, they are involved in the optimisation of these infrastructures. The regional conferences also discuss compensation and measures that can support the desired development of the region (SFOE, 2023).

From the outset, the participatory elements in the Sectoral Plan process were understood as complementary to the democratic processes and instruments (Jordi, 2006). In the conception of the Sectoral Plan process however, the intertwining of democratic and participatory structures and processes elicited crucial questions, which had to be discussed and working compromises had to be found.

One adjustment was the formation of panels on safety issues within the regional conferences ("Fachgruppen Sicherheit"). The Sectoral Plan assigns tasks to regional participation primarily in the area of the design and placement of surface facilities and the socioeconomic impacts of deep geological repositories (SFOE, 2008, p. 34f). In addition, the regional conferences decided to also set up safety panels to examine safety issues (c.f. for example Standpunkt, 2012, p. 7). By installing these panels, members could allocate funds to invite experts of their choice and had the right to read and comment on technical reports. Before the installation of the panels, no public participation on safety issues was planned by the responsible authorities.

With the start of stage 3, some of the tasks of the regional conferences were concluded and new ones were added. As the level of concretion increased, certain communities within the potential siting regions became more directly affected than others. The evaluation process of the application for the general license is work in progress and needs to be well prepared. This applies particularly to the participation of the regional conferences and the involvement of the selected sites (Jordi, 2021).

Even though the regional conferences are contributing to the site selection process in a constructive manner, conflict lines between the local actors represented in the regional conferences can be observed. Indemnities ("Abgeltungen") are payments that the siting region receives for performing a national task. Compensation ("Kompensationen") is used to compensate for negative impacts that arise, for example, during the construction of a deep geological repository. There are various ideas on the use of the indemnities. Therefore, in future, a newly created organisation managed by the siting regions will decide on the use, distribution and management of the payments. Those communes that are designated as infrastructure communes in the Federal Council's decision at the end of stage 3 should be able to use part of the compensation amounts freely (SFOE, 2021).

With the enforcement of the Nuclear Energy Act (SNEA, 2021), the role of the siting region in decision-making processes has changed fundamentally. The veto right, as it was established at cantonal level before the enforcement of the new nuclear energy legislation, can be considered an institutionalized link between the political sphere and the electorate in the Swiss democratic system, which fulfils the same function as public protests or law suits in other democratic systems (Kuppler, 2016). After the events at the Mount Wellenberg- site, political actors were concerned that with the cantonal veto right in place, no repository will ever be built in Switzerland (Kuppler 2017). If suitable sites for deep geological repositories were blocked by cantonal decisions, this could have serious consequences because the radioactive waste could not be disposed of in a sustainable manner (c.f. among others, Nuklearforum, 2002). Finally, the cantonal veto right on underground investigations was abandoned in favour of an optional national veto right on the general license for a deep geological repository (Alpiger, 2019, esp. p. 53; Krütli et al., 2010). This political compromise has endured from 2005 to the present day, but has recurrently been the subject of criticism (cf. for instance SFOE 2018a; UREK-N, 2013). In the consultations that accompanied the development of the Sectoral Plan, concerns were expressed that the envisaged role of the regions in the selection process and their possibilities to raise issues of their interest was too limited. The reasons for this concern were the abandonment of the cantonal veto right and the transfer of responsibility for parts of the general licence application process to the national level. Before the enforcement of the Sectoral Plan, the cantonal authorities were responsible for water permits, for example. Those concerns resulted in the installation of a Committee of the Cantons ("Ausschuss der Kantone") (Kuppler, 2017).

7.3.4 Politics and Administration II—National Politics, Administration and the Implementer

The general political consensus on the Sectoral Plan process in Switzerland has been strong since its inception in 2008. Political initiatives in both chambers of Parliament cover a wide range of specific issues, concerning among others safety, participation, governance and the financing of the disposal of radioactive waste. Since the start of the site selection process, only criticism of the lack of independence between the Swiss Federal Nuclear Safety Inspectorate (ENSI) and the National Cooperative for the Disposal of Radioactive Waste (Nagra), emerging in 2012 after the serious reactor accident at Fukushima, has elicited a significant political and media response (Curia Vista, 2021). Fundamental criticism of the way Switzerland is managing its radioactive waste is not voiced.

In Switzerland, the 'polluter pays' principle applies to the disposal of radioactive waste (SNEA, 2021 Art. 31). Therefore, Nagra, as an organisation founded by the waste producers, is responsible for the safe long-term disposal of the waste (Nagra, 2021a). Nagra proposes geological siting regions and sites, submits an application for a general license (SFOE, 2008, p. 77) and is later in charge of building and operating the deep geological repositories. Nagra can be understood as a boundary organization between the political-administrative and science and technology domains. On the one hand it is part of the public sector, acting as an implementer of radioactive waste policy. On the other hand, it is also part of the sphere of science and technology as it carries out applied research and is responsible for scientific and technical aspects of the site selection process and the following steps of disposal (as described in Sect. 3.4 on science and technology below).

The cost of disposing of Switzerland's radioactive waste is estimated today at approx. CHF 22 billion (approx. EUR 22 billion). A waste disposal fund was created in 2000 to finance the disposal of radioactive waste. Together with the decommissioning fund, which was established in 1984, they constitute the Decommissioning Fund for Nuclear Installations and Disposal Fund for Nuclear Power Plants (STENFO). The bodies of STENFO are the administrative commission, the administrative office and the statutory auditors. The members of the administrative commission and the statutory auditors are appointed by the Federal Council for a term of office of four years (STENFO, 2021).

The political and administrative institutions involved in nuclear waste governance have remained more or less the same since the introduction of the Sectoral Plan in Switzerland, but their role has changed over time. As described in Jost (2012) and Hocke and Kuppler (2015), the central political and administrative actors in Switzerland on the national level are the Swiss Federal Office of Energy (SFOE) and the Swiss Federal Nuclear Safety Inspectorate (ENSI), the Federal Council, and Federal Department of the Environment, Transport, Energy and Communications (DETEC). Several other public institutions bear responsibility for specific topics in the site selection process, supporting the central actors with their expertise. Examples for such institutions are the Federal Office for Spatial Development (ARE) or the Federal Office for Environment (FOEN). In addition, there is a broad network of actors who help to shape the process. They have different responsibilities and different degrees of influence (see Fig. 7.2).

The SFOE has the important role of ensuring that the Sectoral Plan is put into practice in a high-quality manner. The SFOE takes the lead in the site selection procedure and is responsible for centralised operational and administrative activities (SFOE, 2008). Next to overall coordination, this includes the setup of the regional participatory processes. Other federal actors, such as ENSI and ARE remain fully responsible for their specific tasks within the site selection process. ENSI reviews and assesses safety aspects. This includes evaluating applications and reports issued by Nagra as part of the site selection procedure regarding safety issues.

A special aspect of the SFOE's task fulfilment is that a number of active politicians from the Social Democratic Party took and still take leading roles in the site selection process. These individuals bring political experience to the site selection procedure and—due to their specific political orientation—also a particularly good understanding of the concerns of individuals and organisations critical of nuclear energy. The fact that the political orientation of representatives of the SFOE has never played a significant role in public discourse is probably due to the fact that the Swiss political system is generally very consensus-oriented, and most politicians, even the members of both chambers of the Swiss parliament, exercise their mandates in part-time.

In the international context, the Nuclear Safety Commission (NSC) has an exceptional function. This commission consists of seven part-time members who are experts in areas of science and technology that are relevant for nuclear safety. In the field of radioactive waste management, the NSC examines fundamental questions of nuclear safety and issues statements to the licensing authorities. Politically, this commission plays an important role in Switzerland as a second-opinion body, which ensures an independent quality control for the supervisory authorities.

In the Sectoral Plan process, it became apparent early on that many of the potentially suitable sites are located close to the German border for geological reasons. Therefore, German administrative units, municipalities, NGOs and citizens were involved in the Sectoral Plan at an early stage. Communication between representatives of both countries proved challenging at times but has improved over time (cf. for example Besmer, 2021). Challenges are mainly encountered in the areas of political participation, legislation, competences of the authorities and at the political-cultural level. For example, it became clear that participation processes must be embedded in the respective structurally predetermined political processes in both Switzerland and Germany. Parallel structures must not be created that compete with the established political structures. Because the disposal issue has a different status in Germany and a greater potential for conflict than in Switzerland, the Swiss authorities must adapt their conflict management accordingly (El Mohib, 2010).

7.3.5 Science and Technology

Nagra carries the main responsibility for conducting the research, investigations and development needed for ensuring and assessing the safety and feasibility of the deep geological repositories. In addition, ENSI and SFOE conduct their own regulatory research. While ENSI invests in research concerning the safety of radioactive waste management—sometimes embedded in international co-operations (ENSI, 2021a)—SFOE commissions research in the social sciences and occasionally also in the humanities, although to a very limited extent (AGNEB, 2019). This applied research is directly related to the supervisory tasks of both institutions.

Fundamental research on radioactive waste management is conducted at several universities and university-related institutions. The PSI, with its competences in natural and engineering sciences, plays a major role in this. Generally, there is a strong emphasis on natural science research in Switzerland. Fundamental or applied fundamental research on societal aspects of the management of radioactive waste is currently rather marginalized (for one of the rare exceptions see Alpiger, 2019). One explanation for this is that problems related to the management of radioactive waste in Switzerland are solved pragmatically, so far successfully, and—following an internalised and lived principle of subsidiarity—at the lowest possible societal level.[5] The perceived need for social science reflection, articulated e.g. in the context of the Sectoral Plan, is correspondingly low. Social

---

[5] For example, the decisions for a repository in clay in the deep underground and for a site close to the German border in the upper Rhine valley find general acceptance. Other concepts, such as the "Guarding Concept" ("Hüte-Konzept") or maintenance free final disposal are currently not debated.

science studies seem to be noted by implementer and regulator, but exert little (visible) influence on disposal structures and processes.

Further, a number of consultants and consultancy agencies are involved in the site selection process. They usually answer to tenders on specific topics like studies on the socioeconomic consequences of disposal facilities, or carrying out and evaluating deep drillings.

7.3.6 Interactions Between the Spheres

Nuclear waste governance in Switzerland is highly influenced by interactions between the different spheres. The site selection process as described in the Sectoral Plan as a whole can be interpreted as a result of such interactions. As is customary in Switzerland, in the preparations for the Sectoral Plan, a variety of actors were consulted in different ways. Among others, the SFOE conducted focus groups with interested citizens (ISOPUBLIC, 2006). A hearing was organized, in the course of which public actors could hand in their statements and members of the SFOE exchanged views in person with representatives of central stakeholder groups, such as local mayors. These activities led to important adjustments in the Sectoral Plan as described above, which increased its acceptability to a variety of actors (Kuppler, 2017).

A central platform for actors and stakeholders is the Technical Safety Forum (TSF), chaired by the Swiss Federal Nuclear Safety Inspectorate (ENSI). The TSF receives, discusses and answers questions from the public about technical safety aspects. The questions and answers are posted on the Internet after replies have been given. In the TSF, representatives of the federal administration, cantons, communes, communities in neighbouring countries, NGOs, the interested public and others are gathered (TSF, 2021).

The implementer and regulator in Switzerland collaborate intensely with scientific institutions. Every five years, according to Art. 52 of the Nuclear Energy Ordinance, Nagra has to submit its waste management programme. This waste management programme is associated with a research, development and demonstration plan (Nagra, 2016). Both programmes are reviewed by ENSI and SFOE, which also monitor compliance. The review makes it possible to better coordinate the research programmes of implementer and regulator. It also gives the authorities, mainly ENSI and SFOE, the opportunity to bring up their research requirements at an early stage.

With the progress of the Sectoral Plan, new questions move into focus. If Switzerland wants to continue the transparent and inclusive pathway it entered with the Sectoral Plan, discussing and finding an answer to those questions well before they become acute would be key. None of the questions can be classified as belonging in one sphere only. Rather, they need to be answered in close cooperation between the spheres (cf. Fig. 7.1). A particularly important question is what requirements must be imposed on the general license for a repository. This question touches the legal sphere, as laws and regulations have to be adhered to, especially with regard to safety and security of the planned repository. It is also a political question, insofar as the Federal Council and the Parliament decide whether the general license is granted. This means that those political bodies—with the support of the federal administration—have to decide whether in their view one or two safe and secure repositories can be built at the suggested site or sites. It is also a question that touches the public sphere, as an optional referendum can be held on the Parliament's decision if sufficient persons or cantons demand it. It concerns the regional, cantonal and community levels because these levels are most directly affected by the impact of granting a general license. And it is of course also a scientific question, as issues of safety, security, feasibility etc. require scientific assessments.

7.4 Current Topics in Nuclear Waste Governance

The existing governance ecosystem in Switzerland is influenced by further progress on the path of disposal and challenged by current debates that can affect nuclear waste management.

7.4.1 Sectoral Plan—and What Next?

Current issues in radioactive waste management in Switzerland are primarily determined by the status of the site selection procedure. As mentioned above, Nagra has submitted a site proposal in September 2022 (Nagra, 2022a). The sites not included in this proposal are put on hold, i.e. no further investigations are undertaken at these sites for the moment. If the site proposed by Nagra should for some reason prove unsuitable, they can re-enter the process. The evaluation process of the following application for a general license needs to be well prepared. This applies particularly to the participation of the regional conferences and the involvement of the communities where those selected sites are located (Jordi, 2021). Presently pertinent questions are

1. How will Nagra's siting proposal be received in the affected region—and in the regions that have been put on hold in the long-term?
2. How will the mode of governance change in the period between 2022 and the 2030s when the final decision on a general licence application is made? Adaptations can become necessary, for example, because new issues that already refer to the construction and operation of a repository require the inclusion of new competences and responsibilities.
3. The general licence application and the application for determination of a site in the Sectoral Plan are reviewed by the federal authorities. Will they and will the Federal Council and Parliament approve the site and the general licence application? Will the optional referendum that comes at the end of the Sectoral Plan process result in the site being accepted and a general licence being granted to Nagra? What happens if the general licence application is rejected by the electorate?
4. How to continue with public participation after a general license has been granted to Nagra?

Nagra expects to be able to start construction of a repository for low- and intermediate-level waste in 2045 and its operation in 2050. From 2053, the part of the combined repository for high-level radioactive waste will be built and should be in operation from 2060. The entire repository is to be closed at the end of an observation phase, the duration of which is open and which will be terminated by a political decision. Nagra supposes that the repository will be closed around 2125. Then it can be released from nuclear energy legislation. Nagra will have fulfilled its task and can be dissolved (Fig. 7.3).

During this process, the governance ecosystem will have to adapt to additional requirements and new developments. Switzerland benefits from its experience in handling major projects that take decades to complete, such as the New Railway Link through the Alps (NRLA), the planning for which began in 1986 and whose implementation is still in progress. Parts of the NRLA, such as the Gotthard Base Tunnel, took 17 years to build. It can be assumed that over time other pressing political challenges, such as climate change, will bind more resources and take up more space in the political and public debate. At the same time, once a siting decision has been taken and if construction and operation of the repository do not cause any major accidents, the population and politicians will increasingly perceive the nuclear waste disposal project as a "normal" large-scale project that requires negotiations and participation, but does not give rise to fundamental or fierce societal controversy.

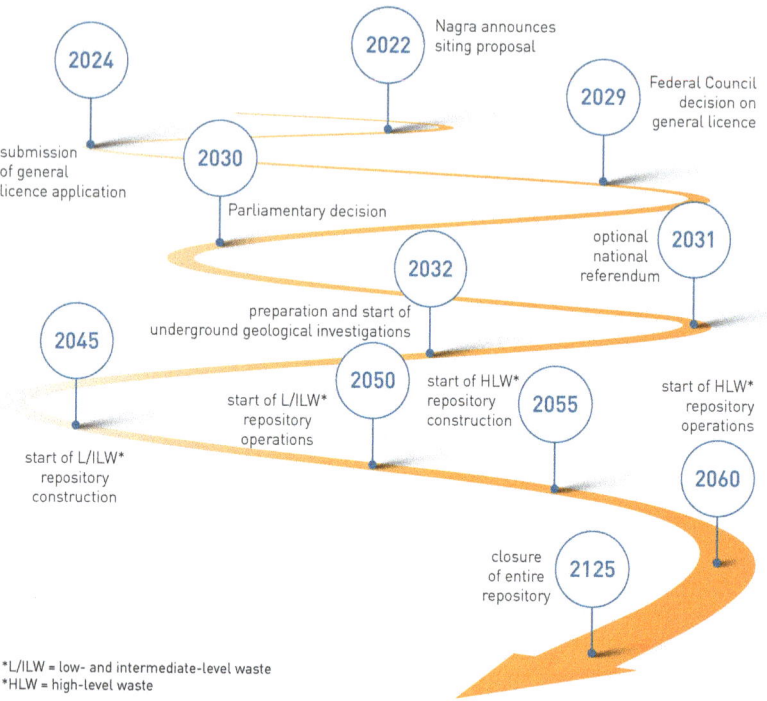

Fig. 7.3 Time plan for a combined repository in Switzerland (Nagra, 2021b, date for start of HLW repository corrected by Nagra June 2022)

However, the further procedure is accompanied by some interesting questions that must be answered by collective actors, such as the communication with future generations: The Nuclear Energy Ordinance (SNEO) obliges the owner of a deep geological repository to "compile documentation that is suitable for securing information about the repository over the long term" (SNEO, 2019, Art. 71). This documentation has to be handed over ultimately to the Federal Department of the Environment, Transport, Energy and Communications (DETEC) (SNEO, 2019, Art. 71). The SNEO also states that the owner must ensure a permanent marking of the repository (SNEO, 2019, Art. 69). Representatives of Nagra and the SFOE participate in international bodies on both issues, for example in the

OECD's Nuclear Energy Agency (NEA). However, no concrete ideas have been presented yet. Following the guideline of the Swiss Federal Nuclear Safety Inspectorate (ENSI), "a concept for permanent marking of the deep geological repository has to be submitted with the construction license application. The permanent marking concept has to be specified in concrete terms in subsequent licensing steps" (ENSI, 2020, p. 7).

7.4.2 Looming Debates

Debates that are already looming could intensify in the future and affect the disposal of radioactive waste. They address for example the following topics:

Dealing with insights from nuclear waste disposal in neighbouring countries
So far, Switzerland is one of the countries worldwide whose disposal programme for high-level radioactive waste is most advanced. Nagra and the Swiss authorities have become accustomed to receiving international visitors interested in the "Swiss model" and to presenting their solutions as exemplary at international conferences. Against this background, the disposal programme in France, which is also at an advanced stage, and the site selection procedure underway in Germany, present entirely new challenges. The larger neighbouring countries maintain programmes of research and development that exceed those of Switzerland. Moreover, France and Germany are currently also gaining experience with participation processes. This means that Switzerland can no longer sell itself as a role model in the long run, but must face the challenges that come with the fact that different, or even better, solutions may be found elsewhere and fuel the discussion on the "right disposal solution" in its own country.

The resurgent use of nuclear technologies
Currently the Nuclear Energy Act stipulates that "The granting of general licences for the construction of nuclear power plants is prohibited" (SNEA, 2021, Art. 12a). However, the Swiss government and Parliament stated that this prescription does not imply a ban on nuclear technology (Swissnuclear, 2019, p. 3). The debate at the World Climate Summits (2021 in Glasgow and 2022 in Sharm el-Sheik) on whether the European Commission should classify nuclear power as a sustainable source of energy and thus encourage future investment in this area, as well as global investment in new small modular reactors, put the rejection of nuclear power in Switzerland into perspective. Extensions of the operating lives of the newer nuclear power plants are already being examined (Meier, 2021), and Swiss media

are taking up the debate on the climate friendliness of nuclear power plants. The current broad social consensus on the disposal of high-level radioactive waste in Switzerland is closely linked to the decision to phase out the use of nuclear energy. Extensions of operating lives or even decisions to build new nuclear power plants could threaten this consensus. The fact that Switzerland, with the European Organization for Nuclear Research (CERN), PSI and École polytechnique fédérale de Lausanne (EPFL), is home to nuclear research facilities gives a particular boost to ideas for new nuclear applications (cf. for example, Transmutex, 2021).

International solutions for the disposal of radioactive waste
Joining an international project or an already existing solution for the disposal of radioactive waste abroad, is a recurrent topic in the political debate in Switzerland (Curia Vista, 2021). If a convincing solution for a joint disposal facility were to emerge in Europe or outside, this would certainly lead to substantial discussions on whether Switzerland should and could join such a solution.

7.5 Conclusions on the Future Governance Ecosystem

7.5.1 Consensus Through Complexity

The governance ecosystem for radioactive waste disposal in Switzerland is complex. The site selection procedure, following the Sectoral Plan, brings together actors with various scopes of responsibility and at different levels of government, institutions with decision-making powers and advisory bodies, science and technology, and a population that is used to having a political say. Prima facie this system raises questions including:

What happens if the Swiss Federal Nuclear Safety Inspectorate (ENSI) and the Nuclear Safety Commission (KNS) disagree in their technical assessment of the proposed repository site for the Federal Department of the Environment, Transport, Energy and Communications (DETEC)? Who is to take on the role of arbitrator here? DETEC does not have the scientific and technical expertise to fulfil this task (IRRS, 2012). Nagra, the implementing body, is largely owned by the cantons. At the same time, the potential siting cantons are following the site selection procedure with a critical eye.

A second look, though, shows that this governance ecosystem is very well adapted to the specific political and cultural environment of Switzerland. The Swiss Federal Chancellor put it this way: "What makes Switzerland special is how we deal with political power. We are world champions in fragmenting power. In restraining and keeping a check on power" (Thurnherr, 2018). In a political culture that is geared towards consensus and consultation with all potentially affected parties, the interaction of many partners with different interests is well-rehearsed. At the same time, the established political culture of consensus and consultation ensures that the Sectoral Plan process functions so far successfully despite the large number of actors involved, and their complicated and not always clearly regulated interactions. Therefore, a general lesson that can be drawn from the Swiss case is that good integration into the specific political culture of a country with a functioning system of checks and balances is both necessary and rewarding.

However, the so far favourable site selection process in Switzerland does not guarantee a smooth and successful continuation in the future. The interaction of all participants must be permanently supported and promoted with great effort, so far especially by the leading SFOE. And ultimately, it is the Swiss electorate that has the say. In the 2030s, Swiss citizens could reject the results of an elaborate site selection procedure that took more than twenty years. Only then will it become clear whether the site selection procedure was ultimately successful. Whether the optional referendum has an enabling effect on the current process is an open question, due to the fact that on the one hand it will be a national referendum that does not give the communities at the selected site any particular veto rights, but on the other hand the national public could sympathize with the host community if they feel that it was not fairly treated. The further steps on the path to deep disposal involve other actors and require new participation procedures. Hence, sustained efforts and significant resources are required over a long time period.

7.5.2 Pragmatism as a Virtue and a Limitation

The relaunch of the search for sites for deep geological repositories in Switzerland at the beginning of the 2000s started with a pragmatic compromise. The newly developed concept of controlled long-term geological disposal combined the final disposal of radioactive waste with control and reversibility. Thereby it met the demands of both advocates of permanent surface disposal and proponents of a final repository. Another example of pragmatism is the Sectoral Plan. For deep geological repositories no specific political instrument for site selection was developed, but it was adapted from an already established instrument in spatial planning. Pragmatism can also be seen in the composition of the regional conferences: The majority of delegates to the regional conferences are members of already existing institutions such as municipalities, regional planning authorities and stakeholder organizations. In addition, representatives of the population can apply to the regional conferences for membership (SFOE 2018c, p. 17). Stakeholders include, for example, regional businesses, agriculture and environmental organisations.

Throughout the Sectoral Plan process, numerous compromises were reached at various levels on topics such as the specific composition of the regional conferences (Planval, 2014, p. 38), the selection of possible siting areas (SFOE, 2018d, p. 9) or even the weighting of flight paths for the safety of surface facilities (Regionalkonferenz Nördlich Lägern, 2013, p. 20). In several cases, however, conflicts emerging within the governance ecosystem have not been resolved in a way that resulted in agreement among all actors involved. Rather, a working compromise has been found that made it possible to proceed with site selection even if the conflict has not been resolved. One example is the debate on whether the abandonment of the veto right at cantonal level was compatible with the Swiss democratic tradition. While no agreement was found, the Sectoral Plan—with its promise of a high degree of transparency and cooperation between the responsible actors at national level, the regional and local authorities as well as the general public—serves as a working compromise in this case.

A downside of pragmatism is a lack of independent applied fundamental research on disposal, especially in the field of social sciences. What has not been addressed so far is, for example, a sketching of the societal resources required to carry through technically demanding monitoring activities, interpret the data collected and take appropriate decisions based on the interpretation. Monitoring and retrievability are socio-technical concepts that require knowledge, skills, financial resources and appropriate decision-making structures—possibly over a long period of time (Hocke & Kuppler, 2019). A forward-looking evaluation and discussion of needs and requirements therefore seems appropriate.

Limits of pragmatism are also revealed by the superficially purely technical question of what kind of repository should be built: a single repository for high, low- and medium-level radioactive waste, or two separate repositories, one for high-level waste and one for low- and medium-level waste. A combined repository would be an efficient solution in terms of the effort required for licenses, compensations, construction and operation, monitoring during the observation phase, marking of the repository, closure etc. On the other hand, a combined repository poses higher safety requirements, for example with regard to potential interactions between the different types of waste or to operation during storage of the wastes. In this context, the questions, "What does the safety, we strive for, look like?", and "How safe is safe enough?", become highly relevant. The central Swiss guiding principle, "Safety First", does not answer how conflicting goals regarding safety should be handled. This also applies to the question of the extent to which compromises in the operational and long-term safety of the repository may be accepted in favour of monitoring in the observation phase, which reduces uncertainties about the development of the deep geological repository. There remains a lack of concrete guidance regarding research needs on, e.g. environmental protection associated with a repository, economic costs of different solutions, and assessment tools regarding safety and side effects.

It is possible that more fundamental reflections on this topic in other countries could reflect back on the Swiss procedure and call into question what has already been achieved. However, due to path dependencies, the hurdles for adjustments in later phases of disposal are very high. It remains to be seen whether accompanying research will play a greater role in the future of the Swiss governance ecosystem than it has to date. In our view, accompanying research is an essential element of any well-functioning governance of radioactive waste management.

7.5.3 Safety as a Socio-Technical Concept

Among the issues affecting several or all of the five spheres, safety plays a pivotal role. The Sectoral Plan sets the focus on safety, "with land use and socio-economic aspects playing a secondary role" (SFOE, 2008, p. 5). What does this mean in practice? Basic requirements for the safety of deep geological repositories are laid down in the nuclear energy legislation. These requirements are specified by ENSI in guidelines (especially ENSI, 2020) and other documents (e.g. ENSI, 2010). However, since Nagra, the implementer, bears the main responsibility for the safety of the deep geological repositories, the requirements of the supervisory authority are generally limited to concise, basic specifications. The Sectoral Plan stipulates that Nagra ("the waste producers") evaluates the proposed geological siting regions and sites, particularly with respect to safety in accordance with the requirements of the Sectoral Plan and the relevant legal provisions (SFOE, 2008, p. 78). The safety authority ENSI (Swiss Federal Nuclear Safety Inspectorate) "reviews and evaluates the siting proposals of the waste producers from a safety viewpoint and advises the SFOE on safety issues" (SFOE, 2008, p. 27). Is it, therefore, Nagra that has to prove the safety of their repository plans and ENSI that has to evaluate this proof of safety?

In the Swiss process, the main responsibility for defining what is safe lies with the scientific and technical experts. Once they have demonstrated and assessed the safety aspects in the application for a general license, the question of what is safe is handed over to the political sphere: The Federal Council and the Parliament decide upon this question as part of their decision on the granting of the general license. However, experience shows that the political institutions rely significantly on the judgement of scientific and technical experts when deciding on topics that touch the safety and security of nuclear installations. But: Safety and security are socio-technical constructs. This implies that public institutions and authorities together with the political and juridical spheres cannot define safety independently of the public debate.[6] Civil society and stakeholders in Switzerland are part, or are actively demanding and working towards becoming a part, of the process of developing a shared interpretation of safety and security—a process that could be characterized as co-creation in decision-making. Should not responsible authorities and scientists therefore put questions of safety and security more actively forward for debate by the public? The sphere of public administration deals with such boundary questions by realizing a high degree of transparency and demanding the same from the other actors involved in the Sectoral Plan, such as Nagra and the regional conferences.

Currently, cantons, municipalities and regions, the Swiss population and civil society have a certain but limited influence on safety-related decisions. The cantons maintain their own working group on safety and an expert group on safety. These groups assess application documents which are submitted by Nagra, as well as other important information for the attention of the Committee of the Cantons. The regions enforced the implementation of safety panels of the regional conferences during the course of the Sectoral Plan. The regional conferences were granted their own budgets for inviting experts of their choice and paying them to write reports about topics they found relevant. If conflicts arise, the Technical Safety Forum (TSF) provides a platform to raise questions about safety and put them up for discussion in a wider circle of experts from different stakeholders. While debates in the TSF are often successfully closed, the question remains open how the results are disseminated and accepted in society—particularly, since the TSF has no officially granted influence on the implementer, i.e. Nagra, to optimize safety standards. No empirical research on the workings and effects of the TSF has been published. However, all of these provisions are so far

---

[6] Sociotechnical constructs of technological safety and security are meaningful interpretations which are well-known and shared by the interested public (for the conceptual framing of sociotechnical processes see Lösch, 2021).

predominantly oriented towards the technical aspects of safety. The socio-technical aspects of safety and security—like providing a strong safety culture, dealing with human failure, intensifying the exchange with related subjects in order to gain new perspectives, ensuring intergenerational justice, dealing with trade-offs between risks and uncertainties or future societal and technological developments—are hardly ever addressed (Hocke, 2015; Kuppler, 2017; Eckhardt, 2021).

In principle, the Safety Case—a methodology developed by the International Atomic Energy Agency (IAEA) to evaluate the long-term safety of a geological radioactive waste disposal facility—could create a link between the different spheres and facilitate discussion. However, in the discourse and perceptions of deep repository projects, there is currently a great deal of scepticism about it—if the Safety Case plays a role in the discourse at all. Therefore, the Safety Case should be better adapted to the needs of stakeholders, and to a certain amount to civil society's expectations. Such an adaptation requires transdisciplinary research on questions like: Which aspects of the safety case (paradigms, objects and results) shape public perceptions of for instance a site selection process? To what extent is it sensible and possible to involve a wide range of stakeholders in the preparation of the Safety Case (Röhlig & Eckhardt, 2017)? This question is currently being investigated in more detail in a research project in neighbouring Germany (Transens, 2021). The research focuses on expectations of civil society members and lay people regarding arguments relevant for safety case studies in nuclear waste governance.

References

AGNEB. (2019). *Forschungsprogramm Radioaktive Abfälle 2017–2020*. Arbeitsgruppe des Bundes für die nukleare Entsorgung. Retrieved June 23, 2022, from https://pubdb.bfe.admin.ch/de/publication/download/9838.

Alpiger, C. (2019). *Evaluation von Beteiligungsverfahren bei der Suche nach Lagerstätten für radioaktive Abfälle*. Nomos.

ARE. (2021). *Konzepte und Sachpläne nach Art. 13 RPG*. Retrieved December 13, 2021, from https://www.are.admin.ch/are/de/home/raumentwicklung-und-raumplanung/strategie-und-planung/konzepte-und-sachplaene.html.

Besmer, A. (2021). *Sachplan Tiefenlager. Wie das Thema auch in Deutschland interessiert*. Retrieved December 07, 2021, from https://energeiaplus.com/2021/11/01/sachplan-tiefenlager-wie-das-thema-auch-in-deutschland-interessiert/.

Curia Vista. (2021). *Geschäftsdatenbank Curia Vista*. Retrieved November 28, 2021, from https://www.parlament.ch/de/ratsbetrieb/curia-vista.

DETEC. (2016). *Volksinitiative «Für den geordneten Ausstieg aus der Atomenergie»*. Federal Department of the Environment, Transport, Energy and Communications. Retrieved November 28, 2021 from https://www.uvek.admin.ch/uvek/de/home/uvek/abstimmungen/atomausstiegsinitiative.html.

Eckhardt, A. (2021). Stressfaktor Mensch. Menschliche Einflüsse auf das verschlossene Endlager—Versuch einer wissenschaftlichen Annäherung. *TRANSENS-Arbeitsbericht-03*.

EKRA. (2000). *Entsorgungskonzepte für radioaktive Abfälle. Schlussbericht. Im Auftrag des Departementes für Umwelt, Verkehr, Energie und Kommunikation*. Retrieved June 09, 2022, from https://www.ensi.ch/fr/wp-content/uploads/sites/4/2012/05/ekra-bericht_entsorgungskonzeptschweiz.pdf.

El Mohib, O. (2010). *Grenzübergreifende Zusammenarbeit zwischen Behörden der Schweiz und Deutschlands*. Projektarbeit eingereicht der Universität Bern im Rahmen des Executive Master of Public Administration (MPA). Retrieved June 23, 2022, from https://www.kpm.unibe.ch/unibe/portal/center_generell/a_title_strat_forschung/k_kpm/content/e69705/e232334/e234053/e234338/e234340/Projektarbeit_OmarElMohib_Dateigroesseverringert_ger.pdf.

ENSI. (2010) *Anforderungen an die provisorischen Sicherheitsanalysen und den sicherheitstechnischen Vergleich*. Retrieved July 13, 2022, from https://www.ensi.ch/de/dokumente/anforderungen-an-die-provisorischen-sicherheitsanalysen-und-den-sicherheitstechnischen-vergleich/.

ENSI. (2020). Specific design principles for deep geological repositories and requirements for the safety case. Guideline for Swiss Nuclear Installations. *ENSI-G03/e*. Retrieved June 23, 2022, from https://www.ensi.ch/en/2009/11/11/g03-specific-design-principles-for-deep-geological-repositories-and-requirements-for-the-safety-case/.

ENSI. (2021a). *Erfahrungs- und Forschungsbericht 2020*. Retrieved June 23, 2022, from https://www.ensi.ch/de/wp-content/uploads/sites/2/2021/05/210427_ENSI_Erfahrungs_und_Forschungsbericht_2020.pdf.

ENSI. (2021b). *Waste Management / Interim storage facilities*. Retrieved December 05, 2021, from https://www.ensi.ch/en/.

Federal Act on the Peaceful Use of Atomic Energy (Atomic Energy Act) of 23 December 1959 (Status as of 27 July 2004). SR 732.0. Out of force since 2005.

Federal Constitution of the Swiss Confederation 1999 SR101. (2021, March 7). https://fedlex.data.admin.ch/filestore/fedlex.data.admin.ch/eli/cc/1999/404/20210101/en/pdf-a/fedlex-data-admin-ch-eli-cc-1999-404-20210101-en-pdf-a.pdf.

Hocke, P. (2015). Nuclear waste repositories and ethical challenges. In M. Wyss (Ed.), *Geoethics: Ethical Challenges and Case Studies in Earth Sciences* (pp. 359-367). Elsevier.

Hocke, P., & Kuppler, S. (2015). Participation under Tricky Conditions. In A. Brunnengräber, M. R. Di Nucci, A. Isidoro Losada, L. Mez, & M. Schreurs (Eds.), *Nuclear waste governance. An International Comparison* (pp. 157–176). Springer.

Hocke, P., & Kuppler, S. (2019). Die Beteiligung der Öffentlichkeit bei der Suche nach einem Endlager: Ein problemorientierter Blick in die Schweiz. In M. Burgi (Ed.), *15. Deutsches Atomrechtssymposium* (pp.299–310). Nomos.

IRRS. (2012). Integrated Regulatory Review Service (IRRS) Mission to Switzerland. *IAEA-NS-IRRS-2011/11*. Retrieved June 23, 2022, from https://www.iaea.org/sites/default/files/documents/review-missions/irrs_mission_to_switzerland_nov_dec_2011_1.pdf.

ISOPUBLIC. (2006). *Sachplan Geologische Tiefenlager. Fokusgruppen. Schlussbericht*. Schwarzenbach. Retrieved July 13, 2022, from https://www.newsd.admin.ch/newsd/message/attachments/4065.pdf.

Jost, M. (2012). Entsorgung radioaktiver Abfälle. Akteure und Aufgabenteilung in der Schweiz. In M. Müller (Ed.), *Endlagersuche auf ein Neues? Der Weg zu einem gerechten und durchführbaren Verfahren* (pp. 138–153). Loccumer Protokolle 25/12.

Jordi S. (2006). *Die Anwendung partizipativer Verfahren in der Entsorgung radioaktiver Abfälle*. Bundesamt für Energie. Retrieved June 23, 2022, from https://pubdb.bfe.admin.ch/de/publication/download/1404.pdf.

Jordi, S. (2021, September 04). *Vollversammlung der Regionalkonferenz Zürichnordost*. Retrieved June 23, 2022, from https://www.zuerichnordost.ch/fileadmin/user_upload/2021_09_04_Vollversammlung_Praesentation_def.pdf.

Jud, B. (2014). Der Sachplan des Bundes—ein unterschätztes Dokument. *Raum und Umwelt*, March 2014, 2–20.

Kool, L., Timmer, J., Royakkers, L. & van Est, R. (2017). *Urgent upgrade: Protect public values in our digitized society*. Rathenau Instituut. Retrieved June 23, 2022, from https://www.rathenau.nl/sites/default/files/2018-03/Urgent_Upgrade.pdf.

Kraft, M. E., & Clary, B. B. (1991). Citizen Participation and the Nimby Syndrome: Public Response to Radioactive Waste Disposal. *Political Research Quarterly*, 44(2), 299-328.

Kreusch, J., Neumann, W., & Eckhardt, A. (2019). *Entsorgungspfade für hoch radioaktive Abfälle: Analyse der Chancen, Risiken und Ungewissheiten*. Springer.

Krütli, P., Flüeler, T., Stauffacher, M., Wiek, A., & Scholz, R. W. (2010). Technical safety vs. public involvement?: A case study on the unrealized project for the disposal of nuclear waste at Wellenberg. *Journal of Integrative Environmental Sciences*, 7(3), 229–244.

Kuppler, S. (2016). Modellfall(e) Schweiz. Was aus der Standortsuche gelernt und generalisiert werden kann. In A. Brunnengräber (Ed.), *Problemfalle Endlager: Gesellschaftliche Herausforderungen im Umgang mit Atommüll* (pp. 337–358). Nomos.

Kuppler, S. (2017). *Effekte deliberativer Ereignisse in der Endlagerpolitik*. Springer.

Linder, W. (2004). Direct Democracy. In U. Klöti, P. Knoepfel, H. Kriesi, W. Linder, Y. Papadopoulos, & P. Sciarini (Eds.), *Handbook of Swiss Politics* (pp. 101-120). NZZ Libro.

Linder, W., & Müller, S. (2017). *Schweizerische Demokratie. Institutionen—Prozesse—Perspektiven*. Haupt.

Linder, W., & Mueller, S. (2021). *Swiss Democracy*. Springer.

Lösch, A. (2021). Welche Unterscheidungen braucht die Endlagerforschung? Soziotechnische Gestaltung zwischen Möglichkeit und Unmöglichkeit. In B. Brohmann, A. Brunnengräber, P. Hocke, & A. M. Isidoro Losada (Eds.), *Robuste Langzeit-Governance bei der Endlagersuche. Soziotechnische Herausforderungen im Umgang mit hochradioaktiven Abfällen* (pp. 25–43). transcript Verlag.

Maissen T. (2015). *Geschichte der Schweiz*. Hier und Jetzt.

Meier, J. (2021, July 3). *AKW sollen zehn Jahre länger laufen—fürs Klima*. NZZ am Sonntag.

Nagra. (2016). The Nagra Research, Development and Demonstration (RD&D) Plan for the Disposal of Radioactive Waste in Switzerland. *Technical Report 16–02*. Retrieved June 23, 2022, from https://backend.nagra.ch/system/files/attachments/ntb/ntb2016/e_ntb16-002.pdf.

Nagra. (2021a). *Our mandate—and who funds us*. Retrieved November 04, 2021, from https://www.nagra.ch/en/mandate-and-funding.

Nagra. (2021b). *What is the procedure for identifying the most suitable repository site?*. Retrieved December 11, 2021, from https://www.nagra.ch/en/site-selection-process.

Nagra. (2022a). *Nagra proposes "Nördlich Lägern" as the site for a repository*. Retrieved February 10, 2023, from https://nagra.ch/en/nagra-proposes-nordlich-lagern-as-the-site-for-a-repository/.

Nagra. (2022b). *Volumes of radioactive waste*. Retrieved February 08, 2023, from https://nagra.ch/en/knowledge-centre/volumes-of-radioactive-waste/

SNEA. (2021). *Nuclear Energy Act* (NEA) of 21 March 2003 (Status as of 1 January 2021). SR 732.1.

SNEO. (2019). *Nuclear Energy Ordinance* (NEO) of 10 December 2004 (Status as of 1 February 2019). SR 732.11.

Nuklearforum. (2002). *Petition: Fachleute wollen geologische Tiefenlagerung und kein kantonales Veto / Ständerat will nationales Referendum für geologische Tiefenlager*. Retrieved November 29, 2021, from www.nuklearforum.ch.

Planval. (2014). *Aufbau der regionalen Partizipation im Sachplanverfahren zur Standortsuche von geologischen Tiefenlagern. Umsetzung und Erfahrungen*. Bundesamt für Energie BFE.

Regionalkonferenz Nördlich Lägern. (2013). *Oberflächenanlagen eines geologischen Tiefenlagers für radioaktive Abfälle. Bewertung der Standortarealvorschläge durch die Regionalkonferenz Nördlich Lägern*. Anhang. Retrieved June 23, 2022, from https://regionalkonferenz-laegern.ch/wp-content/uploads/2018/11/Anhang_komplett_1.pdf.

Röhlig, K. J., & Eckhardt, A. (2017). Primat der Sicherheit: Ja, aber welche Sicherheit ist gemeint? *GAIA - Ecological Perspectives for Science and Society*, 26(2), 103-105.

Saurugger, S. (2010).The Social Construction of the Participatory Turn: The Emergence of a Norm in the European Union. *European Journal of Political Research*, 49(4), 471-495.

SFOE. (2008). *Sectoral Plan for Deep Geological Repositories. Conceptual Part*. Retrieved June 23, 2022, from https://pubdb.bfe.admin.ch/en/publication/download/3437.

SFOE. (2018a). *Sachplan geologische Tiefenlager. Bericht über die Ergebnisse der Vernehmlassung zu Etappe 2 «Auswertungsbericht»*. Retrieved June 23, 2022, from https://www.newsd.admin.ch/newsd/message/attachments/54701.pdf.

SFOE. (2018b). *Ein Tiefenlager in der Wohnumgebung? Einschätzungen der Schweizer Bevölkerung Ergebnisse der Befragung aus dem ImmoBarometer 2012, 2014, 2016 und 2018 von NZZ und Wüest Partner*. Retrieved June 23, 2022, from https://pubdb.bfe.admin.ch/de/publication/download/10399.

SFOE. (2018c). *Sachplan geologische Tiefenlager. Konzept regionale Partizipation in Etappe 3*. Retrieved June 23, 2022, from https://pubdb.bfe.admin.ch/de/publication/download/9480.

SFOE. (2018d). *Sachplan geologische Tiefenlager. Ergebnisbericht zu Etappe 2: Festlegungen und Objektblätter*. Retrieved June 23, 2022, from https://pubdb.bfe.admin.ch/de/publication/download/8908.

SFOE. (2019). *Stakeholders Involved in the Sectoral Plan Procedure. Fact Sheet*. Retrieved June 23, 2022, from https://pubdb.bfe.admin.ch/en/publication/download/8882SFOE. (2020). *Regionale Partizipation*. Retrieved December 07, 2021, from https://www.bfe.admin.ch/bfe/de/home /versorgung/kernenergie/radioaktive-abfaelle/sachplan-geologische-tiefenlager/regionale-partizipation.html.

SFOE. (2021). *Faktenblatt Abgeltungen im Sachplan geologische Tiefenlager*. Retrieved June 17, 2022, from https://www.bfe.admin.ch/bfe/de/home/versorgung/kernenergie/radioaktive-abfaelle/sachplan-geologische-tiefenlager.html.

SFOE. (2023). *Regional Participation*. Website running by SFOE, https://www.bfe.admin.ch/bfe/en/home/versorgung/kernenergie/radioaktive-abfaelle/sachplan-geologischetiefenlager/regionale-partizipation.html. Last access 10.02.2023.

Standpunkt. (2012). Die konkreten Arbeiten haben begonnen. *standpunkt. Das Bulletin der Baudirektion Kanton Zürich zur Entsorgung radioaktiver Abfälle*, 12 (1), 7.
STENFO. (2021). *Faktenblatt Nr. 1: Allgemeine Informationen. Stilllegungsfonds für Kernanlagen und Entsorgungsfonds für Kernkraftwerke*. Retrieved June 23, 2022, from https://www.stenfo.ch/wp-content/uploads/2021/11/Faktenblatt-1-Allg.-Informationen_de_v1.0.pdf.
Swissnuclear. (2019). *Lehre, Forschung und Nachwuchs in der Schweizer Kernenergie. Eine Bestandsaufnahme. Dossier.* Retrieved June 23, 2022, from https://www.swissnuclear.ch/upload/cms/user/20191014DossierErhebenungLehreForschungNachwuchs.pdf.
Swissnuclear. (2021). *Die Schweizer Kernkraftwerke*. Retrieved November 28, 2021, from https://www.kernenergie.ch/de/schweizer-kernkraftwerke-_content---1--1068.html.
Thurnherr, W. (2018, November 13). *Study history* [Keynote address]. Young Leaders Conference. Retrieved December 09, 2021, from https://www.bk.admin.ch/bk/de/home/dokumentation/reden.msg-id-72902.html.
TNS opinion. (2013). *Attitudes towards radioactive waste in Switzerland*. Retrieved July 07, 2022, from https://www.newsd.admin.ch/newsd/message/attachments/32079.pdf.
Transens. (2021). *Transdisziplinäre Forschung zur Entsorgung hochradioaktiver Abfälle in Deutschland*. Retrieved December 08, 2021, from www.transens.de.
Transmutex. (2021). *Reinventing Nuclear Energy from First Principles*. Retrieved December 07, 2021, from https://www.transmutex.com/.
TSF. (2021). *Technical Safety Forum*. Retrieved November 04, 2021, from https://www.ensi.ch/en/technical-safety-forum/.
UREK-N. (2013). *Kein Vetorecht für Standortkantone von geologischen Tiefenlagern. Medienmitteilung der Kommission für Umwelt, Raumplanung und Energie des Nationalrates*. Retrieved December 07, 2021 from https://www.parlament.ch/press-releases/Pages/2013/mm-urek-n-2013-05-07.aspx.

Sophie Kuppler is head of the research unit Radioactive Waste Management as a Socio-Technical Project at the Institute for Technology Assessment and Systems Analysis (ITAS) at the Karlsruhe Institute for Technology (KIT) since October 2022. She has a degree in environmental and resource management, as well as in socio-economic planning, and holds a PhD in sociology. Her work focuses on technology conflicts, technology assessment, and long-term governance. She is an expert in the field of socio-technical analyses of nuclear waste governance with a particular focus on Germany and Switzerland.

Anne Eckhardt is researcher and consultant on safety, risk and uncertainty in sociotechnical systems and on technology assessment (TA). She has a degree in biophysics, and a PhD in natural sciences. In Switzerland she held several mandates in the field of nuclear safety and the management of radioactive waste, most recently as Chairwoman of the Board of the Federal Nuclear Safety Inspectorate. In Germany she is contributing to the project "Transdisciplinary research on the management of high-level radioactive waste in Germany" (TRANSENS). In Technology Assessment, she specializes in studies on new developments at the interface of biomedicine, biotechnology and information technology. Anne Eckhardt is the managing director of the company risicare based near Zurich.

Peter Hocke was head of the research unit Radioactive Waste Management as a Socio-Technical Project at the Institute for Technology Assessment and Systems Analysis at KIT (Karlsruhe, Germany) until October 2022 and is now working there as a Senior Researcher. His research is focused on Technology Assessment (TA), social science-based research on nuclear waste management and public conflicts about advanced technologies. Currently, he is responsible for the transdisciplinary project TRANSENS, which analyses radwaste management within a sociotechnical perspective (www.transens.de). In the 1990s he worked as a junior fellow in the unit Public Sphere and Social Movements at the Social Science Research Center, Berlin (WZB). Since 2006 he has engaged in policy advice (e.g. in the Asse case in 2021). Research fields: TA, socio-technical conflicts in late-modern societies, transdisciplinarity.

Open Access This chapter is licensed under the terms of the Creative Commons Attribution 4.0 International License (http://creativecommons.org/licenses/by/4.0/), which permits use, sharing, adaptation, distribution and reproduction in any medium or format, as long as you give appropriate credit to the original author(s) and the source, provide a link to the Creative Commons license and indicate if changes were made.

The images or other third party material in this chapter are included in the chapter's Creative Commons license, unless indicated otherwise in a credit line to the material. If material is not included in the chapter's Creative Commons license and your intended use is not permitted by statutory regulation or exceeds the permitted use, you will need to obtain permission directly from the copyright holder.

UK Nuclear Waste Policy: 50 Wasted Years

Stephen Thomas

> There should be no commitment to a large programme of nuclear fission power until it has been demonstrated beyond reasonable doubt that a method exists to ensure the safe containment of long-lived, highly radioactive waste for the indefinite future.
> (Royal Commission on Environmental Pollution, 1976, p. 131),

8.1 Introduction

In 2003, an energy policy White Paper, published by Tony Blair's UK government, stated:

Although nuclear power produces no carbon dioxide, its current economics make new nuclear build an unattractive option and there are important issues of nuclear waste to be resolved. Against this background, we conclude it is right to concentrate our efforts on energy efficiency and renewables. We do not, therefore, propose to support new nuclear build now. But we will keep the option open (Department of Trade and Industry, 2003, p. 12).

S. Thomas (✉)
Public Services International Research Unit (PSIRU),
University of Greenwich, London, UK
e-mail: Stephen.thomas@gre.ac.uk

Yet only two years later, Tony Blair told a conference: nuclear energy was *"back on the policy agenda with a vengeance"*, with a review to be undertaken to determine whether the 2003 policy on nuclear should be reversed (Tempest, 2005). This announcement begged the question what actions were planned to resolve the issues on nuclear waste. This chapter focuses on UK nuclear waste policy from 2005 to 2022 and whether the policy on nuclear waste that emerged after 2005 is well founded. The focus is mainly on high-level waste (HLW) and intermediate-level waste (ILW), as these present the most intractable issues.

Sections 2 and 3 provide an overview of the UK's civil and military nuclear programmes and catalogues the attempts up to 2005 to identify sites for waste. Sections 4 and 5 examine the attempt started in 2005 by the Blair government to restart nuclear construction and the corresponding measures taken to deal with waste. Sections 6 and 7 examine the inventory of material that will go into a Geological Disposal Facility (GDF) and the design features of the GDF. The key feature of the current policy on waste, that the site selection process should be driven by consent by host communities rather than imposed by central government, is then examined.

8.2 Military and Civil Nuclear Programmes

Blair's 2005 announcement came after 50 years of nuclear power generation in the UK, which has determined the volume and type of waste that had to be dealt with. The civil nuclear power programme up to 2005 is summarised in Table 8.1.

The military programme predates the civil nuclear programme, and the HLW and ILW from this will be placed in the same repository as the civil waste. Military waste comprises material from the nuclear weapons programme, with the first weapons test taking place in 1952, and spent fuel and waste from submarines, with the first nuclear submarine being commissioned in 1963. These wastes will continue to be generated regardless of any decisions in the civil nuclear sector. The Ministry of Defence is expected to pay its share of the disposal costs.

The first civil reactors used the 'Magnox' design.[1] Twenty-six reactors of this design ranging from 60-600 MWe were built, the first entering service in 1956

---

[1] The Magnox design was named after the magnesium–aluminium alloy used to clad the fuel. The reactors use unenriched uranium and were cooled using carbon dioxide and moderated using graphite.

8 UK Nuclear Waste Policy: 50 Wasted Years

Table 8.1 The UK nuclear programme: Key dates and policy decisions

1956	First of 11 (5 GW) Magnox stations (CO_2 cooled, graphite moderated, natural U) enters service. Last Magnox completed 1972 & closed in 2015. Fuel must be reprocessed because of corrosion
1959	Nuclear Installations Inspectorate, part of the government Health & Safety Executive (HSE), created to regulate nuclear plants. 2011, renamed Office of Nuclear Regulation (ONR) and separated from HSE in 2013
1965	Advanced Gas-cooled Reactor (AGR) technology chosen. CO_2 cooled, graphite moderated, enriched U. 5 stations ordered 1965–1969, entered service 1976–89. First 3 stations to be retired in 2021–22, other 2 closed by 2024. Fuel initially reprocessed.
1977	Dual reactor strategy comprising preparations to build Westinghouse Pressurised Water Reactors (PWRs) & orders for 2 AGRs to give interim work to UK nuclear industry, 1979, in service 1989, to be closed by 2028
1977	Commercial Fast Reactor 1 expected to be ordered soon, put on hold 1982. UK merged FBR expertise with that of France & Germany in 1988, no reactors built.
1979	Margaret Thatcher launches programme of PWR orders, 1 per year for 10 years, first order to be placed 1981. Only 1 PWR (Sizewell B) ordered, 1987, completed 1995
1990	Attempt to privatise electricity industry reveals operating cost alone of Magnox & AGRs double the expected wholesale electricity price. 1990–1996, 10% of electricity bills paid to nuclear to cover costs. Nuclear plants remained publicly owned. Expectation that nuclear would all be closed by 2000
1995	UK Atomic Energy Authority (UKAEA) split and commercial activities privatised. Privatised company ceases nuclear work
1996	AGR reliability improved enough for them to be privatised with Sizewell B, as British Energy
2002	British Energy collapses when wholesale electricity price not high enough to cover costs. Rescued by government & relaunched 2005
2002	British Nuclear Fuels Limited (BNFL) insolvent, plans to privatise it intact abandoned and the company broken up with commercial activities privatised. Ownership of all existing civil nuclear facilities passed to new public organisation, Nuclear Decommissioning Authority (NDA)
2003	Energy White Paper states "[nuclear power's] current economics make it an unattractive option for new, carbon-free generating capacity" and "we conclude it is right to concentrate our efforts on energy efficiency and renewables"
2006	Tony Blair announces nuclear "back on the policy agenda with a vengeance". New nuclear would be competitive & given no public subsidies

(continued)

Table 8.1 (continued)

Year	Description
2008	Nuclear White Paper states 'nuclear is currently one of the cheapest low-carbon electricity generation technologies, so could help us deliver our goals cost effectively.' And 'nuclear power is likely to be cost-competitive with other sources of electricity in most scenarios.'
2009	EDF buys relaunched British Energy comprising 7 AGRs, a PWR and sites to build new reactors
2009	3 competing consortia set up comprising 7 large European utilities each expecting to build 2–3 reactors on each of 5 sites, 16 GW, by 2030
2013	Deal for first project, Hinkley Point C, 2 Areva European Pressurised Reactors (EPRs) agreed with EDF-led consortia, contracts signed, first power 2023, expected construction cost £14bn (£16.4bn 2020 prices), take-or-pay power purchase agreement for 35 years at fixed real price of £92.5/MWh (2012 money)
2013/14	6 European utilities pull out of their consortia and 2 consortia are sold, 1 to Toshiba to build Westinghouse AP1000 and 1 to Hitachi to build *Advanced Boiling Water Reactor* (ABWR)
2015	Government launches attempt to commercialise Small Modular Reactors (SMR) in UK
2016	Bradwell site allocated to China General Nuclear (CGN) to build 2 reactors using Chinese technology
2016/17	Westinghouse & Areva both collapse. Areva taken over by EDF
2018/19	Hitachi & Toshiba abandon their 3 projects. EDF acknowledges it cannot finance its 2nd project, Sizewell C, and proposes Regulated Asset Base model with institutional investors owning the plant
2020	Small amounts of public money for SMR programme given to Rolls Royce PWR SMR, U-Battery HTGR & Westinghouse lead-cooled fast reactor
2021	CGN stops work on Bradwell B project. Dungeness B AGR closed
2022	Hunterston B and Hinkley Point B AGRs retired.5.0 GW of nuclear capacity in operation, 3.2 GW under construction. Remaining AGRs expected to close 2024–2028, Sizewell B will operate till 2045. 3 of 6 new nuclear projects abandoned, 2 of 6 in serious doubt. SMR programme lacking direction. By 2030, maximum nuclear capacity only 1.2 GW
2022	Hinkley Point C delayed to 2027–28 and cost up to £25–26.7bn

Source: Author's research

and the last closing in 2015. Reprocessing the spent fuel to separate the plutonium was required. This was partly because it was assumed the spent fuel was prone to corrosion and could not be disposed of directly. It was also to provide plutonium for the weapons programme,[2] and because of a perception that world reserves of uranium were so limited as to require an early transition to fast reactors fuelled by plutonium. A reprocessing plant (B204) had been in operation since 1952 using fuel from non-power reactors, replaced in 1964 by the B205 plant, which reprocessed Magnox fuel. B205 closed in July 2022 (Her Majesty's Government, 2022).

By 1964, it was clear the Magnox design was not commercially competitive, and a government decision was taken to replace it with another UK design, the Advanced Gas-cooled Reactor (AGR).[3] Five stations were ordered, comprising two reactors each of about 600 MW, but it soon became apparent the design was poor, and the procurement strategy misconceived (Williams, 1979). The five stations are the most delayed and unreliable set of reactors built in the world. This was followed by three more government reactor choices: the Steam Generating Heavy Water Reactor in 1969, the dual AGR/Pressurised Water Reactor (PWR) policy of 1977, and the PWR programme of 1979. However, these attempts all largely failed, and resulted in two more AGRs and one PWR (Sizewell B) being built, completed in 1989 and 1995 respectively.

The fast reactor programme with its need for plutonium remained a strong influence on nuclear policy, and a proposal was made to build a new reprocessing plant to deal with fuel from the AGRs and PWRs[4] as well as imported spent fuel. It was subject to a Public Inquiry in 1977 (The Windscale Inquiry, 1978). The verdict was in favour of the Thermal Oxide Reprocessing Plant (THORP), but construction did not start for another decade, with completion in 1994. THORP only started up in 1997, it never operated as designed, underwent continual breakdowns, and was closed in 2018 when it had fulfilled its contracts to reprocess non-UK spent fuel. Unlike Magnox fuel, which was claimed to require reprocessing, there is no need to reprocess AGR or PWR fuel. By the late 1980s, the fast reactor programme had been essentially abandoned and the need for plutonium for civil reactors no longer existed.

There were several consequences for waste disposal from this history of reprocessing. By 2020, the UK had built up a stockpile of separated civil plutonium

---

[2] It was claimed that civil spent fuel was not used to make weapons plutonium, but the distinction was a materials accounting one. There was one reprocessing plant and there was no segregation of military spent fuel.
[3] The AGR reactors are cooled using carbon dioxide and moderated using graphite and used enriched uranium.
[4] The B205 reprocessing plant was not suitable for fuel from AGRs and PWRs.

of about 140 tonnes, with no apparent use (Fichtlscherer et al., 2020). Despite this, the UK does not categorise spent fuel or plutonium as radioactive waste. The stock of plutonium is sufficient for a significant programme of fast reactors so it is unlikely the spent fuel will not be classified as waste for direct disposal. The 2005 rescue of the collapsed privatised nuclear power company, British Energy (see below), led to an end to reprocessing for AGR fuel because of the high cost (European Commission, 2005, p. 33). In effect, this means that fuel loaded into AGRs after 2005 was not reprocessed, and none of the Sizewell B PWR fuel was reprocessed.

The privatisation of the British electricity industry in 1990, one of the last acts of the Thatcher government, was intended to include the existing nuclear capacity, with a commitment to build at least three more PWRs to follow on from Sizewell B. The information gathered to allow the sale of the nuclear reactors revealed that the operating cost alone of the Magnoxes and AGRs was double the expected wholesale electricity price. It was also clear that private investors were unwilling to take on the risk of building new reactors, and the nuclear sector remained in public ownership. The failure to sell the nuclear capacity was a crushing blow to the credibility of the UK nuclear industry. The performance of the AGRs and Sizewell B had improved sufficiently for them to be privatised in 1996 but with no obligation to build new reactors, while the Magnox plants remained in public ownership. The illusion that nuclear power was cheap was exposed and the decision in 2003 not to pursue nuclear power seemed inevitable.

8.3 Attempts to Identify Waste Disposal Sites

In 1976, the UK government appointed a Royal Commission on Environmental Pollution to examine the environmental impact of nuclear power. Its seminal report, commonly known as the Flowers Report (Royal Commission on Environmental Pollution, 1976), was a comprehensive and thorough review of the impact of nuclear power, but the statement that resonates today is the one quoted at the start of this chapter, that nuclear power should not be pursued until there is a clear solution to the waste issue.

In the wake of this influential report, efforts to identify new sites for disposal of low-, intermediate- and high-level waste (LLW, ILW and HLW) began (see Table 8.2). For LLW, the Drigg site in Cumbria was established in 1959, and by 1980 there was an apparent need to build a new facility. In 1986, four sites, none of which had any existing nuclear facilities, were identified by the Thatcher government as sites for a shallow burial site for LLW. This led to immediate

Table 8.2 The UK nuclear waste disposal programme

Year	Event
1952	B204 reprocessing plant opened to reprocess spent fuel to separate Pu, closed 1964 & converted to pre-handling plant to allow Advanced Gas-cooled Reactor (AGR) fuel reprocessing in B205, re-opening 1969. Explosion in 1973 contaminating the whole plant & 34 workers led to permanent closure of the plant.
1964	B205 reprocessing plant opened to reprocess Magnox fuel, expected to close 2021 when last Magnox fuel reprocessing complete.
1971	British Nuclear Fuels Limited (BNFL) separated from UK Atomic Energy Authority (UKAEA).
1976	Royal Commission on Environmental Pollution recommends: "There should be no commitment to a large program of nuclear fission power until it has been demonstrated beyond reasonable doubt that a method exists to ensure the safe containment of long lived, highly radioactive waste for the indefinite future."
1977	Public inquiry into proposal to build a reprocessing plant, Thermal Oxide Reprocessing Plant (THORP), opened. Approval given 1978. Economic case based on contracts to reprocess foreign fuel. Pu to be sent back to country of origin.
1982	Nuclear Industry Radioactive Waste Executive (NIREX) created to examine options for radioactive waste disposal. Absorbed into Nuclear Decommissioning Authority (NDA) 2007.
1986	4 sites identified as potentially suitable for Intermediate-level Waste (ILW) Geological Disposal Facilities (GDF). Quickly abandoned.
1994	THORP completed, enters service in 1997, but never operates as designed. In 2005 suffered a major leak of Pu, contained but undetected for 10 months. Closed 2018.
1995	Proposal to investigate using Sellafield for GDF by NIREX sent to Public Inquiry. Proposal rejected.
1997	Plant to make Mixed Oxide fuel completed but did not enter service till 2002. Designed to produce 120 tonnes fuel per year but in its 5 years of operation, made only 5 tonnes total.
2001	Committee on Radioactive Waste Management (CoRWM) set up to advise government on best option to deal with *'legacy'* waste.
2003	Energy White Paper states "there are also important issues of nuclear waste to be resolved. These issues include our legacy waste."
2006	CoRWM reports that GDF are the best option for *legacy* waste.
2008	Nuclear White Paper states, "Government believes that it is technically possible to dispose of new higher-activity radioactive waste in a geological disposal facility and that this would be a viable solution and the right approach for managing waste from any new nuclear power stations." And, "We consider that it would be desirable to dispose of both **new and legacy** waste in the same repository facilities."

(continued)

Table 8.2 (continued)

2012	Nuclear Decommissioning Authority (NDA) launches consultation on how to deal with stockpile of separated plutonium, put it 'beyond reach'. 3 options considered: burning in a Hitachi PRISM FBR, burning in a Candu 6, used to make MOX fuel. Consultation not completed but 'burning' options rejected.
2018	THORP closes when foreign contracts fulfilled. Most Pu not sent back to country of origin, but equivalent quantity of radioactivity sent back leaving UK with total stockpile of separated Pu of about 140 tonnes.

Source: Author's research

and determined local opposition. Just before the next General Election in 1987, evaluation of all four sites was abandoned and LLW was expected to be dealt with along with ILW in deep burial sites. Despite Drigg being reportedly close to capacity for decades, compaction has meant it continues in operation, with no immediate plans to close and replace it with a new facility.

In 1982, the nuclear industry, primarily then publicly owned, set up the Nuclear Industry Radioactive Waste Executive, Nirex Ltd, to examine methods for waste disposal. In 1989, Nirex began to look for sites for deep geological disposal of LLW and ILW, and targeted two sites, both with existing nuclear facilities, Dounreay (on the north coast of Scotland) and Sellafield (in Cumbria on the northwest coast of England), both remote and sites of previous nuclear accidents that had contaminated the land with plutonium. This contamination means there is no prospect that either site could be cleaned up sufficiently to allow its release for unrestricted use. In 1992, Nirex announced plans to build a Rock Characterisation Facility at Sellafield. This would monitor conditions at the depth a GDF would be built in order to assess the suitability of the site. The county council for the area, Cumbria, turned down the application, and in September 1995, a Public Inquiry into the rejection of the proposal was opened, running for five months. Nirex's proposal was turned down by the Public Inquiry[5] (Cumbria County Council, 1996), and an appeal by Nirex to the Secretary of State against this verdict was also rejected. The Inquiry Inspector was highly critical of the case made by Nirex.

In 2003, an energy policy White Paper concluded nuclear power was "an unattractive option and there are important issues of nuclear waste to be resolved" (Department for Trade and Industry, 2003, p. 12). To deal with the waste issue,

---

[5] Public inquiries are formal investigations into major developments, convened by a government minister.

the UK government set up the Committee on Radioactive Waste Management (CoRWM) in 2003, with a brief: "to make recommendations for the long-term management of the UK's higher activity wastes that would both protect the public and the environment and inspire public confidence" (Committee on Radioactive Waste Management, 2006, p. 2). The committee emphasised that "CoRWM's recommendations are directed to existing and committed waste arisings. CoRWM believes that its recommendations should not be seen as either a red or green light for nuclear new build" (Committee on Radioactive Waste Management, 2006, p. 13).

CoRWM's main recommendation was:

Within the present state of knowledge, CoRWM considers geological disposal to be the best available approach for the long-term management of all the material categorised as waste in the CoRWM inventory when compared with the risks associated with other methods of management. The aim should be to progress to disposal as soon as practicable, consistent with developing and maintaining public and stakeholder confidence. (Committee on Radioactive Waste Management, 2006, p. 96)

There was disagreement within the Committee about whether the facility should be immediately sealed when it was full or kept open for several hundred years. The Committee was unable to agree on this.

By the time of the 2005 Blair announcement, experience had shown that attempting to site waste facilities even at existing nuclear sites, and even for the technologically relatively straightforward LLWs would be bitterly contested. The moves to fulfil the duty to deal with the existing and committed wastes in an appropriately responsible manner, such as the CoRWM exercise, were immediately derailed by Blair's announcement. Attempts to site waste facilities were, as a result, seen by critics of nuclear power as 'door-opening' measures for new nuclear build, rather than an attempt to deal responsibly with existing waste.

8.4 The Blair Programme

The 2003 energy policy White Paper had promised:

Before any decision to proceed with the building of new nuclear power stations, there will need to be the fullest public consultation and the publication of a further white paper setting out our proposals (Department of Trade and Industry, 2003, p. 12).

So, the 2005 Blair policy speech could not be immediately turned into a programme of new reactor build. A White Paper on nuclear power policy was published in 2008 (Department for Business Enterprise and Regulatory Reform, 2008).

The detailed history of the Blair programme is outside the scope of this chapter but, like the five previous attempts to re-launch a UK nuclear power programme, it largely failed. The 2008 nuclear power policy White Paper led to a government projection that 16 GW of new nuclear capacity, with 11 reactors at five sites, could be in operation by 2025, with an additional site for two reactors, 2.3 GW, added later.

By 2022, only one station, Hinkley Point C (3.2 GW) had started construction and will not be completed before 2027. Three of the sites have been abandoned, and the other two remain in serious doubt. In April 2021, the UK minister Gerry Grimstone said: "*If you read the energy white paper [Department for Business, Energy & Industrial Strategy, 2020] [...] it's by no means certain that this country is going to be building large nuclear power stations.*" (Thomas & Pickard, 2021).

However, in response to high energy prices from 2021, the Boris Johnson government announced a new attempt to restart nuclear ordering, with a target of 24 GW of nuclear capacity to be completed by 2050, with the first new reactor entering service in the mid-2030s (Department for Business, Energy & Industrial Strategy, 2022). It is hard to see why this new attempt should be any more successful than its predecessors.

A major barrier to a relaunch of nuclear power ordering was the financial collapse in 2002 of the two key civil nuclear companies, British Energy (the privatised owner of the newer nuclear power stations) and British Nuclear Fuels Limited (BNFL). British Energy was relaunched in 2005, having satisfied the European Commission that its rescue did not constitute unfair state aid (European Commission, 2005). The price for this public intervention was that 65% of the shares in British Energy were taken by the government. In 2008, EDF (Électricité de France, a multinational electric utility company, largely owned by the French state) bought out the British government, taking an 80% stake in British Energy.[6] This gave it access to the six AGR sites, most of which were seen as suitable for new nuclear capacity.

BNFL was split into eight parts, with the skills and capabilities privatised, but ownership of the sites going to a new government-owned body, the Nuclear

---

[6] The other 20% was taken by and remains with the British energy company, Centrica.

Decommissioning Authority (NDA). Most of these facilities were retired or near retirement and the sites represented major liabilities because of the need to clean them up. At the time of its creation in 2005, NDA's liabilities were estimated to be about £53bn (Nuclear Decommissioning Authority, 2006, p. 70). By 2021, despite 15 years of decommissioning work, the estimated remaining liability had increased to £131.5bn (Nuclear Decommissioning Authority, 2021a, b).

The planning system was seen by the Blair government as a major barrier to large projects, introducing delay and uncertainty. A particular concern was the Public Inquiry system, which was often blamed for the delays building the Sizewell B nuclear power plant and THORP, and the failed attempt to build a deep nuclear waste disposal facility at the Sellafield site. These claims of delays caused by Public Inquiries were however misleading, as the public inquiries represented only a small part of the delays. In 2007, a White Paper introducing a streamlined process was published, *Planning for a Sustainable Future* (Her Majesty's Government, 2007). Under the new procedures, for nationally 'significant infrastructure projects' major Public Inquiries would not take place and there would be a new single consent regime and an independent commission to determine applications.

8.4.1 Resolving Important Issues of Nuclear Waste

The concerns about waste expressed in the 2003 White Paper (Department of Trade and Industry, 2003) needed to be addressed. The 2008 nuclear power policy White Paper (Department for Business, Enterprise & Regulatory Reform, 2008) cited the CoRWM report (2006) as supporting a view that a GDF was the appropriate way to dispose of ILW and HLW but ignored the condition that CoRWM was only mandated to recommend solutions for existing and committed waste. In 2006, CoRWM had reiterated that its conclusions were not applicable to waste from new build:

> The main concern in the present context is that the proposals might be seized upon as providing a green light for new build. That is far from the case. New build wastes would extend the timescales for implementation, possibly for very long, but essentially unknowable, future periods. Further, the political and ethical issues raised by the creation of more wastes are quite different from those relating to committed – and, therefore, unavoidable – wastes. Should a new build programme be introduced, in CoRWM's view it would require a quite separate process to test and validate proposals for the management of the wastes arising. (CoRWM, 2006, p. 13).

In the *Draft National Policy Statement on Nuclear Power Generation* (Department of Energy & Climate Change, 2009, p. 22), the government, then headed by Blair's successor, Gordon Brown, again cited CoRWM as supporting the use of GDFs for ILW and HLW disposal. Four members of the original CoRWM body subsequently wrote to the government expressing dissatisfaction with how their work had been represented.[7]

A White Paper published by the Brown government specifically on waste policy (Department of the Environment & BERR, 2008), elaborated on the nuclear power policy White Paper (Department for Business, Enterprise & Regulatory Reform, 2008), specifically identifying the GDF as the chosen option. Key points from the waste policy White Paper were:

- reflecting the discussions in CoRWM about when the GDF should be closed and the waste made irretrievable, the government said the decision need not be taken now;
- a new division of NDA, the Radioactive Waste Management Directorate (RWM), was set up to replace Nirex using some of Nirex's resources; and,
- while the White Paper sought to stress consultation with the public, it was clear nothing similar to the Public Inquiry system would be allowed. (Department of the Environment & BERR, 2008)

However, the most substantive proposals concerned the site selection and site assessment processes, and while they have been revised several times, the 2008 proposals still form the basis of policy in 2022. At the heart of the proposed process was 'voluntarism and partnership', so that those hosting the GDF would be 'volunteers', unlike the previous process under which a candidate site was selected with no reference to those directly affected. In the 2008 White Paper on waste policy, (Department of the Environment & BERR, 2008), the government identified three sets of local communities: the host community; the town or village where the GDF would be situated; the decision-making body, the local government body for the host community; and wider local interests such as adjoining towns, villages, and districts. The process would begin with a local community making an 'expression of interest', followed by a 'decision to participate' that would commit them to participate in the siting process while still retaining a right

---

[7] http://www.nuclearwasteadvisory.co.uk/wp-content/uploads/2011/06/CoRWM1_Letter_201109.pdf.

of withdrawal, which would apply up to the start of underground testing to determine the suitability of the site. When the decision to participate was taken, a local 'community siting partnership' would be set up.

As incentives, there was an 'engagement package' under which communities' costs would be met and a 'benefits package' provided. The latter included facilities such as transport infrastructure that would be needed for construction, but there would also be 'benefits which may be commensurate with developing the social and economic wellbeing of a community that has decided to fulfil such an essential service to the nation.' Details on what these benefits might be were not specified.

Once the local community had taken a decision to participate, the three stages in the site assessment were a basic screening by means of desk-based studies of the site undertaken to ensure it was suitable, followed by surface investigations and underground operations.

8.5 Developments Since 2008

In 2008, three local councils[8] in the region where Sellafield is sited volunteered to consider hosting a GDF (see Roche et al, 2019). They set up the West Cumbria Managing Radioactive Waste Safely Partnership which met about every six weeks for three years before Cumbria County Council, rejected the plans and the attempt collapsed.

This represented a major setback. Not only had the partnership failed, but the process had revealed serious doubts about the suitability of sites in Cumbria, which are widely seen as by far the most politically feasible because the historic employment offered by the Sellafield complex means there is some local support for new nuclear facilities there.

In 2014, soon after this collapse, the government published another White Paper on waste policy, *Implementing Geological Disposal* (Department of Energy & Climate Change, 2014). This included a national screening process to be carried out by RWM; bringing all facilities associated with a GDF under the 'Nationally Significant Infrastructure Projects' as set out in the planning system reforms introduced in 2008. How relations between government and local communities would operate was also amplified, for example on community representation, how money would be invested in local communities, and establishing a means for local

---

[8] Allerdale Borough Council, Copeland Borough Council and Cumbria County Council.

communities to access independent expertise. No attempt was made to identify potential sites based on this new White Paper.

In 2018, the 2014 White Paper (Department of Energy & Climate Change, 2014) was updated as *Implementing Geological Disposal: Working with communities* (Department for Business, Energy & Industrial Strategy, 2018). This launched the sixth attempt to find a suitable site for a waste disposal facility (see Table 8.3). RWM identified three areas as worthy of investigation for a GDF in England, Cumbria (in the Northwest), Hartlepool and Theddlethorpe (both on the East Coast). By early 2022, three separate Community Partnerships had been set up in Cumbria, in Allerdale (Allerdale Geological Disposal Facility Community Partnership, 2022), Mid Copeland (Mid Copeland GDF Community Partnership, n.d.), and South Copeland (South Copeland GDF Community Partnership, n.d.) and in June 2022 a Community Partnership was set up for the Theddlethorpe site (Theddlethorpe GDF Community Partnership, n.d.). No progress had been made at Hartlepool, and that site seems unlikely to progress. Little has been done other than to set up these Community Partnerships and it is too early to make judgements on them.

8.6 What Material is to Be Disposed of in a GDF?

8.6.1 Legacy Waste

The UK's 2018 White Paper (Department for Business, Energy & Industrial Strategy, 2018), identified three streams of waste that would go into a GDF. HLW is spent fuel or material recovered from reprocessing spent fuel. It generates a large amount of heat as well as a high level of radioactivity. ILW does not generate much heat and arises from reprocessing and from decommissioning of retired reactors. LLW waste can generally be stored in surface stores as the radioactivity decays relatively quickly, but some wastes with long-lived radioactive isotopes are expected to be placed in a GDF.

The position on HLW is complicated by the long history of reprocessing. Spent fuel and separated plutonium are not categorised as waste. The 2018 White Paper says:

> In addition to existing wastes, there are some radioactive materials that are not currently classified as waste, but would, if it were decided at some point that they had no further use, need to be managed as wastes through geological disposal. These include spent fuel (including spent fuel from new nuclear power stations), plutonium and uranium. (Department for Business, Energy & Industrial Strategy, 2018, p. 12)

Table 8.3 Implementation stages for GDF: site selection, site assessment, construction, operation, closure.

Stages in implementing a GDF	Estimated time-line	Main issues/activities
Pre-operation		
Site selection	5 years: Radioactive Waste Management (RWM) identifies potential sites. An individual or a group of people who want to propose an area, be it a few fields or an entire county, for consideration sets up a local group to advance the proposal. RWM reviews the specific sites proposed.	Voluntarism • Expression of interest • Decision to participate • Difficult for communities to object Community Partnership • Gains access to resources. Authorities opposing the proposal have no access to such resources. • Money to build local public facilities Right of withdrawal • In practice it appears to be difficult for members of the partnership to withdraw.
Site assessment	15 years	If, after further investigation by RWM, the site appears promising and there is still local interest, deep investigative boreholes will be drilled by RWM, conditional on consent by the relevant government minister and by the Environment Agency. If these further investigations, expected to take about 15 years, show a Geological Disposal Facility (GDF) is viable, RWM must obtain an Environment Permit from the Environment Agency and a Nuclear Site License from the Office of Nuclear Regulation (ONR) before construction start. If the site proves unsuitable, a new search must start.
Test of public support	Before construction starts	Form of the test not yet determined. If the test fails, the site is abandoned, and a new search must start.

(continued)

Table 8.3 (continued)

Stages in implementing a GDF	Estimated time-line	Main issues/activities
Construction	10 years	Building the GDF is expected to take a further 10 years before the first waste can be emplaced.
Estimated subtotal: 30 years		
Operation		
Waste emplacement	100 years for legacy waste. Much longer, perhaps 250 years, if new-build waste is also disposed of depending on the scale of new-build	It is expected the facility would receive waste for long enough to dispose of only the current volume of 'legacy' waste, about 100 years. If new-build waste is emplaced at the same site, the facility would be open for much longer depending on the scale and timing of new-build. The government (Department of Energy & Climate Change, 2014) states it is: "proceeding on the assumption that only one GDF will be necessary." So given the GDF might be open for 200 years or more from around 2050 and would contain waste generated before 1960, the burden on future generations will be substantial and long-lasting. The facility might not be ready for closure till perhaps 250 years from when it was chosen.
Estimated subtotal: 100–250 years		
Post-operation		

(continued)

Table 8.3 (continued)

Stages in implementing a GDF	Estimated time-line	Main issues/activities
Sealing the facility making waste irretrievable	Seal immediately or after several hundred years	Retrievability: There was disagreement within CoRWM (2006) about whether the facility should be immediately sealed when it was full or kept open for several hundred years. The Committee was unable to agree on this issue. The government claims (Department for Business, Energy & Industrial Strategy, 2018, pp. 25–26): "Permanently closing a GDF at the earliest possible opportunity once operations have ceased provides for greater safety, greater security, and minimises the burden on future generations." The decision can only be taken at the time of closure of the facility.
Estimated subtotal: 0 – 200 years		
Estimated total: 130 – 480 years		

Source: Author's research

This appears to create a major uncertainty about the volume of high-level waste that will be disposed of in the GDF. In 2011, the UK government stated its preferred policy for the stockpile of plutonium was that it should be used in mixed oxide (MOX) fuel that could fuel existing conventional reactor designs such as PWRs. The objective was "to implement approaches to put the inventory of separated civil plutonium beyond reach" (Department for Business, Energy & Industrial Strategy, 2018, p. 14). However, by 2022, attempts to find ways of dealing with the plutonium stockpile, either by 'burning it' in fast reactors or turning it into MOX fuel for conventional reactors had come to nothing.

On spent fuel, the reprocessing plants have been closed and the stock of plutonium seems to be sufficient for a significant programme of fast reactors, so it seems unlikely the spent fuel will not ultimately be classified as waste.

The likelihood is therefore that the plutonium stockpile and the spent fuel will be disposed of directly. So, in practice the likely volume of HLW is known. There is some uncertainty about ILW, as the final stage of decommissioning Magnox reactors that will generate large quantities of ILW was not expected to start until 2075, with decommissioning of AGRs likely to follow sometime after 2100. However, this policy of delay was reviewed in 2020 due to deterioration of the Magnox buildings with a much more rapid timetable likely to be required (Nuclear Decommissioning Authority, Sellafield Ltd & Magnox Ltd, 2021). This will increase the volume of ILW as it will have had less time to decay.

8.6.2 New-Build Waste

The scale and type of waste from new-build is unpredictable because of the uncertainty about the type, number and size of the reactors that will be built. In 2021, four different technologies were being promoted by government: large 1000 + MWe reactors of various designs; the Rolls Royce small (470 MWe) PWR (Rolls Royce. (n.d.); the U-Battery high temperature gas-cooled reactor (3 MWe) (UBattery, n.d.); and the Westinghouse Lead-cooled Fast Reactor (450 MWe) (Westinghouse, n.d.). The latter three options are a decade or more away from commercial deployment with uncertainty about whether they will be pursued. Of the large reactors, there is one station, Hinkley Point C, under construction comprising two European Pressurised Reactors (EPR), expected to be completed before 2030, and two other specific projects (Sizewell C (two EPRs) and Bradwell B (two Chinese-design Hualong One reactors) that might be pursued, but for completion well after 2030.

The 2008 White Paper (Department for Business, Enterprise & Regulatory Reform, 2008, p. 30) stated: "Our view remains that in the absence of any proposals from industry, new nuclear power stations built in the UK should proceed on the basis that spent fuel will not be reprocessed." The Generic Design Assessments by the Office of Nuclear Regulation (ONR) of the reactor designs proposed have been based on disposal of the spent fuel directly into a GDF (see, for example, Nuclear Decommissioning Authority, 2014a). The RWM states: "spent fuel from a new build programme is assumed to be managed by direct disposal after a period of interim storage" (Radioactive Waste Management, 2021, p. 3). The current assumption in government remains that spent fuel would be disposed of rather than reprocessed.

The two EPR projects will use high-burn-up fuel expected to achieve 60+ gigawatt-days per metric ton of uranium (GWd/MTU),[9] more than any commercially operating reactor.[10] High burn-up fuel would be much hotter and more radioactive than conventional spent fuel requiring much longer in intermediate store, perhaps 140 years,[11] before the fuel is stable enough to consider final disposal. There are also concerns that the fuel would become fragile due to fission gases being released in the fuel (see for example Pastore et al., 2017), and that the cladding would become brittle. These factors might make it unwise to dispose of the fuel directly (United States Nuclear Regulatory Commission, 2018), In its assessment of the EPR, the RWM concludes that:

> *ILW and spent fuel from operation and decommissioning of an EPR should be compatible with plans for transport and geological disposal of higher activity wastes and spent fuel. It is expected that these conclusions eventually would be supported and substantiated by future refinements of the assumed radionuclide inventories of*

---

[9] Typical existing reactors have a burn-up of 35–45 gigawatt-days per metric ton of uranium (GWd/MTU). By increasing the enrichment of the uranium in the fuel, it is possible to get to higher burn-ups, meaning the reactor can operate for longer before refuelling is required

[10] Two other designs, the Westinghouse AP1000 and the Hitachi-GE ABWR were approved by the UK safety regulator, ONR, based on using burn-ups of 60 GWd/tU. The projects expected to use these designs have since collapsed although the design approval remains valid. The Hualong One design proposed for Bradwell is expected to have fuel burn-up of about 50 GWd/tU.

[11] RWM states: it would require of order of 140 years for the activity, and hence heat output, of the EPR fuel [with a maximum burn-up of 65 GWd/tU] to decay sufficiently to meet this temperature criterion (NDA, 2014b).

the higher activity wastes and spent fuel, complemented by the development of more detailed proposals for the packaging of the wastes and spent fuel and better understanding of the expected performance of the waste packages (Nuclear Decommissioning Authority, 2014b, p. 8).

The UK White Papers of 2008, 2014 and 2018 on waste disposal make no mention of burn-up and the issues it raises.

8.6.3 Military Waste

Military waste from the weapons and submarine programmes will form a significant part of the waste disposed of in the GDF, but no details have been published about the volume and characteristics of this waste.

8.7 The Proposed Geological Disposal Facility

8.7.1 Design

Only one GDF is proposed, albeit with separate areas to take the different categories of waste. The 2018 White Paper (Department for Business, Energy & Industrial Strategy, 2018) suggested there might be a system of vaults for the disposal of ILW, and an array of engineered tunnels for the disposal of HLW. These could be at different depths, for example 200 m for ILW and 1 km for the higher activity wastes. There would be substantial surface facilities, for example rail and road links for delivery of the waste. The packaged volume of the waste is estimated to be about 750,000 cubic metres, equivalent to 70% of the volume of the Wembley football stadium.

8.7.2 Cost and Employment

The 2018 White Paper stresses the employment impact of the GDF: "Current estimates are it will directly employ around 600 skilled, well-paid staff per year, over the duration of the project, with workforce numbers rising to more than 1000 during construction and early operations." The jobs would be provided for "more than 100 years" (Department for Business, Energy & Industrial Strategy, 2018, p. 54). However, on cost, the White Paper says: "The precise costs of developing a GDF will depend on a number of factors, including the type of rock in which the facility is constructed and exactly how long it operates before being closed." (Department for Business, Energy & Industrial Strategy, 2018, p. 25).In the 2021 GDF annual report, the Nuclear Waste Services (NWS) division of NDA stated the cost of the GDF: "is estimated to be in the region of £20-£53bn", compared to its previous estimate of only £12bn. NWS explained the increase: "This was because that figure [£12bn] only represented a lower-end single-point estimate based on the costs of disposing of legacy waste only alongside some basic assumptions about a single type of geology and depth" (Nuclear Waste Services, 2022, pp. 24–26).

The overwhelming majority of the waste generated will be owned by the NDA, the Ministry of Defence, and the UK government, which will take title to the waste from EDF's nuclear power stations when they are retired.

8.7.3 Timing

The White Paper (Department for Business, Energy & Industrial Strategy, 2018) talks about a period of 15–20 years to identify a site and carry out the technical work necessary to prove its suitability (see Table 8.3). There would then be a period of 10 years to construct the first vaults, at which point emplacement of waste would begin in parallel with construction of further capacity. The White Paper claims a GDF could be open in the 2040s. It is expected the facility would receive waste for about 100 years, long enough to dispose of only the current volume of 'legacy' waste. After 100 years, the 2018 White Paper implies the facility would be closed promptly and waste from new-build plants would need another GDF. However, in discussions between RWM and its stakeholder engagement group, it appears that once legacy waste has been disposed of, new vaults would be constructed for new-build waste using the existing shaft. The Johnson government claims: "Permanently closing a GDF at the earliest possible opportunity once operations have ceased provides for greater safety, greater security, and minimises the burden on future generations." (Department for Business, Energy & Industrial Strategy, 2018 pp. 25–26).

The Cameron government (previously stated it is: *"proceeding on the assumption that only one GDF will be necessary."* Department of Energy & Climate Change, 2014). So given the GDF might be open for 200 years or more from around 2050, and would contain waste generated before 1960, the burden on future generations will clearly be long-lived.

8.7.4 Regulation

The regulatory framework for GDF is expected to be essentially the same as for other nuclear facilities. The ONR will regulate safety and security. The Environment Agency will be responsible for implementing and enforcing environmental protection legislation; its areas of responsibility include environmental pollution, waste management, flood risk management, water resources, fisheries, and conservation. The Health and Safety Executive will ensure the health and safety of workers.

8.7.5 Location

As with previous attempts, the most likely sites to be pursued are those in Cumbria near the Sellafield complex. Proposals to consider sites on the east coast of England (Theddlethorpe and Hartlepool) have attracted little local support and seem unlikely to proceed. RWM have stated: "If the community doesn't want it, it won't be built" (BBC, 2022).

8.7.6 Retrievability

The government states: "The UK Government and regulators agree that the purpose of a GDF is to dispose of waste, not to store it." And that: "Permanently closing a GDF at the earliest possible opportunity once operations have ceased provides for greater safety, greater security, and minimises the burden on future generations" (Department for Business, Energy & Industrial Strategy, 2018, pp. 25–26). However, given that the decision on when to seal the repository will be taken in no less than 150 years from now based on the prevailing conditions, such a statement has little weight.

8.8 Community Consent

Given the hostility previous attempts to impose a disposal facility had generated, ensuring the support of local communities has been at the centre of government proposals since the 2008 White Paper on nuclear waste (Department of the Environment & BERR, 2008). Much of the 2018 White Paper (Department for Business, Energy & Industrial Strategy, 2018) concerns proposals aimed at ensuring this informed consent is given. This raises the issue of how the process can be run without a serious risk that a previously receptive community could end the process if it changed its mind.

The process is initiated by an individual or a group of people who want to propose an area for consideration, be it a few fields or an entire county. If RWM judges that the site is worthy of further consideration, RWM must inform the relevant local authorities. If, after further investigation by RWM, the site appears promising and there is still local interest, deep investigative boreholes will be drilled by RWM, conditional on consent by the relevant government minister and by the Environment Agency. These further investigations are expected to take about 15 years. If they show a GDF is viable, RWM must obtain an Environment Permit from the Environment Agency and a Nuclear Site License from the ONR. Building the GDF is expected to take a further 10 years before the first waste can be emplaced. Including time to identify potential sites, it appears the whole process is expected to take at least 30 years. The claim in the 2018 White Paper (Department for Business, Energy & Industrial Strategy, 2018) that a GDF could be open in the 2040s therefore looks implausible.

The 2018 White Paper proposes that once a site has passed the initial screening, a Working Group should be formed comprising the person(s) who initially indicated an interest, the RWM, an independent chair, an independent facilitator, and all relevant principal (district or county) local authorities should be invited to be members, although things can proceed if they do not join. The job of the Working Group is essentially to identify potentially suitable sites.

The next step is the formation of a Community Partnership comprising community members, organisations, the RWM and at least one principal local authority. This will be backed up by a Community Partnership Agreement specifying working arrangements. The Community Partnership's job is to share information and to seek answers to questions raised by the community. The Community Partnership will be given funding of up to £1 m per year (Community Investment Funding) in the initial stages, rising to £2.5 m if the proposal progresses to drilling boreholes. This fund can be used for local initiatives, for example, enhancing the natural environment.

8.8.1 Right of Withdrawal

The 2018 White Paper claims: "A community can withdraw from the siting process at any time up until it has taken a Test of Public Support." However, it then appears to contradict that statement: "The decision on whether to withdraw the community will be taken by the relevant principal local authority, or authorities where there is more than one, on the Community Partnership. Where there is more than one relevant principal local authority on the Community Partnership, all must agree; no single relevant principal local authority will be able to unilaterally invoke the Right of Withdrawal" (Department for Business, Energy & Industrial Strategy, 2018, p. 58). It will therefore be easier to enter the siting process than to exit it.

8.8.2 Test of Public Support

The Test of Public Support of residents in the Potential Host Community will take place at the point RWM is ready to seek regulatory approval and development consent for the GDF, some 20 years after the process started. The Potential Host Community will be determined by the Community Partnership and will include wards (divisions of towns or cities) that will be physically affected by the GDF, either below or above ground, and including required infrastructure such as transport links. The White Paper (Department for Business, Energy & Industrial Strategy, 2018) does not specify the form the Test might take, but suggests it might be a referendum, a consultation or statistically significant polling. The right of withdrawal ceases once a successful test of public support has taken place.

8.8.3 Engagement Funding

The Community Partnership and its Working Groups will have funding available and access to expert bodies to allow them to commission their own work. The scale of this funding is not specified. However, there is no funding for critical groups. This is unlike Sweden, where the MKG (Swedish NGO Office for Nuclear Waste Review), and an alliance of organisations often critical of nuclear power, receives significant government funding.

8.8.4 Community Investment Funding

The White Paper restates the economic benefits of the project to the area, particularly job creation over more than 100 years. It talks of 600 permanent jobs during the operation of the facility with up to 1000 during construction. It also mentions improvements in infrastructure such as transport links. However, these benefits only begin once construction starts, perhaps 20 years from when the process begins. The government therefore proposes funding of £1 m rising to £2.5 m per year once borehole drilling starts, available to the members of the Community Partnership to be used for projects benefiting the local communities but with no connection to the project.

Once a site has been selected for a GDF and the Community Investment Funding has finished, the local communities will also continue to receive government grants for local projects, amount not specified.

8.8.5 Will the New Policy Yield a GDF?

There is a wide gap between the rhetoric of willing communities volunteering to host a GDF and the reality of the procedures. It seems unlikely that any site apart from one in Cumbria will command local support, and even in Cumbria there will also be significant local opposition. So, while two other areas were proposed in 2021 by local groups, these will be bitterly opposed by other local interests.

The earlier 2008 policy quickly failed when one of the local authorities withdrew support. The government responded by making it easier to set up a Community Partnership, and harder to withdraw from one, with increased incentives to make the lengthy and costly procedure less vulnerable to a precipitate collapse. A proposal can now be set up with support of only one or two local individuals or local groups. Provided it can get support from one or two local authorities and regardless of how many local authorities oppose it, a Community Partnership could be set up and gain access to resources to commission their own studies and receive significant public money to build local facilities unconnected with the proposal. Authorities opposing the proposal have no access to such resources. Once a Community Partnership is set up, despite the promise of a right of withdrawal, in practice, it appears it would be impossible for one member of the partnership to withdraw.

These measures make a mockery of claims that a GDF would not be imposed. They are also unlikely to be politically sustainable if it becomes clear that their effect is to impose a GDF on an unwilling community.

The Test of Public Support would only take place when construction of the facility is ready to start, after up to 20 years of investigations. There will inevitably be boundary problems, with communities close to the proposed facility but outside the boundaries feeling disenfranchised.

8.9 Conclusions

Nuclear power has seldom been a major public policy issue in the UK, with conflicts generally being between the nuclear industry trying to site a facility and the planned host community opposing it. For waste, it has been government bodies promoting the siting of waste facilities. The scientific establishment has not been a major voice.

Like other European countries with significant existing quantities of ILW and HLW, UK policy is to dispose of this in a GDF. Policy statements are designed to promote the view that GDFs are the only responsible policy option for these types of waste, and that there are no doubts that disposal in a GDF is viable and would entail negligible risk that harmful material would leak into the environment over the long period required. This assumption is based on several premises. That:

- A site can be identified that meets the geological requirements over a period of hundreds of thousands of years.
- The complex chemical and radiological changes that will occur over this period are well enough understood.
- The packaging arrangements will be able to withstand the intense heat and radiation they will be subjected to.

Assessing these requirements is beyond the scope of this analysis, but the proposals will not only have to achieve a scientific consensus that they meet requirements; they will also have to convince the public. The poor technological record of the British nuclear industry with many serious technological failures, means its credibility is low.

The Government justifies its advocacy of a GDF based on the recommendations of the Committee on Radioactive Waste Management. Since the start of the Blair attempt to relaunch nuclear construction in 2005 successive governments have never acknowledged that the mandate of this Committee was solely to deal with 'legacy' waste. While this is a historic detail that few will be aware of, the underlying difference between a door-opening decision and a decision to discharge a historic responsibility will continue to be a barrier to getting the local consent needed to select sites. The lack of a proven method for dealing with waste also undermines claims by advocates of nuclear power that it is a sustainable technology.

These issues were exacerbated by the ambitions in 2022 of the UK government under Boris Johnson to expand nuclear power. By 2021, the 2006 Blair programme of building 16 GW of large reactors by 2025 was failing, with the only project to proceed, Hinkley Point C, not forecast to be complete before 2027–28. In its place, the UK government directed public money to Small Modular Reactors (SMR) until 2022, when the Johnson administration launched its own attempt to build large new reactors. The SMR designs are all a decade or more from being deployable and may never be commercially viable. Whether the problems of getting public consent for a GDF would be solved if the UK was to make a decisive decision not to pursue new reactor projects, comparable to the German 'Energiewende', is hard to determine. However, given that the successive failures of nuclear policy dating back to the 1960s do not seem to have dimmed governments of all complexions' appetites to continue to try to launch new nuclear power programmes, such a decision appears implausible.

The history of the British nuclear industry, specifically the policy of reprocessing spent fuel, has also created problems for the UK, notably the huge quantity of separated plutonium. The government's position that spent fuel and plutonium are not categorised as waste causes uncertainty about the quantity and type of high- and intermediate-level waste that will need to be accommodated in a GDF. Radioactive decay of the plutonium means that it will increasingly not be useable as reactor fuel. In practice, it is not clear what the implications over the next decades up to the forecast opening date of a GDF would be, given that a restart of reprocessing and a major fast reactor programme appear to be decades away, if ever. Would the material be stored differently if it was categorised as waste, or as a resource for future use?

The issues raised by the high burn-up fuel, which will be used in Hinkley Point C and any other large reactors built are not addressed by government. These include the very long period, expected to be 140 years, from being removed from the reactor and the spent fuel being ready to be emplaced in a GDF, and the fragility of the fuel and its cladding, which puts into question whether the fuel can be disposed of directly without significant processing.

While RWM has carried out a nationwide survey to identify potential sites, all experience suggests that finding a site that will command local support anywhere other than Cumbria, where the Sellafield complex is sited, will be hard. Sellafield employs about 11,000 people and given the paucity of alternative employment prospects and the closure of many of the facilities at Sellafield, any proposal that offers future employment is likely to receive some support.

The statement in the White Paper that: *"Permanently closing a GDF at the earliest possible opportunity once operations have ceased provides for greater safety, greater security, and minimises the burden on future generations"* (Department for Business, Energy & Industrial Strategy, 2018 pp. 25–26) is rather empty. The facility might not be ready for closure till perhaps 250 years from now.

So, many future generations will have to bear the burden of funding it, operating it and the physical risk that it would pose until it is sealed. When the facility is at the point when it could be permanently sealed, the decision will be taken based on the conditions that prevail then. The intentions stated now will carry no weight.

The alternative to a GDF, of indefinite surface storage, appears to give rise to additional risk because of the accessibility of the material and its vulnerability to natural phenomena such as flooding, and appears to evade our responsibility to clean up the pollution we create. However, it may be the 'least bad' option if emplacement in a misconceived GDF risks radioactive material getting into the environment with no way to mitigate the damage because the material is irretrievable.

The UK has continued to pursue new nuclear power programmes for most of the 45-year period since the Flowers report stated there should be no commitment to new nuclear power plants until there is clear evidence *"that a method exists to ensure the safe containment of long-lived, highly radioactive waste for the indefinite future."* (Royal Commission on Environmental Pollution, 1976, p. 131) There is still no sign this condition can be met, and policymakers continue to make decisions whose consequences will not be known for decades, long after the time they could be held accountable for them.

References

Allerdale Geological Disposal Facility (GDF) Community Partnership. (2022, February 1). *February Newsletter.* https://allerdale.workinginpartnership.org.uk/allerdale-gdf-community-partnership-february-newsletter/.

BBC. (2022, February 8). *Theddlethorpe: Search area for possible nuclear waste site revealed.* https://www.bbc.co.uk/news/uk-england-lincolnshire-60304295.

Committee on Radioactive Waste Management (CoRWM). (2006). *Managing our radioactive waste safely: CoRWM's recommendations to government.* https://assets.publishing.service.gov.uk/government/uploads/system/uploads/attachment_data/file/294118/700_-_CoRWM_July_2006_Recommendations_to_Government_pdf.pdf.

Cumbria County Council. (1996). *Appeal by United Kingdom Nirex* http://www.davidsmythe.org/nuclear/inspector's_report_complete.pdf.

Department for Business, Energy & Industrial Strategy. (2018). *Implementing Geological Disposal: Working with communities.* https://assets.publishing.service.gov.uk/government/uploads/system/uploads/attachment_data/file/766643/Implementing_Geological_Disposal_-_Working_with_Communities.pdf.

Department for Business, Energy & Industrial Strategy. (2022, April 7). *British energy security strategy: Policy paper.* https://www.gov.uk/government/publications/british-energy-security-strategy/british-energy-security-strategy#nuclear.

Department for Business, Enterprise & Regulatory Reform. (2008). *Meeting the energy challenge: A white paper on nuclear power*. CM7296. https://assets.publishing.service.gov.uk/government/uploads/system/uploads/attachment_data/file/228944/7296.pdf.

Department for Trade and Industry. (2003). *Our energy future: creating a low-carbon economy*. CM5761. https://assets.publishing.service.gov.uk/government/uploads/system/uploads/attachment_data/file/272061/5761.pdf.

Department of Energy & Climate Change. (2009). Draft National Policy Statement for Nuclear Power Generation (EN-6). https://assets.publishing.service.gov.uk/government/uploads/system/uploads/attachment_data/file/228630/9780108508332.pdf.

Department of Energy & Climate Change. (2014). *Implementing Geological Disposal: A Framework for the long-term management of higher activity radioactive waste*. URN 14D/235. https://assets.publishing.service.gov.uk/government/uploads/system/uploads/attachment_data/file/332890/GDF_White_Paper_FINAL.pdf.

Department of the Environment & BERR. (2008). *Managing Radioactive Waste Safely: A Framework for Implementing Geological Disposal: A White Paper by Defra, BERR and the devolved administrations for Wales and Northern Ireland*. Cm 7386. https://assets.publishing.service.gov.uk/government/uploads/system/uploads/attachment_data/file/228903/7386.pdf.

European Commission. (2005). *Commission decision of 22 September 2004 on the State aid which the United Kingdom is planning to implement for British Energy plc*. Official Journal of the European Union, 2005/407/EC. https://eur-lex.europa.eu/legal-content/EN/TXT/?uri=uriserv%3AOJ.L_.2005.142.01.0026.01.ENG&toc=OJ%3AL%3A2005%3A142%3AFULL.

Fichtlscherer, C., Friederike F., Kütt, M. (2020, April 17). *Britain has 139 tons of plutonium. That's a real problem*. Bulletin of the Atomic Scientists. https://thebulletin.org/2020/04/britain-has-139-tons-of-plutonium-thats-a-real-problem/ (Accessed July 3, 2022).

Her Majesty's Government. (2007). *Planning for a Sustainable Future*. CM7120. HMSO. https://assets.publishing.service.gov.uk/government/uploads/system/uploads/attachment_data/file/228933/7120.pdf.

Her Majesty's Government (2022). 'Magnox Reprocessing plant achieves final milestone' https://www.gov.uk/government/news/magnox-reprocessing-plant-achieves-final-milestone (Accessed July 12, 2022).

Hon Mr Justice Parker (1978). 'The Windscale Inquiry.' https://fissilematerials.org/library/uk78.pdf (Accessed July 10, 2022).

Mid Copeland GDF Community Partnership. (n.d.). Retrieved July 4, 2022, from https://midcopeland.workinginpartnership.org.uk/.

Nuclear Decommissioning Authority. (2006). *Annual Report and Accounts 2005/6*. https://assets.publishing.service.gov.uk/government/uploads/system/uploads/attachment_data/file/231625/1416.pdf.

Nuclear Decommissioning Authority. (2014a). *Progress on approaches to the management of separated plutonium*. https://assets.publishing.service.gov.uk/government/uploads/system/uploads/attachment_data/file/457874/Progress_on_approaches_to_the_management_of_separated_plutonium_position_paper_January_2014.pdf.

Nuclear Decommissioning Authority. (2014b). *Geological Disposal: Generic Design Assessment: Summary of Disposability Assessment for Wastes and Spent Fuel arising from Operation of the UK EPR NDA Technical Note no. 11261814 rev1*.

Nuclear Decommissioning Authority. (2021). *Annual Report and Accounts 2020 to 2021* https://www.gov.uk/government/publications/nuclear-decommissioning-authority-annual-report-and-accounts-2020-to-2021/nda-annual-report-and-accounts-2020-to-2021.

Nuclear Decommissioning Authority, Sellafield Ltd, and Magnox Ltd. (2021, March 18). *Case study: Timing of the Magnox Reactor Decommissioning Strategy*. https://www.gov.uk/government/case-studies/timing-of-the-magnox-reactor-decommissioning-strategy.

Nuclear Decommissioning Authority, Sellafield Ltd, and Magnox Ltd. (2021). *Timing of the Magnox Reactor Decommissioning Strategy, HM Government*. https://www.gov.uk/government/casestudies/timing-of-the-magnox-reactor-decommissioning-strategy.

Nuclear Waste Services. (2022). *GDF Annual Report 2020–2021*. https://assets.publishing.service.gov.uk/government/uploads/system/uploads/attachment_data/file/1057186/GDF_Annual_Report_2020_21.pdf.

Pastore, G., Folsom, C. P., Williamson, R. l., Hales, J. D., Luzzi, L., Pizzocri, D. & Barani T. (2017). *Modeling Fission Gas Behaviour with the BISON Fuel Performance Code*. Idaho National Laboratory, INL/CON-17–42034-Revision-0. https://inldigitallibrary.inl.gov/sites/sti/sti/Sort_2067.pdf.

Radioactive Waste Management. (2021). *Geological Disposal Generic Design Assessment: Summary of Disposability Assessment for Wastes and Spent Fuel arising from the Operation and Decommissioning of the UK HPR1000 Pressurised Water Reactor. NDA/RWM/172.* https://www.ukhpr1000.co.uk/wp-content/uploads/2021/06/NDA_RWM_172_Decommissioning_of_the_UK_HPR1000.pdf.

Roche, P., Thuillier, B., Laponche, B., Goldstick, M., Ban H., & Alvarez, R. (2019). *The global crisis of nuclear waste*. Greenpeace France. http://www.nuclearwasteadvisory.co.uk/wp-content/uploads/2019/02/REPORT_NUCLEAR_WASTE_CRISIS_ENG_BD.pdf.

Rolls Royce. (n.d.). *Small Modular Reactors*. Retrieved July 4, 2022, from https://www.rolls-royce.com/innovation/small-modular-reactors.aspx/.

Royal Commission on Environmental Pollution. (1976). *Sixth Report: Nuclear power and the environment*. Cmnd 6618. HMSO. https://webarchive.nationalarchives.gov.uk/20110322144120/http://www.rcep.org.uk/reports/06-nuclear/1976-06nuclear.pdf.

South Copeland GDF Community Partnership. (n.d.). Retrieved July 4, 2022, from https://southcopeland.workinginpartnership.org.uk/.

Tempest, M. (2005, November 29). *Blair gives nod to nuclear review*. The Guardian. https://www.theguardian.com/environment/2005/nov/29/energy.greenpolitics.

Theddlethorpe GDF Community Partnership. (n.d.). Retrieved July 4, 2022, from https://theddlethorpe.workinginpartnership.org.uk/.

Thomas, D & Pickard J. (2021, April 28). *UK woos sovereign wealth funds over green investments*. Financial Times. https://www.ft.com/content/f2352470-2bef-4b15-bae8-fb9e002212d0 (Accessed July, 4 2022)

UBattery. (n.d.). Retrieved July 4, 2022, from https://www.u-battery.com/.

United States Nuclear Regulatory Commission. (2018, Oct 1). *Backgrounder on High Burnup Spent Nuclear Fuel*. https://www.nrc.gov/reading-rm/doc-collections/fact-sheets/bg-high-burnup-spent-fuel.html.

Westinghouse. (n.d.). *Lead-cooled Fast Reactor*. Retrieved July 4, 2022, from https://www.westinghousenuclear.com/new-plants/lead-cooled-fast-reactor/.

Williams, R. (1979) *The Nuclear Power Decisions: British Policies, 1953-78.* Routledge.

Stephen Thomas was Professor of Energy Policy at the University of Greenwich, UK, until his retirement in 2015. He has a degree in chemistry. He has more than forty years experience as an energy policy researcher with particular emphasis on nuclear power. He is coordinating editor of the journal, Energy Policy.

Open Access This chapter is licensed under the terms of the Creative Commons Attribution 4.0 International License (http://creativecommons.org/licenses/by/4.0/), which permits use, sharing, adaptation, distribution and reproduction in any medium or format, as long as you give appropriate credit to the original author(s) and the source, provide a link to the Creative Commons license and indicate if changes were made.

The images or other third party material in this chapter are included in the chapter's Creative Commons license, unless indicated otherwise in a credit line to the material. If material is not included in the chapter's Creative Commons license and your intended use is not permitted by statutory regulation or exceeds the permitted use, you will need to obtain permission directly from the copyright holder.

9. The Governance Ecosystem of Radioactive Waste Management in France: Governing of and with Mistrust

Markku Lehtonen

9.1 France as a Forerunner in High-Level Radioactive Waste Management

Together with Finland and Sweden, France is a forerunner in the development of high-level nuclear waste (HLW) management solutions. A deep geological repository for high- and medium-level long-lived waste is being planned for Bure, a very small community in a sparsely populated area in the East of France, with expected operation to start in 2040–2050. The project, led by the national radioactive waste management agency, Andra, and financed via taxes levied on the waste producers, has a long and conflict-ridden history of deep mistrust between proponents and opponents of the project, and faces resistance from an active minority, despite the extensive participatory procedures, especially at the national level (Barthe, 2006; Blowers, 2016; Lehtonen, 2019). In 1998, the government announced reversible deep geological disposal (DGD) as its preferred option—a choice consolidated as the reference option for HLW management in a landmark 2006 waste law, following a public consultation organised by the National Commission on Public Debate (CNDP) in 2005–2006. In 2010, the government approved Andra's plan to site in Bure a deep geological repository, Cigéo,[1]

---

[1] Centre industriel de stockage géologique.

M. Lehtonen (✉)
Universitat Pompeu Fabra, Barcelona, Spain
e-mail: markku.lehtonen@upf.edu

© The Author(s) 2023
M. Arentsen and R. van Est (eds.), *The Future of Radioactive Waste Governance*, Energiepolitik und Klimaschutz. Energy Policy and Climate Protection, https://doi.org/10.1007/978-3-658-40496-3_9

designed to accommodate all high-level and long-lived intermediate-level radioactive waste (ILW) generated by France's operating nuclear fleet throughout its entire lifetime. The mandatory public consultation on Cigéo, in 2013, had to be transformed to an on-line expert debate because of obstruction by local opponents. A law adopted in 2016 specified the criteria of reversibility. Andra submitted its application for a "declaration of public utility" (DUP; demande de déclaration d'utilité publique) in August 2020, and subjected the proposal to a public inquiry in September 2021. Andra hopes to launch the project in 2025 with successive pilot phases, allowing the repository to become fully operational in 2040–2050. Although supported by most parliamentarians, departmental authorities, business organisations, trades unions, and mayors in the region, the project continues to generate controversy and has led to clashes between opponents and the police.

Despite the resistance and controversies, the project has advanced steadily, if somewhat slower than planned. The "participatory turn" inaugurated in 1990 opened up the highly technical planning approach to a broader range of stakeholders, perspectives, and management options. This opening up was triggered largely by the need to manage the considerable public mistrust towards the promoters of the repository project and the nuclear sector in general. Three historically shaped features underpinned the mistrust: the miserably failed communication concerning the Chernobyl fallout in France, the highly technical and non-participatory way in which Andra conducted test drillings in candidate municipalities in the late 1980s, and the longstanding secretive policymaking in the French nuclear sector, led by a small yet powerful group of technocrats, entailing close integration between the scientific and politico-administrative domains of governance.

A number of institutions and practices have been established to manage the pervasive mistrustful relationships between various actors in French HLW governance, to harness mistrust to productive purposes, and to thereby facilitate the articulation across governance domains. This has included the establishment of pluralist multi-stakeholder bodies and institutions, the adoption of the concept of reversibility as the cornerstone of HLW management, and, most recently, experimentation with processes of co-creation of knowledge between institutional and citizen experts. These efforts, in turn, build on the strong tradition of nuclear-sector counter-expertise, developed since the mid-1970s and institutionalised following the Chernobyl disaster. Civic vigilance represented by counter-expertise has forced actors in the political and administrative sphere, as well as industry players, to seek new ways of integrating the civil society and social science expertise into HLW governance.

This chapter analyses these measures and practices adopted in French HLW governance to improve the articulation between the different governance domains, and their impacts on the multiple trust and mistrust relations. In particular, the integration of the societal domain in HLW governance remains controversial and contested, and measures of trust-building have produced a range of partly unanticipated outcomes. Greater transparency and mechanisms of "invited" participation have also generated new forms of mistrust, both between and within the governance domains. For example, sections of the critical civil society and social science community see this engagement as merely another measure employed by the technocracy to maintain control, whereas some voices from the "nuclear community" consider that the engagement with civil society has gone so far as to undermine the integrity and objectivity of science. The French example calls for attention to the complex and multidimensional nature of trust and mistrust, the possibilities and limitations of mistrust in fostering the social robustness of policies and decisions, and the importance of the historical nuclear-sector legacies in shaping the articulation between the domains of HLW governance.

9.2 The Rocky Road Towards Becoming a Forerunner

9.2.1 The Roots of Mistrust: Chernobyl, a Technical Approach to Siting, and the Nucleocracy

The beginning of the institutionalisation of French HLW governance can be traced back to 1979, when the government set up the National Radioactive Waste Management Agency (Andra) to implement geological disposal of HLW and to manage low- and intermediate waste storage. Andra was established as an agency of the Commissariat of Atomic Energy (CEA), at the time still the leader of French nuclear technology development, R&D, and regulation. As such, it closely integrated the politico-administrative and scientific-technological spheres of governance, to the exclusion of the societal domain. HLW management in France is closely conditioned by choices regarding the entire fuel cycle, in particular that of reprocessing of spent nuclear fuel. The La Hague reprocessing site is a key venue for HLW management as the entry into operation of the Cigéo repository is still far off. Three sites for above-ground storage of low-and-intermediate level waste are operational, in the departments of La Manche and l'Aube.

Discontent and mistrust emerged quickly in reaction to the technical and non-participatory way in which Andra conducted its site investigations in 1987–1990. This generated vehement local opposition, with citizens asking why their community should be designated as "France's nuclear wastebasket" (Barthe et al., 2010), and contributed to the quick deterioration of the hitherto relatively high trust in state institutions and engineering elites. The second source of mistrust was the so-called "Chernobyl cloud affair", i.e., the discovery that the authorities had downplayed the true extent of the Chernobyl fallout in 1986 (Kalmbach, 2015; Ambroise-Rendu, 2018; Lehtonen, 2019, pp. 63–75). The public turned sceptical about the ability and willingness of the authorities to manage and communicate on nuclear safety, whereas the media became increasingly critical, and wary of being seen as the mouthpiece of the government and authorities (Ambroise-Rendu, 2018).

The third reason for mistrust had more profound roots in the special place that the nuclear sector has enjoyed within French society since the 1950s. Nuclear energy in France was originally developed to support the atomic weapons industry, and decision-making was secretive, overwhelmingly in the hands of a small number of technocrats, often described as a "nucleocracy"—experts, civil servants and politicians trained in the country's prestigious polytechnics (e.g., Barthe, 2006; Hecht, 2009; Lepage, 2014). However, especially until the Chernobyl accident, the technocracy was not only despised, as the nuclear sector was also seen as a source of pride, export revenue, and a vector of post-War modernization (Hecht, 2009). The civilian nuclear sector took off properly in 1974, with the launching of a massive programme of construction of American pressurised-water reactors (PWRs). There has been significant public scepticism towards nuclear energy in France throughout its history, but politically, nuclear energy enjoyed cross-party support until the mid-1990s, when the uncompromisingly anti-nuclear Green Party became a major player (Brouard & Guineaudeau, 2015).

Today, 56 reactors, operated by the 96% state-owned EDF (Electricité de France)[2], satisfy about 70% of France's electricity demand. The nuclear sector provides an estimated 220,000 jobs in the country (Vie publique, 2022). France holds competence over the entire fuel cycle through the CEA, and above all the

---

[2] "In the midst of the energy crisis triggered by the Russian invasion of Ukraine in February 2022, the French government declared its intention to completely renationalise EDF, most notably to facilitate the construction of new nuclear power plants." This could serve as the source for the 96-percent figure—which is expected to reach 100% sooner or later: https://www.lefigaro.fr/societes/renationalisation-d-edf-l-etatpossede-96-du-capital-a-la-cloture-provisoire-de-l-opa-annonce-l-autorite-des-marches-financiers-20230208.

industry giants EDF, Orano (until late 2017, Areva)[3] and Framatome. The future of the French nuclear sector has during the recent decade become increasingly uncertain. In the aftermath of the Fukushima accident in March 2011, for the first time in French history even some leading politicians evoked the possibility of a nuclear phase-out. Successive governments have sought to ensure the success of the country's nuclear technology exports, which have, however, faced several setbacks over the past fifteen years, most notably in the Asian and American markets. President François Hollande's government made a commitment in 2012 to reduce the share of nuclear electricity from the then 75% to 50% by 2025, but in 2018, Hollande's successor, Emmanuel Macron, postponed the target to 2035. Even this target has since been questioned, as shown by Macron's declaration in 2021 foreseeing the construction of six new European Pressurised Reactors (EPRs) in France, and €1 billion investment in nuclear, with the development of Small Modular Reactors as a priority (Elysée, 2021; Dupont-Calbo, 2021). All this despite the formidable delays, budget overruns, and technical problems on the only current new-build site, Flamanville, where the EDF has been constructing an EPR since 2007. In January 2022, the fuel loading for the reactor was expected to start in 2023, eleven years behind the initial schedule (World Nuclear News, 2022). Significant uncertainties therefore surround the future of the French nuclear sector, and hence also the amount and type of waste that would ultimately be disposed of in Cigéo.

9.2.2 Re-Establishing Trust, Reproducing Mistrust

To re-establish trust and unblock the HLW management stalemate, the government declared a moratorium on site investigations in 1990, and entrusted a parliamentary commission with the task of consulting the actors concerned. The research was reinitiated in 1991 but included three different RWM options, and opened the discussion to a wide range of actors (Barthe, 2006). The landmark Waste Act 1991, the so-called Bataille Law, named after the parliamentarian leading of the preparation of the Waste Act,[4] introduced the ideas of reversible geological disposal and community benefit schemes, and led to the establishment of

---

[3] The French state owns more than 90% of the shares of the full-fuel-cycle nuclear company, Orano.
[4] Loi n° 91-1381 du 30 décembre 1991 relative aux recherches sur la gestion des déchets radioactifs. https://www.legifrance.gouv.fr/loda/id/JORFTEXT000000356548/.

multi-stakeholder commissions, external evaluating bodies, and local information and liaison committees (CLIS). These added further complexity to the multilevel governance of the project.

Towards the late 1990s, local disputes erupted again, in the context of declining public trust in the governance of risk, and following the 1998 government decision to site the underground research laboratory in Bure. The option of burying the waste in granitic formations in the department of Vienne was studied in the 1980s and 1990s, but was abandoned in favour of clay host rock in Bure, because of significant uncertainties concerning the capacity of the Vienne granite to isolate the waste (Patinaux, 2019). Largely because of local opposition, site search was discontinued in the other candidate communities. This quickly turned Bure into the de facto only candidate for hosting a repository (Blowers, 2016). The fifteen-year period of 'opening up' inaugurated in 1991 culminated in a mandatory public debate, organised in 2005–2006 by the National Commission on Public Debate (CNDP), in parallel with debates on a new EPR reactor and the associated high-voltage transmission line project. The waste debate informed the parliamentary discussion leading to the approval of the so-called Planning Act of 2006. The Act instructed Andra to plan a geological repository and apply for a construction licence by 2015. Even many observers critical towards the repository project acknowledged the democratic quality of the CNDP debate—especially its ability to consolidate the legitimacy of CNDP (Bertrand, et al., 2005; Global Chance, 2006, p. 64). However, trust in HLW management institutions was undermined by the exclusion of long-term near-surface storage from the parliamentary preparation of the Planning Act. This option had emerged in the CNDP debate through the demands of a wide range of mainly civil society participants, who argued that keeping the options open would be the only rational solution, given that technological development would most likely bring better solutions, which might even allow turning the waste into a useful resource. A new Act on nuclear transparency and security[5] adopted in parallel in 2006 completed the decades-long gradual process of separation between the promotional and regulatory functions in the French nuclear governance system, by granting the safety authority ASN full independence in relation to both the government and industry.

---

[5] Loi n° 2006-686 du 13 juin 2006 relative à la transparence et à la sécurité en matière nucléaire. https://www.legifrance.gouv.fr/loda/id/JORFTEXT000000819043/.

9.2.3 Towards Implementation: The Cigéo Facility

In March 2010, the government approved Andra's proposal for the creation of the Cigéo repository, after it had been examined by ASN, the National Assessment Board (CNE), and international experts. The HLW would be vitrified, packaged in steel containers, and then placed in tunnels at a depth of about 500 m in a 160-million-year-old Callovo-Oxfordian clay formation (Andra, 2012, p. 4). Cementation or asphalting will be applied to the ILW stored in Cigéo. The repository would be constructed and closed down in a stepwise manner. The project is financed via charges levied on the waste producers: EDF, Orano (until late 2017, Areva), and the national nuclear R&D agency, CEA.[6]

The facility is expected to host about 10,000 m^3 of HLW (about 60,000 waste packages) and 75,000 m^3 of ILW (about 170,000 packages), yet the actual quantity will depend on definitions of waste and on the future of the country's nuclear policy, not least the decisions on whether to continue reprocessing of spent fuel (PNGMDR, 2019, p. 56). Reprocessing has been a cornerstone of France's nuclear policy that since the 1960s has aimed towards a "closed fuel cycle". The 2006 Waste Act[7] defines "the reduction of the quantity and toxicity of radioactive waste especially via reprocessing" as the first of the three key orientations for the National Management Plan for Radioactive Materials and Waste (PNGMDR 2019). Given the ultimate objective of using the reprocessed spent fuel in fast breeder reactors, spent nuclear fuel (SNF) is thus not considered as radioactive waste in France. However, like in most other countries, the fast breeder projects have failed to deliver on their promise, and have faced repeated setbacks since the 1970s. The industrial prototype reactor Superphénix was shut down in 1998, after years of difficult operation, while the Astrid fast reactor project was suspended in 2019 (e.g., Jobert & Le Renard, 2014; Joly & Le Renard, 2021). Moreover, only about 20 of the country's operating reactors can use the mixed oxide (MOX) fuel derived from reprocessing. Given the lack of technological capacity in France to reutilise most of the spent fuel, the safety authority ASN recently called for

---

[6] The French state owns about 96% of the shares of the EDF, the operator of France's 56 nuclear reactors, and more than 90% of those of the full-fuel-cycle nuclear company, Orano.

[7] LOI no 2006-739 du 28 juin 2006 de programme relative à la gestion durable des matières et déchets radioactifs. https://www.legifrance.gouv.fr/download/pdf?id=D9B-tWLBQkp-MfyPyTXr8--nam6aCtsgM2LdqywZyGE=.

a reconsideration of the waste classification, with a view to qualifying the uranium, plutonium, and the residues from the MOX fuel as ultimate waste (ASN, 2020).[8] The latest version of PNGMDR, adopted in 2020, outlined three scenarios for HLW management, based on diverging assumptions concerning the country's future nuclear policy: 1) multiple rounds of waste reprocessing made possible by the deployment of fast breeder Gen IV reactors, 2) continuation of the current policy of one round of reprocessing, and 3) abandonment of reprocessing (PNGMDR, 2019).

After two decades of relative calm, in the context of the 'opening up' of the HLW policy, conflict erupted again in May 2013, when CNDP launched the mandatory public consultation on the siting of the project in Bure. The consultation turned into a farce, following persistent obstruction by opponents (Blanck, 2017). The planned public hearings were cancelled and replaced by on-line expert debates. A relatively successful citizens' consensus conference was organised in early 2014 to "save the face" of the CNDP. The consensus conference suggested that the Cigéo project start with an industrial pilot phase of a minimum of five years, a solution supported by the safety authority's technical support organisation, IRSN (Denoun, 2015). On 25 July 2016, Parliament adopted a law specifying the details of the project, including those relating to safety during operation and after the closure of the repository, as well as the technical criteria for retrievability (see Sect. 9.2.4). Andra submitted its application for a "declaration of public utility" (DUP) in August 2020, and, after a statement from the Environmental Authority, in September 2021 a six-week on-line public inquiry on the project was opened. In December 2021, the public inquiry commission issued a favourable statement on the DUP application.

The government granted Cigéo a DUP, via a decree issued by the Prime Minister, in July 2022.[9] Andra submitted its construction licence application ("autorisation de création") on 16 January 2023, expecting[10] that a government decree will approve the application in 2025, at the earliest (MTE, n.d.). Should this timetable hold, the project would start with a ten-year pilot phase, with waste packages

---

[8] The spent fuel contains about 1% of plutonium, used to produce MOX, with approximately 95% consisting of uranium. About 10% of this uranium is in principle reusable, yet France does not currently possess the requisite technology, and therefore sends the uranium to Russia for enrichment.

[9] Journal Officiel de la République française, no. 0157, text 13, on 7 July 2022. https://www.legifrance.gouv.fr/eli/decret/2022/7/7/ENER2200646D/jo/texte.

[10] https://international.andra.fr/submission-application-authorization-create-cigeo.

which do not contain radioactive material. In 2035–2040, provided that ASN gives its approval, the pilot phase would continue with actual radioactive waste packages. A law defining the conditions for the operation of the repository would allow the repository to become fully operational, in 2040–2050.

9.2.4 Reversible Geological Disposal: A Key Concept for Alleviating and Managing Mistrust

A key concept designed to alleviate public mistrust has been reversible geological disposal—the explicit objective of the French HLW management policy since the late 1990s. Until the late 1980s, the French nuclear elite considered irreversible deep geological disposal as the best and, de facto, the only option for HLW management (Barthe, 2006, pp. 55–57). Irreversibility, portrayed as the impossibility to recover the waste packages, was a central objection of environmental NGOs and local politicians opposed to geological disposal (Cézanne-Bert & Chateauraynaud, 2009, pp. 61–63). Their preferred alternative was temporary near-surface storage at the nuclear sites. In January 1990, a socialist parliamentarian demanded that the reversibility of the geological disposal project be ensured (ibid.).

The National Waste Act in 1991 evoked the notion of "reversible or irreversible geological disposal" but did not clearly define reversibility. In 1998, the government declared reversibility to be an essential requirement and a condition for public acceptance for the radioactive waste management solution (Hoorelbeke 2008, pp. 9–10; Barthe, 2009; Lehtonen, 2010). The Planning Act of 2006 established reversible geological disposal as the reference option and defined reversibility as an umbrella term that covers both the technical and political dimensions of the concept: the ability to retrieve the waste, and the possibility to change and reconsider decisions. Reversibility was again debated in the context of the problematic 2013 CNDP debate on the Cigéo project. Andra's proposal for the practical application of reversibility was debated in Parliament and integrated in July 2016 in the law on reversibility of geological disposal.[11] The law defines reversibility as a concept that allows future generations to choose between

---

[11] LOI n° 2016-1015 du 25 juillet 2016 précisant les modalités de création d'une installation de stockage réversible en couche géologique profonde des déchets radioactifs de haute et moyenne activité à vie longue. https://www.legifrance.gouv.fr/loda/id/JORFTEXT000032932790/.

either continuing the construction and operation of disposal through successive phases, or to re-examine the earlier choices and modify the management solutions accordingly.[12] In addition to reversibility, even after its closure, following some 150 years of operation, the repository and its environment are to remain under monitoring for several centuries.

9.3 Managing Mistrust in Practice: Institutions and Mechanisms for Articulating Between Domains

Since the landmark Waste Act from 1991, numerous legislative acts and milestones have marked the evolution of French HLW governance, and an elaborate legal framework has been set up, consisting of successive key decision points. The 1991 and 2006 laws laid down the key principles of the policy,[13] which is governed by the PNGMDR, a plan revised every three years, informed by the national waste inventory produced by Andra, and ratified by Parliament. The energy ministry and ASN draft the plan, with advice from a multi-stakeholder committee. In 2019–2020, the preparation of the plan was for the first time informed by a public debate organised by CNDP (PNGMDR, 2019).

The politico-administrative system relating to radioactive waste management in France is highly complex, with multiple levels and parallel tracks of state and regional administration. Multiple stakeholders are involved in mutual control and surveillance at state, departmental and local level, across the governance domains. However, the system remains highly centralised: the implementation is delegated to a state agency, Andra, and the state, represented also at the regional and departmental levels by its own "deconcentrated" administrations, holds the ultimate decision-making power. Key local actors include the more than 300 small communes in the planned repository area, and the departmental authorities of the two

---

[12] "permettra aux générations futures de choisir, soit de poursuivre la construction puis l'exploitation des tranches successives du stockage, soit de réévaluer les choix définis antérieurement et de faire évoluer les solutions de gestion".

[13] The three principles are: 1) the sustainable and safe management of radioactive materials and waste; 2) a definite and safe waste management solution that would minimise the burden on future generations; and 3) producer responsibility, i.e., allocation of the main responsibility for HLW management to the nuclear operators.

departments, Meuse and Haute-Marne, which share the underground laboratory and the planned Cigéo facility. The local municipalities have no veto over the siting decision.

National-level policy leadership and coordination is in the hands of the Directorate General for Energy and Climate (DGEC), currently within the Ministry of Ecological Transition, while Andra, since 1991 an industrial and commercial agency independent of the waste producers, is responsible for implementation. Andra has been a forerunner in facilitating the interaction between society and the administration. It has done so by integrating social sciences into its own work, by financing and co-supervising in-house social science PhD work, and especially through its advisory committee on information and consultation, COESDIC,[14] established in response to the 2006 Waste Act. COESDIC is composed of three sociologists from France and Belgium, and a communication and engagement expert from Andra's Swedish counterpart, SKB. Andra can be seen as an international forerunner in integrating social science expertise into its governance.

The largely state-owned waste producers are the EDF (the operator of the country's 56 current reactors), the full-fuel-cycle company Orano, and the Commissariat of Atomic Energy (CEA). The CEA is a state nuclear research institute, the historical leader of the country's nuclear sector, which has since the 1970s gradually lost its earlier leading role in the RD&D, promotion, and regulation of nuclear energy in France. The waste producers seek to strengthen their presence and visibility in the local region through numerous projects designed to foster local socioeconomic development (e.g., Lehtonen & Kojo, 2019).

Among the organisations of control, the ultimate authority on safety rests with the ASN, the national safety authority, independent from the government and industry since 2006. ASN has integrated civil society representatives into its expert advisory groups since 2014. The National Assessment Board, CNE2, is an independent organisation that evaluates the research and studies concerning radioactive waste management. The National Audit Office (Cour des Comptes) has gained an increasingly visible role in nuclear policies, including in the analysis costs and financing of Cigéo. In doing so, the National Audit Office informs debates and decisions within the three-party negotiations. Balancing between the waste producers' desire to minimise the costs of HLW management, and Andra's interest in securing sufficient resources for implementing the project safely, the Directorate General for Energy and Climate (DGEC), acts as the arbiter. The

---

[14] Comité d'Expertise et de Suivi de la Démarche d'Information et de Consultation.

Environment Authority (Autorité environnementale—AE) is mandated to give a statement on Andra's environmental impact study—a part of the request for a DUP for Cigéo. Academic scholars from France and abroad are regularly solicited to review the repository plans.

Numerous institutions and mechanisms mediate and facilitate the articulation across the governance domains. The Parliamentary office for scientific and technological assessment (OPECST), set up in 1983, has played a vital role in shaping the project, as a key organisation integrating science and technology within the domain of politics and administration (e.g. Parotte, 2016). The High-Level Committee (CHN) is chaired by the energy minister and composed of politicians from national, regional, departmental, and municipal levels, representatives from the operators, prefects (department-level representatives of the central government), and other local representatives of the state. It monitors Andra's work, and helps to facilitate the integration of Cigéo in the local and regional socio-economic context. Mediating between society and the political and administrative sphere is the National Commission on Public Debate (CNDP), an independent public organisation created in 1995, and since 2002 an independent administrative authority, which organises public participation in major infrastructure projects of national interest. In each consultation, CNDP invites any interested parties to submit position papers, often asks for counter-appraisals from specific groups, and holds public meetings at various locations deemed as relevant for the project in question. CNDP produces a summary of the debate, but does not have decision-making power, nor does it give recommendations. However, the developer must report the way in which it has taken the debate into account.

Several organisations facilitate interaction across all three domains. The multi-stakeholder High Commission for Transparency and Information on Nuclear Security (HCTISN)—established in 2006 and composed of 40 members representing operators, safety authorities, government, local information and surveillance committees, NGOs, trade unions, parliamentarians, and experts—fosters debate, information and analysis of issues relating to information and transparency in the nuclear area. In the wake of the Chernobyl accident, two still existing organisations of counter-expertise, ACRO[15] in Brittany, and CRIIRAD[16] in Rhône-Alpes in the Southeast of the country, set up their own independent

---

[15] Association pour le contrôle de la radioactivité à l'Ouest.
[16] Commission de recherche et d'information indépendantes sur la radioactivité.

laboratories for measuring radioactivity. The government subsequently accredited these laboratories as entities officially entitled to monitor radioactivity (Topçu, 2008). The Chernobyl accident also spurred experiments in open forms of expertise and civic vigilance, through the local information and surveillance committees (CLIs) and multi-stakeholder expert committees. The CLIS of Bure (Local information and monitoring committee of Bure) was created in 1999, following the selection of Bure to host the underground research laboratory. It is composed of the representatives of the state, Andra, local politicians, and local business and civil society organisations. CLIS informs the public, facilitates dialogue between stakeholders, and monitors the activities of the underground research laboratory and Cigéo.[17] The national umbrella organisation of local information committees, ANCCLI,[18] actively promotes public engagement and serves as a "watchdog". ANCCLI and CLIS have been active in the process, led and coordinated by IRSN (Institute for Radioprotection and Nuclear Safety), whereby institutional and civil society actors have jointly co-constructed risk-related knowledge. In both involved departments, Meuse and Haute-Marne, a multi-stakeholder committee, GIP,[19] manages the distribution of the €30 million available to both Departments to facilitate the integration of the underground research laboratory and Cigéo in the local territory.

Finally, several NGOs and citizen movements are critical towards or actively opposed to the repository project.[20] These organisations have adopted diverse strategies in relation to the institutionalised engagement practices, some (e.g., Greenpeace, WISE-Paris) seeking to participate in all types of dialogue, others participating in CLIS and CNDP debates but rejecting closer collaboration, while many have decided to remain outside of the institutionalised engagement processes (Fig. 9.1).

---

[17] The Bataille Law (1991) made local information and monitoring committees mandatory at each site hosting a nuclear installation in France.

[18] L'Association Nationale des Comités et Commissions Locales d'Information.

[19] Groupement d'intérêt public.

[20] e.g., EODRA, StopBure!, Villesurterre, Réseau Sortir du nucléaire, Robin Wood, WISE-Paris, and Greenpeace.

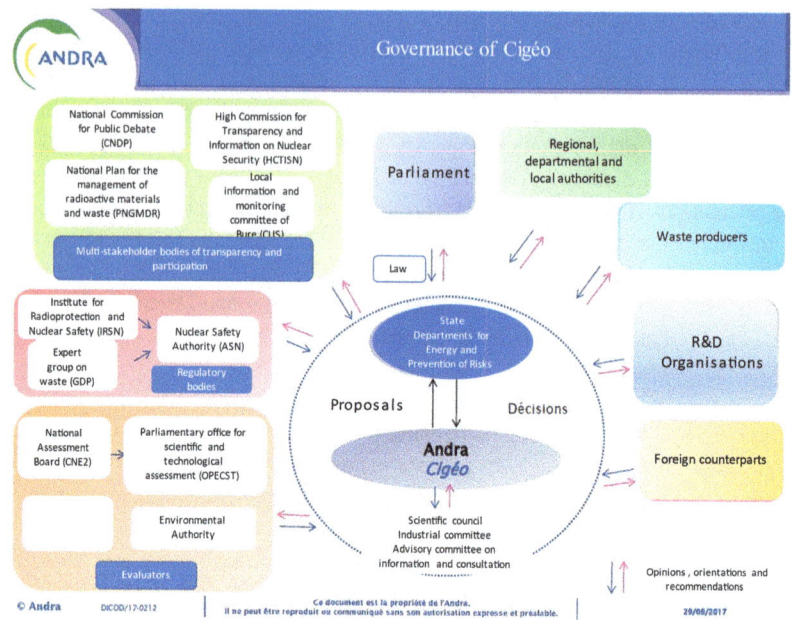

Fig. 9.1 Governance of Cigéo. (Adapted from: https://www.google.com/url?sa=t&rct=j&q=&esrc=s&source=web&cd=&ved=2ahUKEwjDyfWGzvLzAhUyDWMBHQ40BNE4ChAWegQIFBAB&url=https%3A%2F%2Fwww.asn.fr%2FMedia%2FFiles%2F00-PNGMDR%2FPNGMDR-2016-2018%2FLa-demarche-de-concertation-sur-la-gouvernance-et-le-plan-directeur-d-exploitation-de-Cigeo%3F&usg=AOvVaw11IznHx8-AmP_oGw0Hunma)

9.4 Outcomes of Cross-Domain Coordination: Current Debates on Nuclear Waste in France

This section examines the experience of integration across the French HLW governance domains via four key notions: 1) the multiple trust and mistrust relationships that the governance mechanisms described in the previous Sect. (9.3) were designed to manage; 2) the role of the notion of reversibility in the management of mistrust, uncertainties and intergenerational justice concerns; 3) the policy impact of the integration measures; and 4) the role of the nuclear-sector legacies in shaping cross-domain interaction. The section draws on existing literature, as well as on the analysis of parliamentary debates in preparation for the 2006 and 2016 laws relating to HLW management.

9.4.1 Mistrust, Transparency, and "the State vs. Us"

The multiple and elaborate mechanisms and institutions established to reduce dysfunctional mistrust, especially between citizens and the politico-administrative and industrial circles driving HLW management in France, have had varying effects on the trust and mistrust relations. Mistrust is multidimensional, and pervades relations not only between domains of governance, but also within each domain. Moreover, mistrust is not only a governance challenge but also a mechanism for articulating across and within the governance domains.

Mistrust across domains
The mechanisms and institutions of integration have not dispelled the foundational mistrust between the "nucleocracy"—nuclear experts, civil servants and politicians trained to believe in the virtues of nuclear power—and various groups of the broader public. The nucleocracy is frequently blamed for undermining attempts at including civil society, and for seeking to instrumentalise participation to legitimise decisions made behind the scenes. The power of the nucleocracy is frequently evoked, for example in the media (Lehtonen et al. 2021), as an explanation for the failure of participatory and deliberative mechanisms to impact policy, for France's continued reliance on nuclear energy, and for the lack or poor quality of information on HLW (on issues such as waste transports, contrasting repository cost estimates, or job creation estimates). Furthermore, mistrust is reciprocal; some key actors in the nuclear sector are often highly suspicious of citizen and NGO involvement, which they see as a threat to the integrity of science and rational decision-making.

Partly because of the perceived omnipotence of the nucleocracy, mistrust is prevalent also in the relations between the domains of society and science/technology. NGOs that boycott participatory procedures initiated by the authorities and industry often accuse social scientists involved in collaboration with HLW institutions of "acceptology", i.e., for helping the government and industry to persuade local communities and broader publics to accept the repository project.

Mistrust within each governance domain
Mistrust is highly present within each domain.
Amongst the industry and nuclear operators, Andra actively seeks to elicit public trust by maintaining distance from the nuclear operators, to avoid being perceived as part of the nucleocracy. The operators, in turn, are mistrustful of Andra, doubting its ability to implement the industrial repository project, and suspecting Andra for unnecessarily bloating the budget for the construction of the repository.

Within the broader 'nuclear community', tensions have aggravated between the operators and the regulatory authorities ANS and IRSN. Mistrust has emerged in the recent disputes over the safety of the Flamanville EPR reactor, as the ASN and IRSN are both keen to demonstrate their independence in relation to the EDF. Some representatives of the operators have, in turn, mistrusted both Andra's and IRSN's work on co-creation of knowledge, arguing that engagement with civil society and NGOs critical towards the nuclear sector undermine the integrity and objectivity of science.

Within the sphere of science and technology, relations are tense between those social scientists who accept and others that refuse research collaboration with nuclear-sector institutions. In a similar vein, the active civil society is divided between radicals and moderates, the former being quick to condemn their NGO counterparts that collaborate with the state institutions, Andra and IRSN in the first hand. These divisions are particularly sharp in France, probably more so than in most other countries.

Although it is a defining feature of the political sphere in general, mistrust between defenders and opponents of the HLW project has grown in recent years, as demonstrated by the 2016 debates in Parliament concerning the reversibility bill. Both sides of the debate vigorously questioned the trustworthiness of their counterparts. The opponents pointed to the long series of failed safety promises and breaches of procedural justice in HLW management, such as the late-night manoeuvring by the promoters of the project who tried to introduce Cigéo in legislation unrelated to NWM. The project proponents, in turn, blamed the opponents for being motivated only by the desire to end the production of nuclear power, rather than truly seeking a safe solution to the HLW problem.

Mistrust across governance levels

The relations between the state and the local communities in the Bure region are characterised by entrenched perceptions of "us vs. them" and associated mutual mistrust. Andra is often the key target of criticism, perceived as the most visible local-level representative of the state. The lack of previous experience in the nuclear industry, the political and geographical peripherality of the region (Blowers, 2016), and its continuous economic and demographic decline since the 1970s combine to further sharpening the juxtaposition between 'the local' and 'the national' (e.g., Lehtonen & Kojo, 2019). The local-national cleavage manifests itself also in lasting tensions between Andra's headquarters in the Paris region and its local branch in Bure. Local politicians and civil society, but also Andra's local office, mistrust Andra's "Parisians" for their alleged lack of local knowledge.

Mistrust among the locals has been spurred by the failed promise of the state to establish several underground research laboratories, but also by the governance of the community benefit packages via multi-stakeholder committees (GIPs)—in and of themselves designed to reduce mistrust. GIPs have engendered mistrust between the local communities competing for the funding, thus feeding the belief that the state employs divide-and-rule tactics to ensure the acceptance of the Cigéo project. The extension of the boundaries of the "proximity zone" eligible for support added to the tensions: it angered the small communities closest to and most directly affected by the repository, who consider themselves as the obvious priority recipients of support. The GIP support has rather reinforced than dispelled doubts by project opponents who see GIPs as illegitimate bribery, and as yet another proof of the untrustworthiness of the representatives of the state (Lehtonen & Kojo, 2019; Lehtonen et al., 2020). The schemes may have even aggravated some of the state-local-level tensions, as many state, industry and departmental actors blame the local communal leaders for seeking to maximise their commune's share of the benefits, to the detriment of the region's overall good. The nuclear operators, in turn, fear that the GIP funding may dissuade local politicians, who might not accept the project, but instead prefer the status quo which provides them with generous benefit schemes without the possible risks and undesired impacts of the project.

9.4.2 Uncertainties, Intergenerational Justice, and Reversibility

An overarching theme in the French debates concerns the responsibility of the present generation, as the main beneficiary of nuclear power, towards future generations. The analysis of reporting by Le Monde reveals an image of a sceptical and mistrustful "watchdog", newspaper that stresses the multiple outstanding uncertainties that render the entire idea of a "waste solution" illusory (Lehtonen et al., 2021). The newspaper repeatedly stresses that no solution to HLW management has been implemented anywhere—a notion frequently evoked in the parliamentary debates in 2006. The uncertainties discussed concern safety, economics and financing, opposition movements, party politics, and energy policy at large, in a context of multilevel governance and interaction between low-, intermediate- and high-level waste management. Le Monde reported on uncertainties that stem from persistent citizen opposition, growing disagreements between political parties, especially after the Fukushima accident, the uncertain future of reprocessing and nuclear policy, the classification of waste ("recoverable material" vs. ultimate waste), and the cost and financing of the project—between Andra's and waste producers' contrasting estimates, with the government suggesting "compromise figures".[21]

Comparison between the parliamentary debates of 2006 and 2016 reveals changes in the approach to uncertainties. In 2006, the parliamentarians widely agreed on the need for further R&D and "keeping the options open". Ten years later, with the debate now focused on a concrete repository project, the dominant view stressed that "our responsibility" was to act now, trust "our scientists", and recognise that interim storage would provide only a short-term solution. A growing number of parliamentarians now defended the deep geological repository project as the rational and responsible "least-worst option". Continuing to underscore the persistent uncertainties, the opponents claimed that a truly scientific and responsible attitude towards future generations would imply waiting for the better solutions that technological development would certainly bring about (Barthe et al., 2010). The complex role of social sciences emerged in the debate on uncertainties, when Le Monde reported on a sociology PhD thesis, conducted within Andra (Patinaux, 2017) and leaked to the newspaper by a prominent anti-Cigéo activist. Echoing the arguments of the opponents, Le Monde argued that the thesis proved "the impossibility of demonstrating safety"—precisely because of the uncertainties—and thus undermined the credibility and sincerity of Andra. Protracted debates between Andra, the nuclear operators, and opponents ensued, on the uncertainties related to the project but also on the role of social scientists in HLW management policy.

In the face of uncertainties, reversibility features as an overarching "metaframe", a concept that helps to articulate across the domains of governance. In view of the likely technological progress, reversibility would maximise the choices available for future generations and spare them from dealing with the problem: reversibility would allow keeping the options open, while implementing a workable solution. The science and technology domain decisively shapes the debates on uncertainties and responsibility towards future generations. Andra's waste management experts were not enthusiastic when the government announced reversibility as a key requirement. For them, reversibility was a "social and political constraint", an obstacle to rational technical solutions (Andra, 2010,

---

[21] The initial construction cost estimate of €15 billion was revised, first, to nearly €35 billion, and then brought down again—to a politically determined compromise figure of €25 billion.

35; Gilbert and Bourdeaux, 2006, pp. 39–40; Lehtonen, 2010). The experts' preferred way out of the problem was phased, stepwise disposal—advocated by international organisations and today widely adopted in a number of countries—whereby the project would advance through progressive steps towards final irreversible geological disposal (Andra, 2010, p. 36). Opponents pointed out that this would undermine the very idea of reversibility, given that future generations would eventually be faced with a one-off decision to either close the site or keep it open (Barthe, 2009; Cézanne-Bert & Chateauraynaud, 2009). The reversibility debates juxtaposed the natural and engineering sciences with social sciences, the latter gaining influence thanks to international collaboration, directly through Andra's advisory committee on information and consultation (COESDIC), but also via the OECD Nuclear Energy Agency's Forum on Stakeholder Confidence (FSC), established in 2000. Social scientists suggested, among other things, turning interim storage into the reference option, to force continuous exploration of alternatives (Cézanne-Bert & Chateauraynaud, 2009, 84; Gilbert and Bourdeaux, 2006, pp. 37–38). In 2014, COESDIC suggested redefining reversible disposal as deep underground interim storage, in order to overcome the fruitless opposition between the advocates of geological disposal and interim storage.

Although at first a requirement from civil society, reversibility has progressively been appropriated by the dominant actors and integrated into legislation. For those opposed to geological disposal, the concept has come to represent another way used by the nuclear lobby to achieve "social acceptance" for the project and for nuclear energy (Cézanne-Bert & Chateauraynaud, 2009, p. 4). By contrast, local-level actors, including the local information and liaison committees (CLIS) and most local and departmental authorities, increasingly stress the importance of reversibility and monitoring (OECD-NEA, 2009). For Andra, reversibility has become a means of justifying why the Cigéo project can and should go ahead, despite the still numerous uncertainties concerning its safety (Patinaux, 2017, p. 416). Through these processes of articulation, societal demand has been translated into scientifically operationalizable concepts and criteria, with natural and technical sciences at the forefront in defining retrievability, and social science providing options of reversibility. The institutionalisation of the reversibility requirement in legal and administrative texts has been both shaped by, and driven efforts at, defining reversibility scientifically. Finally, the progressive strengthening of the reversibility requirement (from a governmental commitment in 1998, through a legal obligation in 2006, to specific criteria in 2016) has taken place in close interaction with political deliberations concerning the societal values and ideologies that underpin HLW management, in particular intergenerational justice.

9.4.3 Transparency, Openness, and Integration Across Domains: Any Impact on Policy?

Views vary concerning the actual ability of the transparency and engagement mechanisms to facilitate cross-domain interaction. In research interviews, both the pro- and anti-Cigéo HLW stakeholders[22] invariably emphasised the long yet steady evolution towards greater transparency and openness to public engagement in the country's HLW policy. In parliamentary debates of 2006 and 2016, project proponents generally underscored the need to continue along this positive path of greater transparency, while critics denounced the persisting secrecy and opacity, the broken promises, and the lack of impact of transparency and participation on decision-making. This critical perspective gained prominence and intensity over time, with increasingly frequent references to the opacity and excessive power wielded by the "nucleocracy" (see also Lehtonen et al., 2020). The nuclear operators, in turn, have criticised IRSN's and Andra's engagement practices for politicising science. Similarly divided evaluations concern the local-level engagement via CLIS. Its true impact has been contested, both by project opponents who have described CLIS as a paper tiger, and by proponents who blame it for being a platform in which the opponents can spread their "propaganda".

The civil society actors indeed recurrently complain about the weak if not non-existent impact of transparency and participation on decision-making.[23] Patinaux (2017, p. 415) mentions reversibility as the only true concession by Andra to civil society demands, noting that even this demand has over time turned into a mode of governance employed by Andra and the actors driving the Cigéo project. The requirement that Cigéo start with a pilot phase also emanated from the co-construction efforts and the consensus conference of 2014, but Andra translated the pilot phase merely into the first step in the disposal project. This watered-down the idea of a true test phase whose results would inform the decision on whether to implement Cigéo.

The shifting experience of the National Commission on Public Debate (CNDP) illustrates the opportunities and limitations of "invited" participation in fostering engagement across the governance domains, when strong mistrust and asymmetries of power prevail. It also shows the potential virtues of mistrust in

---

[22] Interviewed by the author of this chapter in 2018–2019

[23] Frequently evoked also by key actors of the co-construction experiments piloted by IRSN, interviewed in 2018–2019

spurring integration across governance domains. Already the 2005–2006 waste debate was seen by many critics as a means whereby the nuclear technocracy and the government legitimised the existing policy (Lhomme, 2006; Lehtonen, 2010). However, at the time, CNDP represented an innovation, and even the critics recognised the value of the debate in consolidating the authority of the CNDP as an independent arbiter and social innovator in HLW governance (Global Chance, 2006, p. 64). The immediate impact of the failed 2013 public debate, by contrast, was to undermine CNDP's legitimacy and feed mistrust. Yet, even this seeming failure has also spurred innovation and reform, in the short term through the organisation of a consensus conference as a partial substitute to the lacking CNDP debate, and in the longer term via the adoption of new engagement tools and practices by the CNDP (Blanck, 2017, p. 460).

9.4.4 The Ambiguous French Nuclear Legacies

The articulation across domains takes place in the shadow of multiple material, economic, institutional, and symbolic legacies of the French nuclear sector. Material and economic realities include the need to manage waste from the 56 currently operating reactors and a number of reactors already shut down—the management of the waste from France's early natural uranium graphite gas reactors poses particular and urgent technical challenges. They further encompass the economic and employment heritage of the nuclear sector, and the costs of waste management, which will be high, regardless of policy decisions. Institutionally, the legacy consists of the innumerable organisms set up to support and develop nuclear technology, including its military applications, and the alleged power of the 'nucleocracy'. Among the key symbolic elements features the Janus' face of the nuclear sector as a beloved purveyor of progress, modernity, jobs, and export revenue on the one hand (Hecht, 2009), and as a bastion of secrecy, opacity, and technocracy on the other (Lepage, 2014). In this context, the waste problem represents the nuclear-sector's Achilles' Heel—critical for the continuity of the French nuclear industry and its public acceptance. In the parliamentary debates of 2006 and 2016, proponents highlighted the benefits of the nuclear sector for the French and global society, in supporting France's climate responsibility, technological excellence, job creation, energy independence, and role in developing an internationally applicable waste solution (Lehtonen et al., 2021). For critics, this very progress and French leadership have led to a path dependency that needs to be broken, although the long legacy of waste, resulting from past choices, would nevertheless persist.

These nuclear-sector-specific features are embedded in the broader French governance traditions founded on ideological trust in the state and the public service tradition (the EDF as its incarnation in the energy sector), concentration of decision-making power in the hands of the central government, blended with a profound mistrust and imaginaries juxtaposing the state with civil society (e.g., Saurugger, 2007). Local-level perceptions reveal ambiguous attitudes towards the state as a highly trusted and single legitimate guardian of the public interest on the one hand, and a mistrusted natural adversary of grassroots and civil society on the other. The repeated experiences of "broken promises" of the mistrusted "nucleocracy" have further buttressed mistrust. The nuclear heritage of France is perceived by critics as a succession of broken promises, which have undermined public trust in the nuclear elites. Among the key broken HLW-related promises were that several underground research laboratories would be built, and that community approval for an underground laboratory in Bure would not automatically translate into approval of a repository. Local-level ambiguities are compounded by the region's history, deeply marked by imaginaries of a "sacrificed land", allegedly abandoned by the government as a buffer zone in Franco-German wars in the nineteenth and twentieth centuries (Le Hir, 2017). Nevertheless, the locals frequently criticised the state for its passiveness and failure or unwillingness to take a strong lead on the project. In a region without a nuclear tradition, efforts by project proponents to nurture pride for a nationally vital project face an uphill battle (Lehtonen et al., 2020).

9.5 Conclusions: Interaction Between the Governance Dimensions

French HLW governance has a long, complex, and conflict-ridden history of mutual mistrust relations. These have evolved together with the country's powerful nuclear-military complex, a "nucleocracy" composed of closely integrated politico-administrative and scientific-technological domains, with the societal domain largely excluded until the late 1980s. To manage the mistrust between society and the nucleocracy, and initially to unblock the HLW governance stalemate in 1990, numerous institutions and mechanisms have been established to mediate between the governance domains—in particular to better integrate the societal domain in governance. The articulation between the governance domains in France can be examined through three perspectives: 1) the multiple and mutual mistrust relations across and within the domains as drivers and mechanisms of articulation, 2) reversibility as the key conceptual device of articulation and management of mistrust, and 3) the long-term context and policy landscape, characterised by the longstanding legacies of the nuclear sector policies, decisions, institutions, and material artefacts.

The French HLW sector has been among the pioneers in developing and institutionalising "counter-expertise", multi-stakeholder dialogue, integration of social sciences in HLW management, and most recently, in co-creation of knowledge between institutional and citizen experts. The media has served as an increasingly vigilant watchdog especially since the Chernobyl disaster in 1986. The multiple measures of integration have not eliminated mistrust but have instead further complexified the trust and mistrust relations, both between and within the domains of governance. For example, the experiments in the co-creation of knowledge and the integration of social sciences into HLW institutions have generated tensions and divided opinions within the politico-administrative sphere, among the diverse civil society actors, and within the social science community. On the other hand, reciprocal mistrust relations have served as a driver for greater integration and better articulation between the governance levels. It has spurred the development of mistrustful civic vigilance, and the establishment of a prudent phased approach, with both scientific and societal control embedded in the process—arguably a precondition for socially robust policies of HLW management. The various institutions of coordination and negotiation across domains indeed build on mistrust as a key governance mechanism. As a central concept in French HLW governance, reversibility can be seen as a key conceptual device designed not only to manage mistrust but also to harness this mistrust for the purpose of socially more robust policies and decisions. The fact that reversibility may not succeed in reducing mistrust, given that many opponents consider the concept as an illusion, does not undermine its value in facilitating interaction across the governance domains.

However, mistrust and reversibility operate in a specific and largely problematic context of persisting asymmetries of power between the still powerful "nucleocracy", ambiguous relations of the French society with the state, and the multiple path dependencies generated by the heavy legacy of the nuclear sector in the country. Furthermore, in a society characterised by deep mistrust (e.g., Algan and Cahuc, 2007), the risk is real that the potentially virtuous healthy mistrust might turn into protracted and fruitless conflicts and dysfunctional mistrust. Such dangers are particularly acute given the high uncertainties concerning the French nuclear sector, which finds itself at a crossroads, plagued by recent highly problematic reactor projects and spiralling costs, rapidly declining costs of renewable energy, the government's official commitment to reducing the share of nuclear electricity to 50%, and the possible abandonment of reprocessing for largely economic reasons. Pushed into the corner, fighting for its place in society, the nuclear sector will weigh in on decisions concerning nuclear new-build and the development of advanced reactor technologies that would allow for the "closing of the fuel cycle". Under such conditions, HLW governance continues to face an unstable and unpredictable future, and the nuclear sector may waver in its commitment to openness and cross-domain interaction.

References

ActuEnvironnement. (2022, June 1). Cigéo : l'Andra se met en ordre de bataille avant de déposer la demande d'autorisation de création. https://www.actu-environnement.com/ae/news/cigeo-andra-organisation-maitrise-ouvrrage-cigeo-39735.php4.

Algan, Y., & Cahuc, P. (2007). *La société de défiance*. Editions ENS rue d'Ulm.

Ambroise-Rendu, A-C. (2018). La catastrophe écologique de Tchernobyl : les régimes de fausseté de l'information. *Le Temps des medias*, 30(1), 152–173.

Andra. (2010). *Rendre gouvernables les déchets radioactifs: Le stockage profond à l'épreuve de la réversibilité*. Agence nationale pour la gestion des déchets radioactifs (Andra).

Andra. (2012). *Etude de contexte: Le territoire du projet Cigéo*. Agence nationale pour la gestion des déchets radioactifs (Andra).

ASN. 2020. Avis no 2020-AV-0363 de l'Autorité de sûreté nucléaire du 8 octobre 2020 sur les études concernant la gestion des matières radioactives et l'évaluation de leur caractère valorisable remises en application du plan national de gestion des matières et des déchets radioactifs 2016–2018, en vue de l'élaboration du cinquième plan national de gestion des matières et des déchets radioactifs. https://www.asn.fr/l-asn-informe/actualites/avis-sur-la-gestion-des-matieres-radioactives-et-l-evaluation-de-leur-caractere-valorisable.

Barthe, Y. (2006). *Le pouvoir d'indécision. La mise en politique des déchets nucléaires*. Economica, collection Études politiques.

Barthe, Y. (2009). Les qualités politiques des technologies : Irréversibilité et réversibilité dans la gestion des déchets nucléaires. *Tracés. Revue de sciences humaines*, 16(1), 119–137.

Barthe, Y., Callon, M. & Lascoumes, P. (2010). De la décision politique réversible: histoire d'une contribution inattendue de l'industrie nucléaire (française) a l'instauration de la démocratie dialogique. *Revista Brasileira de Gestão Urbana (Brazilian Journal of Urban Management)*, 2(1), 57–70.

Bertrand, A., Chateauraynaud, F., & Fourniau, J.-M. (2005). Nucléaire et démocratie délibérative. Les technologies nucléaires à l'épreuve du débat public, Rapport de l'étude GRETS/GSPR.

Blanck, J. (2017). Gouverner par le temps: la gestion des déchets radioactifs en France, entre changements organisationnels et construction de solutions techniques irréversibles (1950–2014), PhD dissertation. Institut d'études politiques & Centre de sociologie des organisations, Paris. https://hal.archives-ouvertes.fr/tel-01917434/document.

Blowers, A. (2016). *The Legacy of Nuclear Power*. Routledge.

Brouard, S., & Guineaudeau, I. (2015). Policy beyond politics? Public opinion, party politics and the French pro-nuclear energy policy. *Journal of Public Policy,* 35(1), 137–170.

Cézanne-Bert, P., & Chateauraynaud, F. (2009). *Les formes d'argumentation autour de la notion de réversibilité dans la gestion des déchets radioactifs.* Ecole des Hautes Etudes en Sciences Sociales (EHESS), Groupe de Sociologie Pragmatique et Réflexive (GSPR). Convention Andra EHESS, Rapport final, 15 Decembre. http://gspr.ehess.free.fr/documents/rapports/RAP-2009-ANDRA.pdf.

Denoun, M. (2015). Le "Pilote" de Cigéo: genèse et effets sur la controverse sur l'enfouissement des déchets nucléaires. Carnet Hypothèses, *Portée de la concertation,* 5 septembre 2015. https://concertation.hypotheses.org/1147.

Dupont-Calbo, J. (2021, November 10). Nucléaire : ce qu'EDF propose à Emmanuel Macron et à la France. *Les Echos.* https://www.lesechos.fr/industrie-services/energie-environnement/nucleaire-ce-quedf-propose-a-emmanuel-macron-et-a-la-france-1362501.

Elysée. (2021, October 12). Présentation du plan France 2030. https://www.elysee.fr/emmanuel-macron/2021/10/12/presentation-du-plan-france-2030.

Gilbert, C., and Bourdeaux, I. (eds). (2006). *Recherche et déchets nucléaires: Une réflexion interdisciplinaire.* CNRS.

Global Chance. (2006, November 22). Débattre publiquement du nucléaire? Un premier bilan des eux débats EPR et déchets organisés par la Commission nationale du débat public. *Les cahiers de Global Chance.*

Hecht, G. (2009). *The Radiance of France: Nuclear Power and National Identity after World War II.* MIT Press.

Hoorelbeke, J.-M. (2008). L'appropriation de la notion de réversibilité par l'Andra au fil du temps. In Andra *(Ed.), Réversibilité et sciences sociales. Actes de la journée d'études du 2 octobre 2008* (pp. 9–16) Agence nationale pour la gestion des déchets radioactifs.

Joly, P.B., & Le Renard, C. (2021). The past futures of techno-scientific promises. *Science and Public Policy,* 48(6), 900–910.

Kalmbach, K. (2015). From Chernobyl to Fukushima: The impact of the accidents on the French nuclear discourse. In T. M. Bohn, T. Feldhoff, L. Gebhardt, A. Graf (Eds.) *The Impact of Disaster: Social and Cultural Approaches to Fukushima and Chernobyl* (pp. 67–95). EB Verlag.

Le Hir, P. (2017, January 11). Site d'enfouissement de Bure: "On ne nous atomisera jamais". *Le Monde.* https://www.lemonde.fr/planete/article/2017/01/11/site-d-enfouissement-de-bure-on-ne-nous-atomisera-jamais_5060775_3244.html (Accessed 7 July 2019).

Lehtonen, M. (2010). Opening up or Closing Down Radioactive Waste Management Policy? Debates on Reversibility and Retrievability in Finland, France, and the United Kingdom. *Risk, Hazards & Crisis in Public Policy,* 1(4), 139–179.

Lehtonen, M. (2015). Megaproject Underway: Governance of Nuclear Waste Management in France. In A. Brunnengräber, M.R. Di Nucci, A.M. Isidoro Losada, L. Mez, & M.A. Schreurs (Eds.), *Governance of Nuclear Waste Management: An international Comparison* (pp. 117–138). Springer.

Lehtonen, M. (2019). France Short Country Report (version 2019). HoNESt project deliverable D3.6. https://hdl.handle.net/2454/38269.

Lehtonen, M., & M. Kojo. (2019). "The role and functions of community benefit schemes. Comparison of the Finnish and French nuclear waste disposal projects." In A. Brunnengräber, & M.R. Di Nucci (Eds.), *Governing Nuclear Waste: Conflicts, Participation and Acceptability*. Springer.

Lehtonen, M., Kojo, M., Jartti, T., Litmanen, T., & Kari, M. (2020). The roles of the state and social licence to operate? Lessons from nuclear waste management in Finland, France, and Sweden. *Energy Research and Social Science* 61.

Lehtonen, M., Kojo, M., Kari, M., & Litmanen, T. (2021). Healthy mistrust or complacent confidence? Civic vigilance in the reporting by leading newspapers on nuclear waste disposal in Finland and France. *Risk, Hazards & Crisis in Public Policy*, 12(2), 130–157.

Lhomme, S. (2006). Nucléaire: Débats bidons? Débattre publiquement du nucléaire ? In *Un premier bilan des deux débats EPR et déchets organisés par la Commission nationale du débat public* (pp. 66–67). Global Chance.

Jobert, A., & Le Renard, C. (2014). Framing Prototypes: The Fast Breeder Reactor in France (1950s – 1990s). *Science & Technology Studies*, 27(2), 7–26.

Lepage, C. (2014). *L'Etat nucléaire*. Albin Michel.

MTE. (n.d.). Cigéo, les grandes étapes. Ministère de la transition écologique (MTE), Centre d'informations et de ressources sur CIGEO. https://www.cigeo.gouv.fr/cigeo-les-grandes-etapes-139.

OECD-NEA. (2009). "Repositories and Host Regions: Envisaging the Future Together". Synthesis of the FSC National Workshop and Community Visit, Bar-le-Duc, France, April 7–9, 2009. Paris: OECD Nuclear Energy Agency.

Parotte, C. (2016). *L'art de gouverner les déchets radioactifs: analyse comparée de la Belgique, la France et le Canada*. Doctoral dissertation. Université de Liège.

Patinaux, L. (2017). *Enfouir des déchets nucléaires dans un monde conflictuel. Une histoire de la démonstration de sûreté de projets de stockage géologique, en France (1982–2013)*. PhD dissertation. Centre Alexandre Koyré, Paris.

Patinaux, L. (2019). Enjeux épistémiques et politiques des recherches sur l'évacuation géologique des déchets nucléaires. Étude d'une controverse sur l'implantation d'un laboratoire souterrain dans la Vienne (1994–1998). *Cahiers François Viète*, 3/6, pp. 133–157. https://www.hal.archives-ouvertes.fr/hal-02073628/document.

PNGMDR. (2019). Dossier du maître d'ouvrage pour le débat public relatif à la cinquième édition du plan national de gestion des matières et déchets radioactifs. 5ème édition du PNGMDR. https://pngmdr.debatpublic.fr/images/DMO-synthese/DMO.pdf.

Saurugger, S. (2007). Democratic 'Misfit'? Conceptions of Civil Society Participation in France and the European Union. *Political Studies*, 55(2), 384–404.

Topçu, S. (2008). Confronting Nuclear Risks: Counter-Expertise as Politics Within the French Nuclear Energy Debate. *Nature and Culture*, 3(2), 225–245.

Vie publique. (2022, January 26). Le nucléaire civil: quelle part dans l'énergie de demain? https://www.vie-publique.fr/eclairage/283413-le-nucleaire-civil-quelle-part-dans-lenergie-de-demain.

World Nuclear News. (2022, January 12). Fresh delay to Flamanville 3 blamed on pandemic. https://www.world-nuclear-news.org/Articles/Fresh-delay-to-Flamanville-blamed-on-impact-of-pan.

Markku Lehtonen is an interdisciplinary social scientist, currently working at the Pompeu Fabra University (Barcelona) and at the Universitat Autònoma de Barcelona. Markku is also Adjunct Professor at the University of Jyväskylä, Finland; Associate Researcher at the Groupe de Sociologie Pragmatique et Réflexive (GSPR), Ecole des Hautes Etudes en Sciences Sociales (EHESS) in Paris; and Associate Faculty at the Science Policy Research Unit (SPRU), University of Sussex. He holds a PhD in environmental economics (Université de Versailles, 2005) and an MSc in environmental studies (University of Helsinki, 1994). His research focuses on policies and governance in the areas of energy, environment and sustainability. His recent research projects have analysed controversies and governance of energy policies (e.g., nuclear power, nuclear waste, biofuels), policy evaluation, role of experts and expert knowledge (e.g. indicators, evaluations and assessments) in policymaking, role of trust in policymaking, citizen participation, the role of international organisations in environmental and energy policies, and the social dimension of sustainable development. His current research projects focus on nuclear-sector promises and epistemic communities in Canada, Finland, France, Sweden, and the UK (the PROMISES project, funded by the Kone Foundation and the Academy of Finland), and sustainability in educational institutions in Finland, Portugal, Romania, and Spain (the EU-funded ECF4CLIM project).

Open Access This chapter is licensed under the terms of the Creative Commons Attribution 4.0 International License (http://creativecommons.org/licenses/by/4.0/), which permits use, sharing, adaptation, distribution and reproduction in any medium or format, as long as you give appropriate credit to the original author(s) and the source, provide a link to the Creative Commons license and indicate if changes were made.

The images or other third party material in this chapter are included in the chapter's Creative Commons license, unless indicated otherwise in a credit line to the material. If material is not included in the chapter's Creative Commons license and your intended use is not permitted by statutory regulation or exceeds the permitted use, you will need to obtain permission directly from the copyright holder.

Radioactive Waste Management in Sweden: Decision-Making in a Context of Scientific Controversy

10

Johan Swahn

10.1 Introduction

Sweden has a long military and civil nuclear history, with all the challenges for radioactive waste management (RWM) that this envisages. Despite this, Sweden is one of the countries that have made most progress in developing and implementing technical systems for the management and disposal of radioactive waste, with a relatively advanced governance system since the 1980s.

When in January 2022 the Swedish government decided to allow the construction of a repository for spent nuclear fuel (SNF), the country joined only Finland in having appeared to have found both a site and a method for final management of long-lived high-level nuclear waste (HLW). But the decision was controversial, and it was a challenge to take it as there was severe scientific criticism of the use of copper as a disposal canister material. The canister is the most important barrier in the safety case and there were claims by highly renowned scientists that the copper would only last for some hundreds of years instead of the required 100,000 years.

This controversy stretched the Swedish governance system for RWM to its limit. Only by claiming that long-term safety would always be good enough as a clay buffer and the bedrock provide two complementary if uncertain barriers, could the decision be taken. The decision may still be found to be in conflict with the implementation of Swedish environmental legislation, which requires the precautionary principle to be met and that decisions cannot be taken based on insufficient knowledge about long-term safety.

J. Swahn (✉)
MKG, Swedish NGO Office for Nuclear Waste Review, Göteborg, Sweden
e-mail: johan.swahn@mkg.se

This chapter describes the long process that has led to the decision to allow the construction of a repository for SNF, and the controversies that have arisen and remain. The most important controversy has been the copper canister corrosion issue, which has been central to the discussions of long-term safety of the repository since 2007, as well as to the repository licence review process from 2011 until the January 2022 decision.

Although the final decision was taken by the government, a number of other actors were involved in the process, including regulatory bodies, the environmental court system, the government's scientific advisory board, the scientific research community, the nuclear waste communities, and the environmental movement. The role of different actors has changed over time, and as the discourse became more technical certain actors, including independent scientists and the environmental movement, became influential. Also of interest is that as the government decision grew closer, the repository issue became politicised, something that had been avoided in Swedish politics since the 1970s.

To facilitate the understanding of the developments in recent years, Sect. 10.2 gives an historic background to Swedish nuclear power and nuclear waste management. This is followed in Sect. 10.3 by a description of the Swedish governance and legal framework for RWM. The governance system has some transparency problems that are discussed.

The main focus of this Swedish case study is covered in Sect. 10.4, with a detailed description of the controversies and the decision-making process for the repository for SNF.

In the final section some concluding observations are presented.

10.2 Historic Background

Sweden became a nuclear country quite early and therefore has a long nuclear history. After the Second World War, the military interest in nuclear weapons started a process where a combined military and civil nuclear program developed in the 1950s. The civil program was originally a cover for the military effort and included uranium mining and a plan for a reprocessing plant. A small heavy-water moderated reactor using natural uranium as fuel to produce heat for district heating and electricity was built underground in Ågesta, a suburb south of Stockholm. The reactor also produced plutonium of nuclear weapons quality. The military project was abandoned by the late 1960s when Sweden joined the Nuclear Non-Proliferation Treaty that entered into force in 1970.

As the military interest decreased and the commercial and economic interests increased, the domestic heavy-water reactor programme was converted into a major light-water reactor programme, and 12 nuclear power reactors became operational between 1972 and 1985 at four nuclear power plants (NPPs)—Barsebäck, Ringhals, Oskarshamn and Forsmark.

With the large and fast expansion of nuclear power, a nuclear debate started in Sweden. The opposition to nuclear power allowed the Center Party to lead an opposition coalition in 1976 to break the 40-year political rule of the Social Democratic Party. The anti-nuclear Center Party tried to prevent the start-up of new reactors by the adoption of new legislation. The "Villkorslagen" (Stipulation Act) was formulated so that the industry had to prove that a safe method and a safe site for disposing of HLW existed, before an operational licence could be given.

In parallel to the political developments on nuclear policy, a growing public anti-nuclear movement wanted a referendum on the future of nuclear power, and this was held in 1980. One clear "No" option was put against two different "Yes, for a while" options. When the "No" option did not receive a majority, the result of the referendum was politically interpreted to mean that nuclear power was to be phased out by 2010.

With time, this interpretation was abandoned, but through the years, and more rapidly in recent years, Sweden has reduced its nuclear capacity from 12 to currently 6 reactors supplying about 30% of the total Swedish electricity production of 166 TWh (Energiföretagen, 2021).

Since the political turmoil and wide public debate on nuclear power and nuclear waste management in the 1970s, from the early 1980s onwards there was almost no political interest or public debate in Sweden on nuclear waste issues. The siting process for the SNF repository caused some local political discussions in the mid 1980s, but no actor on the national political level seemed to find nuclear issues interesting enough to stimulate a national debate about nuclear waste. An underlying political understanding developed that the issue of RWM was not to be politicised. Nuclear waste was seen as an issue that had to be resolved because the waste was being produced and something had to be done with it. Also, it was generally felt that the Swedish system for developing a repository for SNF was working well.

After the long political calm on nuclear waste issues, there was an abrupt change around 2020 when nuclear power again became a divisive political issue in Swedish politics. With an upcoming decision on the SNF repository, nuclear waste issues were drawn into a heated political debate.

10.2.1 Early Work Towards a Repository for Spent Nuclear Fuel

As the nuclear waste issue became of increasing political importance in the 1970s, in 1972 the government started a process to investigate the possibilities for permanent disposal of HLW. The result was the AKA (Använt Kärnbränsle och radioaktivt Avfall) report, published in 1976, included a roadmap for the radioactive waste facilities that were later developed.

In 1973, the nuclear industry created a company called SKBF that was to take responsibility for Swedish RWM and disposal. The company was later renamed Swedish Nuclear Fuel and Waste Management Company (SKB), and is owned by the nuclear utilities. After the publication of the AKA report and as a result of the political developments that led to "Villkorslagen", in 1976 SKBF started a project called "Kärnbränslesäkerhet (KBS)": The project published three reports in 1977, 1978 and 1983 presenting different versions of what is still called the KBS method for disposal of radioactive waste. The KBS project and the reports allowed the nuclear industry to show that they had fulfilled the conditions of "Villkorslagen". But according to "Villkorslagen" the industry also had to show that a site could be found that would be safe when using the KBS method. This was quite problematic, but the situation was finally politically "solved" by stating that theoretically it was likely that such a site existed.

The further development of the KBS method and the siting of a repository for SNF, through to the government decision in early 2022 to allow the construction of a repository, is described in Sect. 10.4.

10.3 Governance and Legal Framework: Two Parallel Tracks for Licensing

An application for a license for a repository for radioactive waste in Sweden is processed in two parallel decision-making judicial processes, according to the Nuclear Activities Act (1983)[1] and the Environmental Code

---

[1] Available at: https://www.riksdagen.se/sv/dokument-lagar/dokument/svensk-forfattnings-samling/lag-19843-om-karnteknisk-verksamhet_sfs-1984-3. An older translation into English is available here: https://www.stralsakerhetsmyndigheten.se/en/enactments/acts-and-ordinances. The Nuclear Activities Act is under review and a modernised version will likely be introduced to parliament during 2023.

(1998).[2] There are also clear legal obligations in the decision-making governance system for access to information, access to public participation and consultation, and access to justice.

10.3.1 The Nuclear Activities Act

The 1983 Nuclear Activities Act put all the responsibility for management and disposal of waste onto the nuclear industry. To keep the operational licenses for the nuclear reactors, the industry needs to present so-called "Fud reports" every three years, with the latest translated into English in September 2019 (SKB, 2019). The Fud reports include reporting on and future planning of research development and demonstration (RD&D), and a strategic plan for the future of Swedish RWM and the decommissioning of nuclear facilities.

Each RD&D programme is reviewed by the Swedish Radiation Safety Authority (SSM), which includes a broad societal consultation process. The regulator then makes a report to the government with recommendations. A separate review is provided by an independent scientific advisory board to the government, the Swedish Council for Nuclear Waste. The government then takes a decision on the Fud-report and can give conditions for further RD&D work.

Historically, the Swedish regulator for radiation safety (historically the Swedish Nuclear Power Inspectorate, SKI, and since 2008 SSM) has been relatively positive concerning the SKB work plans as presented in the Fud reports, and has in its review to the government recommended support of the plans. There has been a tendency to refer any perceived problems back to the industry, which has the legal responsibility for resolving them. This means that there has been a risk that problems just "disappear", as it might not be in the industry´s interest to find or examine problems that can hinder its work or plans.

In summary, the legal Fud programme process has been a relatively weak steering process for industry plans or future RD&D work. With a political disinterest in RWM issues and a generally industry-supporting regulator (whether SKI

---

[2] Available at: https://www.riksdagen.se/sv/dokument-lagar/dokument/svensk-forfattningssamling/miljobalk-1998808_sfs-1998-808. More information can be found here: https://www.naturvardsverket.se/en/laws-and-regulations/the-swedish-environmental-code/. An English translation can be found here: https://www.government.se/legal-documents/2000/08/ds-200061.

or SSM), most government decisions on the Fud reports have had no effect on the work of SKB.

10.3.2 The Environmental Code

The Swedish legal framework for decision-making on issues that have an environmental impact was greatly improved in 1998 when the Environmental Code became part of the Swedish judicial system. With the new legislation, a special environmental court system was set up to take licensing decisions on activities that could cause harm to humankind or the environment. The legislation, among other things, regulates the content of the environmental impact statement as well as the consultation process necessary for its development (in Chap. 6). The European legislation on environmental impact assessments and strategic environmental assessments are implemented in the Environmental Code.

A special Chap. 2 of the Environmental Code specifies the criteria for an activity to be allowed. The environmental impact assessment has to include rigorous descriptions of alternative siting and methods. The precautionary principle has to be used, and there is a condition that enough knowledge about the activity and its possible influences on the environment must be had.

Of importance for the parallel decision-making of facilities according to both the Nuclear Activities Act and the Environmental Code is that licensing decisions taken according to the nuclear legislation must follow Chaps. 2 and 6 of the environmental legislation.

Decisions of the Land and Environmental Courts can be appealed to a Land and Environmental Court of Appeal, and the decisions of that court can be appealed to the Supreme Court.

10.3.3 Access to Information, Public Participation, and Justice

Parts of the Environmental Code implement the 1998 Aarhus Convention's second and third pillars of access to public participation and access to justice (UNECE, 1998). The legislation mandates that the implementer of activities that have an environmental impact, including nuclear activities, must carry out and document a process of public consultation while developing the environmental impact statement for a new or changed activity or facility. Part of the decision-making process is that the Land and Environment Court must approve the consultation process and that issues raised have been properly taken into due account. Environmental organisations are given special importance in the legislation and have the right to appeal all decisions taken. MKG, the Swedish NGO Office for Nuclear Waste Review, is a non-governmental environmental organisation established in 2004 to work specifically with nuclear waste issues.[3]

To facilitate the participation of civil society in the decision-making for the repository for SNF, the government has provided resources for environmental NGOs. Between 2005 and 2016 it was possible for environmental NGOs to seek funding from the Nuclear Waste Fund. About EUR 300,000 per year were made available, and since 2017 a similar sum is available through the state budget.

Sweden has a long tradition of open access to official documents of the government, going back hundreds of years. With some exceptions for commercial or security secrecy, and regarding interaction with foreign governments, all documents and even e-mails and messages that concern official business must be registered and made available upon request. Also, the contents of important phone calls have to be noted and registered. This means that the activities of the government, of the nuclear safety regulator and local communities can be followed publicly, together with documents and other information.

However, the nuclear waste company SKB is a private company, which is outside the remit of the legislation and therefore not obligated to disclose any information. This means that SKB, which has the sole legal responsibility for research and development on RWM and repository technology, can keep its work secret; SKB can hide any problems because the documentation or research results never have to be disclosed. In practice, this means that the company publishes only results that support its safety case.

The availability of public information on governmental activities, coupled with lack of access to information from the implementer of RWM, means that the Aarhus Convention's first pillar of access to information is relatively weakly implemented on RWM issues in Sweden.

---

[3] MKG is a collaboration between Nature and Youth Sweden, Friends of the Earth Sweden, The Swedish Society for Nature Conservation in the county of Kalmar, The Swedish Society for Nature Conservation in the county of Uppsala, Oss—the local Public Opinion group for Safe Final Storage of Radioactive Waste and The Swedish Society for Nature Conservation. https://www.mkg.se/en/the-swedish-ngo-office-for-nuclear-waste-review-mkg.

10.3.4 The Two Parallel Tracks for Licensing: A Complex Process

Before a licence application is prepared, the nuclear waste company SKB must carry out a consultation process to prepare the environmental impact assessment document. This document is necessary for both applications, but the application to the Land and Environmental Court does not need to go into the same detail on radiation safety issues. After the two applications are submitted by SKB, the nuclear regulator SSM carries out a review according to the Nuclear Activities Act. The Land and Environment Court (hereafter the Environmental Court), carries out a review according to the Environmental Code. The main focus of the SSM review is the safety analysis document in the application, while the Environmental Court reviews general environmental issues but can decide to what extent radiation safety issues may be of relevance. This parallel track for licensing continues throughout the decision-making process and causes complications. The process is shown in Fig. 10.1, and also described in Bjällås & Persson (2011).

Both reviews start with an analysis of whether the application is sufficiently complete. Both SSM and the Environmental Court carry out a broad external review process. SSM can provide opinions in the Environmental Court review. The Environmental Court process is more open than the SSM process, and SKB is asked to comment on opinions, and in turn interested parties can comment on the opinions of SKB. This can take several iterations and SKB can introduce complementary material at will.

After the applications are considered complete enough in both reviews, they are formally announced by SSM and the Environmental Court. This means that the review on issues formally starts. Again, both SSM and the Environmental Court carry out broad external reviews. SSM continues the regulatory review according to the Nuclear Activities Act on its own after receiving the external comments on issues.

In a more open process, where anyone interested can take part in the review on issues, the Environmental Court passes opinions back and forth between SKB and other interested parties, in the same way as in the earlier review on completeness.[4] In this part of the process, SSM delivers its opinion on the application

---

[4] All the information in the SSM and court processes is publicly available but needs to be requested. MKG has made all the documents in the review of the license application for a repository for SNF available on its website in order to make it more easily accessible. The documents in the court process can be found here: https://www.mkg.se/aktbilagor. The documents in the SSM process can be found here: https://www.mkg.se/myndighetens-diarium.

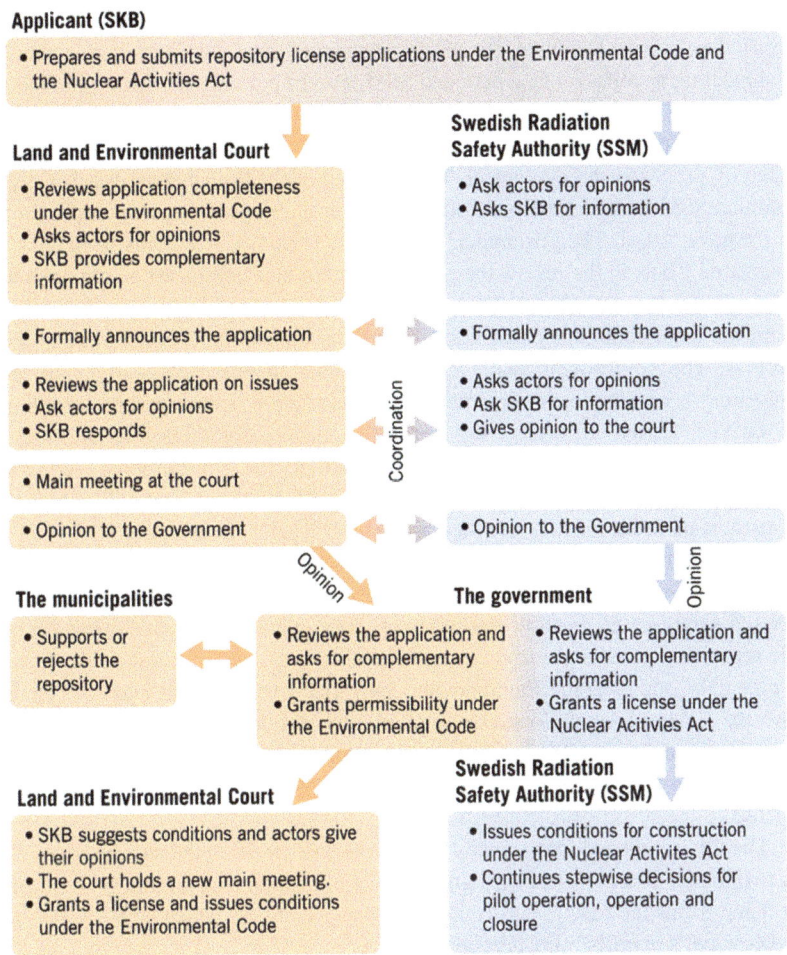

Fig. 10.1 Process for licensing under the Environmental Code and the Nuclear Activities Act. (Source: MKG)

according to the Environmental Code to the Environmental Court. This is an important step as it also gives the first indication of what the final verdict of the regulator will be on radiation safety issues and the safety case.

When the Environmental Court finds that enough information is available to proceed to the next step it announces the main meeting of the Court. In this public oral meeting anyone can take part, and SSM is an important participant. The main meeting ends the Environmental Court's review.

The final decision to allow and license facilities involving radioactive waste is taken by the Swedish government. The next step of the licensing process is therefore that SSM and the Environmental Court give their opinions on the application to the government. The government reviews the opinions. According to the Environmental Code, in the review the government can take comments on the opinion of the Environmental Court.[5] The government also has to get a positive decision from the local community that has can veto the repository, even this late in the process. The government finally decides whether to give permissibility to the repository according to the Environmental Code, and a licence permit according to the Nuclear Activities Act. The government can add conditions to its decisions.

The government decisions can be appealed to the constitutional Supreme Administrative Court, that only considers whether the law has been followed, i.e., it restricts its decisions to issues that have a clear legal connotation.

After a government decision to give a license according to the Nuclear Activities Act, the regulator continues a stepwise decision-making process of examining revised safety cases to allow construction, pilot operation and full operation of the repository. After a government permissibility decision according to the Environmental Code, it is the Environment Court that gives the final license. This is also the Environmental Court's last opportunity to influence the repository project. The Environmental Court will again make a review and ask for opinions, but the review in this part of the process is only of conditions that can be put on the license.

The Environmental Court finally makes a license decision that can be appealed to two higher court levels, based on details in the conditions, but the government decision forms the basis for a license and binds the courts, which must follow the government's permissibility decision.

When SKB has both final licenses for a repository, construction can begin. The present Swedish legal system therefore means that nuclear projects have to have licenses according to both the nuclear and environmental legislation. There can be conflicts between these processes, even though experience and praxis has been developed to allow coordination.

---

[5] MKG also made the documents in the government review available on its website: https://www.mkg.se/regeringens-diarium.

10.4 The Long Decision-Making Process for a Repository for Spent Nuclear Fuel

As described in the Sect. 10.3, the Swedish judicial process for allowing construction of a repository for SNF is complicated and time-consuming. It has taken from 2011 to 2022 just to process SKB's license application. But the start of the project was actually begun in the 1970s, i.e., 50 years ago.

When the KBS concept for a repository for disposal of SNF was developed in Sweden in the mid-1970s by the nuclear waste company SKB, there were three main project reports, in 1977 (SKBF, 1977), 1978 (SKBF, 1978), and 1983 (SKBF, 1983).

The KBS-1 report (SKBF, 1977) was focused on a repository for reprocessed HLW, as at this time reprocessing was the plan for Swedish SNF. The vitrified glass waste was to be encapsulated in a steel container 3 mm thick and then placed in a titanium canister 6 mm thick. Between the steel and the titanium would be 10 cm of lead. The canister was to be surrounded by a buffer of sand and clay. The disposal depth was to be about 500 m. From this concept only the depth of 500 m survived into the final KBS concept used today.

The KBS-2 report (SKBF, 1978) came only a year later when it became unclear whether reprocessing was to be used in Sweden for all the SNF, and provided a similar concept for a repository for direct disposal of unreprocessed SNF. The spent fuel rods were to be taken out of the fuel elements and placed in a copper canister of 20 cm thickness and the whole canister was then to be filled with lead. The canister was to be surrounded by a buffer of blocks of clay. The depth of the repository was to be about 500 m. From this concept the choice of copper as a canister material and the clay buffer survived into the final KBS concept.

The system was further developed and optimised, and in 1983 the KBS-3 concept was presented in a third report (SKBF, 1983), with a 10 cm thick copper canister containing complete fuel elements instead of separated fuel rods, but still with the canister filled with lead. With the final KBS project report, the concept was almost finalised, with copper canisters containing the SNF to be deposited in holes in the floor of tunnels about 500 m underground in granite bedrock (see Fig. 10.2). All tunnels and shafts are also to be filled with clay.

By the mid-1990s the cylindrical canisters were finalised to be 5 m high and 1 m in diameter and made from only 5 cm thick copper. Inside the copper canister is a cast iron insert (instead of lead) to hold the spent fuel elements in place and provide higher strength to the encapsulation (SKB, 1999).

There is always flowing groundwater in the granite bedrock, and even though the copper canister is supposed to be relatively immune to corrosion, it is surrounded by a clay called "bentonite clay" that will swell when subjected to water.

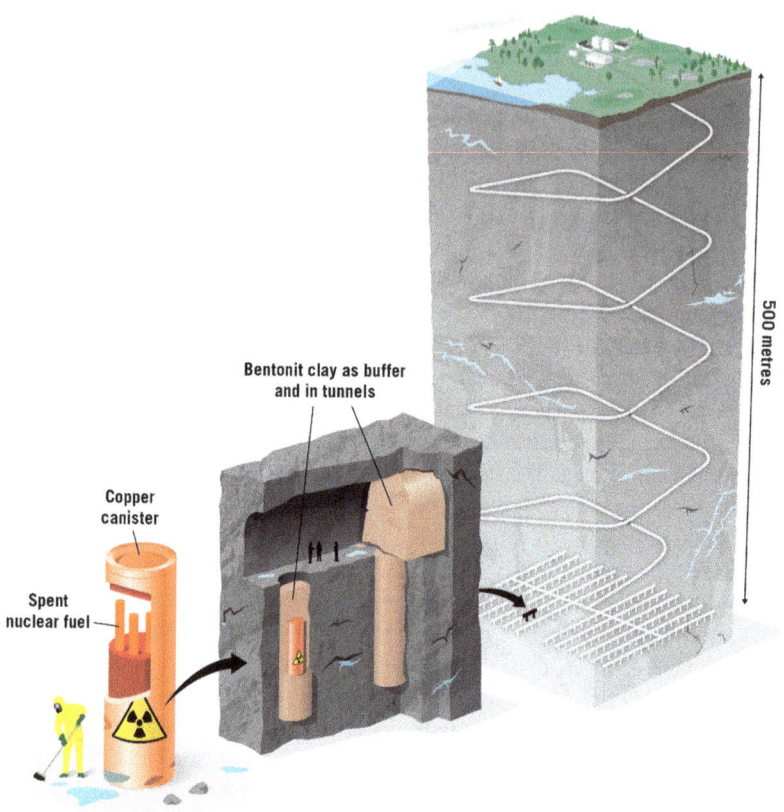

Fig. 10.2 The KBS method. (Source: MKG)

The swollen clay buffer is to provide tight protection of the copper canister from the groundwater. The deposition tunnels and other parts of the repository system will also be filled with bentonite clay so that the whole bedrock system is to become as tight as the bedrock itself to the flow of water.

The long-term safety case for the KBS-3 concept thus relies on two artificial engineered barriers—a copper canister, a bentonite clay buffer—and a semi-natural barrier of the bedrock with tunnels filled with clay. In practice, the tunnels in the bedrock are disregarded in the safety case as it is assumed that no water can flow through them. In the safety case analyses, a rock that has few cracks and fissures therefore becomes a better barrier than a rock with many.

Copper was finally chosen as canister material instead of titanium because theoretically copper is thermodynamically immune to corrosion by water. The immunity of copper to corrosion by water later became an important scientific controversy that became a part of the license review for the repository for SNF.

The reason for originally decreasing the copper thickness from 20 to 5 cm was mainly improved safety analysis modelling, that allowed less and less importance to be put on the copper canister as a barrier. Still, from the 1970s to the early 1990s the bedrock was assumed to be an important barrier in the safety case, meaning that it was important to find the best Swedish bedrock for a repository. This led to a complicated siting process. However, when the siting process made it necessary to be able to site a repository in almost any rock formation in Sweden, the importance of the rock barrier of the bedrock was toned down in the safety case. More emphasis was put on the function of the artificial copper and clay barriers. More information on the siting process is given in Sect. 10.4.1.

10.4.1 Siting of a Spent Fuel Repository—A Long Road to Acceptance

Originally, the bedrock was seen as the most important barrier in the KBS concept. The siting process for a repository for SNF was started in the mid-1970s by the nuclear waste company SKB, with exploratory drilling all over Sweden to find the best bedrock. The arrival of SKB was often met with local resistance, where citizen groups were spontaneously created to oppose the drilling. The opposition to SKB became better organised with time, and a network of local opposition groups called Avfallskedjan (The Waste Network) was formed in order to provide common support. There were almost 20 local groups, and several of them survived long after there was any threat to the local rock becoming a repository.

In 1985, the resistance led to the stop of the siting process. At a demonstration at Almunge, near the city of Uppsala north of Stockholm, police with dogs broke up a demonstration against drilling in a local rock formation. The closeness to the major cities allowed the conflict to become major TV news, and the sight of elderly people being dragged by dogs caused concern, not in the least politically. The Minister of Environment declared that the SKB strategy of selecting a site in conflict with the local community had to stop.

This meant that SKB had to restart the siting work, and a voluntary process was initiated, with all the communities in Sweden contacted to see if they were interested. Two communities in the north, Storuman and Malå saw that a repository could provide jobs and volunteered. In both communities there was political support for the siting projects, but when local referenda were held in 1995 and 1997, the inhabitants of the communities said "No".[6] The remaining conflict within the communities after the referenda took time to heal, and these examples did not encourage other communities to follow.

SKB then moved the search for a site for the repository to communities that already had nuclear facilities or neighbouring communities. By the late 1990s the siting process was focused on two nuclear communities, Oskarshamn and Östhammar, where the Oskarshamn and Forsmark NPPs are situated. At the Oskarshamn NPP there was also already the central intermediate storage site for SNF, Clab, and at the Forsmark NPP there was already the SFR repository for short-lived radioactive waste. At the Oskarshamn NPP, SKB had in 1995 also established an underground hard rock laboratory down to 500 m depth underneath the island of Äspö, where large-scale experiments on copper and clay and on groundwater flows could be carried out.[7]

Both communities were accustomed to nuclear power, nuclear waste facilities and SKB, which undertook large information campaigns to build up trust. This strategy has worked, and a large majority of the population in each community has a positive view of the company. Since 2003, SKB takes yearly polls to measure the popularity of the planned radioactive waste facilities in the communities, and as an example, the support in Östhammar community for a repository for SNF has been between 75 and 84%.

SKB decided to make detailed site investigations between 2002 and 2008 in areas adjacent to each of the NPPs. As discussed above, emphasis in the safety case had shifted in the 1990s from the importance of a tight bedrock to the ability of the artificial barriers of the copper canister and the bentonite buffer to contain the radioactivity in the long-term. This meant that the nuclear waste company could suggest that almost any bedrock could be used for a KBS repository, as the safety case models could show that the artificial barriers of the copper canister and the clay buffer would provide safety for the hundreds of thousands of years needed.

---

[6] In Storuman community, 76% of the population participated and the "No" side won 71 to 28% of the vote. In Malå community, 87% of the population participated and the "No" side won 54 to 44% of the vote.

[7] See: https://www.skb.com/research-and-technology/laboratories/the-aspo-hard-rock-laboratory/.

In 2009, a site just south of the Forsmark NPP in Östhammar community was chosen for a repository in favour of an Oskarshamn site. Interestingly, the reason was that the Forsmark bedrock had fewer cracks than in Oskarshamn, so the safety analysis showed that Forsmark was a little safer. The site for an encapsulation plant (Clink) was to be co-localised with the existing SNF storage facility, Clab, at the Oskarshamn NPP site. The copper canisters were to be transported by ship from Oskarshamn to Forsmark.

Before the decision was announced, most assumptions were that SKB would choose a site just south-west of the Oskarshamn NPP for the repository. This would put it near the encapsulation plant, and the Oskarshamn community appeared to be more politically and administratively well-organised to support a repository decision. But SKB appeared to realise that having a better rock could be more important.

The change in focus over time regarding the importance of the rock barrier in relation to the artificial engineered copper and clay buffer barriers is very important. As is worth repeating, the KBS concept is supposed to rely on three independent barriers for long-term safety. In reality, however, the barriers are not independent of one other, and each may have its problems. The question of to what extent the robustness of the whole system, in a holistic approach, allows the weaknesses of individual barriers to be ignored was to finally become the central issue in the licensing review for the repository for SNF. The long-term-integrity of the copper canister became increasingly questioned throughout the review.

10.4.2 The Copper Corrosion Controversy

Before describing the review of the licence application for the SNF repository, it is vital to understand more about the copper corrosion controversy that has been so important in the decision-making process. The basis for using copper as a canister material is that theoretically, according to classic thermodynamics, copper is as immune as gold to corrosion in a repository environment. The reason for this is that there is no dissolved oxygen in the groundwater at repository depth that can corrode copper. As a comparison, oxygen in the air corrodes copper roofs, turning them green, but without oxygen in the repository, or in the water in the repository, the copper surface will theoretically not be affected and only minor corrosion from other processes will take place (King et al., 2010). In addition, any oxygen in the repository during deposition of the copper canisters will be consumed after the sealing of the holes by bacteria and very fast chemical reactions, with the process taking only a few months.

The problem is that the scientific hypothesis that water without dissolved oxygen (anoxic water) does not corrode copper may be false. This was discovered experimentally by a researcher at the Royal Institute of Technology (KTH) in the mid-1980s (Hultquist, 1986), but the results were ignored by SKB and the Swedish regulator at that time. As the repository consultation process started, the researcher together with colleagues published new experimental results in 2007 and then onwards with new studies (e.g., Szakálos et al., 2007; Hultquist et al., 2009; Hultquist et al., 2013; Hultquist et al., 2015). SKB has strongly contested the research, but the results have been repeated by other researchers (e.g., Becker & Hermansson, 2011; Cleveland et al., 2014). It is now also theoretically understood that water molecules can corrode a copper surface (e.g., Macdonald & Sharifi-Asl, 2011).

As a result of the controversy, there is now an ongoing scientific paradigm shift to the fact that water can directly corrode copper even when there is no oxygen. This raises the question of how fast the reaction can take place at the temperatures and in the complicated water chemistry of the repository. The researchers from KTH claim that some copper canisters can start to collapse after only a few hundred years in the hot and chemically complex repository environment. The issue is not only how fast a general corrosive process occurs but also if pitting corrosion is possible, whereby corrosion can continue relatively fast where it has commenced; much like in a car where rust tends to corrode right through steel once it starts to occur ar a certain spot. Of importance is also that when copper reacts with a water molecule there is a release of hydrogen that can build up inside the copper and make it brittle. Also, the repository gets hot, close to 100 °C, and corrosion proceeds much faster at higher temperatures.

SKB has strongly questioned all criticism and points to its own research, which maintains that of the approximately 6000 copper canisters to be put in the Swedish repository, less than one will start to leak in a million years.

It may appear strange that the scientific controversy of how copper behaves in a repository environment has not been resolved long ago. To the initiated observer it is clear that one problem is that SKB and its sister organisations in Finland and Canada have never carried out experiments in the laboratory or in hard rock laboratories with the purpose of scientifically examining this issue in detail. And when there have been experiments that could give important information, they have not been used to the full extent. An example of this is the LOT experiment operated by SKB in the Äspö hard rock laboratory discussed in Sect. 10.4.5. Another way that SKB has tried to discredit independent research showing copper problems is to claim that the experimenters have been careless, and that oxygen has leaked into the apparatus, even though this has never been shown to be the case.

Sometimes the implementers lose control of the science. At the end of 2017, after the main meeting of the Environmental Court which is discussed in the next Sect. 10.4.3, the results of 18 years of copper corrosion in an oxygen-free repository environment were published, from the international collaboration experiment Full-scale Engineered Barrier EXperiment (FEBEX) in the Grimsel hard rock laboratory in Switzerland. In the experiment, clay and metals were tested in a tunnel that was heated to simulate disposal of HLW. The report showed considerable and unexpected copper corrosion, also pitting corrosion, which is very serious as it means a larger risk of a hole being created through a copper surface (Wersin & Kober, 2017). SKB has claimed that the corrosion must be due to oxygen leaking into the experiment, but this has not been shown.

10.4.3 Consultation, License Application and Review

From 2002 until 2010, SKB carried out a lengthy and thorough consultation process for developing the environmental impact statement for the SNF repository and the encapsulation plant. In March 2011, SKB submitted a license application package according to the Nuclear Activities Act and the Environmental Code (Sect. 10.3.4 and Fig. 10.1) for a SNF repository system using the KBS method at the Forsmark NPP, and an encapsulation plant at the Oskarshamn NPP.

The application review was started by both the regulator, the Swedish Radiation Safety Authority (SSM) according to the nuclear legislation, and the Land and Environmental Court according to the environmental legislation. The initial review for completeness of the application took some time and SKB had to add extra documentation several times. This phase of the review was finished in 2015, and the application was announced as complete by both SSM and the Environmental Court in January 2016.

During 2016 and 2017 the application was reviewed on issues. Many issues were raised, including problems with the site chosen, better alternatives for siting and choice of method (i.e., very deep boreholes), issues concerning the safety case (canister integrity, clay erosion, hydrogeology and seismology), as well as problems with intentional intrusion scenarios and challenges of transferring information about the repository into the future.[8]

---

[8] The interchange of legal briefs with opinions on issues during 2016 and 2017 is presented on the MKG website: https://www.mkg.se/tiden-efter-ansokans-kungorelse). All the documents in the Environmental Court proceedings can be downloaded: https://www.mkg.se/aktbilagor). Some briefs have been translated into English and can be downloaded from the MKG website: https://www.mkg.se/en/Legal-briefs-from-MKG-et-al-with-opinions-in-the-review-of-the-application-for-a-repository-for-spent-nuclear-fuel.

Perhaps most important during the license review process was the issue of possible problems with the long-term integrity of the copper canister. This issue was raised by some actors, including researchers at the Royal Institute of Technology (KTH) in Stockholm and environmental NGOs. The copper corrosion controversy goes back to the 1980s, but became very lively from 2007 onwards with the publication of new studies by researchers at KTH as described in Sect. 10.4.2. The controversy grew to be more and more important during the review process all the way to the end.

An important event in the license review was in June 2016 when SSM presented the nuclear regulator's opinion on the radiation safety issues to the Environmental Court. The regulator had made a large number of demands for additional information from SKB during the review for completeness of the application. SSM had also carried out its own research on the copper corrosion controversy (e.g., Becker & Hermansson, 2011; Macdonald & Sharifi-Asl, 2011; Hultquist et al., 2013). But during the spring of 2016, SSM had to make the first open decision on long-term safety. In a statement to the Environmental Court it declared was that there was a potential that the repository would be safe enough to fulfil the licensing criteria of the Environmental Code (SSM, 2016). This decision bound the regulator to saying "Yes" also later in the process.

In the autumn of 2017, the main meeting of the Environmental Court was held as the final part of the review process. The nuclear safety regulator SSM told the Court that some remaining issues, i.e., the copper corrosion issue, could be dealt with after a government decision, but that the regulator's position was still that there was potential for the repository to be safe enough to fulfil the licensing criteria of the Environmental Code. The Environmental Court questioned SSM's position in the meeting. According to both the Environmental Code and the Nuclear Activities Act, the repository had to be shown to be safe *before* a government decision. The question was: Did SSM mean that there was a potential that the repository could be safe, or that it had *been shown* that the repository would be safe?

At the main Environmental Court hearing, leading corrosion scientists from KTH again strongly questioned the SKB position on copper corrosion and the long-term integrity of the copper canister. The Environmental Court even arranged an extra day for the discussion of copper canister issues.

During the hearing that took in total four weeks it was disclosed through leaks of internal SSM documents to media that the regulator had internal conflicts on the copper canister issue in the spring of 2016, just before the regulator first told the Environmental Court that the repository would likely be safe (Lundell, 2017a; Lundell, 2017b). The documents showed that the leading SSM copper corrosion expert had been opposed to the regulator saying "Yes" to the Environmental

Court, as it was not shown that copper would be a sufficiently good canister material. Documents also showed that there were SSM scenarios on copper corrosion processes that showed regulatory limits for radioactive releases from the repository could be exceeded.

On January 23, 2018, the Environmental Court made its recommendation,[9] that the government say "No" to the application, primarily due to the uncertainties regarding the long-term safety of the planned repository due to possible copper canister problems. These issues would have to be resolved before a government decision could be taken.

On the same date, SSM told the government that it could agree to the repository, as some issues, i.e., possible problems with the long-term integrity of the copper canister, could be dealt with later, after a government decision. The regulator also believed that the repository can be safe enough even if the copper canister barrier does not work exactly as postulated as there are other barriers (bentonite clay buffer and bedrock). This regulatory focus on a holistic approach to the robustness of the safety case is important to understand what happened next in the continued government review.

10.4.4 The Government Review of Copper Corrosion Issues

After the January 2018 statements of the Environmental Court and SSM, the government review started.[10] SKB made a submission of complementary information on copper corrosion in April 2019, stating that the Environmental Court had not understood the copper corrosion issues. Very little new information was provided.

The government sent out the complementary information for consultation, and comments from other parties were provided to the government in late 2019. In its answer, SSM stated that its conviction that the repository would be safe enough was said to have been "strengthened" by the new information, despite information in the regulatory review saying there could be problems with the copper canister (SSM, 2019).

At this time the Swedish Council for Nuclear Waste, the government's scientific advisory body, entered the decision-making process, and said that there may

---

[9] MKG has made an unofficial translation of the summary of the Environmental Court opinion: https://www.mkg.se/en/translation-into-english-of-the-swedish-environmental-courts-opinion-on-the-final-repository-for.

[10] All the documents in the government review can be found on the MKG website: https://www.mkg.se/m201800217me-regeringsprovning-enligt-miljobalken.

be problems with the copper canister, and also with the cast iron insert, which may show that the KBS concept will not work as intended.

The researchers at KTH persevered in their criticism of using copper as a canister material. They were joined by the SSM corrosion expert who had opposed the regulator saying "Yes" to the court in 2016, who had subsequently left SSM. MKG also stated that it would be wrong to use copper as a canister material.

10.4.5 An Unexpected Development: New Experimental Packages from the LOT Project Retrieved with 20 years of Copper Corrosion

In the middle of the government review an unexpected possibility occurred that had the potential to clarify the issue of whether copper was a good enough canister material for the Swedish SNF repository.

The so-called LOT (Long-term test of buffer material) experiment operated by SKB has been ongoing at 400 m depth in the Äspö Hard Rock Laboratory near the Oskarshamn NPP since around the year 2000. In total there were seven experimental packages with copper and clay in a very good simulation of real repository conditions. Three 1-year packages were retrieved early, but when SKB retrieved one 5-year package in 2006 an unexpected amount of copper corrosion had occurred. However, the reporting on the corrosion that had taken place in these packages was very limited. There were only estimated general corrosion data and no cross-sectional metallographic studies that are necessary in order to understand how much corrosion has taken place and of what type (Karnland et al., 2009; Wersin, 2013).

As results about copper corrosion from the LOT experiment could be important for the understanding and possible resolution of the copper corrosion controversy, MKG had repeatedly demanded that the next package be retrieved and analysed. These demands were not met by SKB, and the regulator SSM has shown little interest in the copper corrosion results from experiment.

Then came the surprise. In the early autumn of 2019, SKB secretly retrieved two 20-year-old experimental packages. This was disclosed by SKB at a meeting organised by the regulator SSM in early October 2019. The disclosure was likely unintentional, and while SKB started to provide more information about the retrieval, the company originally stated that it had no intention of revealing results from the retrieved packages until after the government had taken a decision on the repository.

During the autumn of 2019, MKG worked to get SKB to disclose all relevant corrosion results as soon as possible, so that SSM could check the results by carrying out a scientific quality review. MKG kept the government informed of the developments concerning the LOT packages. Its recommendation was that the government should wait for the corrosion results before taking a decision on the repository results, as if the corrosion was as bad the FEBEX experiment, something could be very wrong with using copper as a canister material.

These efforts were successful, and SKB published a report on the copper corrosion results in October 2020 (Johansson et al., 2020). Although there is a large amount of information on copper corrosion in the report, it was clear that the reporting was scientifically lacking in quality. Even though it was clear from pictures in the report that some surfaces were very corroded, these were not examined. The most heated surfaces where the corrosion was expected to be the largest were not examined in detail, and SKB claimed that other surfaces were examined instead as it was easier to do so. The corrosion on the most heated surfaces was indirectly estimated by measuring the corrosion products in the clay adjacent to the surfaces; a method that gives only a rough estimate. Cross-sectional metallographic studies in the report from less heated areas show signs of pitting corrosion. There is a very high likelihood that such images of the corrosion of the most heated areas would have shown deep pitting corrosion, and that SKB would have had big problems explaining how this had occurred.

During the autumn of 2020, SSM carried out a quality assurance project with the support of the UK consultancy Galson Sciences, and published a report in early 2021 (Hicks et al., 2021). MKG sent four inputs to the regulator to support the review.[11]

Using the report, SSM made a statement on the LOT results to the government in March 2021. Unfortunately, SSM accepted the SKB reporting of results without much analysis of its own. The researchers at KTH pointed out to the government that if the reporting of the LOT results lacked scientific quality, then "the anoxic copper corrosion rate in Swedish groundwater is catastrophic with respect to the KBS-3 model and this conclusion can be made without further considering

---

[11] MKG has published all the documents in the SSM act on the review on its website, and the comments and some responses from SSM can be found here: https://www.mkg.se/ssm-20205740-kvalitetsgranskning-av-skbs-lot-experiment. There is also a separate correspondence between SSM and MKG: https://www.mkg.se/ssm-20199556-korrespondens-om-kvalitetssakring-av-lot-forsoket-mkg-och-ssm.

the radiation induced corrosion (radiolysis), stress corrosion cracking and hydrogen embrittlement".[12]

10.4.6 The Government Decision

Despite the copper corrosion controversy Östhammar community in October 2020 told the government that it approved the siting of the repository and would not use its veto. All formal conditions were fulfilled for a government decision. But since 2018 the government had been a Social Democrat and Green Party minority coalition, with a Minister of the Environment from the Green Party who was reluctant to approve any SNF repository.

In the spring of 2021 the political discourse on nuclear power and nuclear waste management became increasingly politicised. Pressure from the pro-nuclear political parties in opposition increased throughout the year. All the parties in the conservative block (Liberal Party, Conservative Party, Christian Democrats and Sweden Democrats) that has been forming in Swedish politics for a few years have nuclear power as central to their climate policies.

The copper corrosion controversy became more intense in the autumn of 2021. MKG told the government that more scientifically produced results from the LOT experiment should be used to provide vital copper corrosion information necessary before a decision. The Swedish Council for Nuclear Waste stated that more research is needed to understand how the copper canister behaves in a repository environment, but that this could be done after a government decision. The Council also suggested that according to the Environmental Code, the government would be able to give only a construction license, and an operational license could be given separately at a later time. Such a legal construction would, however, be unprecedented and lacked any previous praxis. The Environmental Code states that there should be enough knowledge about the possible environmental effects of a project before a licence is given.

Because of the controversy that had put into doubt whether the copper canister would work as intended in the repository, towards the end of the license review SKB and SSM were forced to emphasise the importance of seeing the KBS

---

[12] In a letter to the government on 23 March, 2021, Professor Christofer Leygraf from KTH summarises their view on a number of copper corrosion issues. It is act document 158 and can be found here: https://www.mkg.se/m201800217me-regeringsprovning-enligt-miljobalken. The LOT experiment results are commented in the letter and in appendices E and F.

concept in a holistic perspective. Both organisations were convinced that there were no copper problems which could be important enough to question the long term-safety of the repository. In their common opinion the safety case with the three barriers (copper canister, clay buffer and the rock/clay in tunnels) that work together proves the repository will be robustly safe. In fact, there are scenarios in the SKB safety analysis that show that even if there are small holes in many of the canisters from the beginning, the regulatory limits will only be exceeded in the very long term if the clay buffer works as intended and the rock of the tunnels is very tight to water flow.

In November and December 2021 there was political parliamentary turmoil regarding the government budget process for 2022. This resulted in the Green Party leaving the government. The new Social Democrat Minister of the Environment almost immediately promised a decision on the SNF repository in January 2022.

On January 27, 2022, the Social Democrat government took the decision to approve the repository. The decision relied almost exclusively on statements from SSM based on the view that in a holistic perspective the three barriers together provide sufficient long-term safety.

MKG and member environmental organisations have appealed the government decision to the Swedish Highest Administrative Court (constitutional court) for judicial review (Naturskyddsföreningen et al., 2022). The organisations primarily want the court to review whether the government has followed the preconditions for a decision according to the Environmental Code (i.e., that the repository has been shown to be safe at the time of the license and that the precautionary principle has been followed) when the government decision so strongly relies only on support from the regulator.

In the appeal, the organisations also question the holistic industry and regulatory approach that the robustness of the whole KBS barrier system means that individual barriers need not function as intended. Their case is that there is strong evidence that the copper canister will not work as foreseen due to corrosion and other processes. If this is so, then the clay buffer will likely be destroyed by the copper corrosion products and will not be tight to water. The clay buffer barrier is not independent of copper canister problems. If the final barrier of the rock/clay in tunnels does not work, there is then a big problem.

In fact, it is not the rock itself that is the weakest part of this final barrier, but rather the clay in the tunnels. If the clay does not completely stop the flow of water as intended, and there is relatively little research to show that it will, then the "rock barrier" is not as strong as envisioned in the safety case. According to the organisations, it is too simple to give each of the three barriers a high protective function in the safety case and claim that as long as one barrier is intact everything is fine. An important issue for the constitutional court to ponder is how big can problems with individual barrier problems be, compared to the "robustness" of the total barrier system, for an environmental project to receive approval.

If the appeal is unsuccessful, the next step in the decision-making process will be the return of the case to the Land and Environment Court for a final licence decision and conditions. This process will not start until mid-2023 and will take several years, with the possibility to appeal any decisions taken.

If everything goes as SKB hopes, there would be a construction start in perhaps five years, and the first copper canister containing spent nuclear fuel would be placed in the repository in fifteen years' time; unless the science of copper corrosion and/or a better understanding of the weaknesses of clay barriers come back to haunt the decisions taken so far.

10.5 Some Final Observations

There may be some lessons to learn from the Swedish system for governance of RWM, especially from the controversial case of the repository for SNF.

Firstly, the Swedish SNF repository project is a clear example of when over time a project becomes too big to fail. With complete regulatory support from the industry, at times confirmed in weak governmental oversight, there were never any alternatives other than to move forward with the project.

Secondly, it is clearly a problem to have all the responsibility for research and development for radioactive waste facilities attached to a private industrial entity that is not part of the national public access to information system. If the work of private nuclear waste company SKB had been open to public scrutiny it is likely that the copper corrosion controversy would have been resolved much earlier. It would also have been better to have more resources, and a better mandate for the regulator to carry out its own independent research. And to have more general public funding for research on RWM.

Thirdly, the science behind the SNF repository safety case seems to have gone into a mode of confirmation bias early on. It is of course possible that SKB actively avoided doing the necessary research to prove that the copper canister would work as intended. But what has happened can perhaps be explained instead by a tunnel vision based on early basic assumptions that were just thought not needed to be tested, even when there were clear signs that the assumptions might be wrong.

Fourthly, the quality of the decision-making process was improved considerably by the implementation of good consultation processes and systems for access to justice. Even though the final outcome of the decision-making for the SNF repository may have been disappointing to some parties, it is hard to argue that not all voices were heard or were able to influence the process. The quality of the decision-making process was further improved by resourcing local communities and environmental NGOs to be able to participate fully in the process.

Finally, it is of vital importance that all problems that arise during the development and decision-making process for a repository for high-level radioactive waste are fully examined as far as possible. And even more importantly, as early as possible. The challenge is to find a governance system that both encourages and enables this.

References

Becker, R., & Hermansson, H. P. (2011). *Evolution of hydrogen by copper in ultrapure water without dissolved oxygen, SSM report 2011:34*. Swedish Radiation Safety Authority. Retrieved September 18, 2022 from https://www.stralsakerhetsmyndigheten.se/contentassets/825ec315628349c4b53750ff467c4440/201134-evolution-of-hydrogen-by-copper-in-ultrapure-water-without-dissolved-oxygen.

Bjällås, U., & Persson, I. (2011). *Licensing under the Environmental Code and the Nuclear Activities Act of a final repository for spent nuclear fuel, Report 2011:2e*. Swedish Council for Nuclear Waste. Retrived September 18, 2022 from https://www.karnavfallsradet.se/sites/default/files/documents/report_2011_2.pdf.

Cleveland, C., Moghaddam, S., & Orazem, C. (2014). Nanometer-Scale Corrosion of Copper in De-Aerated Deionized Water. *Journal of The Electrochemical Society, 161*(3), C107–C114.

Energiföretagen. (2021, December 31). *Elåret 2021: Från rekordlågt till rekordhögt elpris*. https://www.energiforetagen.se/pressrum/pressmeddelanden/2021/elaret-2021.-fran-rekordlagt-till-rekordhogt-elpris.

Hicks, T., Baldwin, T. D., & Scully, J. R. (2021). *Quality Assurance Review of the Swedish Nuclear Fuel and Waste Management Company's LOT Experiment (Phase S2 and A3) at the Äspö Facility in Sweden, SSM report 2021:06*. Retrieved September 18, 2022 from https://www.stralsakerhetsmyndigheten.se/contentassets/4dcbd2560af543449febb508dc2e9ce9/202106-quality-assurance-review-of-the-swedish-nuclear-fuel-and-waste-management-companys-lot-experiment-phase-s2-and-a3-at-the-aspo-facility-in-sweden.pdf.

Hultquist, G. (1986). Hydrogen Evolution in Corrosion of Copper in Pure Water. *Corrosion Science, 26*(2), 173–177.

Hultquist, G., Szakalos, P., Graham, M. J., Belonoshko, A. B., Sproule, I., Grasjo, L., Dorogokupets, P., Danilov, B., Aastrup, T., Wikmark, G., Chuah, G. K., Eriksson, J., & Rosengren, A. (2009). Water Corrodes Copper. *Catalysis Letters, 132*, 311–316. https://doi.org/10.1007/s10562-009-0113-x.

Hultquist, G., Graham, M. J., Kodra, O., Moisa, S., Liu, R., Bexell, U., & Smialek, J. L. (2013). *Corrosion of copper in distilled water without molecular oxygen and the detection of produced hydrogen, SSM report 2013:07*. Swedish Radiation Safety Authority.

Retrieved September 18, 2022 from https://www.stralsakerhetsmyndigheten.se/content assets/70967b190f57464fad1a741eb88a2b41/201307-corrosion-of-copper-in-distilled-water-without-molecular-oxygen-and-the-detection-of-produced-hydrogen.

Hultquist, G., Graham, M. J., Kodra, O., Moise, S., Liu, R., Bexell, U., & Smialek, J. L. (2015). Corrosion of copper in distilled water without O2 and the detection of produced hydrogen. *Corrosion Science*, (95), 162–167.

Johansson, A. J., Svensson, D., Gordon, A., Pahverk, H., Karlsson, O., Brask, J., Lundholm, M., Malmstrom, D., & Gustavsson, F. (2020). *Corrosion of copper after 20 years exposure in the bentonite field tests LOT S2 and A3, SKB TR-20-14*. Retrieved September 18, 2022 from https://www.skb.com/publication/2496000.

Karnland, O., Olsson, S., Dueck, A., Birgersson, M., Nilsson, U., Hernan-Hakansson, T., Pedersen, K., Nilsson, S., Eriksen, T. E., & Rosberg, B. (2009). *Long term test of buffer material at the Äspö Hard Rock Laboratory, LOT project: Final report on the A2 test parcel, SKB TR 09-29*. Swedish Nuclear Fuel And Waste Management Company. Retrieved September 18, 2022 from https://www.skb.com/publication/1961944/TR-09-29.pdf.

King, F., Lilja, C., Pedersen, K., & Vahanen, M. (2010). *An update of the state-of-the-art report on the corrosion of copper under expected conditions in a deep geologic repository, SKB TR-10-67*. Swedish Nuclear Fuel And Waste Management Company. Retrieved September 18, 2022 from https://skb.se/upload/publications/pdf/TR-10-67.pdf.

Lundell, K. (2017a, October 11). Strålsäkerhetsmyndigheten mörkade risker med slutförvaret. *Sveriges Natur*. Retrieved September 18, 2022 from https://www.sverigesnatur.org/aktuellt/stralsakerhetsmyndigheten-morkade-risker-med-slutforvaret.

Lundell, K. (2017b, October 23). *Dokumentet avslöjar: Så allvarliga är riskerna. Sveriges Natur*. Retrieved September 18, 2022 from https://www.sverigesnatur.org/aktuellt/dokument-avslojar-riskerna-ar-allvarliga.

Macdonald, D. D., & Sharifi-Asl, S. (2011). *Copper Immune to Corrosion When in Contact With Water and Aqueous Solutions?, SSM report 2011:09*. Swedish Radiation Safety Authority. Retrieved September 18, 2022 from https://www.stralsakerhetsmyndigheten.se/contentassets/d23a452aa5db46b196c729f0c94375db/201109-is-copper-immune-to-corrosion-when-in-contact-with-water-and-aqueous-solutions.

Naturskyddsföreningen, Jordens Vänner, MKG & Fältbiologerna. (2022). *Ansökan om rättsprövning av regeringens beslut om anläggningar i ett sammanhängande kärnbränsleförvarssystem i Forsmark och Oskarshamn*. Retrieved September 18, 2022 from https://www.mkg.se/uploads/Naturskyddsforeningen_mfl_begaran_om_rattsprovning_karnbransleforvar_220427.pdf.

SKB. (1999). *Deep repository for spent nuclear fuel, SR 97—Post-closure safety, Main Summary Report, SKB TR-99-06*. Swedish Nuclear Fuel And Waste Management Company. Retrieved September 18, 2022 from https://www.skb.com/publication/2488114.

SKB. (2019). *RD&D Programme 2019: Programme for research, development and demonstration of methods for the management and disposal of nuclear waste, SKB TR-19-28*. Swedish Nuclear Fuel And Waste Management Company. Retrieved September 18, 2022 from https://skb.se/wp-content/uploads/2020/01/RDD-Programme-2019.pdf.

SKBF. (1977). *KBS 1—Handling of spent nuclear fuel and final storage of vitrified high level reprocessing waste, I General, KBS—Kärnbränslesäkerhet (Nuclear Fuel Safety Project)*. Swedish Nuclear Supply Company. Retrieved September 18, 2022 from https://www.skb.com/publication/4377/722+KBS-1+Eng+1.pdf.

SKBF. (1978). *KBS 2—Handling and final storage of unreprocessed spent nuclear fuel, I— General, KBS—Kärnbränslesäkerhet (Nuclear Fuel Safety Project)*. Swedish Nuclear Supply Company. Retrieved September 18, 2022 from https://www.skb.com/publication/4390/KBS-2+General.pdf.

SKBF. (1983). *KBS 3—Final storage of spent nuclear fuel—KBS-3, Summary, KBS—Kärnbränslesäkerhet (Nuclear Fuel Safety Project)*. Swedish Nuclear Supply Company. Retrieved September 18, 2022 from https://www.skb.com/publication/1678004/716+5+KBS-3+Summary.pdf.

SSM. (2016). *Consultation response on the licence application under the Environmental Code from the Swedish Nuclear Fuel and Waste Management Company (SKB) for a system for management and final disposal of spent nuclear fuel*. Swedish Radiation Safety Authority. 29 June. Retrieved September 18, 2022 from https://www.mkg.se/uploads/SSM_Consultation_response_on_the_licence_application_160629.pdf.

SSM. (2019). *Technical Note, SSM's external experts' reviews of SKB's report on supplementary information on canister integrity issues, SSM Report 2019:22*. Swedish Radiation Safety Authority. Retrieved September 18, 2022 from https://www.stralsakerhetsmyndigheten.se/contentassets/b8881783acf14def9409d9d48789a0e2/201922-technical-note-ssms-external-experts-reviews-of-skbs-report-on-supplementary-information-on-canister-integrity-issues.pdf.

Szakálos, P., Hultquist, G., & Wikmark, G. (2007). Corrosion of Copper by Water. *Electrochemical and Solid State Letters*, 10(11).

UNECE. (1998). *Convention on Access to Information, Public Participation in Decision-making and Access to Justice in Environmental Matters* (Aarhus Convention). Retrieved September 19, 2022 from https://unece.org/environment-policy/public-participation/aarhus-convention/text.

Wersin, P. (2013). *LOT A2 test parcel. Compilation of copper data in the LOT A2 test parcel, SKB TR 13-17*. Swedish Nuclear Fuel And Waste Management Company. Retrieved September 18, 2022 from https://www.skb.com/publication/2682520/TR-13-17.pdf.

Wersin, P. & Kober, F. (Eds.). (2017). *FEBEX-DP: Metal Corrosion and Iron-Bentonite Interaction Studies. Arbeitsbericht NAB 16-16*. Swiss National Cooperative for the Disposal of Radioactive Waste (Nagra). Retrieved September 18, 2022 from https://www.mkg.se/uploads/FEBEX-DP_Metal_Corrosion_Iron-Bentonite_Interaction_Studies_Wersin_Kober_NAB_16-16_Nagra_October_2017.pdf.

Johan Swahn has worked academically for many years in the field of Science, Technology and Global Security at the Chalmers University of Technology in Göteborg, Sweden, mostly on issues that concern military and civil nuclear technology. Since 2005 he has been working for the Swedish environmental movement on nuclear waste issues as the director of Miljöorganisationernas Kärnavfallsgranskning, MKG. He has written extensively about the governance of radioactive waste.

Open Access This chapter is licensed under the terms of the Creative Commons Attribution 4.0 International License (http://creativecommons.org/licenses/by/4.0/), which permits use, sharing, adaptation, distribution and reproduction in any medium or format, as long as you give appropriate credit to the original author(s) and the source, provide a link to the Creative Commons license and indicate if changes were made.

The images or other third party material in this chapter are included in the chapter's Creative Commons license, unless indicated otherwise in a credit line to the material. If material is not included in the chapter's Creative Commons license and your intended use is not permitted by statutory regulation or exceeds the permitted use, you will need to obtain permission directly from the copyright holder.

11 The Finnish Solution to Final Disposal of Spent Nuclear Fuel

Jarmo Vehmas, Aleksis Rentto, Jyrki Luukkanen, Burkhard Auffermann and Jari Kaivo-oja

11.1 Introduction

Finland is the first country in the world to be in the implementation phase of geological final disposal of spent nuclear fuel (SNF). The implementing company, Posiva Oy, owned by two nuclear power companies Teollisuuden Voima Oy (TVO) and Fortum, has marketed its concept ONKALO and the facilities as a "final solution" to the problem of high-level nuclear waste (HLW). A third Finnish nuclear power company, Fennovoima, is not included in the ONKALO project.

Finland's political culture is based on structural corporatism and high trust of citizens in the state and its institutions, which partly explains the progress of Posiva's project and the relatively minor opposition to it. Public debates have focused more on new nuclear power plants (NPPs), which have been on the political agenda at the same time as the final disposal facility and its expansions. The

J. Vehmas (✉) · A. Rentto · J. Luukkanen · B. Auffermann · J. Kaivo-oja
University of Turku, Finland Futures Research Centre, Tampere, Finland
e-mail: jarmo.vehmas@utu.fi

J. Luukkanen
e-mail: Jyrki.luukkanen@utu.fi

B. Auffermann
e-mail: burkhard.auffermann@utu.fi

J. Kaivo-oja
e-mail: jari.kaivo-oja@utu.fi

© The Author(s) 2023
M. Arentsen and R. van Est (Eds.), *The Future of Radioactive Waste Governance*, Energiepolitik und Klimaschutz. Energy Policy and Climate Protection, https://doi.org/10.1007/978-3-658-40496-3_11

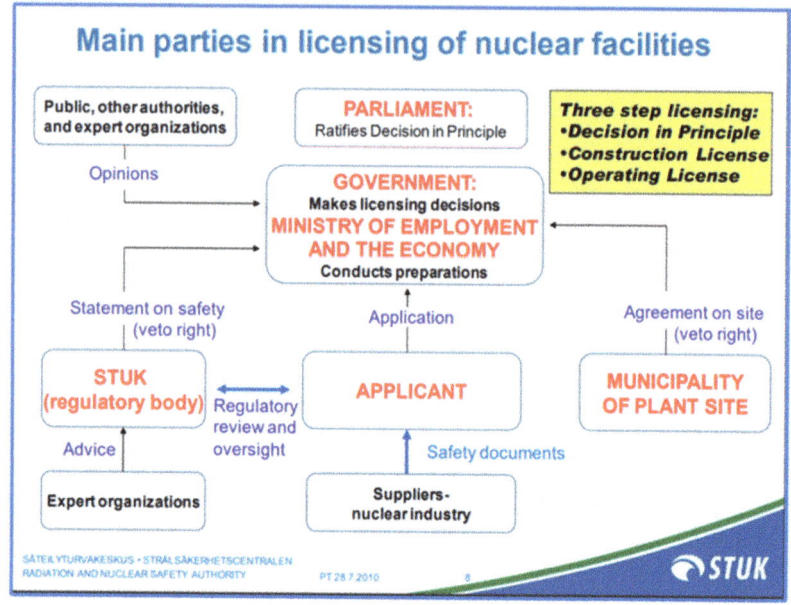

Fig. 11.1 Major actors in the licensing procedure of nuclear facilities in Finland (STUK, 2019)

licensing procedure is the same for all nuclear facilities,[1] including both NPPs and final disposal repositories (Fig. 11.1).

During the process of Posiva becoming the first holder of an operating license for a final disposal facility for SNF, public participation has not been very active and has been considered ineffective by various social scientists. This was one reason to strengthen the role and potential for public participation in the revised Act on Environmental Impact Assessment Procedure (252/2017), which has not yet

---

[1] According to the Nuclear Energy Act (990/1987), a nuclear facility refers to facilities to produce nuclear energy, facilities for large-scale final disposal of nuclear waste, and facilities for producing, manufacturing, using and storing of nuclear materials and nuclear wastes. A decision-in-principle (DiP) is required for (1) a nuclear power plant with a heat efficiency of 50 MW or more, (2) a facility for final disposal of nuclear waste, and (3) other facilities with a significant amount of nuclear material, nuclear waste, or nuclear radiation, comparable to (1).

Table 11.1 The amount of radioactive waste in Finland (MEE, 2022)

Type of radioactive waste	Stored by the end of 2019	Final disposal by 2019	Final disposal by 2030	Final disposal by 2050
Very low level	204 m^3	n. a.[a]	2,300 m^3	6,900 m^3
Low level	1,691 m^3	6,541 m^3	8,761 m^3	10,661 m^3
Intermediate level	1,970 m^3	2,117 m^3	8,278 m^3	9,078 m^3
High level	2,261 t[b]	0	3,200 t	4,200 t

[a] Included in the figure of low level waste
[b] Amount in temporary storage at the nuclear power plant sites

been applied to nuclear facilities. Furthermore, according to the Ministry of Economic Affairs and Employment (MEE),[2] processing Posiva's application for an operating license for ONKALO will include possibilities for public participation (MEE, 2021), which is new in granting an operating license for a nuclear facility in Finland.

Table 11.1 shows the amount of nuclear waste by 2019 and estimates for 2030 and 2050, Table 11.2 provides information on the Finnish NPPs, and Table 11.3 shows the amounts of SNF in these plants by 2019 and the maximum licensed amounts.

This chapter provides a view of Finnish nuclear waste management (NWM) from the governance ecosystem perspective (see chap. 1 of this volume) and describes how the first final disposal facility for SNF in the world, ONKALO by Posiva Oy, has been smoothly implemented. Section 11.2 describes the development of Finnish NWM. Section 11.3 discusses technological challenges related to the geological disposal of SNF, i.e. stability of the Finnish bedrock, the Swedish KBS-3 V concept, and a less discussed issue—temporary storage of SNF lasting up to 50 years. Section 11.4 looks at the financial side of NWM based on the State Nuclear Waste Management Fund, which also provides resources for scientific research on NWM.

Section 11.5 provides background to Finnish consensus-seeking decision-making by focusing on essential characteristics which enable Finnish govern-

---

[2] To simplify the English translation of the name(s) of the Finnish Ministry of Economic Affairs and Employment over the historical period described in this chapter, the acronym MEE is used throughout.

Table 11.2 Basic information on the nuclear power plants in Finland

Nuclear power plant	Reactor type and current capacity	Operating license in force
Loviisa 1 (Fortum)	Atomenergoexport VVER-440, 507 MW_e	31.12.2027
Loviisa 2 (Fortum)	Atomenergoexport VVER-440, 507 MW_e	31.12.2030
Olkiluoto 1 (TVO)	AB Asea Atom BWR, 890 MW_e	31.12.2038
Olkiluoto 2 (TVO)	AB Asea Atom BWR, 890 MW_e	31.12.2038
Olkiluoto 3 (TVO)	Areva NP EPR, 1,600 MW_e [a]	31.12.2038
Hanhikivi 1 (Fennovoima)	Rosatom AES-2006 PWR, 1,200 MW_e [b]	

[a] Started on 21 December 2021, grid connection expected in 2022
[b] Reactor in the 2015 construction license application. Fennovoima withdrew the application on 24 May 2022

Table 11.3 Total quantity of spent nuclear fuel produced until decommissioning of the nuclear power plants in Finland (MEE, 2022; Posiva 2021; Fennovoima, 2015)

Nuclear power plant	Quantity of spent nuclear fuel by the end of 2019 (t)	A total maximum quantity of SNF until decommissioning (t)
Loviisa 1–2	690	1,096
Olkiluoto 1–2	1,565	2,904
Olkiluoto 3	–	2,500
Hanhikivi 1	–	(1,800)
Total	2,261§	6,500 (8,300)

ance—structural corporatism, high trust in technology and experts, and the subservient role of the public. These are reflected in NWM via typical Finnish characteristics, including strong energy elites, cross-ownership of nuclear power companies, and the so-called Mankala principle applied in many Finnish energy companies, among them TVO, Fennovoima, and Posiva. Section 11.6 describes an important part of the governance ecosystem, namely weak social inclusion in the Finnish NWM. Public participation in decision-making, the role of anti-nuclear movements, and the media's role are addressed. Section 11.7 concludes and looks at the future of NWM in Finland.

11.2 History of Nuclear Waste Management (NWM) in Finland

Figure 11.2 presents the most recent schedule from the Ministry of Economic Affairs and Employment (MEE, 2022) regarding (1) use and decommissioning of the licensed NPPs, (2) operation and closure of storage facilities for low- and intermediate-level nuclear waste (LILW) at the NPP sites, (3) interim storage of SNF at the NPP sites, and (4) final disposal of SNF.

11.2.1 NWM Before Finland Entered the EU in 1995

Finland began preparing for NWM during the procurement and construction phase of the first NPPs. In 1969, a bilateral agreement was concluded with the Soviet Union, including a principle that the Soviet Union takes back the SNF used in the Soviet-based nuclear reactors. This export of SNF from the two Loviisa reactors started in 1981 and ended when the ban on nuclear waste exports and imports (included in a 1994 amendment to the Nuclear Energy Act) entered into force in 1996. Since then, SNF from Loviisa 1–2 has been first placed in a cooling pool beside the reactor, and then in temporary storage located at the NPP site.[3]

TVO had a different situation with its Swedish nuclear reactors in Eurajoki (Olkiluoto 1–2). According to Raumolin (2011), TVO considered final disposal of SNF in Finland as its preferred option.[4] However, the TVO Board had rejected international negotiations on reprocessing tenders in 1979 for economic reasons (Kojo, 2009). TVO made a schedule for NWM, which allowed temporary storage of SNF for 40 years before its final disposal (Table 11.4).

In 1983, the government made a decision on NWM. It included two basic options. According to MEE (2015a, p. 7), the first involved "centralised international final disposal solutions and contract arrangements that would allow reprocessing SNF to be irrevocably located abroad". In the second option, nuclear

---

[3] A final repository for LILW in Loviisa came into use in 1998. Expansion for the waste generated during decommissioning of the VVER reactors is expected.

[4] TVO has built cooling pools and an interim storage for SNF in the Olkiluoto site. A final repository for LILW was also built in Olkiluoto and came into use in 1992. Enlargement of this repository has been included in the construction license granted for Olkiluoto 3.

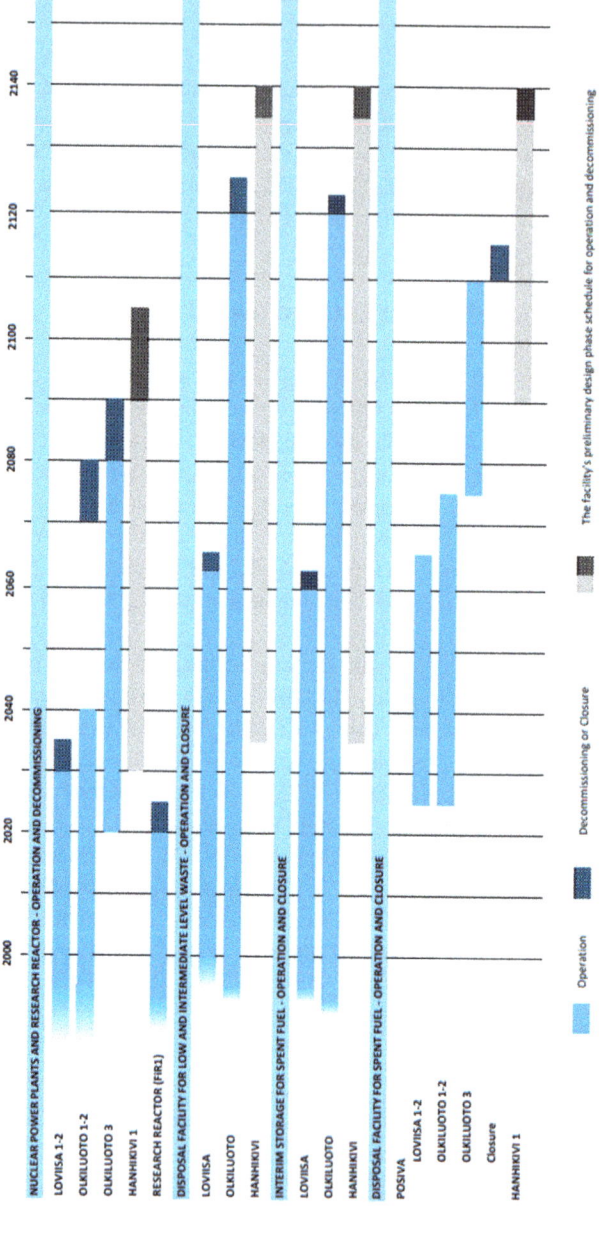

Fig. 11.2 Timetable regarding the use of Finnish nuclear power plants and nuclear waste management. (MEE, 2022)

Table 11.4 Schedule for the final disposal of spent nuclear fuel by TVO (Raumolin, 1982, as cited in Kojo, 2009, p. 167; Kojo et al., 2010, p. 170)

Period	Activity
1980–1982	Suitability study with safety analyses
1983–1985	Preparation for the preliminary site characterisation
1986–1992	Preliminary site characterisation in chosen site areas (5–10 sites)
1993–2000	Additional siting studies (2–3 sites)
2001–2010	Detailed studies on the chosen disposal site and pre-planning of the siting and the encapsulation plant
2011–2020	Planning and construction of the final disposal site and the encapsulation plant
2021–2050	Final disposal facility in operation
2051–2060	Closing of the final disposal site

power companies prepared for final disposal of SNF in Finland. The 1983 decision preferred international solutions, but demanded that the nuclear power companies are prepared for final disposal of SNF in Finland, if necessary (Kojo, 2009).

TVO's original schedule of NWM has been followed without major exceptions. Screening of possible sites started in a large number of areas but dropped to 85 by using extra-geological criteria, e.g., land ownership and municipal acceptability. TVO selected five areas for preliminary site characterisation studies in 1987: Olkiluoto, Veitsivaara, Kivetty, Romuvaara, and Syyry (Fig. 11.3). Olkiluoto as a NPP site had a special position, because the proximity of the facilities would reduce the transportation of SNF. Detailed site characterisation studies started in Olkiluoto, Romuvaara, and Kivetty in 1992 (Kojo, 2009).

11.2.2 Decision-In-Principle and Licensing of ONKALO

In 1995, Fortum and TVO established a joint company Posiva Oy for the final disposal of SNF from their NPPs in the new context of banned exports and imports of nuclear waste and a mandatory Environmental Impact Assessment (EIA) process. Posiva continued the siting process started by TVO, and added Loviisa to the potential final disposal sites in 1997 (Fig. 11.3).

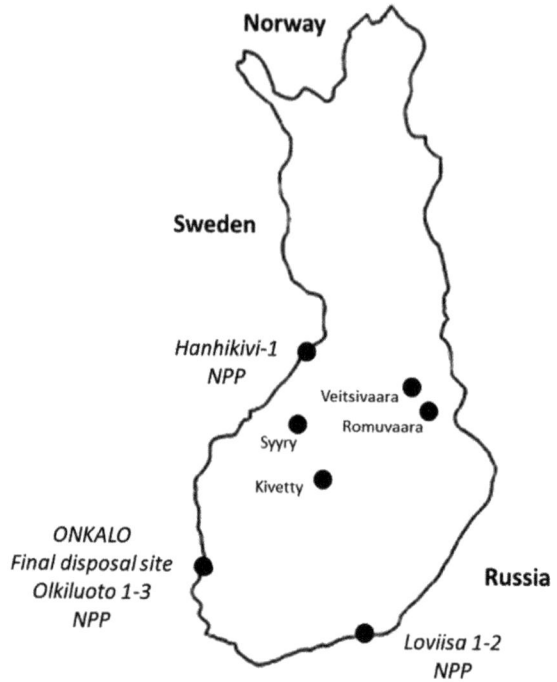

Fig. 11.3 Locations of the final disposal sites for spent nuclear fuel with site characterisation studies and the existing nuclear sites

In the preparatory phase of the DiP application, local acceptability of the SNF repository became a decisive factor for Posiva, especially acceptability by the municipal council of the host municipality. Posiva and the municipality of Eurajoki started negotiations on mutual economic benefits of choosing Olkiluoto as the site for final disposal of SNF. A well-known result of these negotiations is the "Vuojoki agreement". Among other things, Eurajoki agreed to lease a real estate, the Vuojoki Manor, to Posiva, and Posiva agreed to finance construction of a new senior centre in Eurajoki. The municipal council of Eurajoki approved the Vuojoki agreement on 9 May 1999 (see Kojo, 2009).

On 26 May 1999, Posiva applied a DiP to construct an encapsulation plant and final disposal facility for SNF. The only site included in the application was

Olkiluoto in Eurajoki. Posiva stated that "an essential factor regarding the implementation is also to gain local acceptance for the operation" (Kojo, 2009, p. 173).

Posiva estimated the maximum amount of HLW to be 9,000 tons (t)[5] covering the SNF produced in Loviisa 1–2, Olkiluoto 1–2, and two planned new NPPs. Because TVO had submitted an application for a DiP to construct Olkiluoto 3, Posiva changed its DiP application in November 2000 to cover SNF only from the reactors in operation (4,000 t), and submitted a new application for a DiP to extend the repository by 2,500 t of SNF from Olkiluoto 3. Moreover, Posiva asked the government to decide on Olkiluoto 3 and the extension of the final disposal repository at the same time (MEE, 2013; Kojo et al., 2010).

The government issued a favourable DiP on the final disposal facility for 4,000 t of SNF in December 2000. The government stated that, "of the studied disposal options, deep disposal in the bedrock, i.e. geological disposal, offers the best and most realistic possibilities to isolate high-level nuclear waste from the biosphere and the human habitat" (Government of Finland, 2000). The parliament approved this DiP on 18 May 2001 with votes 159–3.

The government made the DiPs regarding the construction of Olkiluoto 3 and extension of the repository for 2,500 t of SNF from Olkiluoto 3 in January 2002, and the parliament approved both in May 2002 (MEE, 2013; Kojo et al., 2010).

In 2004, Posiva introduced the Finnish name ONKALO for the underground research facility excavated in the Olkiluoto bedrock, meaning a cavity or a hidden cave, which sounds "safer" than a normal cave (Auffermann et al., 2015; cf. El-Showk, 2022). Soon it became widely-used for the whole project on final disposal of SNF in Finland. Since 2018, ONKALO has been a registered trademark of Posiva Oy.

In 2007, a group of Finnish power companies and the German E.ON established a new nuclear power company, Fennovoima. Two years later, Fennovoima submitted an application to the government for a DiP to construct a new NPP, Hanhikivi 1, in Pyhäjoki, on the north-western coast of Finland (Fig. 11.2). In the same year, TVO and Fortum submitted applications for DiPs on two new NPPs, Olkiluoto 4 (TVO) and Loviisa 3 (Fortum). At the same time, Posiva submitted two applications for a DiP to extend ONKALO for SNF, one from Olkiluoto 4 and another from Loviisa 3.

---

[5] 9,000 tons of SNF is around 900 m^3 in volume. The amount of HLW such as SNF is documented in metric tons only.

The MEE processed all five DiP applications during 2009–2010, and the government made the DiPs in May 2010. Construction of TVO's Olkiluoto 4 and Fennovoima's Hanhikivi 1, as well as the extension of ONKALO for SNF from Olkiluoto 4, were deemed to be "in line with the overall good of the society", but Fortum's Loviisa 3, and Posiva's related extension of ONKALO were not.[6] The parliament left the three favourable DiPs in force in July 2010.

In December 2012, Posiva submitted an application for a construction license for ONKALO with a total capacity of 6,500 t of SNF. The final disposal facility will be constructed in such a way that its safety will not be monitored after the repository has been decommissioned and the ownership of and responsibilities for nuclear waste have been transferred to the state (Posiva, 2012). The government granted the construction license in November 2015. On 30 December 2021, Posiva submitted an application for ONKALO's operating license. According to the application, the operation would start in March 2024 (Posiva, 2021). The MEE will organise a public consultation, request statements from authorities, organisations, and municipalities in the affected area, and provide citizens and communities with an opportunity to express their opinions (MEE, 2021).

11.2.3 Cooperation Between Posiva and Fennovoima

In the application for the Hanhikivi 1 DiP, Fennovoima (2009) planned the NWM in cooperation with other licensees responsible for NWM. The MEE appointed a working group in March 2012 to coordinate the three nuclear power companies' joint investigation into alternatives for final disposal of SNF. The working group compared construction alternatives and recommended utilising the competence and field experience accumulated during Posiva's project (MEE, 2013). Moreover, the working group recommended that Posiva and Fennovoima should continue cooperation to solve Fennovoima's NWM—the number of facilities for final disposal of SNF is not an issue (MEE, 2013, p. 15). In 2017, MEE appointed a new working group to investigate future alternatives for long-term NWM, but the working group excluded the final disposal of SNF and stated that the previous working group report is up-to-date (MEE, 2019a).

---

[6] In 2015, TVO decided not to apply for a construction license, so the DiPs related to Olkiluoto 4, granted in 2010 for TVO and Posiva, lapsed.

11 The Finnish Solution to Final Disposal of Spent Nuclear Fuel

In 2016, Fennovoima and Posiva signed a mutual agreement on using Posiva's expertise in planning and developing Fennovoima's NWM activities (Fennovoima, 2016).[7] Fennovoima also submitted its EIA plan as required by the MEE in the Hanhikivi 1 DiP, and announced that the location of the final disposal site will be selected in the 2040s (Fennovoima, 2016).

In 2017, the MEE requested additional information on Fennovoima's NWM before giving its statement on the EIA plan. Fennovoima informed MEE that the location will be decided "after receiving the construction license for Hanhikivi 1 at the earliest, and when applying for the operating license at the latest" (Fennovoima, 2018, p. 4). Fennovoima prefers only one final disposal facility of SNF in Finland (Fennovoima, 2018; MEE, 2019a), but keeps open two siting options Olkiluoto and Pyhäjoki. Posiva, on the other hand, is willing to offer expertise but does not support a joint project in Olkiluoto, which might require a shareholder position for Fennovoima in Posiva Oy.

11.3 Scientific and Technological Challenges

11.3.1 Stability of the Bedrock

Posiva has chosen deep geological storage as the method for the final disposal of SNF. The bedrock of the Olkiluoto site consists of Svecofennian metasediments and plutonic rocks, 1,800–1,900 million years old (Anttila et al., 1999). In Posiva's solution, the bedrock acts as a natural barrier. Its safety functions are intended to (1) isolate the SNF from the surface environment and normal habitats for humans, plants and animals, limit the possibilities of human intrusion, and isolate the repository from changing conditions at the ground surface, (2) provide favourable and predictable mechanical, geochemical and hydro-geological conditions for the engineered barriers, and (3) limit the transport and retard the migration of harmful substances that could be released from the repository (STUK, 2015).

Posiva has accumulated practical experience related to the stability of the bedrock in Olkiluoto from the test drillings started in 1989 by TVO, and during the excavation of the underground rock characterisation facilities from 2004. Posiva considers the bedrock to be sufficiently stable around the deposition tunnels and

---

[7] In 2016, Posiva established a subsidiary, Posiva Solutions, offering expertise and consulting services on the management of nuclear waste and radioactive materials.

deposition holes. Posiva has studied the geological structures of the bedrock at the disposal site and estimated that at a depth of 400–450 m, the requirements for post-closure safety and the constructability of the disposal facility are fulfilled. According to STUK (the Finnish Radiation and Nuclear Safety Authority), the understanding and measurements of the baseline stress of the bedrock are sufficient at the construction license stage; however, Posiva will have to reduce specific uncertainties and deficiencies before construction of the disposal facilities. Moreover, further investigations are required related to the impact of the heterogeneity of the bedrock on the stability of the bedrock and concerning the rock mechanical properties of the fracture zones on various scales. However, STUK (2015) concludes that the characteristics of the bedrock in Olkiluoto are favourable for ensuring the post-closure safety of SNF final disposal.

The changes of conditions due to an ice age as well as permafrost are seen by Posiva as the most important above-ground natural phenomena regarding final disposal. Based on its own modelling, Posiva has estimated that the permafrost would reach a depth of 60–240 m during a dry, cold period lasting 10,000 years. Using the same analysis, Posiva has estimated that permafrost extending to a depth of 400 m would require a dry, cold period of 100,000 years, which it considers unlikely.

There are uncertainties related to climate evolution analyses that extend far into the future. For this reason, Posiva has also estimated the effects of permafrost that reaches a disposal depth on the performance of the fuel canister and other engineered safety barriers (STUK, 2015; see Sect. 11.3.2 on the KBS-3 V final disposal concept). However, there has been criticism towards the disposal concept, on geological grounds: "All the forecasts of the safety of the disposal site after the next glacier period (55,000–65,000 or 90,000–100,000 years from present) are speculations and are not based on scientific factors" (Saarnisto, 2008, as cited in a popular magazine by Ukkola, 2010).

STUK (2015, p. 41) states that the amount of collected seismic data needs to be extended during the construction and operation of the facility since the safety of the disposal will be evaluated "over timespans that exceed the data coverage presented". STUK does not define the timespans, but the seismic data presented in Posiva's application for the ONKALO construction license covers 1965–2012. Moreover, seismic risks need to be further investigated by taking into account the bedrock structures and their properties in Olkiluoto more diversely, as well as by assessing further magnitudes and frequencies of earthquakes under various geological circumstances (STUK, 2015).

11.3.2 The KBS-3 V Concept

Posiva plans to pack the SNF inside copper-steel canisters at an above-ground encapsulation plant from where they will be transferred into the deep underground tunnels of the repository and placed in the holes excavated in the final disposal tunnels (Fig. 11.4).

The KBS-3V concept was originally developed by the Swedish Nuclear Fuel and Waste Management Company (SKB). Posiva adopted the concept and has elaborated it further together with SKB. KBS-3V has three safety barriers (copper capsule, bentonite clay, and bedrock granite) designed to keep the HLW isolated from the biosphere for at least 100,000 years (Fig. 11.5). According to Posiva (2018), a shortcoming of one barrier does not endanger the safety of the insulation.

Finland proceeds as the first implementer of KBS-3V, as ONKALO is expected to start operating in 2024. About one hundred final disposal tunnels will be excavated during the 100-year operational period of ONKALO. The repository will total a length of 35 km with each tunnel being about 4.5 m high, 3.5 m wide, and 350 m long, each holding about 30 canisters of SNF.

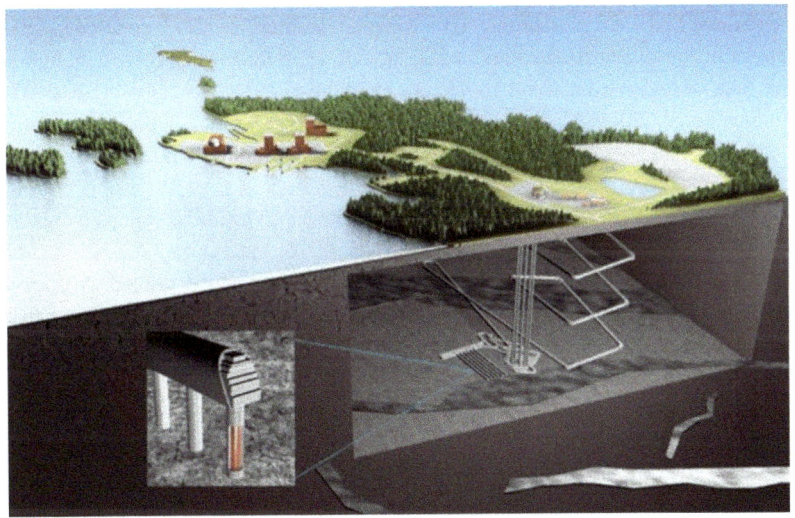

Fig. 11.4 Concept image of the KBS-3V final disposal solution. (Source: Posiva Oy)

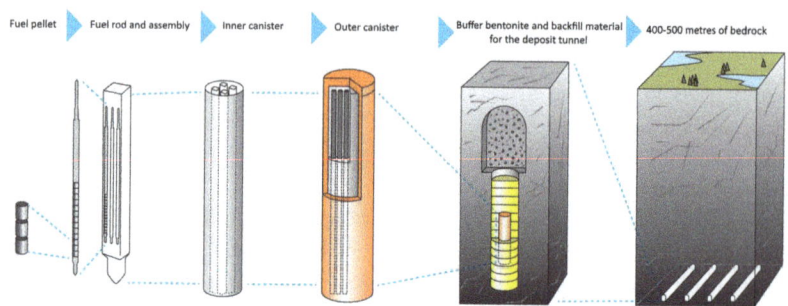

Fig. 11.5 The multi-barrier principle in Posiva's final disposal concept

The copper canister is the most important barrier against the release of SNF (MEE, 2019b). The final disposal concept relies on the assumption that copper does not corrode in anaerobic conditions. Therefore, the canisters used for disposal should corrode extremely slowly when buried deep in the bedrock with bentonite clay surrounding them.

Researchers at the Swedish Royal Institute of Technology (KTH) have repeatedly questioned the KBS-3V method by highlighting greater copper corrosion risks than SKB acknowledges. Experimental studies at KTH concluded that copper in the disposal canisters could corrode even under anaerobic conditions if it takes oxygen from water molecules (Hultquist, 1986; Szakálos et al., 2007; Hultquist et al., 2009; Szakálos et al., 2018). Therefore, contact with groundwater could risk a higher corrosion rate for the copper canisters than is considered safe for SNF disposal.

Posiva and SKB rejected such claims by referring to a similar repeated experiment where no corrosion was detected (SKB, 2016; Ottosson et al., 2017). The appropriateness of experimental test conditions for sensitive copper corrosion research have been disputed. Posiva (2018) has nevertheless been confident that their ongoing research and modelling together with SKB is enough to guarantee the safety of the repository project.

The scientific dispute over copper corrosion has not received much media attention in Finland, while in Sweden it is a potential "showstopper" in the country's own final SNF disposal plans (Litmanen et al., 2017b; Lehtonen, 2021). In 2018, the Swedish Land and Environmental Court of Appeal stated to the government of Sweden that SKB's application for a SNF repository should only be approved if the company can provide further evidence of long-term safety regarding the durability of the copper capsules.

11.3.3 Temporary Storage of Spent Nuclear Fuel

The SNF of a NPP is stored in cooling pools of the reactor for at least two years. Then it will be transferred to an interim storage facility (Becker, 2017). The cooling pool is a vulnerable part of a NPP with a considerable radioactive inventory. If a terror attack causes a breach of the concrete walls of a SNF pool, the cooling water will pour out. This causes the SNF to heat up due to the decay heat. Once the SNF reaches a temperature of 900 °C, the zirconium cladding of the fuel starts to burn in the air (Becker, 2017). This can cause high radioactive releases (National Academy of Sciences, 2016).

According to US National Research Council (NRC) estimates (NRC 2006), a fire in a dense-packed SNF pool could release 100 times as much cesium-137 into the atmosphere as the three reactor meltdowns released in Fukushima. Such an accident would cause a relocation of 3.5 million people (von Hippel & Schoeppner, 2016). NRC (2006) has examined the risks of a terrorist attack on temporary storage of SNF for using these materials for a radiological dispersal device. A successful terrorist attack on SNF pools, though difficult, is possible. A propagating fire in a pool could release large amounts of radioactive material, but rearranging SNF in the pool during storage and providing emergency water spray systems would reduce the likelihood of a propagating fire even under severe damage conditions.

In Finland, the need for modification of the SNF temporary storage has been assessed by the Finnish Radiation and Nuclear Safety Authority (cf. STUK 2021). In Olkiluoto, all SNF from Olkiluoto 1–2 is in the interim storage after being cooled enough in the pools of reactor units. TVO decided to double the number of cooling pools due to the additional operating time of the reactors and the new Olkiluoto 3.[8] The capacity of the enlarged SNF storage is considered to be sufficient for the three Olkiluoto units. The enlargement of the interim storage was included in the most recent operating license of Olkiluoto 1–2. The licensing of the enlargement was conducted as a major plant modification with approval from STUK. When conducting changes in an old nuclear facility, the new safety requirements have to be followed. The major challenge in designing the enlargement of the SNF storage was to modify it to withstand a large airplane crash. The operator chose to cover the pools with protective slabs dimensioned to be light

---

[8] The government granted TVO an operating license for Olkiluoto 3 in March 2019. All nuclear reactors Olkiluoto 1–3 have an operating license in force up to the end of 2038 (Table 1.2).

enough to ease their handling but strong enough to withstand the impacts followed by an airplane crash to the storage building, and to build a landfill embankment and concrete structures outside the storage, dimensioned to be high enough to protect the pool structures from a direct airplane impact (Maaranen, 2013).

After the 2011 Fukushima accident, STUK required the nuclear power operators to investigate how the NPPs are prepared to withstand exceptional natural phenomena and other unpredictable disturbances in the external power supply, such as a war. Some modifications to the interim storages of SNF were planned after the stress tests.

11.4 Financing of Nuclear Waste Management

In Finland, the nuclear operators TVO, Fortum, and Fennovoima are financially responsible for the management of radioactive waste and decommissioning of their NPPs (Nuclear Energy Agency, 2021). The legal instrument for this is the State Nuclear Waste Management Fund (SNWMF), independent from the state budget but controlled by the MEE (Nuclear Energy Act, 990/1987, Chap. 7). The nuclear operators pay an annual fee to the SNWMF to cover their liabilities. In practice, the SNWMF acts as a kind of guarantee fund from which potential remaining decommissioning and nuclear waste management measures are paid if a nuclear operator does not fulfil its obligations (Nuclear Energy Agency, 2021).

The nuclear operators and their shareholders are entitled to borrow back a part of the accumulated assets from the SNWMF in exchange for the provision of securities. This was a maximum 75%, but was decreased to 60% in 2021, based on recommendation by a working group set up by MEE to improve the investment activity of the SNWMF (see MEE, 2019c). Fortum and TVO have actively used their right for back-borrowing. Regarding the remaining assets, at least 20% must be available for the State, and the SNWMF must actively invest at least 20% to increase the assets against collateral security yielding the best possible return (Nuclear Energy Act, 990/1987, Sect. 52).

The costs of the final disposal of SNF depend on the time horizon of permanent disposal. At the end of 2019, €2.6 billion had been accumulated in the SNWMF from charges on generated electricity, which account for 10% of the production costs of nuclear electricity (Jalonen, 2021, private communication). The SNWMF is expected to cover all the costs of the final disposal of SNF and decommissioning of the NPPs in operation. The total estimated cost is €3.3 billion, which includes

€2.4 billion for the operation of the SNF repository until 2120 and €200 million for decommissioning of the NPPs (Conca, 2021).

Co-ordinated, publicly administered research programmes on nuclear waste have been in operation since 1989 (VTT, 2006). Financing came mostly from the Ministry of Trade and Industry (currently MEE), Radiation and Nuclear Safety Authority (STUK), Technical Research Centre of Finland (VTT), and the nuclear power companies. Since the funding for research on NWM was institutionalised in 2003, national research programmes have been organised by the MEE and financed by the Nuclear Safety Research Fund and the Nuclear Waste Research Fund, which were established in 2003 to guarantee the sufficient availability of new scientific information about nuclear waste and its management (Nuclear Energy Act 990/1987, Sect. 53).

According to Litmanen (2008), the funding for social scientific research on nuclear waste was first introduced in the JYT2 programme (1994–1996). During that time, the ban on imports and exports of nuclear waste, the introduction of legislation on EIA, and controversy about TVO's siting plans for final disposal facility held by the residents of different municipalities created a political need for social scientific research. The importance of social sciences was emphasised, "as the public debate on nuclear waste had started and opposition to the plans seemed to be increasing" (Litmanen, 2008, p. 435).

After the favourable DiP on Posiva's repository for SNF in 2000 and the extension in 2002, the political need for social scientific research decreased. It dropped out from the first KYT research programme but returned in 2008 under the title "sociological research" (MEE, 2011; Table 11.5). The political need for social scientific research increased because Posiva had started preparing an application for the construction license for ONKALO.

Table 11.5 Total research funding and the share of social sciences according to the final reports of the completed KYT research programmes (VTT, 2006; MEE, 2011, 2015b, 2019b)

Research pro-gramme	KYT2005 (2002–2005)	KYT2010 (2006–2010)	KYT2014 (2011–2014)	KYT2018 (2015–2018)
Total research funding	4,157,000 €	7,044,000 €	6,612,000 €	7,391,000 €
Research funding for social sciences	n. a.	150,000 €	100,000 €	285,000 €
Share of funding for social sciences	n. a.	2.1%	1.5%	3.9%

11.5 Structural Corporatism in Finnish Decision-Making

Finland can be characterised more as a consensus democracy than a majoritarian democracy (cf. Lijphart, 1999), or as a coordinated market economy instead of a liberal market economy, following the typology of varieties of capitalism in the theory of Hall and Soskice (2001). The political system of Finland is influenced strongly by corporatist pluralism (Nousiainen, 1985), whereby many interest groups play an important role in national, regional, and municipal decision-making. This includes both employer/entrepreneur organisations and employee/trades unions, as well as a broad spectrum of NGOs, institutions, and interest groups.

Legislation at the top level of the state requires the formally established body of committee hearings with external experts and their consultation on several stages of the law-making process. The preparation of legislation within the ministries requires the consultation of outside experts and stakeholders (Auffermann, 2009). Consequently, at a very early stage of preparation, interest/pressure groups have both formal and informal possibilities to direct the planning of new legislation. In a small country like Finland, with 5.5 million inhabitants, the political, legal, and industrial elite is very small, and "everybody knows each other" (cf. Ruostetsaari, 2010; 2017). Below the state level, this phenomenon continues, and the striving for a consensual solution is distinctive in any political decision-making.

Mainly for historical reasons, the Finnish political system and the political culture of Finnish democracy can be described as a de-politicised system, with of citizens' high trust in the state and expert authority based on knowledge and integrity. The background is the very deep split in Finnish society after the revolution and the civil war in 1918. The division between "reds" (left-wing working class) and "whites" (right-wing bourgeoisie) could still be felt in the whole society in the 1970s and 1980s, going as far as people buying their food either in the workers' cooperative food stores or in the privately-owned stores of the bourgeoisie. This has been overcome, however.

Part of the development in the 1970s and 1980s was the consolidation and rapid expansion of a comprehensive social security system and the welfare state following the Nordic model. This process can be characterised as successful, but from the perspective of critical voices it leads to a de-politicisation of Finnish democracy and consequently to a relatively low level of (radical) political opposition movements, including the environmental and anti-nuclear movements. These societal movements, in turn, led to the formation of a new political party. In 1983, two representatives of the societal movement were elected to parliament.

The Green League (since 2006, the Greens) was first registered as an association in 1987, and as a political party in 1988. The Greens quickly became part of the broad societal consensus and has, in 1995–2002, 2007–2014, and since 2019, taken governmental responsibility as a conformist force regarding e.g., environment, human rights, equality, and feminism. The Greens has left the government twice, both times because parliament left a DiP on constructing new NPPs in force (TVO's Olkiluoto 3 in 2002, and Fennovoima's Hanhikivi 1 in 2014).

The traditionally relatively strong post-communist left-wing party overcame its split into radical and reformist wings and over the years joined the government several times, mainly as a representative of the poorer part of the population, but in recent years increasingly as a party favouring reconciliation between environmental and social interests in policymaking.

A Finnish "Untertanengeist", a spirit of subservience, resulting from 700 years of first Swedish and later Russian rule can still be perceived today (Auffermann, 2009). As Lehtonen (2021) puts it, the Finnish post-War policy culture has been characterised by a certain civil passiveness and weak legitimacy of radical citizen activism.

When looking at energy policy in Finland, some typical characteristics reflect structural corporatism. Finland industrialised relatively late compared to many other European countries (Myllyntaus, 1991), and was based largely on state-owned companies. These were established especially in the energy sector. First for producing hydropower (Imatran Voima Oy, currently Fortum) and domestic fuels such as peat and wood (Vapo Oy), then for oil refining (Neste Oy, currently Fortum) and importing natural gas (Neste Oy, currently Gasum Oy), and finally nuclear power production was started by Imatran Voima Oy.

However, private industries established several energy companies, such as Pohjolan Voima Oy for hydropower production and Teollisuuden Voima Oy (TVO) for nuclear power production. Many were originally co-owned by several companies from energy-intensive fields such as the forest industry, base metal industry, and chemical industry. The idea of cooperation was simple: to improve the predictability of the price of an important production factor by investing jointly in electricity production. The purpose of these companies was to produce electricity for the shareholders, not making profit or distributing dividends.

A major boost for industrial power companies was a 1963 Supreme Administrative Court decision that a hydropower company Mankala Oy (established in the 1930s) was not guilty of hidden dividends when its shareholders received the produced electricity at cost price in relation to their shares in the company (Ialenti, 2020). Correspondingly, the shareholders covered all fixed and variable costs in the same way, as indicated in the articles of association of Mankala Oy.

After the 1963 decision, many similar companies were established in the Finnish electricity supply system, and cross-ownership increased. Nuclear power companies TVO and Fennovoima operate under this "Mankala principle", as well as the NWM company Posiva Oy. The future of the Finnish Mankala principle, which is a unique feature in the global energy markets, has been questioned from the perspective of EU competition law (Puikkonen, 2010; Ialenti, 2020), since the shareholders of Mankala-type companies receive electricity at cost price, which usually is below the market price and has been considered to distort competition. However, Mankala principle has been applied successfully to NWM in the ONKALO project by the Posiva shareholders TVO and Fortum, which has been an important part in the Finnish governance of NWM.

11.6 Weak Social Inclusion in Decision-Making on Nuclear Waste

11.6.1 Limited Public Participation

Positive public governance prioritises stakeholders, advances democratic values, and produces widely-valued societal outcomes (Douglas et al., 2019). Open information exchange between stakeholders and public debate is needed to address the challenges of NWM (WNWR, 2019). Public participation is important because citizens and NGOs can bring new perspectives and help to legitimise the process. However, one challenge is how to overcome the largely artificial technical-social divide that characterises NWM, "the definition of waste and safety are political statements and choices" (Nurmi et al., 2012). Recent research has argued for the importance of nuanced public engagement in ensuring socially stable and sustainable nuclear waste policies (Litmanen et al., 2017a; Lehtonen et al., 2021b).

Raittila et al. (2002) have characterised Finland's experience as a "nuclear waste wonder" due to the smooth progress in decision-making and licensing of Posiva's ONKALO. The degree of citizen engagement in nuclear waste issues has been low. According to Lammi (2009) and Lehtonen (2010b), low public participation is partly because too few actors are able to produce reliable information on the subject. This reflects the high trust in the state authorities and experts among the Finns (see Sect. 11.5). The parliament exercises political power when it ratifies or rejects DiPs, while MEE influences the framing and agenda-setting of energy issues, and exercises, together with STUK, considerable administrative power continuously in their regulative and supervisory roles.

In addition to little public debate, there is a high level of trust in technology and technological development among Finnish citizens (Ruostetsaari, 2017). This has served to further de-politicise NWM and weaken civic vigilance by favouring a dominant narrative of an "engineering nation" (Lehtonen et al., 2021b), where the nuclear regime, i.e. the nuclear companies, energy department of the MEE, STUK, and part of the academia studying energy issues, is depicted as by far the most competent and reliable in assessing nuclear waste safety issues. After ratification of the DiP on constructing Posiva's ONKALO by parliament in 2001, requests for increasing public dialogue between different stakeholders almost disappeared.

Although public engagement in Finnish nuclear waste policy has been limited, it has been discussed and developed over time. Posiva's site selection strategy changed from geological criteria to acceptance by the council of the host municipality (Kojo, 2009). The site selection started by TVO was first highly technical and generated opposition in all the selected municipalities. TVO had to reconsider its approach, not only due to local opposition but also due to legislative changes during the process. The Nuclear Energy Act (990/1987) gave a veto right to the selected host municipality and introduced a wide range of statements and a mandatory public hearing. In addition, the Act on Environmental Assessment Procedure (468/1994) made an EIA mandatory before assessing (in the DiP phase) if the proposed nuclear facility is "in line with the overall good of the society".

The EIA procedure is the main venue for public participation in large construction projects in general, and NWM in particular. During the site selection processes, Posiva invested heavily in public participation, most notably within the two-year EIA, allowing citizens to be informed and making their voices heard. However, many questioned if the EIA had any real impacts. In those days, the role of EIA was only advisory, the number of participants was low, and the framing of the discussion included only the already-decided concept of deep geological disposal (Lehtonen, 2010a). Posiva's project was considered too big for an EIA to influence the outcome (Hokkanen, 2002). It has also been argued that in EIA, purposes of public participation are vague and open to industrial bias, manifesting itself in specific institutional arrangements which receive little scrutiny (Strauss, 2012).

Partly for these reasons, the EIA legislation was revised in 2017. The purpose of the Act on Environmental Impact Assessment Procedure (252/2017) is to improve the availability of information and possibilities for public participation, as well as to ensure that the EIA procedure will be taken into account in decision-making. A contact authority (for nuclear facilities the MEE), makes a "reasoned conclusion" on the EIA process, informs the public on the availability of various reports (the EIA plan, the EIA report, and the reasoned conclusion), and organises public hearings on them (Act on Environmental Impact Assessment Procedure, 252/2017). The applicant must include the EIA report and the reasoned conclusion in the DiP application, and the Government has to explain how the EIA documents and results from the related public hearings have been taken into account in the DiP.

11.6.2 Weak Anti-Nuclear Movement

The national portrayal of Finland's nuclear history is characterised by a firm belief in technology, engineers, and authorities; people tend to be more sceptical about the expertise of anti-nuclear movements. However, this has not always been the case. In 1993, the anti-nuclear movement successfully influenced some members of parliament, and finally the parliament rejected a favourable government DiP on constructing a new (fifth) NPP. Since then, the Finnish anti-nuclear movement has weakened due to e.g. organisational discontinuity and a stronger emphasis on the potential of nuclear power in climate strategies and welfare production in the political discourse (cf. Lammi, 2009). Today, a majority of the parties in parliament are in favour of nuclear power, not least because of the "solved waste problem".

The smooth implementation of Posiva's ONKALO project in Olkiluoto has raised the question of why nuclear waste has mobilised so little citizen action in Finland (Kojo, 2014). According to Lammi (2009), the selection of Olkiluoto in the municipality of Eurajoki to host of the SNF repository ended anti-waste-nuclear movements in other potential host municipalities. Similarly, the unused veto right by the municipal council of Eurajoki marginalised the local anti-nuclear-waste movement. Opinions on the final disposal of SNF have been polarised among the Eurajoki inhabitants; 42% favoured and 36% opposed it (Kojo et al., 2012). However, active public participation and expression of criticism still went against the prevailing norm, which could be explained by fatigue, adaptation, and tolerance—Eurajoki has hosted NPPs including the temporary storage of SNF from the 1970s (cf. Kojo, 2014).

These circumstances have led to an asymmetry between pro-nuclear and anti-nuclear views, meaning that comprehensive critical evaluation in terms of contrasting expert views on the project and counter-expertise is more or less excluded from nuclear policy formulation (Lammi, 2009; Litmanen et al., 2017a). This raises a question of whether a final solution to the nuclear waste problem has been found, or if the discursive pro-nuclear dominance has only mitigated the impact of disputes in the public debate on NWM.

11.6.3 The Role of Media

Key actors in Finnish NWM are frequently framed as trusted and neutral sources of information by the print media, which gives them considerable agenda-setting power in a closed communication culture (Kojo et al., 2020). Journalists tend to turn to the regulator and the nuclear waste company for official information (Litmanen et al., 2017a). A longitudinal analysis of two large print media, Helsingin Sanomat and Aamulehti, shows that nuclear waste reporting has become more positive (Kojo et al., 2020). For example, Helsingin Sanomat's news coverage on SNF management mainly stresses performance-relevant information that underpins confidence in the repository project, as "most news articles take it practically for granted that the project can proceed as envisioned" (Lehtonen et al., 2021b, p. 141).

According to Litmanen (2009), two major changes in mass media have led to the situation where the nuclear industry feeds journalists with information regarding nuclear waste issues. Firstly, the structural changes of modern media have decreased pluralism through multi-channel communication strategies that aim to reach as many target audiences as possible through significant news items (Litmanen, 2009). Secondly, the changes in the journalistic profession towards highly educated "workers of the information society" who process results from scientific research and integrate them into their writing. Journalists also lean towards neutrality in their reporting, while news topics are mainstreamed and factualised, which can pose a problem for anti-nuclear views in a small country like Finland, with few independent experts. This lack of alternatives has become something of a journalistic norm. Finnish media tends to de-politicise SNF issues (Lehtonen et al., 2021a), which indicates that the nuclear industry has been particularly successful in its efforts at managing publicity concerning nuclear waste (Kojo et al., 2020).

11.7 Conclusions: The Future of Final Disposal of Spent Nuclear Fuel in Finland

ONKALO, the disposal facility for SNF by Posiva Oy, a joint company of nuclear power companies TVO and Fortum—currently waiting for the operating license—is known as a final solution for the problem of NWM in Finland. However, some challenges remain, such as the safety of cooling pools for SNF assemblies inside the NPP building and tens of years of temporary SNF storage at the nuclear sites. It is also possible that ONKALO will not cover all SNF produced in Finland in the future. A third nuclear power company, Fennovoima, is not involved. Increasing the capacity of ONKALO has not been a problem for Posiva, but it is not yet known to what extent the planned capacity of ONKALO can be realised in practice because final disposal tunnels and holes will be excavated when needed.

From the governance ecosystem perspective, some general conclusions on Finnish NWM can be drawn. First, Finland is a society where citizens' trust in the state and its institutions is very high. The overall governance system of energy policy is dominated by the scientific and technological domain, where energy industries are an important host. Strong connections between energy companies and technical universities are well-established. The same holds for the connections between energy companies and energy administration in the MEE. Representatives of the energy industries, energy administration, and the scientific community are central parts of the energy elite that emerged during the state-driven industrialisation of the country after World War II.

Because of the high trust among the citizens, political decision-making on nuclear facilities can be managed effectively in the existing decision-making institutions. Next to the democratic representative institutions, no additional quest for public participation is voiced. Therefore in Finland, the preparation and decision-making processes, as well as their outcomes, are highly acceptable among citizens.

Finland's political culture, based on structural corporatism, has been central in all national, regional, and municipal/local decision-making. The complex licensing procedure for new nuclear facilities and the high trust of citizens in the state and its institutions are combined with civil subservience and the dominating tendency to prefer decisions in broad consensus. Public and political opposition to nuclear energy projects has been minor, and public debates have focused more on new NPPs than the final disposal of SNF, which have usually been simultaneously on the agenda. This has been a successful tactical choice by Posiva and its shareholders.

However, regular polls on energy attitudes (e.g. Finnish Energy Industries, 2020) have shown that negative opinions on the safety of geological disposal of SNF have been more common than positive ones. This has been poorly reflected in the decision-making processes, partly because surveys in Eurajoki have shown more positive opinions. Arranging a possibility for public participation has been mandatory in the preparation phase of the decision-in-principle, but participation has not been very active, with no impact, as described in Sect. 11.5. The revised EIA legislation (Act on Environmental Impact Assessment Procedure Act 252/2017) will hopefully improve public participation. Posiva's application for ONKALO's operating license, submitted in December 2021, is now in the pipeline, and MEE has made announcements about providing opportunities such as a public hearing and statements to express public opinions (MEE, 2021). This is not mandatory, but the Nuclear Energy Decree (161/1988) allows taking into account other information considered as necessary by the authority (e.g. MEE) before decision-making.

Recently, the NWM of Fennovoima and the construction of Hanhikivi 1 NPP have dropped off the agenda due to the war started by Russia in Ukraine. On 2 May 2022, Fennovoima decided to terminate the contract for the delivery of Hanhikivi 1 NPP with Rosatom. The official reason was "RAOS Project's significant delays and inability to deliver the project" (Fennovoima, 2022a). Three weeks later, Fennovoima withdrew its application for a construction license of Hanhikivi 1 (Fennovoima, 2022b).

The most current issue for Finnish NWM is the operating license of the ONKALO project, for which Posiva applied in December 2021. The political decision-making will take its time, but as learned from history, significant changes to Posiva's plan cannot be expected. Based on a recent survey (Finnish Energy Industries, 2021), public opinion on favouring increased use of nuclear power is at the highest level in Finland since surveys began. The next Finnish nuclear project is likely to be a benchmark of applying the revised EIA legislation in its full form.

References

Act on Environmental Impact Assessment Procedure 1994 (468/1994). https://www.finlex.fi/en/laki/kaannokset/1994/en19940468_20091812.pdf.

Act on Environmental Impact Assessment Procedure 2017 (252/2017). https://www.finlex.fi/fi/laki/ajantasa/2017/20170252.

Anttila, P., Ahokas, H., Front, K., Hinkkanen, H., Johansson, E., Paulamäki, S., Riekkola, R., Saari, J., Saksa, P., Snellman, M., Wikström, Lisa., & Öhberg, A. (1999). *Final disposal of spent nuclear fuel in Finnish bedrock. Olkiluoto site report.* Posiva 99–10. https://www.osti.gov/etdeweb/servlets/purl/693888.

Auffermann, B. (2009). Das politische System Finnlands. In W. Ismayr (Ed.), *Die politischen Systeme Westeuropas*. VS Verlag für Sozialwissenschaften, Wiesbaden.

Auffermann, B., Suomela, P., Kaivo-oja, J., Vehmas, J., & Luukkanen, J. (2015). A final solution for a big challenge? The governance of nuclear waste disposal in Finland. In A. Brunnengräber, M.R. Di Nucci, A.M. Isidoro Losada, L. Mez, & M. Schreurs (Eds.), *Governance of Nuclear Waste Management: An International Comparison* (pp. 227–247). Springer.

Becker, O. (2017). *Working Paper on possible terrorist threats and necessary nuclear security measures for NPPs and interim storages. Nuclear Risk & Public Control—The Joint Project*. http://www.joint-project.org/upload/file/WorkingPaper_NuclearSecurity_2017_final.pdf.

Conca, J. (2021, May 21). Finland Breaks Ground on World's First Deep Geologic Nuclear Waste Repository. *Forbes*. https://www.forbes.com/sites/jamesconca/2021/05/31/finland-breaks-ground-on-its-deep-geologic-nuclear-waste-repository/?sh=1684001a6103.

Douglas, S., Hart, P.'t, Ansell, C., Anderson, L.B., Flinders, M., Head, B., Moynihan, D., Nabatchi, T., O'Flynn, J., Peters, B.G., Raadschelders, J., Sancino, A., Schillemans, T., Sorense, E., & Torfing, J. (2019). *Towards Positive Public Administration: A Manifesto*. https://www.researchgate.net/publication/336362499_Towards_Positive_Public_Administration_A_Manifesto.

El-Showk, F. (2022). Final resting place. *Science, 375*, 6583.

Fennovoima. (2009). *Application for a Decision-in-Principle Regarding a Nuclear Power Plant*. https://issuu.com/fennovoima/docs/application_for_a_decision-in-princ.

Fennovoima. (2015). *Application for a Construction License pursuant to Section 18 of the Nuclear Energy Act (990/1987) for the Hanhikivi 1 Nuclear Power Plant*. https://issuu.com/fennovoima/docs/construction_license_application_pu.

Fennovoima. (2016). *Fennovoima and Posiva signed a Service Agreement—Environmental Impact Assessment begins*. https://www.fennovoima.fi/en/news/fennovoima-and-posiva-signed-service-agreement-environmental-impact-assessment-begins.

Fennovoima. (2018). *Täydennys Hanhikivi 1 –ydinvoimalaitoksen rakentamislupahakemukseen*. https://tem.fi/documents/1410877/2615913/K+Fennovoiman+ydinj%C3%A4tehuoltoa+koskeva+lis%C3%A4selvitys%2C+29.1.2018.

Fennovoima. (2022a). *Fennovoima has terminated the contract for the delivery of the Hanhikivi 1 nuclear power plant with Rosatom*. https://www.fennovoima.fi/en/press-releases/fennovoima-has-terminated-contract-delivery-hanhikivi-1-nuclear-power-plant-rosatom.

Fennovoima. (2022b). *Fennovoima has withdrawn the Hanhikivi 1 Construction License Application—focus is now on preserving the Pyhäjoki site*. https://www.fennovoima.fi/en/press-releases/fennovoima-has-withdrawn-hanhikivi-1-construction-license-application-focus-now.

Finnish Energy Industries. (2020). *Kansalaisten energia-asenteet 2020*. https://energia.fi/files/5537/Energiateollisuus_-_Energia-asenteet_2020.pdf.

Finnish Energy Industries. (2021). *Popularity of nuclear power reaches a record high in Finland*. https://energia.fi/en/newsroom/popularity_of_nuclear_power_reaches_a_record_high_in_finland.5419.news.

Government of Finland. (2000). *Valtioneuvoston periaatepäätös 21 päivänä joulukuuta 2000 Posiva Oy:n hakemukseen Suomessa tuotetun käytetyn ydinpolttoaineen loppusijoituslaitoksen rakentamisesta*. https://www.eduskunta.fi/FI/vaski/Documents/m_7+2000.pdf.

Hall, P.A., & Soskice, D.W. (Eds.) (2001). *Varieties of Capitalism: The Institutional Foundations of Comparative Advantage*. Oxford University Press.

Hokkanen, P. (2002). Kansalaisosallistumisen muodot ydinjäte-YVA:ssa. In P. Raittila, P. Hokkanen, M. Kojo, & T. Litmanen (Eds.), *Ydinjäteihme suomalaisittain* (pp. 20–35). Tampere University Press.

Hultquist, G. (1986). Hydrogen evolution in corrosion of copper in pure water. *Corrosion Science*, 26(2), 173–177.

Hultquist, G., Szakálos, P., Graham, M.J., Belonoshko, A.B., Sproule, G.I., Gråsjö, L., Dorogokupets, P., Danilov, B.A, Astrup, T., Wikmark, G., Chuah, G.-K., Eriksson, J.-C., & Rosengren, A. (2009). Water Corrodes Copper. *Catalysis Letters*, 132(3–4), 311–316.

Ialenti, V. (2020). Mankala Chronicles: Nuclear Energy Financing and Cooperative Corporate Form in Finland. *Nuclear Technology*, 107, 1377–1393.

Kojo, M. (2009). The Strategy of Site Selection for the Spent Nuclear Fuel Repository in Finland. In M. Kojo, & T. Litmanen (Eds.), *The renewal of nuclear power in Finland* (pp. 161–191). Palgrave Macmillan.

Kojo, M. (2014). Ydinjätepolitiikan osallistava käänne. Acta Universitatis Tamperensis 1987. Tampere University Press. https://urn.fi/URN:ISBN:978-951-44-9605-9.

Kojo, M., Kari, M., & Litmanen, T. (2010). The socio-economic and communication challenges of spent nuclear fuel management in Finland. The post site selection phase of the repository project in Eurajoki. *Progress in Nuclear Energy, 52*, 168–176.

Kojo, M., Kari, M., & Litmanen, T. (2012). Nuclear community considering threats and benefits of final disposal. Local opinions regarding the spent nuclear fuel repository in Finland. *International Journal of Environmental Technology and Management*, 15(2), 124–145.

Kojo, M., Kari, M., Litmanen, T., Vilhunen, T., & Lehtonen, M. (2020). The critical Swedes and the consensual Finns: Leading newspapers as watchdogs or lapdogs of nuclear waste repository licensing? *Energy Research & Social Science*, 61, 101354.

Lammi, H. (2009). Social Dynamics behind the Changes in the NGO Anti-Nuclear Campaign, 1993–2002. In M. Kojo, & T. Litmanen (Eds.), *The Renewal of Nuclear Power in Finland* (pp. 69–87). Palgrave Macmillan.

Lehtonen, M. (2010a). Deliberative decision-making on radioactive waste management in Finland, France and the UK: influence of mixed forms of deliberation in the macro discursive context. *Journal of Integrative Environmental Sciences*, 7(3), 175–196.

Lehtonen, M. (2010b). Opening up or Closing down Radioactive Waste Management Policy? Debates on Reversibility and Retrievability in Finland, France, and the United Kingdom. *Risk, Hazards & Crisis in Public Policy*, 1(4), 139–179.

Lehtonen, M. (2021). *Das Wunder von ONKALO? Zur unerträglichen Leichtigkeit der finnischen Suche nach einem Endlager*. Bundeszentrale für politische Bildung. https://m.bpb.de/apuz/333368/das-wunder-von-onkalo-zur-unertraeglichenleichtigkeit-der-finnischen-suche-nach-einem-endlager?s=03.

Lehtonen, M., Kojo, M., Kari, M., & Litmanen, T. (2021a). Healthy mistrust or complacent confidence? Civic vigilance in the reporting by leading newspapers on nuclear waste disposal in Finland and France. *Risk, Hazards & Crisis in Public Policy*, 12(2), 130–157.

Lehtonen, M., Prades, A., Espluga, J., & Konrad, W. (2021b). The emergence of mistrustful civic vigilance in Finnish, French, German and Spanish nuclear policies: ideological trust and (de)politicization. *Journal of Risk Research*.

Lijphart, A. (1999). *Patterns of Democracy: Government Forms and Performance in Thirty-six Countries*. Yale University Press.

Litmanen, T. (2008). The changing role and contribution of social science to nuclear waste management in Finland. *Energy & Environment,* 19(3–4), 427–453.

Litmanen, T. (2009). The temporary nature of societal risk evaluation: understanding the Finnish nuclear decisions. In M. Kojo, & T. Litmanen (Eds.), *The renewal of nuclear power in Finland* (pp. 192–217). Palgrave Macmillan.

Litmanen, T., Kari, M., Kojo, M., & Solomon, B.D. (2017a). Is there a Nordic model of final disposal of spent nuclear fuel? Governance insights from Finland and Sweden. *Energy Research & Social Science,* 25, 19–30.

Litmanen, T., Kojo, M., Kari, M., & Vesalainen, J. (2017b). Does technical risk dialogue entail socioeconomic evaluation? The case of scientific dispute over copper corrosion in a spent nuclear fuel disposal project. In M. Lehtonen, P-B. Joly, & L. Aparicio (Eds.), *Socioeconomic Evaluation of Megaprojects: Dealing with uncertainties* (pp. 134–158). Routledge.

Maaranen, P. (2013). *The Spent Fuel Management in Finland and Modifications of Spent Fuel Storages*. In Safety of Long-term Interim Storage Facilities. [Workshop Proceedings]. Munich, Germany, 21–23 May 2013. https://www.oecd-nea.org/jcms/pl_19345/safety-of-long-term-interim-storage-facilities-workshop-proceedings.

MEE. (2011). *KYT2010 Finnish Research Programme on Nuclear Waste Management 2006–2010. Final Report*. 26/2011. https://tem.fi/documents/1410877/3346190/KYT2010+Finnish+Research+Programme+on+Nuclear+Waste+Management+2006-2010+10062011.pdf.

MEE. (2013). *Ydinjätehuoltoyhteistyön selvitys. Työryhmän loppuraportti*. 1/2013. https://tem.fi/documents/1410877/2414631/Ydinj%C3%A4tehuollon+selvitys+loppuraportti+2013.pdf/2d91fecb-f2c6-4477-906e-7f8f19457b3f/Ydinj%C3%A4tehuollon+selvitys+loppuraportti+2013.pdf.

MEE. (2015a). *Management of spent fuel and radioactive waste in Finland—national programme in accordance with Article 12 of the Council Directive 2011/70/Euratom*. 39/2019. https://www.stuk.fi/documents/12547/554501/National+Programme+072015docx+14072015a+English+translation+21082015a.pdf.

MEE. (2015b). *KYT2014 Finnish Research Programme on Nuclear Waste Management 2011–2014. Final Report*. 60/2015. https://julkaisut.valtioneuvosto.fi/handle/10024/74994.

MEE. (2019a). *Final Report of the National Cooperation Group on Nuclear Waste Management*. 45/2019. https://julkaisut.valtioneuvosto.fi/handle/10024/161763.

MEE. (2019b). *KYT2018 Finnish Research Programme on Nuclear Waste Management 2015–2018. Final Report*. 30/2019. https://julkaisut.valtioneuvosto.fi/handle/10024/161514.

MEE. (2019c). *Valtion ydinjätehuoltorahaston sijoitustoiminnan kehittäminen—loppuraportti*. 47/2019. https://julkaisut.valtioneuvosto.fi/handle/10024/161764.

MEE. (2021). *Posiva to apply for an operating licence for a spent nuclear fuel disposal facility first in the world*. https://tem.fi/en/-/posiva-to-apply-for-an-operating-licence-for-a-spent-nuclear-fuel-disposal-facility-first-in-the-world.

MEE. (2022). *Management of spent nuclear fuel and radioactive waste in Finland*. 20/2022. https://tem.fi/documents/1410877/86271436/Management+of+spent+nuclear+fuel+and+radioactive+waste+in+Finland.pdf.

Myllyntaus, T. (1991). *Electrifying Finland: The Transfer of a New Technology into a Late Industrialising Economy*. Macmillan & ETLA.

National Academy of Sciences. (2016). *Lessons Learned from the Fukushima Nuclear Accident for Improving safety and Security of U.S. Nuclear Plants, Phase 2; Committee on Lessons Learned from the Fukushima Nuclear Accident for Improving Safety and Security of U.S. Nuclear Plants.* https://www.nap.edu/catalog/21874/lessons-learned-from-the-fukushima-nuclear-accident-for-improving-safety-and-security-of-us-nuclear-plants.

National Research Council. (2006). *Safety and Security of Commercial Spent Nuclear Fuel Storage. Public Report.* The National Academies Press.

Nousiainen, J. (1985). *Suomen poliittinen järjestelmä.* WSOY.

Nuclear Energy Act (990/1987). https://www.finlex.fi/en/laki/kaannokset/1987/en19870990.

Nuclear Energy Agency. (2021). Ensuring the Adequacy of Funding Arrangements for Decommissioning and Radioactive Waste Management. NEA/OECD. https://www.oecd-nea.org/jcms/pl_59705/ensuring-the-adequacy-of-funding-for-decommissioning-and-radioactive-waste-management.

Nuclear Energy Decree (161/1988). https://www.finlex.fi/en/laki/kaannokset/1988/en19880161.

Nurmi, A., Kojo, M. & Litmanen, T. (2012). *Working paper: Identifying remaining sociotechnical challenges at the national level: Finland.* European Commission. https://jyx.jyu.fi/handle/123456789/38353.

Ottosson, M., Boman, M., Berastegui, P., Andersson, Y., Hahlin, M., Korvela, M. & Berger, R. (2017). Copper in ultrapure water, a scientific issue under debate. Corrosion Science, 122, 53–60.

Posiva. (2012). *Rakentamislupahakemus Olkiluodon kapselointi- ja loppusijoituslaitoksen rakentamiseksi käytetyn ydinpolttoaineen loppusijoitusta varten.* https://tem.fi/documents/1410877/2412863/Posivan_rakentamislupahakemus.pdf/3d8fae76-9866-3c3d-272e-8909b93111fe/Posivan_rakentamislupahakemus.pdf?t=1609153067984.

Posiva. (2018). *News from the world: Review procedure on final disposal project proceeds in Sweden.* https://www.posiva.fi/en/index/news/pressreleasesstockexchangereleases/2018/news_from_the_world_review_procedure_on_final_disposal_project_proceeds_in_sweden.3383.html.

Posiva. (2021). *Operating Licence Application, Spent Nuclear Fuel Encapsulation Plant and Disposal Facility.* https://www.posiva.fi/en/index/media/reports.html.

Puikkonen, I. (2010). Cooperative Mankala-companies—The Acceptability of the Company Form in EC Competition Law. *Helsinki Law Review,* 2010/1, 139–156.

Raittila, P., Hokkanen, P., Kojo, M. & Litmanen, T. (2002, Eds.). Ydinjäteihme suomalaisittain. Tampere University Press. https://trepo.tuni.fi/bitstream/handle/10024/65721/951-44-5485-5.pdf.

Raumolin, H. (2011, April 5). *Ydinjätehuolto.* [Presentation] Finnish Nuclear Society, Young Generation (ATS YG) seminar. https://ats-fns.fi/images/files/presentations/2011/YG_seniorit_seminaari_2011_raumolin.pdf.

Ruostetsaari, I. (2010). Changing Regulation and Governance of Finnish Energy Policy Making: New Rules but Old Elites? *Review of Policy Research,* 27(3), 273–297.

Ruostetsaari, I. (2017). Stealth democracy, elitism, and citizenship in Finnish energy policy. *Energy Research & Social Science,* 34, 93–103.

SKB. (2016). *Kopparkapseln klarar korrosionen i ett slutförvar [The copper canister handles corrosion in a final repository].* https://www.skb.se/halla-dar/kopparkapseln-klarar-korrosionen-i-ett-slutforvar/.

Strauss, H. (2012). For the overall good of society: decision-making processes for energy projects in Finland. *Nordia Geographical Publications*, 41(5), 35–43.

STUK. (2015). *Safety assessment by the Radiation and Nuclear Safety Authority of Posiva's construction license application.* https://www.stuk.fi/documents/88234/963503/stuk_safety_assessment_of_posiva_construction_application.pdf/b01e5c91-2944-4d8a-a5dd-0d9b48a2b509?t=1444844110542.

STUK. (2019). *Finnish report on nuclear safety. Finnish 8th national report as referred to in Article 5 of the Convention on Nuclear Safety. International Atomic Energy Agency.* https://www.iaea.org/sites/default/files/finland_nr-8th-rm.pdf.

STUK. (2021). *Radiation and Nuclear Safety Authority Regulatory Guide on Security of a nuclear facility.* https://www.stuklex.fi/en/ohje/YVLA-11.

Szakálos, P., Hultquist, G., & Wikmark, G. (2007). Corrosion of copper by water. *Electrochemical and Solid-State Letters*, 10(11): C63–C67.

Szakálos, P., Åkermark, T., & Leygraf, C. (2018). Comments on the paper "Copper in ultrapure water, a scientific issue under debate" by M. Ottosson, M. Boman, P. Berastegui, Y. Andersson, M. Hahlin, M. Korvela, and R. Berger. *Corrosion Science*, 142, 305–307.

Ukkola, J. (2010). Ydinjätteen loppusijoitus: Ei sittenkään turvallista? *Suomen Kuvalehti*, 28.5.2010. https://suomenkuvalehti.fi/jutut/kotimaa/ydinjatteen-loppusijoitus-ei-sittenkaan-turvallista/.

von Hippel, F.N., & Schoeppner, M. (2016). Reducing the Danger from Fires in Spent Fuel Pools. *Science & Global Security*, 24, 141–173.

VTT. (2006). *The Finnish Research Programme on Nuclear Waste Management (KYT) 2002–2005. Final Report.* VTT Research Notes 2337. https://www.vttresearch.com/sites/default/files/pdf/tiedotteet/2006/T2337.

World Nuclear Waste Report. (2019). *The World Nuclear Waste Report. Focus Europe.* Berlin & Brussels. https://worldnuclearwastereport.org/.

Jarmo Vehmas is a Regional Manager at the Finland Futures Research Centre (FFRC) at the University of Turku. He holds a PhD in administrative sciences (2002) and a BSc in power engineering. He is an international expert in the assessment of sustainable development, energy and environmental policies, interdisciplinary approaches, and foresight methodology. For over 30 years, he has been involved in international and national research projects and coordinated two EU framework programme projects. He is an Adjunct Professor of Environmental Policy at the University of Helsinki, Finland.

Aleksis Rentto was employed as an intern to work on nuclear waste governance research at the Finland Futures Research Centre (FFRC) at the University of Turku. He holds a BSc in social sciences (political science) from the Åbo Akademi University and is currently working on his Master's thesis. In addition to his work experience as a researcher, Rentto has worked with research funding in the public sector. His research interests are focused on democratic theory and innovations, as well as public participation.

Jyrki Luukkanen is a Senior Advisor at the Finland Futures Research Centre (FFRC) at the University of Turku. He earned a Doctor of Technology in systems theory at Tampere University of Technology (1994). Luukkanen is an Adjunct Professor of Future Studies at the University of Turku. He has directed more than 50 international and domestic research projects and has served as a consultant in international organisations. His research interests include: energy and climate policy, sustainable development indicators, modelling, material flow analysis, and development studies, and he has authored a large number of publications on these issues.

Burkhard Auffermann is a Senior Research Fellow at the Finland Futures Research Centre (FFRC) at the University of Turku. He holds a PhD in political science from the Freie Universität Berlin (1994). He was a Professor of International Relations at the Universities of Tampere and Helsinki, Jean-Monnet Chair for European Integration and a Research Fellow in the Ministry for Foreign Affairs, Helsinki. Auffermann is an expert in future studies and security research, with specific research interests in energy and climate policies.

Jari Kaivo-oja is a Research Director at the Finland Futures Research Centre (FFRC) at the University of Turku. He holds a PhD in administrative sciences (2004) and an MSc in social sciences (international economics). He is an Adjunct Professor at the Faculty of Science at the University of Helsinki and the Faculty of Social Sciences at the University of Lapland. His main research interests include foresight research, energy and climate policy, low-carbon/renewable energy transitions, innovation research, the service economy, management and planning sciences (especially transition management), sustainable development, ubiquitous Industry 4.0 r/evolution, robotics, conflict management, and global development issues.

Open Access This chapter is licensed under the terms of the Creative Commons Attribution 4.0 International License (http://creativecommons.org/licenses/by/4.0/), which permits use, sharing, adaptation, distribution and reproduction in any medium or format, as long as you give appropriate credit to the original author(s) and the source, provide a link to the Creative Commons license and indicate if changes were made.

The images or other third party material in this chapter are included in the chapter's Creative Commons license, unless indicated otherwise in a credit line to the material. If material is not included in the chapter's Creative Commons license and your intended use is not permitted by statutory regulation or exceeds the permitted use, you will need to obtain permission directly from the copyright holder.

12. European Lessons for the Governance of Long-Term Radioactive Waste Management

Rinie van Est and Maarten Arentsen

12.1 Introduction[1]

In the introductory Chap. 1, we indicated that in many European countries radioactive waste management (RWM) governance has been confronted with great social resistance since the 1970s, especially when it came to the siting of storage facilities. During recent decades these events have led to a reassessment and a search for new, more inclusive forms of knowledge production and decision-making, new institutional arrangements and common policy principles. This paradigm shift is sometimes characterised as the 'participatory turn' in RWM governance (Bergmans et al., 2014).

To gain insight into the practical implementation of this new, more inclusive governance approach, this book has presented how ten countries in Europe organise and plan decision-making regarding long-term RWM. Taken together, these country studies provide practical examples of policy principles, policy

---

[1] The authors would like to thank all other authors who have contributed to this volume for their very helpful comments on earlier versions of this chapter.

R. van Est
Rathenau Instituut, The Hague, Netherlands
e-mail: q.vanest@rathenau.nl

M. Arentsen (✉)
Emeritus University of Twente, Terborg, Netherlands
e-mail: m.j.arentsen@utwente.nl

© The Author(s) 2023
M. Arentsen and R. van Est (eds.), *The Future of Radioactive Waste Governance*, Energiepolitik und Klimaschutz. Energy Policy and Climate Protection,
https://doi.org/10.1007/978-3-658-40496-3_12

instruments and institutional arrangements. This chapter therefore addresses the book's central question: What lessons do the European country studies teach us about the governance of long-term radioactive waste management?

To draw lessons from the country studies, we make use of the multi-level governance ecosystem framework, as outlined in Chap. 1. This framework assumes that decision-making takes place within a complex field of political, social, scientific, technological, economic and legal actors and institutions. More specifically, the framework distinguishes four interacting social domains: politics and administration, laws and regulation, science and technology, and civil society. By applying this framework we aim to gain insights into how the decision-making process concerning long-term management of radioactive waste can be organised in such a way that it leads to effective and democratic solutions.

The structure of this concluding chapter takes a cue from the governance ecosystem framework. Section 12.2 discusses the participatory turn in RWM governance, and describes how the thinking of various actors about organising democratic and effective decision-making around RWM has changed drastically in recent decades. All ten country case studies show that RWM governance is strongly influenced by developments in the field of nuclear energy. Section 12.3 therefore discusses important characteristics of this relationship. Section 12.4 argues that all ten country case studies show that the governance of radioactive waste is a multi-level governance issue. We reflect on the interactions between both international and national governmental levels as well as national, regional and local levels. The subsequent four sections each focus on one of the four domains of the governance ecosystem framework: politics and administration (Sect. 12.5), law and regulation (Sect. 12.6), science and technology (Sect. 12.7), and civil society (Sect. 12.8).

Each section identifies a number of generic lessons that follow from the ten European country studies on RWM governance. The lessons are briefly described under the bold headings in each section and illustrated with examples from the country chapters. Finally, we provide an overview of 17 main lessons drawn from this book. The lessons are intended for policymakers, stakeholders and concerned citizens, and provide insight into ways in which RWM governance can be organised more inclusively, so that civil society and local authorities can play a suitable role. This often requires strengthening the governance ecosystem from a democratic participatory perspective.

12.2 The Participatory Turn in RWM Governance

The contributions to this volume show that in determining suitable locations for long-term radioactive waste disposal facilities, national governments in Europe initially opted for an expert-dominated top-down policy implementation strategy, in combination with a decide-announce-defend (DAD) communication strategy. In Finland this strategy was only to a limited extend challenged by civil society. Its consensus-seeking political culture, in combination with trust in science and experts, facilitated effective decision-making featuring final disposal. In contrast, in most other European countries studied here, societal resistance developed against siting processes. Faced with social resistance most countries have started to look for a more open, inclusive, transparent and participatory way of interacting with civil society. Within this new approach, the relationship between state and civil society is no longer described in terms of power-over, but more in terms of co-creation and power-with. And the same applies to the relationship between the science and technology domain and civil society.

Lesson 1: RWM governance currently tries to experimentally shape the participatory turn
We thus see a paradigm shift in the relationship between civil society and the scientific and technological and political-administrative domains. This shift illustrates a transition from a DAD strategy towards an engage-deliberate-decide (EDD) strategy. This significant change in the governance of RWM is also being referred to as the 'participatory turn' (Bergmans et al., 2014) or the 'experimental turn' (Parotte, 2020), in which RWM is seen as a 'real-world experiment'; an ongoing process of sociotechnical innovation, where the 'living laboratory' is the country in which the radioactive waste is to be stored. Numerous lessons are drawn below that fit within the participatory turn and can give further substance to it. From the perspective of the governance ecosystem framework, this may involve strengthening interactions between different layers of government and between civil society and governmental and scientific authorities.

12.3 RWM Governance in the Context of Nuclear Energy

The task of dealing with long-lived high-level radioactive waste (HLW) is related to the use of nuclear technology, in particular nuclear energy (see Box 12.1). It therefore seems obvious that all ten country chapters show that RWM governance is influenced in various ways by nuclear energy developments. The intertwined debates about RWM and nuclear energy can provide both opportunities and barriers for RWM governance.

Lesson 2: RWM governance is affected by planned and unplanned nuclear energy developments

The broad public and political support for nuclear energy, or the lack of it, can form opportunities and barriers for RWM governance. In Finland, the long-standing broad support for nuclear energy creates a favourable social and political climate for RWM governance (see Chap. 11). In Germany, the Fukushima disaster in 2011 led the Christian Democratic/liberal government to reverse its plan for a 12-year extension of the phase-out period, and decree the 'definitive' phase-out by 2022 (see Chap. 5). This political decision paved the way to develop a new, more open and inclusive way of dealing with RWM governance. A political decision not to expand or phase out nuclear energy can be important with regard to the strategic involvement of opponents of nuclear energy in the field of RWM governance. This is because a solution for long-term RWM also has potential to increase the chances of expanding nuclear energy. For example, in Spain, environmental groups are opposed to any type of nuclear waste policy, as long as nuclear power plants remain in operation (see Chap. 6). Opponents of nuclear energy can thus demand a change of policy with regard to nuclear energy, before they start engaging with RWM governance.

History shows that the political and social climate surrounding nuclear energy can change over time. For example, in various European countries, national or international nuclear accidents have had a strong negative impact on public and political support for nuclear energy. For example in Sweden, the 1979 Three Mile Island (Harrisburg) accident in the USA provoked a change in the position of the Social Democratic party and led to a national referendum on nuclear power in 1980, of which the outcome was politically interpreted to mean that nuclear power was to be phased out by 2010 (see Chap. 10). In Italy, the outcomes of the 1987 and 2011 referenda on nuclear power generation were strongly influenced by the nuclear accidents in Chernobyl (Ukraine) in 1986 and Fukushima (Japan) in 2011 (see Chap. 3). In the Netherlands, political support for investments in two new nuclear power stations faded away after the Chernobyl accident, and although the idea of new nuclear investments emerged again in the early 2000s, these then disappeared after the Fukushima accident, only to reappear in the 2020s due to the climate crisis (see Chap. 2).

But there may also be historical developments that seem to promote political and social support for nuclear energy. For example, in 2022 the energy transition in combination with geopolitical tensions in Europe, including the Russian invasion of Ukraine, brought nuclear energy back into the debate on the future of the European energy system. Mid-2022, the Dutch government announced a feasibility study of two new nuclear power plants in the country. The gas crisis made the Belgian and German governments reconsider the question whether a complete nuclear phase out is timely. At the time of writing (August 2022), in Belgium this has already led to an extension of the lifespan of some nuclear power plants, and Germany is considering to keep two out of three NPPs (the ones located in Southern Germany) that are planned to be phased out at the end of 2022, as a reserve in order to stabilise the grid.

> **Box 12.1 Nuclear energy as the major source of HLW**
> In all ten countries the vast majority of radioactive waste originates from nuclear power stations. Despite reprocessing and upgrading of spent nuclear fuels (SNF) in the nuclear cycle, in the end, all current operational nuclear energy reactors produce HLW. A country's nuclear energy position is thus a good indicator of the HLW challenges it faces.
>
> Considering the 56 operational reactor units and 69% share of electricity generated in the country originating from nuclear power, France is a clear outlier in the group of countries included in this book (see Table 12.1). The United Kingdom (UK) has 12 reactor units and all other countries have 7 or less. The UK and Sweden have similar amounts of installed capacity, but with a different number of reactors (12 vs. 6) and nuclear share in national electricity generation (14.8% vs. 30.8%). Finland and Switzerland each have 4 reactor units and around 30% share in national electricity generation. Spain and Belgium each have 7 reactor units, but are quite different in share in electricity generation (20.8% vs. 50.8%). Germany progressively disconnected reactors from the grid, with only 6 left in 2020, and 3 at the end of 2021 producing 4055 MWe. Italy has no operational nuclear capacity, and the Netherlands has 1 reactor with 482 MWe installed capacity.
>
> New reactors are under construction in Finland (whose fifth reactor unit Olkiluoto 3 was connected to the national grid in March 2022), France, and

the UK. Some countries, such as the Netherlands, are considering more nuclear energy in the context of climate change mitigation. These initiatives and considerations also impact the production of radioactive waste in Europe. In 2019, before Brexit, the European Commission forecasted an increase of radioactive waste in all classes of radioactive waste (see Table 12.2). The UK case shows that the dynamics of the public and political debate about the management of existing and committed—and, therefore, unavoidable—waste, may differ from the discussion about radioactive waste from nuclear power plants which are yet to be built (see Chap. 8).

Table 12.1 Overview of nuclear power reactors and nuclear share on 31 December 2021, in the ten countries described in this book (based on IAEA, 2022, pp. 7–8)

Country	Reactors in number of units	Operation net capacity (MWe)	Nuclear electricity supplied (% of total)
Netherlands	1	482	3.1
Italy	0	0	0
Belgium	7	5.942	50.8
Germany	3	4.055	11.9
Spain	7	7.121	20.8
Switzerland	4	2.96	28.8
United Kingdom	12	7.343	14.8
France	56	61.37	69.0
Sweden	6	6.882	30.8
Finland	4	2.794	32.8

Table 12.2 Estimated future amounts of radioactive waste and spent nuclear fuel (SNF) (m^3) in the EU (Source: European Commission, 2019, p. 27)

	Very Low Level Waste (VLLW)	Low Level Waste (LLW)	Intermediate Level Waste (ILW)	High Level Waste (HLW)	Spent Fuel (SF)
2016	603	2,519,000	338	6	58
2030	1,360,000	3,322,000	455	9	76

12.4 RWM as a Multi-Level Governance Phenomenon

The ten country studies show that RWM is characterised by different forms of multi-level governance. Vertical interactions take place between the public authorities of different administrative layers, as well as horizontal and diagonal interactions between public and private actors, within a particular tier of government and across different tiers of government. In Sect. 12.8 we reflect on the role civil society plays within RWM (the so-called horizontal interactions). Here, we mainly focus on the interactions between different tiers of government (the vertical interactions). We first draw lessons about the interaction between the international, European, and national levels. Subsequently we discuss the interactions between national, regional and local levels of government.

Lesson 3: The interaction between international and national levels with regard to nuclear safety and radiological protection is well-coordinated and institutionally embedded
With regard to nuclear safety and radiological protection, the interactions between international, European and national layers are well-coordinated. The guidelines, rules, and regulations developed by international organisations, like the International Atomic Energy Agency (IAEA), OECD's Nuclear Energy Agency (NEA), and the European Union Directives, are transmitted into national rules and regulations in all countries included in this book. This also shows that the division in responsibility for nuclear development and nuclear safety, advocated at international level, has been implemented in almost all countries studied. In some countries this took more time than in others. Separating responsibilities turned out to be a trust-strengthening factor in national debates, whereas diffused responsibilities encourage mistrust and complicates decision-making processes.

Lesson 4: The option of a multinational geological waste disposal facility is seriously considered and explored
Several countries, such as the Netherlands, Italy, Denmark, and Belgium, are interested in jointly exploring the option of a multinational geological disposal facility, partly for financial reasons, opportunities to share knowledge, and limited availability of space and suitable geology. To further explore this route, RWM operators have institutionalised their collaboration in the European Repository Development Organization (ERDO), which was established in 2021 after ten years of preparation (cf. Di Nucci & Isidoro Losada, 2015). RWM organisations from several European Member States work within this international association on multinational radioactive waste solutions.

Lesson 5: There is a need to achieve more coordinated interaction between national, regional and local levels
In contrast to the well-established interactions between international, European and national governmental tiers, the coordination between national, regional and local layers is far less mature in most countries. Moreover, these relationships are often specific to a particular country, and its political-administrative structure and culture. The relationships between the national and regional and local tiers of government are particularly tested in siting issues, where local interests clearly play a role.

In most countries studied, the search for geologically suitable and socially acceptable locations for the storage and disposal of radioactive waste has a history of local political protest, with citizens and civil society organisations working together with regional and local authorities. For example, at the end of the 1970s, widespread political and socially-supported regional and local protests in the northeast of the Netherlands ensured that exploratory drilling planned by the national government could not take place. In particular, the feeling that certain developments that are seen as undesirable from a local perspective are imposed from above (from the national level) can lead to strong local protest. In Germany, massive resistance from the anti-nuclear-movement developed against the national government and the planned geological repository at Gorleben. In Italy, the local civic and political protest in Scanzano in 2003 is another strong example. The protest, which lasted for about two weeks and in which some 150,000 people took part, had political effect, and paved the way a decade later for a more participatory national approach. In Switzerland, underground investigations for a repository for low- and intermediate-level waste at the Mount Wellenberg site had to be abandoned due to two Cantonal vetoes against this endeavour (see Chap. 7). That event also eventually led to a new policy approach (see Lesson 6).

Lesson 6: Reliability and validity of research on technological safety and risks play a central role in the siting process for a geological disposal facility
At the local level, a siting process for a geological disposal facility raises various technical and risk questions for political and social actors. Why especially is this location perceived as suitable, based on what criteria? To what extent can a geological disposal facility be regarded as safe for a very long time, and how is the transport of radioactive waste to the facility to be managed? To answer such questions, local actors often rely on scientific and technical expertise. This raises the question to what extent local actors trust such expertise and the (often national) organisations that develop and contribute to that knowledge. Distribution of knowledge across various administrative layers and the institutionalisation

of checks and balances in the field of scientific and technical knowledge, therefore, has become an important issue. This topic, as well as the participation of local actors in the decision-making process surrounding the siting of radioactive waste disposal facilities, will be discussed further in Sect. 12.8.

Lesson 7: A siting process for a geological disposal facility raises the question to what extent it fits in with local development visions
Apart from scientific and technical topics, the question to what extent the installation of a radioactive waste disposal facility fits in with the local area development vision is relevant. From that perspective, several countries studied haven chosen to store and dispose of radioactive waste in places where there is already a tradition of nuclear activities. In both Italy and Spain, various regions have highlighted the incompatibility between the national repository and local development strategies based on tourism, agriculture, and the valorisation of local traditions and landscape. Regional visions on the development of the economy, landscape and nature will also jointly determine to what extent local communities can agree with proposed financial rewards and compensations, or be convinced that work related to the construction and operation of the facility benefits the local economy. The Spanish Chap. 6 shows that the ideas and interests of the ruling political coalition at national and regional levels can collide, that this can shift over time, and that HLW management is used by political parties to profile themselves politically, which according to the authors has led to a 'nuclearization of politics'.

Some countries, such as Finland (since 1987), Spain (since 2006), the UK (since 2008), and Italy (since 2021) follow the principle of local voluntarism, which involves a local informed consent, with right of withdrawal or veto over the creation of a radioactive waste storage facility. In the UK, the relevant principal local authority has this right, or the relevant Community Partnership can use this right, but it is limited to cases where all members agree to withdraw. Switzerland is a federal state in which the cantons retain a high degree of autonomy. At the beginning of the 2000s, however, the Swiss Parliament, the Federal Assembly, abolished the cantonal veto rights on deep geological disposal in favour of an optional national veto right on the general license for such a repository. The idea behind this is that finding a site for a geological disposal facility is a joint federal problem that will likely never be solved if citizens can use their veto right at the level of individual cantons.

Finally, Finland is an exception to the challenges outlined above. The original plan for the construction of a geological disposal facility has been followed closely since the 1980s. The main explanatory factor seems to be the high level of trust throughout the Finnish civil society towards state authorities, experts, technological development, and the electricity sector. While in France, for example, the relationship between local and national actors is often seen as a battle between 'us and them' (see Chap. 9), Finnish citizens generally seem to assume that governments act in the common public interest, based on technical and scientific knowledge that can be trusted.

12.5 Politics and Administration: Working on Shared Principles and Separation of Responsibilities

The ten country studies show the importance of, and the general possibility to formulate, widely-supported principles for policy. Such policy principles can strongly guide the implementation of policy. The national cases indicate that a clear division of institutional responsibilities is crucial for the governance of RWM. These two political-administrative lessons are described below.

Lesson 8: There is a need to clearly separate institutional roles and responsibilities for site selection, organising public participation, and managing the radioactive waste disposal facility
For decades, the responsibility for both stimulation of nuclear power, and nuclear safety and radiation protection, supervision and licensing of nuclear activities has rested with the same government organisation. This was for example the case in France, Italy, and the Netherlands. In such a situation, potential conflicts of interest could arise. Assigning conflicting responsibilities within a particular organisation can thus accelerate public mistrust in the related institutions and undermine their public legitimacy. As a result, in 1994, the IAEA Convention on Nuclear Safety stipulated that each Member State had to ensure a separation between organisations in the fields of nuclear safety and radiation protection, and nuclear energy. This task has been followed up by many countries, although sometimes it has been very slow, as in Italy and the Netherlands. In 2006, France granted the safety authority ASN full independence from both the government and industry. The Spanish Nuclear Safety Council (CSN) is another insightful example. This public body, which was established in 1980, is independent from the General State Administration, with a legal personality and its own assets, which is not accountable to the government, but to the Spanish Parliament.

The clear division of potentially conflicting roles and responsibilities is also important in the field of RWM. To avoid any conflict of interest, and create conditions in which societal trust in institutions may grow, it is therefore strongly preferred to have separate organisations for site selection, organising public participation, and managing the radioactive waste disposal facility. In Germany, for example, the ultimate responsibility for the site selection procedure and for public participation currently lies within the same authority, namely the Federal Office for the Safety of Nuclear Waste Management (BASE). BASE itself has raised this issue, since for site selection it must be completely independent, but for its other task, public participation, it must cooperate with many other parties. In Italy, the operator SOGIN has a similar dual role, both as implementer and future operator of the radioactive waste repository, and as the main actor responsible for the whole public participation process. Such a mix of potentially conflicting responsibilities does not inspire confidence among local authorities and citizens.

Lesson 9: It is important to develop widely-supported policy principles
A relevant insight from the ten country studies is the importance of formulating and internalising certain widely-supported policy principles regarding the decision-making process on RWM. Policy principles are important in structuring and guiding the public and political debate and decision-making processes. Because various principles can be fleshed out in various ways, clarification via debate, policy, and possibly legislation and regulations is desirable. The guiding power of policy principles can be strengthened by giving them a legal basis (see Sect. 12.6). Shared policy principles do not arise overnight, but are often the result of decades of social and political learning processes. Public protest was often the reason to start such a learning process.

The Dutch National Programme from 2016 listed four general policy principles for RWM: (1) minimisation of the generation of radioactive waste; (2) safe management of radioactive waste; (3) no unreasonable burdens on the shoulders of future generations; (4) the producers of radioactive waste are responsible for the costs of its management. Interwoven in various ways with the above four principles, the National Programme specifically mentions three requirements with regard to the final disposal of radioactive waste: passive safety, retrievability and reversibility. In the Belgian Chap. 4 a wide range of stakeholders—from concerned citizens, scientists, policymakers, civil society representatives, and public administrators, through to environmental associations—considered the following five principles to be important for HLW governance: (1) a flexible and stepwise approach, (2) practicing transparency, (3) providing clarity about the link between participation and decision-making, (4) ensuring monitoring and control, and (5) robust financing. In this list, public information and participation emerges as a policy principle, coupled with the need for clarification of what this will mean in concrete terms for the decision-making process.

Elements from this partially overlapping and cohesive set of policy principles are reflected in other countries. Similar principles, however, can be implemented in different ways in different countries, as is the case with reversibility and retrievability. In France, reversibility, which includes both reversibility of decision-making and retrievability of waste, forms a cornerstone of HLW management and helps to manage trust and cross-domain interaction. The French criteria for reversibility were legally established in 2016. This law was the result of a decades-long discussion from the early 1990s, surrounding the necessity for and precise meaning of the term 'reversibility'. The law now defines reversibility as a concept that allows future generations to choose between either continuing the construction and operation of disposal through successive phases, or to re-examine the earlier choices and modify the RWM solutions accordingly. In France, retrievability is also part of the implementation of the reversibility policy principle. It is assumed that when, after an operational time of some 150 years, a geological disposal facility will be closed, the repository and its environment are to remain under monitoring for several centuries. Germany decided by law that such a repository should be sealed with the possibility of retrieval for 500 years after closure. In the UK there is discussion about the usefulness of such a monitoring period. In 2003 there was disagreement within the UK Committee on Radioactive Waste Management (CoRWM) about whether the facility should be immediately sealed when it was full, or kept open for several hundred years. In 2018 the UK government decided that the waste sites should be irreversibly sealed at the end of their operational time, arguing that permanently closing a geological disposal facility at the earliest possible opportunity provides for greater safety, greater security, and minimises the burden on future generations (see UK Chap. 8).

Reversibility of decision-making and retrievability of waste are thus strongly linked to the policy principle of intergenerational justice. In France, this has been an overarching theme, starting from the observation that current generations benefit from nuclear energy while many future generations will be burdened with HLW. The response to this issue has changed over time. While in 2006, most parliamentarians stressed keeping options open and the need for further research, ten years later the dominant view pointed at the current generation's responsibility to take care of the concrete construction of a geological disposal facility, since an interim storage would provide only a short-term solution. In the Netherlands, the first-mentioned interpretation of intergenerational justice is still used: keeping options open for future generations. Correspondingly, the Dutch government is still opting for long-term interim above ground storage until 2130, when a geological disposal facility is assumed to be operational, and to keep options for final disposal open.[2]

In almost all countries the 'polluter pays' principle undergirds the financing of disposal of radioactive waste. This applies regardless of whether the operator of RWM is owned by private companies (e.g., Finland and Sweden) or by the state (e.g., Germany and the Netherlands). Several countries have established nuclear waste management funds, which are supposed to continue until the far future to guarantee adequate financial resources for current and future RWM. Belgium has articulated reliable financial management for HLW as a core policy principle (see Chap. 4). This also includes the financing of research and development. A fund for the German Nuclear Waste Management was established in 2017 as a foundation (KENFO) under public law. This means that any financial risk associated with a centralised interim and final storage has been taken up by society. The payments for the liabilities of the 25 nuclear power plants in Germany totalling € 24.1 billion were transferred by the NPP operators to the KENFO foundation in July 2017. Finland separated three sections in the State Nuclear Waste Management Fund, established in 1988: the Contingency Fund, the Nuclear Safety Research Fund, and the Nuclear Waste Research Fund. The Contingency Fund is for nuclear waste management in the future. In this way funding for current and future RWM is guaranteed, as well as the continuation of funding for scientific research to cope with scientific uncertainties. Not every country has established such a fund.

12.6 Laws and Regulations: Creating a Legal Basis for Decision-Making Around RWM Options

The ten European countries included in this book are all democratic constitutional states in which the law, as a result of democratic decision-making, functions as a codifying instrument to (temporarily) settle societal debate, including disagreement and conflict. Laws, if seen as fair, can thus counteract societal mistrust, and help to develop codified elementary agreement in societies on RWM. In this section, we distinguish the legal underpinning of, firstly, certain policy principles and

---

[2] The decision-making process surrounding the EU taxonomy may influence this, as the current draft suggests that Member States are expected to develop and operate storage facilities for LLW and ILW and geological disposal for HLW by 2050.

technological design requirements for RWM, and secondly, decision-making procedures on RWM and the tasks of the organisations and actors involved in these.

Lesson 10: It is important to anchor policy principles and technological options in law
Above we gave some examples of countries that have established certain policy principles in legislation and regulations: in France, retrievability; in Germany, the retrieval period; and in Belgium and Finland, passive safety. The latter refers to the repository being safe 'by itself', i.e. unmediated by human actors and actions. The legal grounding of key principles is often the result of long periods of debate, and often marks the societal and political closure of such a debate. Technological options and requirements can also be laid down through legislation. Already in 2014, Italy legally laid down 15 criteria for excluding locations as potential disposal sites in Technical Guide no. 29. This has been complemented in 2021 by the CNAPI, the National Map of Potentially Suitable Areas for the National Repository, which identifies areas whose characteristics meet the criteria set out in the Technical Guide 29 and by the proposed National Map of Suitable Areas (CNAI) in 2022.

Moreover, the German *Repository Site Selection Act* (StandAG, 2017) states that all three host rock types (salt, clay and crystalline rocks) can be considered for a geological disposal facility, and that such a facility should be able to guarantee the safe containment of the waste for a period of one million years. In Switzerland, the broad political agreement on a specific model of deep geological repositories for HLW, ILW, and LLW, paved the way for and became part of the nuclear energy legislation that came into force in 2005.

Lesson 11: It is important to legally underpin decision-making procedures
Laws and regulations are major mechanisms to embed decision-making processes in society, by clarifying and legally framing the democratic principles that underpin it. Since in Finland the preparation of legislation within ministries requires the consultation of external experts and stakeholders, interest groups have ample opportunities to participate in the legislative process, e.g. on RWM, at an early stage. In France, the "Bataille law" from 1991 was probably the most fundamental foundation for subsequent advancement towards a repository project (see Chap. 9). The process of elaborating the law was triggered by the conflict and stalemate reached, because of an excessively "technical" approach to siting that had prevailed until the end of the 1980s. As the result of decades of deep societal resistance and conflict, Germany promulgated the StandAG to regulate the siting process, including public participation and norms for transparency. The goal

of the German law is that a suitable final disposal site for HLW will be found "through a science-based and transparent procedure and is to be carried out in a participatory, science-based, transparent, self-questioning and learning process" (StandAG, 2017, §1(1)).

Belgian law also aims to strengthen the transparency of procedures and responsibilities. On April 2, 2022 the federal government agreed on a Draft Law requiring the Belgian RWM agency ONDRAF-NIRAS to "draw up a step-by-step plan for the R&D activities for deep disposal in Belgium of high-level and/or long-lived waste", to "sound out neighbouring countries and other interested countries on the possibility of developing shared disposal facilities", and "to organise a participatory process and public debate" on this matter (Council of Ministers 2022; see Belgian Chap. 4). The Belgian law makes it clear that there must be participation, and leaves a lot of room for implementing this. The contours of a decision-making process can be laid down in law, but also in policy plans. Switzerland presents a good case-in-point, where the Sectoral Plan for Deep Geological Repositories of 2008 arranges the process of finding locations for the final disposal of LLW, ILW, and HLW. The Sectoral Plan discerns three phases: phase 1 is devoted to the selection of suitable geological areas, in phase 2, at least two potential siting areas for respectively high-level waste and low- and intermediate-level waste, or one site for a combined repository, had to be proposed and public participation had to be realized, especially with regard to the siting of the near surface facilities, in phase 3 the nomination of two disposal sites or the site for a combined repository is planned to be approved by parliament and the electorate in 2031 at the latest. In 2004, the NEA argued for such a step-by-step approach to decision-making, in which the public should be meaningfully involved (OECD, 2004). Such an approach would be in line with the principle of reversibility of decision-making.

12.7 Science and Technology Domain: Towards an Institutionally Diverse Knowledge Landscape

In a deep geological repository, a series of natural, engineered, and social barriers are assumed to work together to contain and isolate long-lived radioactive waste to protect people and the environment for extremely long periods of time. Such a multi-barrier system consists of natural elements (that provide passive safety), namely the geosphere, and human-made technical and social elements (that provide active safety) (cf. OECD, 2003). The function of the selected geosphere is to act as a natural barrier, which is expected to protect the repository from disruptive natural events, water flow, and human intrusion for hundreds of thousands of years. The engineered materials placed within a repository include waste containers or canisters, and buffer boxes that are used to encase the waste containers.

When making choices with regard to, for example, the geological layer, the construction of a storage or disposal facility, and the organisation of RWM, both political decisions and scientific and technological knowledge (and the lack thereof) play a role. The scientific and technological domain thus plays various pivotal roles in the democratic governance of RWM, such as identifying problems and developing solutions, and informing the political and public debate about these, so that actors from the political and administrative domain and civil society can make science-informed decisions. This section examines four aspects: the need to take scientific uncertainties seriously, the way the political debate on retrievability has blurred the technological distinction between passive and active safety, the need for social scientific knowledge, and the need for the institutional distribution of knowledge. A fifth important topic will be covered in the Sect. 12.8, and concerns ways to generate socially robust scientific knowledge, which can provide a credible scientific basis for democratic decision-making.

Lesson 12: It is important to be transparent about and openly debate scientific uncertainties about suitable RWM methods and geological formations, as knowledge development is dynamic

Finland, France, and Sweden are forerunner countries in the process towards final disposal. These three countries have chosen a geological host rock, a repository site, and the disposal technology. In the other seven countries, research into the appropriate geological formation for the final storage of radioactive waste is ongoing, and the final disposal technology is still undecided.

Choosing a geological subsurface is a politically sensitive issue because it helps determine where geological disposal can or cannot take place. For the selection of a suitable geological subsoil, the type of deep geological subsurface and numerous other design criteria may play a role. As noted above, Italy, in the initial siting phase, has already legally defined 15 criteria for excluding locations as potential disposal sites, which include inter alia volcanic and seismic activities, locations within 5 km of the coastline, unsuitable distance from residential areas, hydrology and hydro-resources, and safeguarding biodiversity.

The country studies show that scientific insights about the suitability or unsuitability of certain types of geological host formations can shift over time. For example, in the 1970s, scientists in the Netherlands assumed that geological disposal could best take place in salt rock layers (which are mainly found in the northeast of the Netherlands). Clay layers (which mainly occur in the south of the Netherlands) were considered unsuitable at the time. After retrievability of the waste had become a policy requirement in the early 1990s, the research also came to include Boom Clay, which is mainly found in the southern part of the Netherlands. In Germany the initial focus was also on salt rock formations. The StandAG has widened the search perspective to include salt, clay and crystalline rocks as potentially suitable for a geological disposal facility. In the 1970s, the salt dome Gorleben was regarded by the German government as a suitable place to build a national deep geological repository for radioactive waste. Finally, after decades of conflict, in 2020, the federal company for radioactive waste disposal BGE assessed the overall geological situation in Gorleben as 'unfavorable'. In Sweden, the KBS concept for disposal of SNF was developed in the early 1980s. The KBS-3 concept from 1983 has various safety barriers: the HLW is encapsulated in cast iron canisters, which are encapsulated in copper capsules that are deposited in a layer of bentonite clay, in a circular hole, eight meters deep and with a diameter of two meters, drilled in a tunnel 500 m down into crystalline rock. At that time, the bedrock was seen as the most important passive safety barrier. But by the late 1990s, the emphasis in the safety case shifted from the importance of a tight bedrock to the ability of the human-made engineered barriers to contain radioactivity in the long term.

In France, geological site investigations turned out to stir controversy and heavily local opposition during the 1990s. Although sceptics are still active, the project has progressed to such an extent that any criticism at this point in time seems to have little chance of stopping it. In the Cigéo nuclear waste project, vitrified HLW would be packaged in steel containers which would be placed in tunnels at about 500 m depth in a 160-million-year-old Callovo-Oxfordian clay formation in Bure (department Meuse), with the entrance to the repository situated in the neighbouring municipality Saudron (department Haute-Marne). By the way, this was a result of negotiations between the departments Meuse and Haute-Marne, which both wanted to benefit from the economic support and expected investments (see Lesson 7). Cementation or asphalting will be applied to the ILW that will be stored at the Cigéo repository. The repository would be constructed and closed down in a stepwise manner, in line with the compromise agreement reached in the societal dispute on reversibility in France.

Based on the Swedish KBS concept, Finland decided on deep geological disposal with the granite bedrock as a passive safety measure, and copper capsules and bentonite clay as human-made safety measures in the early 1980s. In January 2022, the Swedish government allowed the construction of a geological repository for SNF based on the assumption that they had found both a suitable site and method for the final disposal of long-lived HLW. But the decision was controversial and was challenged by various independent scientists because of the corrosion risk of the copper capsules, as part of the KBS-3 system. Interestingly, this scientific dispute has been hardly an issue in Finland. The high trust in the Finnish society in industry experts seems to prevent attention for academic counter expertise. In contrast, in Sweden independent experts and NGOs have brought the issue to the table and pushed proponents of the envisaged geological disposal facility for answers. The RWM company SKB responded to the copper capsule erosion controversy by arguing that long-term safety is not just about the safety of the HLW capsule, but of the entire multi-barrier system.

Lesson 13: The policy principle of retrievability implies a significantly longer period of active safety before moving on to passive safety
HLW will remain hazardous for hundreds of thousands of years. It is however hard to imagine that social institutions will be stable for even thousands of years to actively ensure the safety of HLW. Therefore, for the very long-term, passive safety of a final disposal method is seen as desirable. Long-term aboveground storage is seen as an active safety option, and thus as temporary. In contrast, geological disposal is presented as a passive safety option. However, the policy principle of retrievability means that geological disposal must first be actively managed for a considerable period of time before it is closed-off and considered to be passively safe. The length of the retrievability period is determined politically and can therefore differ from country to country.

As illustrated in this book, several European countries have embraced the policy principle of retrievability since the early 1990s. The political and technological implementation of this means that even when choosing a deep geological disposal facility, the safety of the waste must be actively managed during the period of retrievability. This is exemplified by the way in which retrievability is currently imagined and determined in France and Germany. In France, it is assumed that a geological disposal facility will be closed after an operational period of some 150 years, after which the repository and its environment will be monitored for several centuries. During this period, the waste may still be retrieved. Officially Germany is expected to decide on a site for a geological disposal facility by 2031. After its operational period, the repository should be sealed with the possibility of retrieval for 500 years. If Germany were to take a geological storage facility into operation by 2050, and operate this for 100 years, it would only become a passive active safety option in the year 2650. So if all goes well, in Germany, geological disposal will become a passive safety option only after more than six centuries; by reckoning 25 years per generation, this would mean 24 generations into the future. The principle of retrievability in Germany therefore means active safety of radioactive waste for many centuries to come.

Lesson 14: There is a need for interdisciplinary and transdisciplinary knowledge, and social science can play a central role in this
In response to decades of strong social resistance, policymakers and radioactive waste disposal operators in some countries came to realise that RWM is not only a technological challenge, but also requires understanding of the social dynamics accompanying the decision-making process. That is why in 2000 the OECD established the Nuclear Energy Agency's Forum for Stakeholder Confidence (FSC). The French national radioactive waste management agency (Andra) can be considered a frontrunner in integrating social science expertise in its governance. Andra contracted social scientists to facilitate the interaction with society and administration. It established an advisory committee consisting of social scientists in 2006. Social knowledge is also commissioned in other countries, but is still rather limited, as for example the Dutch case shows (Chap. 2).

In contrast, it has become common social scientific sense that the governance of radioactive waste is a socio-technical issue, which requires multi- and transdisciplinary knowledge, as reflected in all country chapters. An important added value of social scientific research is its ability to address questions regarding RWM options in a broad political and social context. While technical research is often instrumentally focused on a particular solution, social scientists often look at the interactions between problems and solutions, between means and ends. The authors of the Belgian Chap. 4 for example, state that over recent decades research and decision-making has focused on one envisioned solution, namely a geological disposal facility. They propose starting a discussion regarding the high-level and long-lived radioactive materials that are present in society—some declared as waste, others not (yet)—and asking societal actors and stakeholders how to deal with them. This example shows that social science could play a crucial role in critical reflection on RWM policy and engagement with society by clarifying what is going on in civil society, and analysing and reflecting on the outcomes of public participation.

Lesson 15: There is a need for the institutional distribution of knowledge
Knowledge, and thus experts and research institutes, play an important role in decision-making around RWM. In all the countries studied, perhaps with the exception of Finland, RWM (and nuclear energy) are politicised knowledge areas. In such a situation, doubts may be expressed as to whether experts reach

an opinion independently of economic, political or social interests, and this can undermine political and public confidence in the independence of science.

Scepticism and critical reflection are central features of science. That is why adequate peer review of scientific research and knowledge is common. In order to hold a social and political discussion about a controversial issue, informed by scientific knowledge, it is important that the actors involved have confidence in the relevant knowledge and experts. In addition to scientific quality, attention is therefore also required for the (different) relationship(s) between the scientific and technological domain and politics, public administration and civil society. This requires, for example, broadening social involvement in research. In Italy, for instance, regions can mobilise 'Scientific and Technical Committees' with experts from universities and the research community conducting independent research. There thus is a need for the institutional distribution of knowledge, so that a more level playing field is created in the field of knowledge, in which various actors can speak with each other on a more equal footing. The country studies show that this is not yet the case in most countries.

Switzerland seems to be a positive exception, and therefore it is instructive to further elucidate the contours of its knowledge landscape. Within the Swiss scientific domain, research on RWM is conducted at several universities and related institutions, as well at the Paul Scherer Institute (PSI), the largest research institute for natural and engineering sciences in Switzerland. Within the political-administrative system, knowledge about RWM is spread over various institutions. On the federal level, the Swiss Federal Office of Energy (SFOE) and the safety authority ENSI each conduct their own regulatory research. There is also a Nuclear Safety Commission, with seven nuclear safety experts, which plays an important role as a second-opinion body, which is meant to ensure independent quality control for the supervisory authorities. Moreover, at the level of the cantons there is a Safety Workgroup and an Expert Group on Safety with a budget for research. In addition, Nagra, founded by the nuclear waste producers, is responsible for safe long-term disposal, and carries the main responsibility for R&D on deep geological disposal. Last, but not least, the Technical Safety Forum, chaired by ENSI, gathers representatives of the federal administration, cantons, communes, communities in neighbouring countries, NGOs, the interested public and others. The Technical Safety Forum receives, discusses and answers questions from the public about technical safety aspects, and publicises its answers on the internet. This distribution of knowledge in Switzerland empowers actors within different levels of government, as well as economic and civil society actors, as well-informed participants in the democratic debate on RWM.

12.8 Civil Society: The Challenge of Informing and Engaging Civil Society

Above, we stated that RWM governance currently takes its cue from the EDD (engage-deliberate-decide) strategy (see Lesson 1). This new governance perspective is about ways of informing and engaging with civil society that encourage social learning and may build mutual trust. The chapters in this book show that while some countries are still in a preparatory design phase (such as Belgium and the Netherlands), countries like Germany and Italy are in the early phase of implementation, and Finland, Sweden, France and Switzerland are already in a more advanced phase of implementation. Moreover, degrees and methods of participation can differ greatly by country. Below, we draw a number of lessons in the field of informing and engaging civil society.

Lesson 16. There is a need for joint production of socially robust knowledge
This insight is in line with Lesson 15, although the emphasis here is on the involvement of civil society actors and the crucial role information plays within this. From an inclusive perspective, the development and application of knowledge is seen as an interactive process in which science, politics and policy, and civil society are closely linked, each with its own role, but feeding each other in the process. There is therefore a need for more interactive forms of knowledge development, sharing and use. The country studies show several interesting examples through which socially robust knowledge can be generated in a joint manner in the field of a politically controversial subject, such as RWM.

With the exception of Finland, civil societies in the countries studied here assumed a more critical position vis-à-vis the information about the field of nuclear technology and the related risks which was provided by experts, politicians and governmental authorities over the course of the 1970s and 1980s. This has led to bottom-up social initiatives in various countries for the establishment of documentation centres and counterexpertise organisations, often in collaboration with critical scientists. In the Netherlands, for example, the National (Anti) Nuclear Energy Archive (LAKA) was established in 1988. In France, the 1986 Chernobyl accident spurred the founding of counterexpertise organisations (such as ACRO and CRIIRAD, dedicated to monitoring radioactivity around nuclear installations), as well as the establishment of local information and surveillance committees (CLIs). Civil society actors therefore need reliable information as well as the possibility and capacity to produce, acquire and check knowledge themselves.

The Belgian survey reported in Chap. 4 used the Delphi method—a series of questionnaires that allow participants to develop ideas about potential future developments around an issue. The results showed the need for a high-quality and varied information system, in which current and historical knowledge can be found, as well as knowledge about the actors involved and their positions, and in which contributions from multiple knowledge sources, including counterexpertise, are brought together. Besides collecting and preserving information, the purpose of such a desired "Pluralist Documentation Centre" was to distribute this to diverse audiences: civil society, politicians and subject experts. An important question is how to set up such an information centre. A public body is one option, another is joint management by a broad range of stakeholders as already practiced in Switzerland (Technical Safety Forum). In 2006, France established the multistakeholder High Commission for Transparency and Information on Nuclear Security (HCTISN), composed of 40 members representing operators, safety authorities, government, local information and surveillance committees, NGOs, trades unions, parliamentarians, and experts, to foster information, analysis and debate on issues in the nuclear area, including RWM.

Some countries provide examples where the government offers civil society parties the opportunity and resources to gather information, put research on the agenda, and set it up or carry it out themselves. In the UK, on the local level, the so-called engagement funding allows a Community Partnership and its Working Groups to initiate and define their own, completely independent research, on (local) issues of their preference. However, there is no funding for critical groups. Conversely, in Sweden, the Financial Act of 2006 enables environmental NGOs to seek funding from the Nuclear Waste Fund. The NGO funding has allowed the Swedish environmental movement to participate more fully both in the consultation process and the licensing process for the repository for SNF. The funding has allowed the organisations to build up competence and they have raised issues on siting, alternative methods and on the safety case. France has also experimented with research commissioned by or on behalf of civil society actors. For example, the local information and surveillance committees (CLIs) and their national umbrella organisation (ANCCLI), together with the Institute for Radiological Protection and Nuclear Safety (IRSN), have jointly co-created risk-related knowledge.

Lesson 17: There is a need to clarify and enhance the role of societal engagement in various steps of the political decision-making process
In recent decades, all ten countries studied in this volume have been arguing for the meaningful involvement of civil society in a step-by-step decision-making

process around long-term RWM (cf. OECD, 2004), and thus the institutionalisation of engagement practices. Critical civil society organisations will relate to this differently: some will trust the process while others will mistrust it, and some will participate while others decide to remain outside of the institutionalised engagement processes (cf. German Chap. 5). This means that the public debate on long-term RWM is often more comprehensive than the organised one. From a democratic perspective, decision-makers should therefore always consider both bottom-up as well as top-down participatory initiatives (cf. Belgian Chap. 4).

Before discussing concrete country examples of engagement processes, we would like to mention three more fundamental issues related to societal participation. First, based on the core idea within the EDD-strategy that civic engagement processes should be co-constructed in collaboration with civil society, it follows that defining the function and form of a participatory process already requires a participatory process. In the same vein, it is important that the forms of participation are regularly assessed so that continuous critical reflection and social learning can take place. Secondly, the strong link between the debate about RWM and the role of nuclear energy within the energy transition raises the question of how these debates relate to each other sequentially. For example, in Germany, the discussion on the governance of RWM was preceded by a public debate on national energy policy. The outcome of this, the phasing out of nuclear energy, created a new context for the governance of RWM. Each country must decide how to deal practically with the relationship between the discussion about RWM and nuclear energy. A third fundamental issue concerns how open the debate may be—pragmatically put: Can the debate go beyond the solution of a geological disposal facility and how can that be achieved? The authors of the Belgian Chap. 4 claim that the societal debate can be reactivated by broadening the initial question from "What should be the solution?" to the question "What is the problem that needs to be solved?".

One of the biggest challenges for politics and policy is to clarify the role of public participation in the different steps of the political decision-making process. This is preceded by clarifying the various steps of the political decision-making process. In Finland a decision-making process was determined in the early 1980s, which gave parliament a central role in decision-making, at a relatively early stage in the process, and vested the involved local municipality with a veto power over the repository siting decision. In practice, the authorities did little to actively spur participation. In Switzerland, it was decided in 2008 to link the decision-making process around finding a geological disposal facility to the methodology of a Sectoral Plan, which is an established spatial planning instrument of the Swiss Confederation. The Sectoral Plan for Deep Geological Repositories has thus guided the decision-making process in Switzerland since 2008, and the role of public participation therein, which formally takes shape by means of regional conferences. In Germany, France and Italy, regulation has been used to formalise the legal base for participation. In Germany, public participation is legally grounded in national law, the StandAG, which states that participation should not be limited to information and consultation modes. Instead, concerned citizens and stakeholders should be empowered to participate in a way that goes beyond previous participation patterns. In the UK, Italy and Spain the idea of volunteered participation in return for compensation of local communities is considered or practised. The UK draws on participation by temptation and reward, through compensating regional communities which volunteer nomination to host a disposal site. It is important to note that none of the forms of public participation currently developing or already practiced in Europe has actually achieved dominance. Therefore, this crucial aspect of decision-making must continue to be closely monitored.

12.9 Overview of European Lessons for Radioactive Waste Governance

In this book, we have looked at the governance of long-term RWM from a multi-level governance ecosystem perspective. We acknowledged that the top-down expert-based RWM governance from the 1970s to the 1990s led to much social resistance and public distrust. The ten country studies show that a new, more inclusive and participatory governance mindset has emerged over the last decennia, in which the involvement of civil society and building better relationships between civil society and the domains of science and technology, and politics and administration, are central. Based on the ten country chapters, this final chapter looked for important elements or puzzle pieces of an effective and democratic governance ecosystem. The 17 lessons from Europe formulated above are intended for policymakers, stakeholders and concerned citizens. We believe they represent important design elements for a type of RWM governance that stimulates public participation, social learning, co-production of knowledge, and confidence-building political and policy action, with the aim of dealing with radioactive waste in a responsible way for a very long time to come (see Table 12.3).

Table 12.3 Overview of European lessons for the governance of RWM

The participatory turn in RWM governance
Lesson 1: RWM governance currently tries to experimentally shape the participatory turn
RWM governance in the context of nuclear energy
Lesson 2: RWM governance is affected by planned and unplanned nuclear energy developments
RWM as a multi-level governance phenomenon
Lesson 3: The interactions between international and national levels with regard to nuclear safety and radiological protection is well-coordinated and institutionally embedded
Lesson 4: The option of a multinational geological waste disposal facility is seriously considered and explored
Lesson 5: There is a need to achieve more coordinated interaction between national, regional and local levels
Lesson 6: Reliability and validity of research on technological safety and risks play a central role in the siting process for a geological disposal facility
Lesson 7: A siting process for a geological disposal facility raises the question to what extent it fits in with local development visions
Politics and administration: Working on shared principles and separation of responsibilities
Lesson 8: There is a need to clearly separate institutional roles and responsibilities for site selection, organising public participation, and managing the radioactive waste disposal facility
Lesson 9: It is important to develop widely-supported policy principles
Laws and regulations: Creating a legal basis for decision-making around RWM options
Lesson 10: It is important to anchor policy principles and technological options in law
Lesson 11: It is important to legally underpin decision-making procedures
Science and technology domain: Towards an institutionally diverse knowledge landscape
Lesson 12: It is important to be transparent about and openly debate scientific uncertainties about suitable RWM methods and geological formations, as knowledge development is dynamic
Lesson 13: The policy principle of retrievability implies a significantly longer period of active safety before moving on to passive safety
Lesson 14: There is a need for interdisciplinary and transdisciplinary knowledge, and social science can play a central role in this
Lesson 15: There is a need for the institutional distribution of knowledge
Civil society: The challenge of informing and engaging civil society
Lesson 16: There is a need for joint production of socially robust knowledge
Lesson 17: There is a need to clarify and enhance the role of societal engagement in various steps of the political decision-making process

References

Bergmans, A., Sundqvist, G., Kos, D., & Simmons, P. (2014). The participatory turn in radioactive waste management: Deliberation and the social-technical divide. *Journal of Risk Research,* 18, 347–363.

Council of Ministers. (2022a, April 1). *Nationale beleidsmaatregel inzake langetermijnbeheer van hoogradioactief en/of langlevend afval.* news.belgium. Retrieved May 2, 2022a from https://news.belgium.be/nl/nationale-beleidsmaatregel-inzake-langetermijnbeheer-van-hoogradioactief-enof-langlevend-afval.

Di Nucci, M.R. & Isidoro Losada, A.M. (2015). An open door for spent fuel and radioactive waste export? The international and EU framework. In: Brunnengräber, A., Di Nucci, M.R., Isidoro Losada, A.M., Mez, L. and Schreurs, M.A. (Eds.) (2015). *Nuclear waste governance: An international comparison.* Springer VS. pp. 79–97.

European Commission. (2019). *Inventory of radioactive waste and spent fuel present in the Community's territory and the future prospects.* European Commission.

IAEA. (2022). *Nuclear power reactors in the world. Reference Data Series no. 2, 2022 edition.* International Atomic Energy Agency.

OECD. (2004). *Stepwise approach to decision making for long-term radioactive waste management: Experience, issues and guiding principles.* Organisation for Economic Co-operation and Development, Nuclear Energy Agency.

OECD. (2003). *Engineered barrier systems and the safety of deep geological repositories: State-of-the-art report.* Organisation for Economic Co-operation and Development, Nuclear Energy Agency.

Parotte, C. (2020). A nuclear real-world experiment: Exploring the experimental mindsets of radioactive waste management organisations in France, Belgium and Canada. *Energy Research & Social Science,* 69, 101761.

StandAG. (2017). *Gesetz zur Fortentwicklung des Gesetztes zur Suche und Auswahl eines Standortes für ein Endlager für Wärme entwickelnde radioaktive Abfälle und anderer Gesetzte: StandAG.*

Rinie van Est is a research coordinator at the Rathenau Instituut, the Dutch parliamentary technology assessment (TA) and science systems assessment (SciSA) organisation in The Hague. He has a degree in applied physics and public administration, and a PhD in political science. He is a global expert in the field of TA, politics of innovation and public participation. For more than twenty-five years he has been involved in the energy and digital transitions, with special attention to the role of emerging technologies, such as robotics and AI. He is part-time Professor of Technology Assessment and Governance at Eindhoven University of Technology.

Maarten Arentsen was Associate Professor of Innovation in Energy Supply at the University of Twente in the Netherlands until his retirement in 2020. He has a degree in political science and a PhD in engineering sciences. His many years of research focused on change and innovation in European energy markets, among others, the transition towards renewable energy. He has published numerous articles, papers and book chapters, and has co-edited several books on the topics. He is a member of REFORM, an international academic network on innovation and change in energy markets.

Open Access This chapter is licensed under the terms of the Creative Commons Attribution 4.0 International License (http://creativecommons.org/licenses/by/4.0/), which permits use, sharing, adaptation, distribution and reproduction in any medium or format, as long as you give appropriate credit to the original author(s) and the source, provide a link to the Creative Commons license and indicate if changes were made.

The images or other third party material in this chapter are included in the chapter's Creative Commons license, unless indicated otherwise in a credit line to the material. If material is not included in the chapter's Creative Commons license and your intended use is not permitted by statutory regulation or exceeds the permitted use, you will need to obtain permission directly from the copyright holder.

GPSR Compliance

The European Union's (EU) General Product Safety Regulation (GPSR) is a set of rules that requires consumer products to be safe and our obligations to ensure this.

If you have any concerns about our products, you can contact us on

ProductSafety@springernature.com

In case Publisher is established outside the EU, the EU authorized representative is:

Springer Nature Customer Service Center GmbH
Europaplatz 3
69115 Heidelberg, Germany

www.ingramcontent.com/pod-product-compliance
Ingram Content Group UK Ltd.
Pitfield, Milton Keynes, MK11 3LW, UK
UKHW022119230426

12048UKWH00010BA/603